TRANSFORMING ADMINISTRATIVE PROCEDURE

TRANSFORMING ADMINISTRATIVE PROCEDURE

JAVIER BARNES
(Editor)

EBERHARD SCHMIDT-ASSMANN
HANS CHRISTIAN RÖHL
FRANCISCO B. LÓPEZ-JURADO
RICARDO GARCÍA MACHO
JAVIER BARNES
JOSÉ Mª RODRÍGUEZ DE SANTIAGO
PETER L. STRAUSS
JENS-PETER SCHNEIDER
LUCIANO PAREJO
WINFRIED KLUTH / JANA NUCKELT

GLOBAL LAW PRESS
EDITORIAL DERECHO GLOBAL

SEVILLA • 2015

Instituto Andaluz de Administración Pública
CONSEJERÍA DE JUSTICIA Y ADMINISTRACIÓN PÚBLICA

Research Projet SEJ-740
(Junta de Andalucía - Spain)

2ª edición

© Javier Barnes (Editor)

© 2015: Editorial Derecho Global–Global Law Press
C/ Virgen de Luján, 19. 2º B
41011-Sevilla (SPAIN)
info@globallawpress.org / www.globallawpress.org

Design: Los Papeles del Sitio

ISBN: 978-84-941426-4-2
DL: SE-911-2015

(Printed in Spain)

CONTENTS

REFORM AND INNOVATION IN ADMINISTRATIVE PROCEDURE

Javier Barnes

INDEX

The editor would like to thank William Saindon for his commendable assistance in the translation and editing of this book.

My thanks to Professor Michael Nimetz for reading the first draft of this article.

THIS introduction argues for the necessity of a wide-sweeping reform of traditional statutes on administrative procedure. Many national procedural laws are out of date, as they fail to recognize the new modes and methods of governance, and are still based on an antiquated approach to procedure akin to traditional "courtroom" processes. More importantly, they do not reflect current administrative activities: they either lack any provisions for rule-making, or the provisions that do exist are incomplete or superannuated. Furthermore, the first-generation statutes on administrative procedure say little or nothing about *informal*, *international*, or *private* actions of the administration.

The new strategies of regulation and governance require new procedural mechanisms and rules that are much more collaborative, flexible, and informal than those now in use in traditional hierarchical models of regulation. Administrative procedures must promote openness, citizen and interagency participation, accountability, effectiveness, and coherence in governance. Furthermore, the proper development of constitutional requirements, particularly those derived from and necessary to democracy and the rule of law, must be embedded in these new methods of regulation.

Beyond these questions lies a more fundamental issue: the new face of administrative procedure should be understood as a system facilitating the exchange of information and communication between agencies and citizens, not merely a decision-making process or a tool of application and enforcement of the law.

I
ADMINISTRATIVE PROCEDURE IN TRANSFORMATION

A. ADMINISTRATIVE PROCEDURE, THE BACKBONE OF ADMINISTRATIVE LAW

Procedure, as an institution, embodies the status quo of public law in any given time or place. It shows where the citizen stands before the administration and how different public bodies interact among themselves. Procedure is one of the basic building blocks of today's administrative law. It is the first to be affected in times of transition[1] becouse it is effectively "the way administrative law is made a reality."[2] As a result, an institution so fundamental must be subject to constant legislative and theoretical revision.

The importance of procedure has only increased with the advance of time. This is due to many factors, which include the following:

– Administrative procedure is the primary "conveyor belt" of the constitutional values and guarantees set forth by the principles of the rule of law, democracy, and efficacy in the interactions of the Administration and the citizen.[3]

– It establishes a mechanism of control and structural steering of the public Administration in the hands of the legislator.[4] Given that it is the legal framework that defines the procedure, this has multiple effects on how the administration makes future decisions and may indirectly determine what these decisions shall be.[5]

---

1. Javier Barnes, *Sobre el procedimiento administrativo: evolución y perspectiva* in INOVACIÓN Y REFORMA DE DERECHO ADMINISTRATIVO 277, 331 (J. Barnes, ed., 2006).

2. *"Verwiklichungsmodus des Verwaltungsrecht,"* as expressed in R. Wahl, *Verwaltungsverfahren zwischen Verwaltungseffizienz und Rechtsschutzauftrag* in 41 VVDStRL 151 *passim* (1983).

3. Thus, for example, procedure is the mechanism by which society guarantees control, transparency and accountability; the justification of administrative decisions; the democratic legitimacy of administrative actions; the balancing of complex interests and points of view from differing levels of government; public-private partnership; a reasonable administrative response time; a search for consensus; and so on.

4. *See generally* Matthew D. McCubbins, et al., *Administrative Procedures as Instrument of Political Control*, 3 J. L. ECON & ORG. 243 (1987) (providing a positive political theory perspective); Eberhard Schmidt-Aßmann, DAS ALLGEMEINE VERWALTUNGSRECHT ALS ORDNUNGSIDEE 203, 305 (2004) (examining this question through the lens of administrative law, particularly steering and efficiency).

5. For example, a legislator cannot foresee what may be necessary in every possible case concerning sustainable development. Nevertheless, he can decide what the administrative procedure used to resolve the issue is to be, and, to this end, calculate the weight to be given to the input received from the scientific community, the general public, the affected agencies within the Administration as a whole, etc., in order to determine the most environmentally sound solution. The relative weight given to each of these sources of information may well affect the outcome of the process.

– It compensates for the lack of legal standards in many laws via public participation;[6] thus conferring greater *democratic legitimacy* on administrative actions.

– It is the manner by which the administration adopts its most relevant decisions. These decisions can take on a *formal* or *informal* character. Examples of formal decisions are individual resolutions or "administrative acts" (i.e., adjudications); rules (i.e., regulations or territorial planning); and the award process leading to the procurement of contracts. Informal decisions are those described as soft law: guides, recommendations, manuals, interpretations, and so on. In sum, administrative procedure is not solely a decision-making process, although this is one of its more traditional and transcendental aspects. It also extends into other areas and serves to establish the criteria that guide the private activities of Public Administration, transnational administrative actions, and standards of care and conduct regarding the provision of services or mediation.[7]

– It is an instrument for interagency relations that transcend national boundaries, *i.e.* at the European[8] or global level.[9]

B. THE SHORTCOMINGS OF TRADITIONAL ADMINISTRATIVE PROCEDURE LEGISLATION

Administrative procedure laws were introduced to regulate and standardize administrative procedure during a period of rapid administrative expansion, especially after World War II (*i.e.*, U.S. Administrative Procedure Act of 1945). The initial laws and their suc

---

6. *See* E. Schmidt-Aßmann, *infra* Ch I, *and* H.C. Röhl, *infra* Ch II, *for examples concerning the environmental, food safety, and social sectors, etc., of the European Union. See also* J. Barnes, *supra* note 1, at 324.

7. *Id.*

8. *Id.*

9. Actions beyond national boundaries require the establishment of decisive procedures that satisfy in every case the necessities of the inherent values found in the principles of democracy and the rule of law (transparency, participation, motivation, control, etc.). *See* J. Barnes, *supra* note 1, 279 *passim.*

cessors have been repeatedly reformed and updated as needed with the passage of time.[10]

Nonetheless, the vast majority of national administrative procedure laws dating from the second half of the twentieth century are now out of step with regard to their *content,* considered insufficient, their *conceptual basis,* for the most part obsolete, and their *regulatory method,* restricted to traditional patterns (See Tables 1 and 2). All this spurs the need for reform, that is, a complete renovation or transformation of these laws because:

– First and foremost, many relevant issues are not even dealt with.[11] In general, administrative procedure law is no longer representative of the activities of the contemporary administration.[12]

– Second, administrative procedure law was designed for situations more closely resembling trial proceedings rather than for the realities of current administrative action. This antiquated model includes a bilateral and adversarial procedure, a sequence of administrative actions geared toward a final decision, and a process designed to merely apply a solution dictated by a material law.[13] Administrative procedure laws follow a judicial schematic conceived to guarantee certain rights in determined conflicts, but have no bearing on many other scenarios,[14] much less so in situations where the administration carries out a creative or innovative function, *i.e.,* planning regulations or decisions of a technical or scientific nature that are not the simple result of the application of solutions or standards dictated by statutes. In these cases, the solution must be found within the mechanics of the procedure itself.[15]

---

10. *See, for example, the study of* US APA, E. Schmidt-Aßmann, *infra* Ch. I.

11. *See* Table 1.

12. *See* Table 1.

13. *See* J. Barnes, *supra* note 1, *for an in-depth analysis.*

14. For example, many administrative procedure laws have no bearing on the elaboration of regulations. *See* E. Rubin, *It's Time to Make the Administrative Procedure Administrative,* 89 CORNELL L. REV. 95, 135 (2002).

15. *See infra,* Table 1.

– Third, they do not represent any method of regulation, other than that *classically* defined by an administration in the form of a rigid, hierarchical pyramid that renders unilateral and binding decisions mandated by norms dictated by a superior central power (the "command and control" regulation).[16] There is no mention made of new forms of regulation and governance, nor of their impact on modern administrative procedure.[17]

In short, the institution of administrative procedure and its reform are faced with the following challenges:

– The insufficient or nonexistent representation of administrative activities at the legislative level,
– The obsolescence or inefficiency of the "courtroom" method in many cases,
– The lack of new administrative procedures governing the new models of regulation and governance.

C. THE NEGATIVE CONSEQUENCES OF INSUFFICIENT THEORETICAL AND LEGISLATIVE PROGRESS IN ADMINISTRATIVE PROCEDURE

The negative consequences of this triple challenge can be resumed in three problem sets:

– Legal insecurity and uncertainty, in that many relevant actions taken by the administration either lack any clear normative reference or have a normative reference unresponsive to the institutional dynamics of that action.

---

16. *See infra* Part III and Table 2.

17. Here we take regulation in its broadest sense, equivalent to the steering and governance of a given sector through the framework and instruments provided by the State.

– Inefficient and ineffectual results stemming from the use of outmoded models, techniques or instruments.[18]

– The relaxation of the principles of democracy and the rule of law, as a consequence of an insufficient understanding of the requirements these place on new and different types of procedures and regulatory mechanisms.

Rulemaking, one of the most formidable instruments of contemporary government, and one of the outstanding activities of contemporary administrations in the latter half of the twentieth century,[19] serves as a perfect example of these consequences in any kind of regulations: territorial and urban planning; technical norms concerning health, welfare, security or the environment; executive regulations; or independent agency regulations, among many others. These negative effects are most evident if:

– The legislator is unaware of or ignores the establishment of procedures concerning rulemaking,

– The legislator is unfamiliar with the diversity of regulatory models[20] and strategies[21] available to him, or

– The legislator acts in accordance with an archaic concept of the normative process.[22]

---

18. For example, a "linear" courtroom method is not appropriate in procedures designed as exchanges of information, round tables, group discussions, conferences, or other collaborative procedures. *See, e.g.,* J.P. Schneider, *infra* Ch. VIII, (discussing the "star-shaped" procedure in German legislation).

19. *See P. Strauss, infra* Ch. VII, Introduction.

20. Regulations of a technical or scientific character, for instance, may require the participation of experts to a different extent than those that concern territorial planning.

21. For example, regulatory strategies based on the achievement of a consensus and on public-private cooperation (agreements and accords, negotiated regulations, etc.) require an alternative to the strategy often found in traditional adversarial, bilateral procedures. In more abstract terms, it is one thing to negotiate, and quite another to argue. Each function requires a very distinct procedural framework.

22. For example, this is the theory upheld by E. Rubin regarding the rulemaking procedures of the APA, which, in his opinion, are excessively influenced by procedural elements. *See,* E. Rubin, *supra* note 14, at 95–110. *See also,* P. Strauss, *infra* VII, Introduction and Part III.

D. THE SCOPE AND EXTENT OF REFORM OF
ADMINISTRATIVE PROCEDURE

In this context, we will not consider a conventional evolution placed on traditional concepts and methodologies. If one could measure the reform of administrative procedure by using an idealized scale representing the various levels of reform according to the degree and depth of change necessary, one would reach the following conclusions:

- First, the present need for change cannot be met by a piecemeal revision of traditional procedures or of their final "product," be it adjudication, a contract or a regulation.

- Moreover, it cannot be fully resolved by merely creating a patchwork of regulations for new situations[23] or procedures,[24] although this is a crucial element.

- The legislator must design an administrative procedure, broadly understood as a *tool* to construct a heterogeneous reality in which procedure exists as a medium of exchange of information between the administration and the citizen, and between the various administrations themselves.[25] The growing exchange of information provided by administrative procedure can be considered a hallmark of our times. As opposed to the old concept with emphasis on the final resolution, that is to say the formal product of an essentially bilateral procedure (adjudication, regulation, etc.), the most recent doctrine contemplates an informative dimension, wherein the exchange of information and communication between all parties involved is as important as a final result, if not more so.[26]

---

23. One example is the elaboration of the instruments of indicative or "soft" law, such as recommendations, guidelines, interpretations, etc.

24. *I.e.*, transboundary administrative action, both within the EC and internationally, eGovernment, etc.

25. *See* E. Schmidt-Aßmann, *infra* Ch. I, *and* J.P. Schneider, *infra* Ch. VIII. *See also* J. Barnes, *supra* note 1.

26. *See* H. HILL, DAS FEHLERHAFTE VERFAHREN UND SEINE FOLGEN IM VERWALTUNGSRECHT (1986), F. HUFEN, FEHLER IM VERWALTUNGSVERFAHREN (2nd ed., 1991), F. Schoch, *Der Verfahrensgedanke im allgemeinen Verwaltungsrecht*, in 25 DV (1992).

– At the highest level, reforms must take into account emergent methods of regulation, steering, and governance in order to reflect these new models and their impact on new administrative procedures.[27]

In short, the current legal regime needs a profound renovation of its provisions and underlying conceptions, and a new, up-to-date and all-inclusive "blueprint." This is the basic premise of this book.

---

27. *See infra* Part III.

II
OUR OBJECTIVE

As stated above, all the studies in this volume arise from the following assertion: traditional administrative procedure legislation and the theories that sustain it are no longer sufficient. Today's complex reality has surpassed the limits of classic administrative procedure.

Classic administrative procedure legislation is silent in the face of a rapid succession and interrelation of phenomena of wide scope and impact, such as the globalization and transnationalization of inter-administrative relations, or the collaboration of the public and private sectors. Each of these cases gives rise to new forms of regulation, steering and governance.

If we look closely at this question, we realize that the *administrative space* of national administrations no longer stops at national boundaries, but enters a regional (*i.e.*, European) or international area.[28] At the same time, the relationship state-society or administration-citizen has clearly changed, not only because the division between the two has already undergone a notable shift, as demonstrated by the disappearance of state monopolies or the emergence of self-regulation, but also, and more importantly, because the entire vision of a rigid, equidistant, and formal division between the two spheres is being gradually displaced by a new concept of increased interaction and cooperation.[29] Administrative law, as a whole, and not only administrative procedure in particular, must admit two decisive transitions: one, from that of a nationally focused state administration to a *transnational* administration and, two, that of an Administration as a service provider to one that becomes the acting guarantor of services and public-private cooperation.[30]

---

28. *See* E. Schmidt-Aßmann, *infra* Ch. I.

29. *See* H.C. Röhl, *infra* Ch. II.

30. This two-fold transitional process is further discussed in H.C. Röhl, *supra* note 29, *and* E. Schmidt-Aßmann, *supra* note 28.

The essays in this book share a common goal: to elaborate as well as inspire a more ample and integrated understanding of administrative procedure, based on a multiform sectoral regulation at a national, supranational, and international level; and to suggest a precise, well-developed systematization and understanding of the diversity of procedural structures, objectives, models and types. The contents of this volume comprise a debate that is far-reaching in both time and substance. Herein we address the procedures of scientific and technological "uncertainty management" that characterize the "risk society,"[31] the consequences of the information society on procedure,[32] the provision of health services as an example of the new procedural model,[33] the role of administrative procedure in European Law,[34] the requirements procedure places on inter-administrative cooperation at a national level,[35] the extensive experience of the United States in rule-making and forms of soft law,[36] and the much-needed expansion of the scope of national administrative procedure legislation, with the cases of Spain and Germany as examples.[37]

---

31. Borja López-Jurado, *infra* Ch. III.

32. R. García Macho, *infra* Ch. IV, and W. Kluth, *infra* Ch. X.

33. J.Mª Rodríguez de Santiago, *infra* Ch. VI.

34. E. Schmidt-Aßmann, *supra* note 28 and H.C. Röhl, *supra* note 29.

35. J. Barnes, *infra* Ch. V.

36. P. Strauss, *infra* Ch. VII.

37. J.-P. Schneider, *infra* Ch. VII, and L. Parejo, *infra* Ch. IX.

III
THE MODEL OF REGULATION, STEERING, AND GOVERNANCE AS A CONCEPTUAL FRAMEWORK FOR ADMINISTRATIVE LAW

A. THE TRADITIONAL METHOD OF REGULATION AND CLASSIC ADMINISTRATIVE LAW

The regulation model has long been monopolized by the traditional method, known in Anglo-American literature as "command and control regulation." The rules and laws are based on positive legal commands and prohibitions, and the Administration implements, enforces and controls the application of these by means of coercive sanctions.

Classical administrative law evolved under these conditions. The characteristic legal institutions and techniques of traditional administrative law as we know them today are a result of this framework and were conceived as instruments for its design and maintenance. It consists of binding laws that take everything into account, programming and steering all administrative action down to the smallest detail. It is a pyramidal administrative hierarchy, whose procedures are merely tools to apply the law, as part of a centralized top-down regulatory process.

The validity of this model is indisputable; not so, however, its monopoly. The administrative law developed after the nineteenth century was based fundamentally on the model or method of "command and control." The administrative law of the twenty-first century finds a new basis in a multiplicity of models, instruments, and regulatory strategies: public-private and inter-agency cooperation, "soft law" mechanisms, and so on. As a rule, these are hybrids which complement the classical system, at times merely isolated instruments or strategies inserted when necessary into the traditional framework. A single public policy (water, environment, parental leave, part-time work, etc.) can combine various elements from different models: binding laws passed down from a higher, central authority *and* forms of soft law, coercive sanctions *and* mechanisms of decentralized cooperation and consensus to facilitate development and implementation,[38] etc.

The adoption of innovative methods of steering and governance demands, as a matter of course, a rethinking of the traditional institutions of administrative law.[39] The administrative law that adjudicates or prohibits is now only part of the reality. There is also an administrative law of cooperative action and voluntary compliance, of economic and fiscal incentives, and of information regulation, among many others.[40]

Once this hypothesis is accepted, administrative procedure, like so many other techniques, tools, and categories of traditional administrative law, can be molded and adapted in as many ways as there are models or methods of steering and governance. The need to investigate how and how much these new models modify the structure, relation and function of administrative procedure should be apparent by now.

---

38. *See, i.e.,* Directive 2000/60/EC of the European Parliament and of the Council of 23 October 2000 establishing a framework for Community action in the field of water policy. By means of this Framework Directive, the EU provides for the management of inland surface water, groundwater, transitional waters and coastal waters in order to prevent and reduce pollution, promote sustainable water use, protect the aquatic environment, improve the status of aquatic ecosystems and mitigate the effects of floods and droughts. "Designed to replace a series of centralized and traditional command and control directives that dealt separately with groundwater, surface water, drinking water etc, the WFD mixes classic top-down regulatory modes and legally binding requirements with decentralized, bottom-up, participatory and deliberative processes; iterative planning; horizontal networks; stakeholder participation; information pooling; sharing of best practices; and non-binding guidance." *See* David M. Trubek & Louise G. Trubek, *New Governance & Legal Regulation: Complementarity, Rivalry, and Transformation,* 13 COLUM. J. EUR. L. 539 (2007). *See also* C.F. Sabel & J. Zeitlin, *Learning from Difference: The New Architecture of Experimentalist Governance in the European Union,* in European Governance Papers (EUROGOV), No. C-07-02, 42 *passim,* at http://www.connex-network.org/eurogov/pdf/egp-connex-C-07-02.pdf.

Council Directives on parental leave or on part-time work are other examples. *See* O. Treib, H. Bähr, G. Falkner, *Modes of Governance: Towards Conceptual Clarification,* in Eurogov, N-05—02, 7 at www.connex-network.org/eurogov/pdf/legp-newgov-N-05-02.pdf.

39. Richard B. Stewart, *Administrative Law in the Twenty-First Century,* in 78 N.Y.U. L. REV. 437, 454 (2003).

40. *See* E. Schmidt-Aßmann, *supra* note 4.

B. FROM A TRADITIONAL MONOPOLY TO A PLURALITY AND FUSION OF SYSTEMS.

The shortcomings and deficits of traditional methods of government, firmly entrenched in the old legal framework of prohibitions, commands and enforcement tools, have given way to other deeply interconnected *models, mechanisms,* and *instruments* that complement one another and have become one of the hallmarks of our times in many areas.

The interaction that exists today between the administration and the citizen, working together as associates in the interest of reaching the common good, is just one of these signs. Another important example can be found in the cooperation and coordination of all administrations implicated in an issue, on all levels of government: domestic, supranational, or international. We can also include: "regulated self-regulation," private self-regulation, privatization, the active participation of a well-informed public, the simplification of the administrative burden stemming from reduced regulatory requirements, principles and practices designed to create better regulation of intrinsically complex or uncertain scenarios, laws that establish general objectives while leaving to the discretion of the administration a decision as to the most suitable means to achieve them, decisions conceived from their outset to be of the most efficient application possible, forms of soft law, impact assessments, new paths of transparency and accountability, and a long list of etceteras.

Along with the more traditional methods, there have arisen new forms of governance, based on decentralized, participative, deliberative, bottom-up processes. These include the constant monitoring and revision of plans and programs; horizontal administrative networks; shared information, experiences and good practices manuals; non-binding recommendations and guidelines, etc.[41] As a result, new public and private actors have come into being, along with continuous experimentation regarding regulatory models and strategies. Within

---

41. *See* Table 3.

these new confines, the state must first renounce the use of hierarchic, and binding instruments as the only means of action and, second, cease to function as a self-contained, self-sufficient entity.[42]

Briefly, both state and administration have undergone tremendous changes since the last decades of the twentieth century, resulting in new methods of steering and governance. These new methods are the product of a fusion of regulatory reform movements and revolutionary new tendencies such as globalization, deregulation, privatization, and the knowledge-based society.

C. SOME EXAMPLES OF PROCEDURAL ADAPTATION WITHIN THE CONTEXT OF REGULATORY STRATEGIES AND MODELS

1. THE PRIVATIZATION OF PROCEDURE

Citizen participation in the investigation of facts in the context of administrative procedure - a stage dominated until recently by the administration - is an example of privatization. This participation occurs, for example, when the citizen is required to present environmental impact assessments while applying for a permit.[43] The private party assumes the costs of investigation and elaboration of this impact assessment. The administration need only verify the integrity, reliability, and quality of the information generated, processed, and submitted by the applicant. In this sense, privatization represents *a transition from one model of steering and regulation to another*. This privatization is borne of a new regulatory strategy - the transference of transaction costs to the private sector and a shared responsibility between state and society in the promotion of the public interest,

---

42. *Id.*

43. *I.e.*, Council Directive 85/337/EEC of 27 June 1985 on the assessment of the effects of certain public and private projects on the environment, article 5.

while the ultimate control of the final result remains in the hands of the administration.[44]

More to the point, the new investigation principle, which transfers the gathering and processing of information, as well as their costs, to the citizens, must implement these new strategies and abandon the traditional model, which is now seriously outdated. This posits the incorporation of other elements and a framework more suitable to contemporary demands. Thus, laws must establish a more open, decentralized and transparent procedure, where the information gathering and processing will be subject to greater debate and control by all interested parties, including the public at large.[45]

2. Rulemaking in the Context of Scientific and Technical Issues

In the face of so many challenges with respect to the regulation of scientific or technological issues, characterized by uncertainty, vertiginous changes and innovations, one possible solution is to formulate complex administrative procedures designed to establish a rulemaking process akin to the scientific method. The scientific community defines the threshold that differentiates accepted and proven facts from what is unknown or uncertain through investigation and study, the promotion of transparency and consensus when dealing with doubtful situations, and the use of hypotheses or models to prove or disprove possible theories and solutions. The object of the scientific method is to investigate data and facts that are by their very nature debatable or disputed. This is an obvious and radical departure from the legal processes that serve as a means of exercising political will.

Thus, in questions that require regulations of a scientific or technical nature, such as those concerning tolerable levels of ozone expo-

---

44. *See* G. F. Schuppert, Verwaltungswissenschaft, Verwaltung, Verwaltungsrecht, Verwaltungslehre 805-22 (2002)

45. *See infra* Tables 1 and 3.

sure, food safety, emission limits, or pharmaceutical product approvals, the structure and organization of the decision-making procedure should be analogous to the scientific method.[46] It needs to follow a process of investigation, transparent debate, and the search for an expert consensus in risk management, including all doubts and uncertainties. This administrative procedure is one of broad-based, active participation, based on the publication of all pertinent and available scientific facts, analyses, studies, expert opinions, evaluations, etc.[47], in an easily accessible and comprehensible manner to facilitate public discussion and accountability.[48]

3. ADMINISTRATIVE GOVERNANCE IN THE EUROPEAN UNION

Among other issues, there is a need to improve the procedures of comitology systems,[49] those carried out entirely within a given agency, or those that follow the open method of communication[50] by means of

---

46. *See infra* Chapter VII Part 2.b (discussing US Rulemaking,).

47. *See* M. Shapiro, *The Globalization of Law* in 1 Ind. J. Global Legal Stud. 37, 48 (1993).

48. *Id.*

49. Council Decision 1999/468/EC laying down the procedures for the exercise of implementing powers conferred on the Commission (28 June 1999). Amended by Council Decision 2006/512/EC. The participation of experts in committees, for example, requires specific forms of transparency. Thus, to ensure debate and discussion, the method by which the experts' opinions are selected, unified, evaluated, etc. must be made public, as should the actual list of participating experts. *See* Alexandra Gatto, *Governance in the European Union: a Legal Perspective* in 12 Colum. J. Eur. L. 487, 501 (2006), *for a general introduction.*

50. C.F. Sabel & J. Zeitlin, *Learning from Difference: The New Architecture of Experimentalist Governance in the EU* in 14 Colum. J. Eur. L. 3, 271-327 (2008) *at* http://papers.ssrn.com/sol3/papers.cfm?abstract_id=1106732.
I.e., the European Medicines Agency (EMEA) is a decentralized body of the European Union. The EMEA is responsible for the scientific evaluation of applications for the European marketing authorization of medicinal products (centralized procedure). Under the centralized procedure, companies submit a single marketing authorization application to the EMEA. The Agency brings together the scientific resources of some 40 national authorities in 30 EU and EEA/EFTA countries in a network of over 4.000 European experts. It contributes to the European Union's international activities through its work with the European Pharmacopoeia, the World Health Organization, and the ICH and VICH trilateral (EU, Japan and US) conferences on harmonization, among other international organizations and initiatives

incorporating new patterns of procedural transparency, control, participation and efficacy, while safeguarding the flexibility and informality characteristic of these procedures.[51] The principles guiding the procedure are relevant to public involvement, interest groups and experts at all stages of the policy cycle.

4. Participation and Transparency in the Interest Representation Model and Expertise Model

The method used as a basis for rulemaking procedures, be this the "interest representation model"[52] or a model based on expert opinion[53] to cite two examples, produces very different modes of participation and transparency. In either case, this participation aims to steer *and rationalize* the exercise of an administration's discretionary powers, especially in rulemaking. Increasingly, the interplay between policy-makers, interested parties and the public is part of policy-making, and

(http://www.emea.europa.eu/htms/aboutus/emeaoverview.htm). *See* article 30 *passim* of Regulation (EC) No 726/2004 of the European Parliament and of the Council of 31 March 2004 laying down Community procedures for the authorization and supervision of medicinal products.

51. The "open method of cooperation" has enhanced the transparency and participation of all the actors, both public and private, in the design, application and control of the public policies that employ the method (social welfare and security, employment, etc.). In its initial stages it was an opaque and technocratic method. *See* David M. Trubek & James S. Mosher, *New Governance, Employment Policy, and the European Social Model* in Governing Work and Welfare in a New Economy: European and American Experiments 33, 38-41 (Jonathan Zeitlin & David M. Trubek, eds., 2003). The procedure varies in each sector (*in re:* structure, instruments, duties, etc.) *Id.* 551.

52. Administrative procedure legislation must define, for example, those participating (interest groups, public opinion, agencies, etc.) and must indicate how to assure participation from the outset of the plan, program norm or public policy, *i.e.*, by means of sufficient notice and publication, open channels of participation, etc. *See* R. Stewart, *The Reformation of American Administrative Law*, 88 Harv. L. Rev. 1667 (1975) and *Administrative Law in the Twenty-First Century*, 78 N. Y. U. L. Review 437(2003), *for examples of U.S. Law.*

53. *See, for example,* Regulation (EC) No 178/2002 of the European Parliament and of the Council of 28 January 2002, laying down the general principles and requirements of food law, establishing the European Food Safety Authority and setting procedures in matters of food safety.

our attention must focus not just on the outcome of policy, but also on the process and procedures undertaken.[54]

D. FINAL CONSIDERATIONS

1. PROCEDURE AS A CONTROL AND STEERING TOOL OF DISCRETION

For more than two centuries, the "command and control" method has ruled as a complete monopoly. During its long reign, the procedure as law-applying tool, the "courtroom-style" procedure, and the standard procedure for adjudication[55] were the only protagonists in both *legislation* and the *general theory of administrative procedure.* In less than two decades, this method has been forced to co-exist with an ample variety of new models of steering, regulation, and governance. The administrative procedure of these new models does not mesh with the traditional method and, to avoid spurious imitation or contamination, cannot be constructed from the traditional premises.

For many decades, classic administrative procedure has taken a *defensive* attitude towards abuses of power and arbitrary actions. Its aim, in these cases, has been to protect the citizen by emphasizing control of its discretionary powers, mainly through judicial review. More recently, administrative procedure has also assumed *affirmative* tasks (as has administrative law in general[56]). Henceforth, discretionary power will be exercised not only according to the minimal material or procedural legal standards, when and if they exist, but will take into account the complex economic and social circumstances involved as well, in order to reach the best possible decision. Logically, then,

---

54. *See Better Regulation,* European Commission at http://ec.europa.eu/governance/better_regulation/expertise_en.htm

55. *See infra* Table 1.

56. *See* Richard B. Stewart, *Administrative Law in the Twenty-First Century,* 78 N.Y.U. L. REV. 2, 437 (2003).

administrative law must also implement an efficient steering of the administration's discretionary powers to achieve the highest standard of services for citizen and society.

In other terms, it is not enough to prevent or *control* the legality of ever increasing discretionary powers of the public administration. This is the defensive view and only constitutes a first step. The second step demands that administrative law also steer and rationalize these discretionary powers in the name of a more productive and efficient administrative action. This is the affirmative view. In this context, as significant a central tool as administrative procedure must help achieve the affirmative tasks required by new methods of governance.

2. THE ADMINISTRATIVE NATURE OF PROCEDURE

Administrative procedure in the *context of the new forms of governance* can no longer emulate "courtroom procedure," as in the case of adjudication, nor "legislative procedure," as seen in traditional executive regulations.[57] Contemporary administrative procedure is searching for its own identity in the legal world, evolving into a cyclical unity, a process without a clear beginning or end. As a result, administrative procedure begins in the preliminary phases[58] and continues during the activity in question, whether it be rulemaking, decision-making or any other, until it reaches its eventual effects or consequences.[59] The new administrative procedure legislation must acquire a marked "administrative" nature, as opposed to a "judicial" or "legislative" one. It must be capable of representing the peculiarities of the new forms of governance, and encompass the *entire cycle* of public policy. The new regu-

---

57. The first is merely a system of application; the second only concerns itself with the creative process.

58. See *infra* Ch. 8.

59. The concern here is reaching goal, and to this end, includes control and supervision of the decision, its modification and revision, etc.

latory methods, in many cases, have made obsolete the traditional separation between establishing a regulation or a law and its implementation.

In sum, it is clear that the reform of administrative procedure legislation, along with the subsequent modernization of its theoretical underpinning, cannot be found in the complete codification of existing administrative procedure laws, or in the simple addition of new procedures to the traditional laws, or, even less, in an extension of the sphere of classic administrative procedure statutes into new areas such as public-private collaboration, self-regulation, or administrative activities subject to private law.[60] On the contrary, there is a crucial need to elaborate criteria or principles of procedure suited to these new situations, and to include qualitatively distinct procedures or characteristic actions that more faithfully represent today's administrative reality. One must fit these new administrative procedures into the puzzle that makes up the framework of today's regulatory architecture.

---

60. See *infra* Ch. 1 II.2, and J. Barnes, *supra* note 1.

TABLE 1

CHARACTERISTICS AND DEFICITS OF TRADITIONAL ADMINISTRATIVE PROCEDURAL LAWS

CHARACTERISTICS OF TRADITIONAL ADMINISTRATIVE LAW	SOME EXAMPLES OF SHORTCOMINGS AND SOLUTIONS
The scope of administrative procedure laws refers only to the administration when exercising public powers, and therefore subject to administrative law.	Legislation does not contemplate principles and standards for the administration and agencies when acting as private entities subject to private law
Administrative procedure is a decision-centered process. - Adjudication - Contracts - Rules and Regulations	Legislation does not consider procedures that are not decision-making in nature, such as those involving information gathering and processing. - Control of Administrative Funds and State Aid - Drafting of Environmental Maps
Procedure is a formal process. The law only contemplates administrative actions subject to a formalized procedure and which end in a formal decision, *i.e.*: - Contract - Regulations - Adjudication	Legislation excludes administrative activities that are not formalized, *i.e.*: - Preliminary Negotiations - Consultation - Counseling Non-binding rules and other forms of soft law are also excluded in many countries, *i.e.*: - Recommendations - Interpretations - Guidelines - Good Practice Manuals
The standard result of procedure is an individualized administrative decision, especially in adjudication.	Rulemaking is often relegated to a second level of importance, with the notable exception of the U.S. APA.
Administrative procedure is a tool for the proper application and implementation of substantive rules and standards. It fulfils a secondary or auxiliary function in relation to substantive law.	Procedures that do not implement substantive law, such as those designed to create rules, plans, programs, etc. or to investigate the best available decisions are often not considered standard procedure and are excluded from general legislation, *i.e.*: - Urban Planning Procedure - Strategic Environmental Assessment

The application and implementation of law are accomplished through limited enforcement tools. 　Creation and application are seen as two strictly separate stages.	Legislation disdains many other relevant channels to achieve effective application and implementation of the law, *i.e.*: 　- Public-private cooperation: Agreement, Mutual Learning, etc. 　- Voluntary compliance mechanisms 　- Incentives 　- Monitoring, Control and Revision of the Decision to ensure Efficacy
Administrative procedure legislation concerns itself with domestic administration and its relationships within the state.	Administrative procedure legislation has little concern for interagency relationships at the supranational and international levels.
The procedure establishes rigid and limited channels of communication exchange between the administration and the citizenry. 　- The citizen's participatory duties and rights are formalized and strictly defined. 　- The administration alone establishes common interests and needs. 　- Investigation and information gathering is carried out *ex officio*.	Investigation and information gathering done by the private sector is not deemed worthy of consideration in traditional administrative procedure law.
The principle of separation of powers is expressed as a system of *rivalry*. 　According to this view, the executive (government and administration) limits itself to the execution and administration of the law and thus does not form public policy. As a consequence, administrative procedure only works as an *application tool* resembling courtroom procedure (*i.e.*, U.S. "due process," English "natural justice," or French "rights of defense"). Procedure is not considered an instrument that can be used in all stages of public policy.	The three functions of public power are not *complementary*, as contemporary administrative procedure requires. 　The new forms of steering and governance call for a new understanding of administrative procedure that encompasses *all aspects of public policy*.
Classic administrative procedure is seen as a *defense* mechanism against incidental abuses of power and arbitrary action. It aspires to guarantee decisions that are: 　- Impartial, 　- Adopted according to the system of the allocation of powers,	Administrative procedure does not fulfill affirmative tasks that guarantee a correct and efficient exercise of discretionary power. It should guarantee: 　- The best decision available, 　- Decisions made within the framework of broad participation and transparency,

- Respectful of the rights of private parties.	- Decisions that balance the rights and interests of all participants.
Administrative procedure is a tool to *control* power.	Administrative procedure should be seen as a *steering* tool of discretionary power.

Administrative procedural requirements are *rigid* and *hard*.
  They establish fixed requirements regarding:
  - Who may participate, and when,
  - The means and channels of information exchange,
  - The ways and methods of decision-making.
	Administrative procedures lack *flexibility* and *softness*.
	  Their requirements should contemplate:
	  - Open communication,
	  - Fluid participation,
	  - A deliberative process based on the exchange of experiences and good practices, leading to consensus.

Administrative procedure, in the context of the classic division between the *creation of law* and its *implementation*, is designed as an instrument in the service of the latter.	Administrative law has no procedures that consider public policy as a continuous cycle, beyond the traditionally strict dichotomy between *creation of the law* and its *implementation*. Unlike the traditional model, the governance model does not insist that legislation, implementation, enforcement, and adjudication are separate stages. Instead, it seeks to form dynamic interactions among these processes.

TABLE 2

THE ADMINISTRATION AS REFLECTED IN ADMINISTRATIVE PROCEDURE LAW

ADMINISTRATION MODEL IN TRADITIONAL LEGISLATION OF ADMINISTRATIVE PROCEDURE	SOME EXAMPLES OF MODELS AND FORMS OF ADMINISTRATION NOT CONSIDERED IN TRADITIONAL LEGISLATION
The administration that emerges from traditional legislation has a "command and control" nature.	Other forms and models of administration are ignored, for example those administrations: - Acting in cooperation with the private sector, - Working at the transnational or international level with other administrations, - Providing services, - Guaranteeing the activities and services of self-regulating providers.
The administration is structured as a hierarchical, closed pyramid, designed to transmit commands and information from the top down.	Network administration and its horizontal collaborative relationships with other administrations are not regulated.
The administration is a public organization that makes binding decisions and enforces them.	Traditional administrative procedure law does not consider the administration when: - It produces "soft law" (guidelines, manuals, interpretations, etc) - It engages in informal activities (provision of services, etc.), - It negotiates (i.e., negotiated rule-making, agreements, etc.), - It gives pre-procedural advice.
The flow of information within the internal structure of the administration is of little interest to the law. Interagency collaborative procedures are isolated exceptions in the system. The participation of other administrations in the procedure is infrequent and not of primary importance.	Inter-agency gathering, processing, and exchange of information are not sufficiently regulated in traditional administrative procedure law, particularly in supranational and international relationships between administrations. Because of this, administrative procedure law does not involve itself in situations such as constant system-wide cooperation, as in the case of composite administration in the EU.

The administration is "state-centered" and does not act beyond national boundaries.	The contemporary reality of transnational and international administrative actions is not sufficiently developed in traditional administrative procedure law.

TABLE 3

FROM TRADITIONAL REGULATION TO GOVERNANCE

	TRADITIONAL REGULATORY MODEL	NEW GOVERNANCE MODEL
NATURE OF LAW	- Centered - Substantive - Centralized - Command-and-Control - Rigid and Fixed - Uniform rules Generalized	De-centered and Proliferated Procedural Reflexive Decentralized Coordination and Orchestration Flexible and Adaptable Diversity Contextualized Variances
INSTITUTIONAL ORGANIZATION	Top-down Hierarchy Formal	Horizontal Network Informal
CENTRAL ACTORS	State National level Public	- Multiple levels of government (local, + transnational + international) - Multiple public and private participation - Decentralization and Principle of Subsidiarity
MODES OF ACTION	Formal avenues of activism	Proliferation of modes of activism
LAW-MAKING PROCESS	Static, One-shot Ossified, Entrenched	Dynamic, Iterative, Repeat learning, Experimental, Promotes innovation
MOTIVATOR FOR PRIVATE ACTION	Liability (Fear)	Reform Problem-solving Improvement
FORM OF ENGAGEMENT	Discrete actions, Distinct cases, Separate fields of law	Holistic, systemic approach Integration of policy domains

ROLE OF PRIVATE ACTORS	Individuals are the object of regulation--can comply or not	Individuals are norm-generating, Active citizenship
USE OF KNOWLEDGE AND INFORMATION	Information is selective for fear of liability	Integrated approach: All information should be considered over a long period of time and shared, Regularized continuous reflection
PROCEDURAL FRAME	Reactive Defensive Ex post	Proactive Ex ante
ADJUDICATIVE APPROACH	Before and after the fact judgment	Ongoing Benchmarking
SOURCE OF NORMS	Legal regime as primary source of norms	Legal regime as part of a range of factors that are considered together-- economic, ethical, customary
POWER OF LAW	"Hard" Coercive Rules Mandatory Sanctioned	"Soft" Aspirational Guidance Voluntary Structured but unsanctioned
ROLE OF LAWYER	Professionalized Operates in legal arena	Multi-disciplinary engagement Operates in diverse social arenas
CONCEPTUAL FRAMEWORK	Haves/have-nots struggle for a share of the static pie Law asks: how to divide the pie	Win-win framework Law asks: how to enlarge the pie

THIRD TABLE REPRODUCED FROM: Orly Lobel, The Renew Deal: the Fall of Regulation and the Rise of Governance in Contemporary Legal Thought, 89 Minn. L. Rev. 342 (2004).

CHAPTER I

STRUCTURES AND FUNCTIONS OF ADMINISTRATIVE PROCEDURES IN GERMAN, EUROPEAN AND INTERNATIONAL LAW

Eberhard Schmidt-Aßmann*

*Professor of Administrative Law, Institute of German and European Administrative Law, University of Heidelberg, Germany.

INDEX

Translated from the German by Lenka Dzurendova, Institute of German and European Administrative Law, University of Heidelberg.

I
ADMINISTRATIVE PROCEDURE: CHARACTERISTICS, FUNCTIONS, CONCEPTS

A. DEFINITION

ADMINISTRATIVE procedures are intertwined processes carried out by public bodies designed to gather, manage, and analyze information. Administrative procedures should increase the rationality of decision-making and service provision by agencies. Such procedures do not always result in a concrete, formal decision. Administrative services, internal administrative coordination, and periodic reporting duties can also be the goal of administrative procedures. The traditional and marked distinction between the decision-making process and the final decision dissolves even more when the relevance of information and communication between administrations, and between administrations and citizens, for the creation of a modern administrative law, is accentuated.[1] The decision becomes "proceduralized:"[2] that is to say, integrated into, as well as shaped by the procedure.[3]

This broad concept of administrative procedure stems from intensified administrative communication. Accordingly, legal provisions shaping the procedure are just as complex as the procedure itself. Administrative procedure law is made up of procedural rules which aim to provide a solution to a concrete situation (*situation-based* procedures), usually regulated by administrative procedure acts,

---

1. *See also* VERWALTUNGSRECHT IN DER INFORMATIONSGESELLSCHAFT (Wolfgang Hoffmann-Riem & Eberhard Schmidt-Aßmann, eds., 2000),

2. *See* ARNO SCHERZBERG, DIE ÖFFENTLICHKEIT DER VERWALTUNG, 126 *passim* (2000),

3. *Cf.* HERMANN HILL, DAS FEHLERHAFTE VERWALTUNGSVERFAHREN UND SEINE FOLGEN IM VERWALTUNGSRECHT, 1986, 193 *passim*.; HANS JULIUS WOLFF, ET AL., VERWALTUNGSRECHT I, § 58 para. 1 (12th. ed., 2007); 25 FRIEDRICH SCHOCH, DER VERFAHRENSGEDANKE IM ALLGEMEINEN VERWALTUNGSRECHT, DV, 21 *passim* (1992).

and rules on procedures independent of concrete occasions (*situation-independent* procedures), usually regulated by open government provisions on nondisclosure, data protection and access to information in general.

B. DIVERSITY OF FUNCTIONS

Administrative procedures fulfill several functions. They:

– ensure protection of individual rights,
– allow for participation,
– provide for balancing of interests,
– serve administrative transparency and clarity,
– make cooperation among various agencies and actors possible,
– enhance administrative efficacy.

Most procedures fulfill several functions (multi-functionality). The general concept of procedure is meant to secure the rationality of state action. It is about intelligent arrangements to enhance the transparency of decision-making, the quality of decisions reached, and the readiness of the authorities in charge to improve their performance. This is the case with environmental impact assessment procedure, for example, in which there is not only an "external" decision-making process, but also an "internal" one. In such proceedings, external participation—comments and involvement by the public and other agencies—is followed by an internal administrative process of careful assessment and consideration of the collected data, comments, and information, resulting in systematic collation of facts and balanced analysis of the impact on the environment. In a third step, the data, comments, and information must be thoroughly analyzed by the administration responsible for environmental issues (or "consultant administration") under the varied and specific statutes involving environmental issues. As a whole, the environmental impact assessment serves the purpose of gathering and managing information and knowledge by means of administrative procedure law.[4]

C. STRUCTURAL ELEMENTS AND ARRANGEMENTS

Procedures can be subdivided into several stages and consist of a combination of diverse elements:

- Public hearing, submission of data, consultation,
- Exchange of information, collecting evidence,
- Instruments or mechanisms for clarification, granting consent, and decision-making.

Administrative procedure law has modeled these elements into solid structures: public hearings, the right to access records and information, the obligation to give the reasons and motivations for administrative decisions, the obligation to provide inter-agency assistance and collaboration, and rules on preclusion. The correct inclusion of these structures within a certain administrative procedural function –the creation of procedural *arrangements*– is not accomplished through mechanical implementation or application. It is rather a skill possessed only by those who are able to combine experience in dealing with administrative procedure law with creativity.

Administrative procedures are part of the major tools that Administrative Law uses to steer and control the actions of agencies and administrations; such control constitutes *context-based direction,* as will be explained below. In a broader perspective involving not only national administrative law, but also European and international law, the rele-

---

4. *Cf.* Karl-Heinz Ladeur, *Privatisierung öffentlicher Aufgaben und die Notwendigkeit der Entwicklung eines neuen Informationsverwaltungsrechts* in VERWALTUNGSRECHT IN DER INFORMATIONSGESELLSCHAFT *supra* note 1, 225, 235.

vance of informal administrative procedure exceeds the relevance of the German doctrine on so called "formal instruments" in administrative law (that is, instruments that are governed by a set of rigid and formal rules: administrative decisions and adjudications, contracts, etc.). Administrative procedures and standards or criteria to be taken into account by the agency when taking action (*e.g.*, protection against discrimination, principles of proportionality and good faith, legitimate confidence) are the two most important tools of administrative regulation.

D. ISSUES TO BE DISCUSSED

A broad concept of administrative procedure involving many other things than adjudications, the idea of multifunctionality of administrative procedure, and the centrality of procedure in administrative law is the basic cornerstone of the legal research of most modern administrative law scholars in Germany and Spain.[5] Thus, the German-Spanish legal comparison is nowadays a *process of mutual and reciprocal learning.*[6] This article, which I hope will contribute to this process, deals– as the heading suggests – with the *three levels* of German (Part II), European (Part III), and international administrative Law (Part IV) successively. In dealing with these *three levels,* the doctrine of administrative procedure law corresponds to modern doctrine on legal sources, which has also been extended beyond the national level to European and international law.[7]

---

5. *Cf.* Oriol Mir, *Das Verwaltungsverfahren in Spanien: Eine Einführung* in DIE ÖFFENTLICHE VERWALTUNG [DÖV] 841 *passim* (2006), ; JAVIER BARNES, *Sobre el procedimiento administrativo: evolución y perspectivas,* in INNOVACIÓN Y REFORMA EN EL DERECHO ADMINISTRATIVO 263 *passim* (Javier Barnes, ed., 2007).

6. *See* Mariano Bacigalupo & Francisco Velasco, *Wirkungen der deutschen Verwaltungsrechtslehre nach außen – Am Beispiel Spaniens,* in *DÖV* 333 *passim* (2003); Barnes, *supra* note 5.

7. *See* Matthias Ruffert, *Rechtsquellen und Rechtsschichten,* in GRUNDLAGEN DES VERWALTUNGSRECHTS I [GVwR I] § 17 para. 8, 30, 121, 149, 171 (Wolfgang Hoffmann-Riem et al. eds., 2006).

II

ON THE CHARACTERISTICS OF ADMINISTRATIVE
PROCEDURE ACT IN GERMANY

ADMINISTRATIVE procedure law is characterized by the concept of procedure, the constitutional requirements of due process, and by relating procedure to the two major legal regimes of administrative law, public and private law. The concept of procedure will be dealt with in detail by Jens-Peter Schneider in this volume. This allows me to focus on (1) the constitutional requirements and (2) the questions of public and private procedural law.

A. CONSTITUTIONAL REQUIREMENTS OF DUE PROCESS

Unlike the Spanish Constitution, the German Basic Law, or *Grundgesetz* (GG), does not contain specific provisions on administrative procedure. Nonetheless, its relevance in terms of administrative procedure law has been generally recognized.[8] Traditionally, the principle of rule of law has been construed as the fundamental basis for administrative procedure.[9] The right to be heard, the obligation to give reasons and motivate administrative decisions, and the duty to give notice and publish all administrative decisions follow from this principle. The same applies to matters of transparency of "composite procedures" or "staged procedures" (*e.g.*, those carried out partly on the national level and partly on the EC level) and the obligation to administer a procedure in a way that does not render impossible or

---

8. *See also* Hermann Pünder, *Verwaltungsverfahren*, in *13 ALLGEMEINES VERWAL-TUNGSRECHT* § 12 para. 10 *passim* (Uwe Erichsen & Dirk Ehlers, eds., 13th ed. 2006)

9. Eberhard Schmidt-Aßmann, *Der Rechtsstaat*, in *2 HANDBUCH DES STAATSRECHTS* § 26 para. 76 *passim* (Josef Isensee & Paul Kirchhof, eds., 3d ed. 2004).

unreasonably impede subsequent judicial review. The values that underlie § 19.4 of the German Basic Law,[10] although initially designed for judicial review, have also had a profound impact on administrative procedure. Moreover, democracy and welfare-state principles lend administrative procedure a specific character.[11] The *model of democratic legitimacy* is primarily a procedural one.[12] The *welfare-state principle* requires that administrative procedures account for the individual situation of the beneficiary and provide for all necessary care and assistance, but it also requires that the procedures take into account administrative efficiency. In short, there are a number of constitutional requirements, but as a rule they do not require a specific design or method of administrative procedure. Fundamental rights shall serve as an example.[13]

In German tradition, particular significance is attached to *fundamental rights* ("procedure as a means of fundamental rights protection").

A judgment of the Federal Constitutional Court in the year 1969 stated: "According to the concept of the *Grundgesetz* (Basic Law), effective legal protection, securing the preservation of property, constitutes a significant element of the fundamental right as such."[14] Ever since, most of the substantive fundamen-

---

10. "Should any person's right be violated by public authority, recourse to the court shall be open to him. If no other court has jurisdiction, recourse shall be to the ordinary courts."

11. *Cf.* Peter J. Tettinger & Jens-Peter Schneider, *Verwaltungsrechtliche Instrumente des Sozialstaates,* in 64 VEROFFENTLICHUNGEN DER VEREINIGUNG DER DEUTSCHEN STAATSRECHTSLEHRER [hereinafter VVDStRL] 199 *passim,* 238 *passim* (2005) (*in re* the procedural aspects of the social-welfare principle).THOMAS GROSS, *DAS KOLLEGIALPRINZIP IN DER VERWALTUNGSORGANISATION* 280 *passim* (1999); see also EBERHARD SCHMIDT-ASSMANN, *DAS ALLGEMEINE VERWALTUNGSRECHT ALS ORDNUNGSIDEE,* ch. 2 para. 102 *passim* (2nd ed. 2004) (*in re* the principle of democracy).

12. *See also* HANS-HEINRICH TRUTE, Die demokratische Legitimation der Verwaltung, *in* GVwR I, *supra* note 7, § 6 para. 47 *passim.*

13. *See* Eberhard Schmidt-Aßmann, *in* INNOVACIÓN Y REFORMA EN EL DERECHO ADMINISTRATIVO, *supra* note 5, 15, 46 *passim* (*in re* the constitutionalization of administrative law).

14. *Bundesverfassungsgerichtsentscheidung* [Judgement of the German Federal Constitutional Court, hereinafter BVerfGE] 24, 367 (401).

tal rights have had to be assessed and researched in terms of their "procedural-organizational components."[15]

The other German courts have accommodated this doctrine, which adds a procedural guarantee to the substantive content of fundamental rights. This view of procedure as tied to the nature of the underlying fundamental right certainly contains considerable productive potential, which can inspire a jurist's creativity and imagination. For example, in the judgment of the Federal Administrative Court of 2 July 2003, the Court derived from the occupational freedom laid down in GG Article 12 (1),[16] a constitutional right to information for any "potential participant in the procedure," independent of his formal procedural position and standing.[17]

Analyzing the significance of administrative procedure for material fundamental rights has, admittedly, lead also to confusion and controversial disputes. For example, the formula of "best possible protection of basic rights"– used in a famous dissenting vote in the Mülheim-Kärlich Decision[18] – has turned out to be of little help in resolving these disputes. The term "best possible" bears many meanings. In some cases it has been far too easily construed as the "maximum" of administrative procedural requirements. However, in my opinion, the proper understanding of the "best possible protection of fundamental rights" formula is that it requires neither a specific model of administrative procedure to protect those substantive rights nor the most time-consuming procedure; the formula leaves room for legislative flexibility. Nonetheless, it often may be unclear where to draw the line between constitutional requirements and the freedom of parliament to design administrative procedural guarantees.

---

15. *See* Johannes Masing, *Der Rechtsstatus des Einzelnen im Verwaltungsrecht, in* GVwR I, *supra* note 5 § 7 para. 53 *passim (in re* evidence on the current stage).

16. "All Germans shall have the right freely to choose their occupation or profession, their place of work, and their place of training. The practice of an occupation or profession may be regulated by or pursuant to a law."

17. *Bundesverwaltungsgerichtentscheidung* [Federal Administrative Court of Germany Decision, hereinafter BVerwGE] 118, 270 *passim.*

a) Uncertainty as to what the constitution requires stems from, first, the openness and indeterminate nature of the respective constitutional guarantees of each fundamental right. These guarantees are limited to substantive statements and do not indicate *what* procedural safeguards are considered necessary for their effective enforcement. The difficulties resulting from this lack of concrete procedural provisions are considerably increased by the procedure itself. Procedures consist of a number of actions and interactions that evolve in a flexible way according to their internal dynamics. This evolution is often unpredictable. Procedures have proven to be variable arrangements. Their elements and schemes are not determined from the very beginning, but instead change during pursuit of the stated goals as well as during their incorporation into different and broader contexts. A complaints procedure must be necessarily structured in a different way than a local town planning procedure designed to create a balance between all relevant interests. Administrative procedure as a means of social direction and political control of agencies becomes reality through direction of an entire "context."[19]

b) Secondly, the ambiguities are often rooted in the existence of several dialectical tensions:

- This applies, for example, to so-called *multi-polar or multilateral legal relations*, which are characterized by the opposing and adversarial interests of the parties, who – as neighbors or competitors – invoke their respective fundamental rights. The procedural possibilities constitute here a kind of system of communicating vessels. What brings profit to the *one* puts a burden on the *other*. More often, administrative procedures do not have a bipolar structure, but include a variety of interests. The Federal Constitutional Court has pointed out the special characteristics of these procedures and, in recent cases, has derived from them distinctive restrictions related to judicial review in public procurement procedures.[20]

- Finally, functionality and effectiveness of agencies also are relevant for the Constitution. Procedures are to be implemented in an easy, appropriate

---

18. BVerfGE 53, 30 (75) (HELMUT SIMON, H & HEUSSNER, H, dissenting).

19. *Cf.* Wolfgang Hoffmann-Riem, *Verwaltungsverfahren und Verwaltungsverfahrensgesetz – Einleitende Problemskizze*, in VERWALTUNGSVERFAHREN UND VERWALTUNGSVERFAHRENS-GESETZ 9, 38 *passim* (Hoffmann-Riem & Schmidt-Aßmann, eds., 2002).

20. BVerfGE 116, 135 *passim*; also BVerfGE 111, 1 *passim*.

and timely fashion. The requirement of timeliness follows not only from the goal of efficacy, but also from the Constitution itself.[21] During the last ten years, the legislature has focused on shortening the procedure. There is a remarkable gap between what has been written by legal scholars on the procedural dimension of fundamental rights and the pragmatic approach applied by the legislature.

B. MAIN QUESTIONS ABOUT PUBLIC AND PRIVATE PROCEDURE LAW

In discussing administrative procedure, we usually think of procedures regulated by public law, and carried out by public bodies. Procedures implemented by private persons under private law do not fall into the category of administrative procedure. However, several relationships may be discerned among the two main types of procedure that are also of some interest in respect to administrative law.

In the first place, it must be noted that private law comprises a whole range of rich procedural experience. Procedural law is not exclusive to public law. For example, some procedural rules of corporate law, mainly rules regarding stocks and shares, are very interesting; they provide a starting point for an analysis of procedural balancing of private interests, and sometimes include procedural balancing with public interests. Balancing can be achieved by procedural rules. The range of procedure in private experience is, however, not what I plan to discuss. I am instead going to focus on two spheres in which the interactions between procedures under public and private law are significant:

---

21. Efficacy (*effet utile*) also constitutes a requirement set by EC law to the procedures executed by the Member States. The German and EC concepts of efficacy have, however, different points of reference and they also differ in their consequences.

– Procedures in which public administrations or agencies act under private law (A),

– So-called private procedures in a narrow sense (B).

1. Public Bodies Acting in Procedures according to Private Law

There is a gap in the literature on the interaction of public and private in administrative law; only a few authors have addressed this interaction.[22] The basic presumption must be that public bodies acting under private law must abide by the procedural rules of private law. If there are no private rules, the question then becomes whether one can draw an analogy to the rules of "standard procedure" under the Administrative Procedures Act. Some possible analogies may involve rules on conflict of interest, on the obligation of the authorities to investigate the facts of a case *ex officio*, and, presumably, also on the right of an individual to access records and information. In addition, rules on situation-independent procedures such as data protection and general rights to access information apply to both public-law and private-law activities undertaken by the administration. That is to say, nowadays there is considerable emphasis on procedural law binding on the Administration in *all* its actions – under both public and private law.

During the last ten years, *public procurement law* has gained even greater importance. According to traditional German understanding, a public procurement procedure consists of concluding a contract under private law, after a procedure belonging to administrative law (i.e., state budget law). This first procedural stage subject to administrative law comprises a variety of procedural provisions, but it has been traditionally regarded as *internal law* that, according to prevailing opinion, does not bestow any subjective rights on the other bidders. This traditional understanding has been shattered by the European Directive on public procurement. Today, we still do not have a statute on public procurement in

---

22. *See also* Ulrich Stelkens, Verwaltungsprivatrecht 1015 *passim* (2005).

Germany. Nonetheless, anti-trust law provides in detail for the level of legal protection available to the bidders both during the procedure and during any later challenge contesting the results. On the other hand, these specific procedures also guarantee that due allowance is made for the interests of the administration in acting in an efficient manner. For example, in Germany, as a rule, adjudication procedures and judicial review suspend decisions taken by agencies. This principle is of limited validity here, because such European Directives on public procurement aim to avoid delay in reaching a final decision. But the new procurement law is only applicable to projects that reach the thresholds set by EC law.

Interestingly enough, the changes EC procurement law has induced in procedural requirements for projects above EC thresholds have also led to questioning of the commensurability of traditional German procurement law in the sphere below EC thresholds. EC law has once again shown its capability to trigger "*spillover effects.*" Some administrative courts have tried to model the procurement procedures in the sphere below EC thresholds following a *Two-Step Solution.*[23] According to this solution, an authority first selects a bidder under public law in the form of an administrative act (a formal administrative decision). This decision can be challenged by filing an action for annulment. The private contract is concluded between the chosen bidder and the agency in the second step, which releases the procedure from issues of competitor protection. By applying this solution to the "below-threshold" projects, which are of lesser importance in economic terms, these projects are furnished with more effective legal protection than those above the thresholds, since an action filed with an administrative court has, as a rule, the ability to suspend the decision, following VwGO § 80 (1) (the Code of Administrative Court Proceedings, concerning judicial review). Two recent judgments by supreme courts carry forward the distinction established between the legal protection standards applicable to procedures on projects *below* and *above* the EC thresholds:

– First, the Federal Constitutional Court held on June 13, 2006, that differentiation based on the EC thresholds does not infringe upon the principle of equality[24] under GG Article 3 (1).[25] The Court stated that public procurement

---

23. *Oberverwaltungsgericht* [Higher Administrative Court, hereinafter OVG] Rheinland-Pfalz, Judgment of 25 May 2005 (DVBl 2005) 988 *passim*; OVG Nordrhein-Westfalen, Judgment of 11 August 2006, (VergabeR 2006) 771.

24. BVerfGE 116, 135 (149 *passim*.).

25. GG § 3 (1) "All persons shall be equal before the law."

serves the aim of effective distribution of public funds in terms of economics; that the constitutional right of occupational freedom (GG Article 12 (1)) does not bestow on the participants in a tender a right to be chosen, and that a negative decision affects an unsuccessful bidder's prospective profit, but not his personal legal position. Therefore, the Federal Constitutional Court concludes that usually statutes are not bound to provide, in the sphere below EC thresholds, the same level of "primary legal protection" as applies to projects above the thresholds, where decisions may be challenged by filing an action for annulment of the selection of a bidder. Effectiveness and economic rationality in reaching a procurement decision is in the eyes of the Court a sufficient reason for declining to follow the EC example. In that context, the Federal Constitutional Court underlines the potential risk of improper use or even misuse of legal protection rights by unsuccessful bidders – an aspect that has so far incorrectly received little attention in other areas, such as stock corporation law.

– The Federal Administrative Court has adopted this doctrine and, in its judgment of 2 May 2007, overruled the Two-Step-Solution referred to above.[26] Public procurement in the sphere below the EC thresholds in future will be considered following the rules of contract under private law, irrespective of the applicability of specific public law provisions in the same procedure. However, the Federal Administrative Court has notably emphasized the right to proper legal protection (judicial review) that is to be granted to unsuccessful bidders in projects that fall below the thresholds. Future developments in these areas remain uncertain. In view of the fundamental right to effective judicial review,[27] it shall be important to inform all bidders of the intended selection decision in time, to enable them to apply for interim measures in civil courts. This is ultimately an improvement owing to the "spillover effect." Nonetheless, these recent judgments have not assessed properly the overall significance of public procurement procedures for administrative law.[28]

---

26. BVerwGE *(NvwZ)* 820 *passim* (2007).

27. GG § 19.IV "Should any person's right be violated by public authority, recourse to the court shall be open to him. If no other court has jurisdiction, recourse shall be to the ordinary courts."

28. See Martin Burgi, Von der Zweistufenlehre zur Dreiteilung des Rechtsschutzes im Vergaberecht, in NVwZ 737 *passim* (2007).

2. "PRIVATE PROCEDURES"

Private procedures are procedures enforced by private persons. They are of interest under administrative law insofar as they influence or control administrative decisions.

– This happens when procedures or at least parts of procedures that traditionally have been subject to administrative law are conferred to private parties. *Privatization of procedure*, that is, outsourcing of some procedural elements or pieces such as gathering of information or investigation of any facts, is intended to remove the strain from public authorities and to allow for use of external knowledge. Examples can be found in Europe in local town planning and environment laws.

– *Vice versa*, the category of private procedures also contains procedures that initially belonged solely to the private sector and the results of which have been subsequently adopted by the state. This applies, for example, to procedures on product safety (certification and accreditation) that were previously only subject to liability according to private law. Procedures of technical standardization also fall into this category. *Publification of previously private procedures requires solving some problems.*

The problems that arise in the field of private procedure concern a new model of state cooperation with civil society (public-private partnership), enforced self-regulation (publicly-supervised industry self-regulation), and a new division of responsibilities between administration and citizens.[29] In this collaborative relationship between society and state, the essentials of public and private law must be preserved. It is important on the one hand to preserve creativity, expertise, and rationality of autonomous action by private legal persons. To make them part of the public administration would not be an appro-

---

29. Martin Eifert, *Regulierungsstrategien in* GVwR I, *supra* note 5, § 19 para. 52; Martin Burgi, *Rechtsregime in* id. § 18 para. 79 *passim.*; Schmidt-Aßmann *in* BARNES, *supra* note 5, 15, 69 *passim.*

priate solution. Principles applicable to public administration, namely the requirements of democratic legitimacy and the rule of law, cannot be simply and directly extended to private procedures.

On the other hand, the incorporation of certain aspects of private procedure brings social welfare into a broader administrative context. By adopting the results of private procedures into administrative decision-making, issues of social welfare come into play and the public interest must be duly considered. This guarantee of consideration of the public interest is provided by the administration in collaboration with society. The administration thus must guarantee a legitimate decision-making in the whole process, even though it is carried out by private persons.[30] An administration must examine whether neutrality, parity of interests, transparency, and competence are also characteristic of private participants in the private procedure. The extent to which issues of public interest, traditionally protected by public law, will be taken into account depends on the degree to which input from the private procedure is central to administrative decision-making. Liability risks can be covered by requiring the private participant in the procedure to have liability insurance. Public procurement law regarding the selection of private partners for administrative cooperation has become crucial in the service sector.

---

30. *Cf.* Ruffert, *Rechtsquellen und Rechtsschichten*, in GVwR I, *supra* note 7, § 17 para. 93.

III
EUROPEAN DIMENSIONS OF
ADMINISTRATIVE PROCEDURE LAW

IN discussing the European dimensions of administrative procedure, we must not restrict our view just to the European Union, although the most relevant issue for us is certainly European Union law (within its legal jurisdiction), and particularly European Community law, always allowing for supranational competence.

– A second European dimension of administrative procedural law has been shaped within the framework of the *Council of Europe*, especially under the Convention for the Protection of Human Rights and Fundamental Freedoms. Of particular importance have been the right to file a complaint under ECHR Article 13, the jurisdiction of the ECHR on procedural aspects of Article 2 (right to life) and Article 8 (right to privacy),[31] as well as several resolutions by the Committee of Ministers of the Council of Europe.

– The third dimension represents a pool of procedural guarantees to be found in the legal orders of all European countries. They can be traced back to principles valid under Roman law, such as *audiatur et altera pars* and *nemo judex in causa sua* and constitute the basic stock of a "common European administrative law."[32]

A. SIX COMPONENTS OF EC ADMINISTRATIVE PROCEDURE LAW

EC procedural law, which we shall now focus on, consists of six major components:

---

31. Judgment of 8 July 2003 "Hatton and others vs. UK" Europäische Grundrechte-Zeitung [hereinafter EUGRZ] 584 *passim* (2005).

32. *See also* RUFFERT, Rechtsquellen und Rechtsschichten, GVwR I, *supra* note 7, § 17 para. 143 *passim*.

(a) First, there is the procedural law applicable to organizational units within the administration (see below 2): *Procedural law of direct administration.*

(b) A second type represents the *uniform procedural* law to be observed by all national administrations. Some examples of uniform procedural law are the Customs Code (Regulation No. 2913/92) and the Schengen Borders Code (Regulation No. 562/2006). National procedural laws have been completely replaced by these legal acts.

(c) In other policy spheres, such as in internal market and environmental protection policies, a *harmonization of procedure* has been carried out under EC law. EC directives provide for regulation of the structure of national administrative law in order to enhance the implementation of the substantive aims pursued by EC law. This regulation is based on the concept of a particular steering potential of procedure in terms of reaching substantive targets such as the creation of market transparency, enhancement of use of resources, and establishment of mutual political confidence.

(d) Where no uniform procedural laws apply (b) and harmonization of national law has not yet taken place (c), EC law must at least provide minimum standards for implementation by national administrations. When-ever national public authorities implement substantive EC law applying their own procedural rules, they act, as is said, in "organizational and procedural autonomy." Nonetheless, this autonomy is restricted and national rules are synchronized with the rules of other nations by the imperatives of equivalence and effectiveness.[33] Following this doctrine based on the *effet utile* principle, the ECJ has in many cases interfered substantially, but often in a quite unsystematic manner, with long established doctrines of national law. For example, the ECJ has in the past interfered with national statutes of limitations. This phenomenon has been referred to as *instrumentalization* of national procedural law (*Scheuing*).

(e) A fifth component is represented by *common procedural standards,* applicable to the EC direct administration and to national administrations whenever they implement EC law. These are elementary legal guarantees like the right to be heard, the right to a fair procedure, the principle of impartiality, the right to a timely decision, and the right to contest adverse administrative deci-

---

33. Pünder, *Verwaltungsverfahren, in* ALLGEMEINES VERWALTUNGSRECHT § 12 para. 18 *passim* (Erichsen & Ehlers ed., 2007) Jörg Gundel, *Verwaltung, in* EUROPARECHT § 3 para. 194 *passim* (Reiner et al., eds., 2006).

sions. Taken together, these rights and principles constitute the core of the *right to good administration.*[34]

(f) Lastly, cooperation between EC administrative authorities and national administrations must be provided with procedural frames in their horizontal and vertical dimensions. The processes of comitology, mutual administrative assistance, supervision, and creation of networks are major cornerstones of the European composite administration (made up of the EC and the national administrations and their mutual interrelations).

The issues of the European composite administration will be dealt with in detail by Hans Christian Röhl in this volume. I will focus on the procedural law of EC direct administration (in Part III.B) and make some comments on common European procedural standards (in Part III.C).

B. ADMINISTRATIVE PROCEDURE LAW
OF EC DIRECT ADMINISTRATION

The procedures used by the direct administration have not yet been *codified*, although the EC has the legislative authority to do so. Some requirements are entailed in the *EC Treaty, e.g.*, the obligation to state reasons (Art. 253), to publish (Art. 254), to enforce the decisions of the Council or the Commission (Art. 256). These have been supplemented by rules on data protection (Art. 286) and general access to records (Art. 255). Further procedural law has been derived from the general legal standards mentioned above (see Part III.). Some examples of such derivation include the right to be heard and the right to legal privilege, which follow from the notion of defense rights and become relevant in adversarial procedures.

However, important procedural provisions for administrative action have been created in the first place in *secondary law, e.g.*, in antitrust and merger control law. Numerous provisions are included in legal acts establishing European

---

34. *Cf.* PAUL CRAIG, EU ADMINISTRATIVE LAW Chs 10 - 11 (2006).

agencies, *e.g.*, the Aviation Safety Agency (Regulation No 1592/2002) and the Food Standards Agency (Regulation No 178/2002). Also interesting in this context are the provisions on the general budget of the European Communities (Regulation No 1605/2002), on public procurement procedures (Art. 91 *passim*), and on EC funding procedures (Art. 108 *passim*). Outside Germany, this procedural law is, quite rightly, not considered to be purely internal administrative law.

The applicability of most procedural provisions is restricted to a certain policy field. *Provisions of more general applicability* are laid out in Regulation 1049/2001 regarding public access to documents of Community organs and Regulation 45/2001 on the protection of personal data by Community institutions and bodies. Procedural standards detailed in these legal acts recall those imposed by the EC on the Member States in the field of environmental protection. The establishment of parallel standards expressly provided for in EC Art. 286 (1) pays homage to the fact that procedural law of the European Union must enact the same principles on all levels. Administrative procedure is a footprint of administrative culture, and culture is not divisible.

A third source of procedural law is represented by the *codes of good practice* issued by the EC organs and the Ombudsman. These codes contain a large variety of provisions: recognized legal standards, recent rules on citizen-friendly administration, but occasionally also banalities. The doctrinal relevance of such codes is difficult to assess. They represent a combination of case-law and soft law. The "right to good administration" under Art. 41 of the EU Basic Rights Charter offers a "gateway" to this pool of rules, the passing of which could transform individual, not yet legally recognized rules into binding legal provisions.

The variety of procedural rules certainly bars any general conclusions on the role of administrative procedural law within the EC legal system. Administrative procedural law certainly constitutes an important means of integration. However, we must keep away from a procedural euphoria or a system based purely on procedural justice. This is reflected in the various methods of remedying procedural irregularities. It is true that the remedies for procedural irregularities are more restricted under EC than under German law. Nonetheless, even in EC law a procedural irregularity must rise to the level of a violation of 'substantial' procedural rules to provide a basis for an action for annulment under EC Art. 230 (2). Thus far, participation rights, the rights to be heard, and the obligation to provide reasons have been considered 'substantial' procedural rules. There is also a harmless error rule: When it is established that the outcome of a certain procedure would have been the same even if a hearing had taken place, then its omission does not result in the nullification of the administrative decision.[35] In general, the European Courts flexibly construe the relevant procedural provisions—such as the obligation to state reasons or the right to access records—in favor of the Administration, so as to find no procedural irregularity.[36]

C. COMMON EUROPEAN LAW ON ADMINISTRATIVE PROCEDURE

Some resolutions and recommendations of the Committee of Ministers of the European Council deal with major procedural issues:

The foundation was laid on 28 September 1977 when the Resolution (77)31 on the Protection of the Individual in Relation to the Acts of Administrative Authorities[37] was adopted. Other examples followed: recommendations about the exercise of discretionary powers by public bodies (1980), administrative procedures affecting a large number of persons (1987), provisional court protection in administrative matters (1989), and administrative sanctions (1991).[38] Among the more recent recommendations, particularly significant are the recommendations on alternatives to litigation (2001), on the execution of administrative and

---

35. ECR 1990, I-307 para. 31.

36. ECJ, judgment of 1 February 2007, EuGRZ, *supra* note 1 173 para. 64 *passim* (2007).

37. *Verwaltungsverfahrensgesetz* [hereinafter VwVfG] app. 7 (Stelkens et al. eds., 2008) (The five principles construed as procedural rights are: public hearing, access to records, legal assistance, statement of reasons, remedies.)

38. Rec (80)2E of 11 March 1980, concerning the exercise of discretionary powers by administrative authorities; Rec(87)16E of 17 September 1987, on administrative procedures affecting a large number of persons; Rec(89)8E of 13 September 1989, on provisional court protection in administrative matters; Rec(91)E1 of 13 February 1991, on administrative sanctions; downloadable at the webpage of the Committee of Ministers www.coe.int/t/cm/home-en.asp.

judicial decisions (2003), and on judicial review of administrative acts (2004).[39] A semi-official survey initiated by the Swedish government contains a list of ten principles of good administration that are recognized in most member States of the Union through constitutional and/or sub-constitutional legal provisions.[40]

Even though a uniform "procedural philosophy" has not yet emerged and legal orders of the European states and EU law differ in their assessment of the relevance of procedural law (*e.g.*, regarding procedural violations or irregularities), the idea of procedure constitutes basic expression of a common European administrative law.[41,42] The convergences will grow primarily in the sphere of influence of EU law: "In the integration-oriented European Community, the diverse national legal orders are in a constant and close interaction mediated by European legislative and jurisprudential institutions."[43]

---

39. Rec (2001)9E of 13 February 2003, on alternatives to litigation between administrative authorities and private parties; Rec (2003)16E of 9 September 2003, on the execution of administrative and judicial decisions in the field of administrative law; Rec (2004)20E of 15 December 2004, on judicial review of administrative acts; see www.coe.int/t/cm/home-en.asp.

40. STATSKONTORET, PRINCIPLES OF GOOD ADMINISTRATION 71 *passim* (2005).

41. JÜRGEN SCHWARZE, EUROPÄISCHES VERWALTUNGSRECHT 1135 *passim* (1993).

42. *See also The Procedure of Administrative Acts, in* EUROPEAN REVIEW OF PUBLIC LAW (Supp. 1993).

43. Rainer Wahl, *Das Verhältnis von Verwaltungsverfahren und Verwaltungsprozeßrecht in europäischer Sicht, in* EUROPÄISCHES VERWALTUNGSVERFAHRENSRECHT 357, 381 (Hermann Hill & Rainer Pitschas eds., 2004); see also Matthias Schmidt-Preuß, *Gegenwart und Zukunft des Verfahrensrechts, in* NvwZ 489, 493 (2005); Pünder, *Verwaltungsverfahren, in* ALLGEMEINES VERWALTUNGSRECHT § 12 ¶ 26 (Erichsen & Ehler eds., 2007).

IV
PROCEDURAL ASPECTS OF INTERNATIONAL ADMINISTRATIVE LAW

A. THE NOTION OF INTERNATIONAL ADMINISTRATIVE LAW

THE international law requirements for administrative procedures are extremely difficult to define. While legal provisions and concepts of national administrative law are for the most part clearly defined and a conception of the scope and contents of European administrative law has developed over the last two decades, it is still uncertain what the scope of international administrative law is or should be.[44]

– By "international administrative law" many scholars mean the administrative law of international organizations. So far, international administrative law is composed mainly of organizational law, the law on civil servants, and budgetary law; despite being assigned to international law, it has been somewhat depreciatively referred to as "internal law."

– Second, prevailing doctrine in Germany has, quite differently, defined international administrative law in analogy to international private law as conflict of laws principles. According to this doctrine, international administrative law is in its substance national administrative law that determines when a particular state's substantive administrative provisions are applicable.

The two definitions, as well as the concepts they are based upon are insufficient, though. The international-law notion is based on the right presumption: international administrative law is *international*, not national law. The definition of internal law is, however, too narrow to cover all the relevant legal provisions and legal issues concerning international organizations and international administrative

---

44. See also Ruffert, supra note 7, § 17 para. 169 passim.

cooperation. The notion based on conflict of laws is fundamentally flawed. There is no parallel to international private law since national administrations, unlike private legal persons, do not enjoy the freedom of choice of law that is characteristic of international private law. This does not mean that issues of conflict of laws cannot play a role in public law. On the contrary, their role has been constantly increasing. These rules should be, however, referred to as public conflict laws[45] rather than as – in a mistaken analogy to international private law – international administrative law.

This essay uses the term "international administrative law" to designate *all rules on typically administrative regulatory structures of international intercourse.* "Administrative law" stands for the actions and activities of administrations as well as legal provisions applicable to them. This "administrative law" is "international" since it goes beyond national jurisdictions.

B. THE SPECIFICS OF INTERNATIONAL ADMINISTRATIVE LAW

Any attempt to develop a concept that can encompass these manifold legal norms, administrative activities, and organizational structures and to establish a system of international administrative law as a third pillar of a universal administrative legal order – next to national and European administrative law – must take into account the specific characteristics of the international administrative regulatory structures discussed above. There are enormous differences between, on the one hand, the intensified administrative relations on the *national* and more recently on the *European* levels, and, on the other hand, the administrative structures on the *international* level. These differen-

---

45. *Cf.* Christoph Ohler, *Die Kollisionsordnung des Allgemeinen Verwaltungsrechts* 2 *passim* (2005).

ces make it impossible to simply transfer our traditional administrative legal doctrine to the novel third pillar. I shall point out three of them:

– First, the relevant *sector-specific* legal sources are to a high degree *fragmented*. Each of them is restricted to a specific field of action, whether fishing, emissions trading, or social security systems. Comprehensive legal regulations typical of administrative action have been rare thus far; they can be discerned, if at all, in the sphere of human rights protection.

– Second, there is also *spatial or regional* fragmentation. Administrative regulatory structures concern various areas: cooperative organizations of neighboring states, treaties tailored to certain regions, or subjects of global scope. Many treaties have their origins in the common legal and cultural traditions of the parties involved. Other treaties try to accommodate deeply divergent concepts of the law, and what is to be accomplished by means of law. International Administrative Law is not applicable to only one homogeneous *administrative space*, as is National or European administrative law.

– Third and last, international administrative law lacks any type of unifying jurisdiction that could provide a basic foundation of law and create progress in times of stagnation. There might be a whole range of courts and court-like institutions on the international level, but these far from constitute a juridical system to compare with the Union's Courts in Luxembourg and national administrative courts. In particular, the difference in the ability to influence administrative law enjoyed by the International Court of Justice and the European Courts could not be greater.

International Administrative Law, understood as something more than application of respective relevant legal acts, at first will evolve slowly and without centralization, and will be fragmented into various fields. A great variety of administrative structures and an enormous amount of legal sources have yet to be analyzed. Nonetheless, "international administrative law as a research task" according to Ruffert seems to be a very promising endeavor.[46] Two

_____

46. *See also* INTERNATIONALES VERWALTUNGSRECHT (Christoph Möllers et al. eds., 2007).

developments in international law have made this multifaceted field of law a uniform research object:[47] For one thing, there is the evolution from a law of coordination to a law of cooperation, followed by a dramatic increase in cooperation between national administrations and administrative activities of international organizations. In addition, the increasing importance of both the international protection of human rights and the international protection of common goods has led to the creation of administrative structures. International administrative law has in this way become an "implementation tool" of the law of nations in a more universal understanding such as was advanced by the classic school of Salamanca.[48] Systematic scholarly work in a field of such complexity is both possible and desirable. It will have positive effects on the practical issues of treaty interpretation under international law and on the evolution of customary international law.[49]

C. CONCEPT OF THREE FUNCTIONAL SPHERES

In an earlier paper, I attempted to assign the structures of international administrative law to three functional spheres.[50] Here, I will continue this approach and will draw on the development and structure of European administrative law. In doing so, this section highlights the above differences between European and international

---

47. ANGELIKA EMMERICH-FRITSCHE, VOM VÖLKERRECHT ZUM WELTRECHT, 686 *passim* (2007)

48. *Cf.* ALFRED VERDROSS & BRUNO SIMMA, UNIVERSELLES VÖLKERRECHT, §§ 10 and *passim* (3d ed. 1984) (*Bonum commune generis humani* as a target pursued by international law by Vitoria and Suarez).

49. *See* KLAUS FERDINAND GÄRDITZ, UNGESCHRIEBENES VÖLKERRECHT DURCH SYSTEMBILDUNG (AVR 2007).

50. Eberhard Schmidt-Aßmann, *Die Herausforderung der Verwaltungsrechtswissenschaft durch die Internationalisierung der Verwaltungsbeziehungen,* in DER STAAT 315 *passim* (2006), also in REVISTA DE ADMINISTRACIÓN PÚBLICA 7 *passim* (Oriol Mir, trans., 2006).

administrative law resulting from the initial status quo. The three functional spheres are "law of action," "law of determination," and "law on cooperation."

a) *Law of action* is international administrative law applicable to the actions of international actors, particularly international organizations. It covers *internal* administrative law, which governs traditional matters such as civil servants and budget law. The rules on internal administrative decision making, usually laid down in the organizations' statutes and in internal organizational law, also belong in this category. As in the law of EC direct administration, law of action has been dramatically evolving into a law of external administrative relations vis-à-vis other actors (states, enterprises and private persons). Official Development Assistance, particularly in the World Bank and the United Nations Development Program (UNDP),[51] (ODA) is a prime example which typically exemplifies the use of structural elements of national and European subsidy law in international law: program schemes, project assessment, contracts, and conflict resolution schemes. Law of action only partly originates in international treaties. The secondary legislation of respective international organizations is also an important source, as are, in a broader sense of "law," their recommendations and guidelines, published in manuals. Having recourse to these instruments of "soft law" is characteristic of international law of action.

b) *Law of determination* is that part of international administrative law that sets standards for national administrative law. Again, a parallel to EC law can be drawn, although there are no supranational legal instruments like EC directives in the international context. Law of determination originates mainly in international treaties, for example, in global and regional covenants on human rights or in the Geneva Refugee Convention. In the sphere of environmental protection, the Aarhus Convention is of particular note. It obliges the signatory states to provide public access to environmental information, environmental impact assessments, and the right to file a class action. Beyond the use of administrative law in treaties, some general principles of international law now incorporate elements of the traditional content and meaning of administrative law.

c) Finally, international administrative law is to a considerable extent *law on administrative cooperation.* As a result, the relevance of international administrative conflict rules has been constantly dropping behind that of transnational

---

51. Philipp Dann, *Grundfragen eines Entwicklungsverwaltungsrechts*, in INTERNATIONALES VERWALTUNGSRECHT, *supra* note 7, 7 *passim.*

administrative cooperation.[52] The meaning of agency cooperation and pro-blems associated with these specific issues are also dealt with in European law. Rules on agency cooperation can be found in law of action as well as in law of determination. The notion of law on cooperation does not introduce a new or independent branch of law, but points to a particular problem with the issues of efficacy and transparency that emerge at the intersections of spheres of agency action. Any form of cooperation generates its own particular questions and pro-blems apart from the common issues present in the law of action and the law of determination.

Cooperation takes place *vertically*, between international organizations and states, and *horizontally*, between two or more states or agencies. The parties involved act, as long as they do not resort to private law, under different legal regi-mes: international organizations according to international public law, and natio-nal administrations according to their respective national law that may in some cases have been harmonized by the international law of determination. Thus, legal sources of cooperation law diverge. The term "administrative cooperation law" should, with regard to legal sources, remain restricted to legal acts of inter-national law. Of decisive importance will be interrelation and coordination bet-ween the two legal regimes in both their procedural and substantive aspects. Whether transnational cooperation law will evolve into an autonomous regime equivalent to national and international administrative law remains to be seen.

D. ADMINISTRATIVE PROCEDURES UNDER INTERNATIONAL LAW

Procedures are extraordinarily important instruments for the con-trol and direction of organizations, particularly with regard to interna-tional administrative law. This applies especially to the direct admin-istration of international organizations and to cooperation law. The distinction between rules of diplomatic and administrative intercourse is hardly possible at times. For instance, the lines are blurred in the area of information-provision and reporting duties of states under

---

52. *See* Matthias Ruffert, *Rechtsquellen und Rechtsschichten, supra* note 7, § 17 para. 170.

international treaty regimes that focus on monitoring state behavior. Overall, an increase in typically administrative elements can be discerned. On the other hand, procedural law on rule-making by international bodies (secondary legislation) is regarded, as always, as classical diplomatic international law.

Administrative procedures in international law aim to achieve the goals and functions entrusted to them. *International mutual assistance* constitutes the basic type of procedure under international administrative law. In national administrative law, public hearing procedure is the most basic type of procedure. The reasons for this difference between the two levels are hidden in their respective histories: national administrative law has acquired its current shape thanks to judicial review by the courts that secured civil rights. Procedures of international administrative law have their origins in the need for administrative cooperation. Hence, *effet utile* or efficacy is the dominant feature. Accordingly, the idea of procedure at each level leads to a different function: citizen protection, at the national level, and inter-agency cooperation, at the international level.

Nonetheless, there have also been harmonizing tendencies. In national administrative law, the significance of effective administration has been recognized by accepting the so-called "double function" of administrative law (protection of the interests of the individual and effective administrative performance). Similarly, protection of the individual has become more important in international administrative law. Nowadays, schemes of mutual assistance, as in social, tax and police law, involve, as a rule, provisions on data protection. This applies even to the politically highly sensitive issues of repatriation and readmission agreements in migration law.

The Court of First Instance of the EU discussed exactly this issue in its judgment in the *Yusuf* case, while applying elementary standards of legal protection to the administrative actions of the UN Security Council and considering these standards to be current *ius cogens*.[53]

---

53. EuGRZ 592 *passim* (2005).

International human rights protection, long ago incorporated into law of determination and transformed into procedural standards to be observed by national administrations, must, in the same way, be valid under the law of action applicable to international organizations. The law of administrative procedure is an expression of administrative culture, and that culture may at last be understood as indivisible, regardless of the numerous differences between the states and regions of the world.

CHAPTER II

PROCEDURES IN THE EUROPEAN COMPOSITE ADMINISTRATION

Hans Christian Röhl*

* Professor of Administrative Law, University of Konstanz, Germany.

INDEX

I
THE ROLE OF PROCEDURE IN THE LAW
OF THE EUROPEAN UNION

A. THE FURTHER DEVELOPMENT OF ADMINISTRATIVE
PROCEDURE LAW BY THE EUROPEAN UNION

ADMINISTRATIVE procedure law in the European Union absorbs the dominant tendencies of public law: external Europeanization and internationalization of the state as well as internal development of processes of coordination between public authorities and private persons. European administrative procedure law conveys new approaches of regulation to the law of the Member States and leads to a "re-orientation."[1] At the same time it benefits the harmonization of enforcement in a federal European Administration.

1. NEW APPROACHES TO ADMINISTRATIVE PROCEDURE LAW

The innovations brought about by European administrative procedure law induce new outlooks in the Member States' systems of administrative law, thereby contributing to a "re-orientation" of national concepts of administrative procedure. A primary component of the new European procedural orientation is the concept of an informed public or the involvement of private persons in the execution of administrative tasks ("Selbstverantwortung" – self-responsibility). One significant example of this is the strategic environmental assessment procedure introduced by the EC.[2]

---

1. Eberhardt Schmidt-Aßmann, *Der Verfahrensgedanke im deutschen und europäischen Verfahrensrecht*, in II GRUNDLAGEN DES VERWALTUNGSRECHTS § 27 MN. 71 (Hoffman-Riem et al., ed., 2008).

2. *See* Javier Barnes, *Collaboration among Public Administrations through Domestic Administrative Procedure*, in this Volume.

This innovative force of European Law is considerable and might be due to its character as new law. New law can more easily absorb the current state of debate and is less dependent on old concepts. In contrast, national law is sometimes resistant to novelty. German law's central focus on codification vividly illustrates how inertia may be inherent in a national legal system.

2. FEDERAL HARMONIZATION OF ENFORCEMENT THROUGH PROCEDURE

At the same time, European administrative procedure law is supposed to harmonize national administrative enforcement. The EC has entrusted the majority of the enforcement of Community Law to Member States' authorities.[3] Administrative enforcement is "a momentous process of realization and above all a strong source of different results in the application of law."[4] In any given area of administration, these varying results have to be harmonized, bearing in mind the interests of the Community as a whole. Therefore, it is not sufficient to enact uniform or harmonized substantive laws; European Law becomes concerned with rules of procedure and organization.

---

3. Reinhard Priebe, *Die Aufgaben des Rechts in einer sich ausdifferenzierenden EG-Administration*, in STRUKTUREN DES EUROPÄISCHEN VERWALTUNGSRECHTS 71 *passim*, (Schmidt-Aßmann & Hoffmann-Riem, eds. 1999).

4. Rainer Wahl & Detlef Groß, *Die Europäisierung des Genehmigungsrechts am Beispiel der Novel Food-Verordnung* in DVBl 2, 3 (1998); *see generally* Udo Di Fabio, *Verwaltung und Verwaltungsrecht zwischen gesellschaftlicher Selbstregulierung und staatlicher Steuerung* in 56 VVDStRL 235, 266 (1997); ARMIN HATJE, DIE GEMEINSCHAFTSRECHTLICHE STEUERUNG DER WIRTSCHAFTSVERWALTUNG 111-114 (1998). *See* GERNOT SYDOW, VERWALTUNGSKOOPERATION IN DER EUROPÄISCHEN UNION, 117 *passim* (2004), *for extensive discussion of individual models of enforcement.*

3. The Interaction of Different Functions

These different functions of European administrative procedure law as a requirement for the Member States' legal systems can be realized and reconciled by certain procedural rules, but they can come into conflict as well:

– The promotion of greater public participation or allocation of responsibility for the achievement of political objectives to private persons, as has been done in environmental law, is part of the modern understanding of administrative procedure. At the same time the movement toward inclusion offsets the self-interest of national administrations and directs them towards the achievement of European political objectives.

– Conversely, a modern understanding of procedure can lead to greater administrative discretion. However, if national self-interests regain priority in a system of localized discretion, the federal European system may be weakened.

B. THE ROLE OF ADMINISTRATIVE PROCEDURE IN THE FEDERAL ADMINISTRATIVE STRUCTURE OF THE EUROPEAN UNION

The harmonization of the Member States' administrative activity also takes place through the medium of procedure, by judicial minimal harmonization with the aid of the legal concept of "effet utile," by legislative harmonization of procedural rules and finally by the involvement of member states' administrations in an composite administration.

1. Basic Harmonization by the ECJ: "Effet Utile"

The current state of Community Law provides for the application of general national administrative law and national law on administrative justice when national administrations are used for the enforcement of European Law.[5] It is obvious that due to the different systems and needs of any particular national administration, these areas of law must be subject to change.[6] Therefore, the requirements of European Law go beyond precise requirements derived from secondary legislation and include general unwritten principles of administrative law and the law on administrative justice.[7]

Through the application of these general principles, the Community Law perspective has often revealed inherent weaknesses in the doctrines of national general administrative law.[8] This development is less an innovation than a critical scrutiny of traditional doctrines triggered by Community Law.[9] In known cases regarding interim relief, implementation of directives by administrative guidelines, and standing,[10] the requirements of community law have acted as a rationalizing element and have thereby caused a "productive irritation" of national administrative law.[11] Such change does not, however, amount to uncritical adoption of Community Law ideas. The case law of the European Court of Justice may well be at the limits of its jurisdiction.[12] Its decisions are not always of a precision capable of convincing practi-

---

5. Another solution is conceivable in a federal system: see the provision of § 1 Abs. 2 S. 1 BVwVfG (Federal Administrative Procedure Act), which is not to be applied because of the exclusion clause of § 1 Abs. 3 BVwVfG.

6. See GIOVANNI BIAGGINI, THEORIE UND PRAXIS DES VERWALTUNGSRECHT IM BUNDESSTAAT..., summary 308 passim. (1996), in re a parallel "blindness towards federalism" regarding general administrative law in the European Union, as in the case of Switzerland.

7. See ROBERTO CARANTA, Judicial Protection against Member States: A New Jus Commune Takes Shape in 32 CMLR 703(1995), in this context.

8. See also Jean-Marie Woehrling, NVwZ 462-467 (1998) ; Karl-Heinz Ladeur, EuR 227 passim (1995); Friedrich Schoch, 2 DV Beih. 135, 144 (1999).

9. Schoch, Auflösen von Verkrustungen, also gleichsam ... die Beseitigung eines rechtlichen Reformstaus DV Beih. 2, 135, 144 (1999).

10. Ladeur, EuR 227 passim (1995); Schoch, supra note 9, 144.

11. Ladeur, supra note 8, 229 passim, in re: the implementation of directives through administrative provisions.

12. See SCHOCH, DIE EUROPÄISIERUNG DES VERWALTUNGSGERICHTLICHEN RECHTSSCHUTZES 47 passim (2000).

tioners and academics.[13] To meet these concerns regarding general administrative law, legal concepts must be scrutinized in advance for their persuasive force on the European level and must contain clear points of reference and reasonable patterns of thought.[14]

2. HARMONIZATION OF ADMINISTRATIVE PROCEDURE IN THE MEMBER STATES

Fewer legal challenges are created by the requirements of secondary legislation that reshape the administrative procedure law of the Member States or—as in the cases of the Community Customs Code[15] and the Schengen Borders Code[16] —even replace it completely.

3. COMPOSITE ADMINISTRATION

The last step of federal harmonization of enforcement is reached by the composite administration. Composite administration is the community's response to the need for a coherent European administration. It is mainly created and safeguarded by procedure. The need for a composite administration grows proportionately to the increase in transnational administrative activities of the member states ("Entgrenzung"). The administrations in Europe come together to form networks of public authorities and thereby take over tasks and functions which could have been carried out by a different and more unified organization.[17] The processes described below take place

---

13. For example the decisions in Emmott (Rec.1991,p.I-4269) and Ciola (Rec.1999,p.I-2517).

14. *See* ANDREAS VOSSKUHLE, KOMPENSATIONSPRINZIP 86 *passim* (1999), *for a national perspective on such developments,*

15. Regulation (EC) 2913/92.

16. Regulation (EC) 562/2006.

17. *See* Schmidt-Aßmann, in HOFFMANN-RIEM ET AL, I GRUNDLAGEN DES VERWALTUNGSRECHTS § 5 Mn. 25 ff. (2006); *for a more concise account,* see *also* Helmuth Schulze-Fielitz,

under the cover of administrative procedure law because in this instance we are dealing with the cooperation of organizationally separate administrations. But they essentially approximate a single organization, as the involved parties, i.e. the Commission and some or all member states, are determined in advance and do not change depending on the subject matter. Because of administrative procedure law, a *unified structure of enforcement* is developed.

Something like this is to a large degree unknown to current German legal thinking, which is rooted in the idea of a federal state. Here, there are hardly any federal mechanisms of control of the state administration.[18]

Die Verwaltung im europäischen Verfassungsgefüge, in VERWALTUNG UNTER DEM EINFLUSS DES EUROPARECHTS 91 *passim* (Wilfried Erbguth & Johannes Masing eds., 2006).

18. *Möllers*, GVwR I, § 3 Mn. 27.

II
PROCEDURES IN THE EUROPEAN COMPOSITE ADMINISTRATION

A. FUNDAMENTAL STRUCTURES OF THE EUROPEAN COMPOSITE ADMINISTRATION

"THE administration of the area of the Union is carried out in a composite of information, decision making and control between the executives of the member states and the Union."[19] This section addresses the links between decision-making and administrative procedure law.[20] We find such connections in varying intensity throughout the European Composite Administration. Most obvious are the cases in which the Commission acts as supervisory authority towards the member states. Supervision may be on a case-by-case basis or may in some areas be extended to continuous control.

Most cases involving planning take place in a vertical relationship of supervision and control. The Member States' authorities which apply European Law are connected to a genuine composite administration where their decisions, particularly about the common area of competition, have sustained effects on the other Member States. Finally, special procedural requirements ensure that decisions which apply throughout the Community will be structured and legitimized.

---

19. Schmidt-Aßmann, GVwR I (note 17), § 5 MN. 16.

20. See V. Bogdandy, GVwR II § 25, *supra* note 1., for further discussion of informational interlocking (the informational relationships between different branches of the European Administration).

1. VERTICAL ADMINISTRATIVE LINKS

a) Case-Related Supervision

Case-related supervision is the situation where the lawfulness of a measure of a member state depends upon the cooperation or approval of the European Commission.[21]

– *Customs Procedure:* In principle, customs authorities of the member states are responsible for the enforcement of the customs provisions of Community law.[22] Certain decisions which are significant for tax law or are likely to have sustained effects on the Community budget (additional charges, refunds, or remissions) demand a prior decision of the Commission.

– *Supervision of State Subsidies:* Subsidies by national governments are determined according to national administrative procedure law. However, if state aid falls into the scope of Article 87 EC, the Member State is under an obligation to stay the allocation proceedings and to notify the Commission of the subsidy in question.[23]

– *Control of Individual Decisions in Commercial Law:* The Commission has a right to determine cases which are of relevance to the Common Market. Examples are decisions concerning *traffic or energy infrastructure.*

– *Competing Permissions:* A similar structure can be found in merger control law in the case of competing permissions under the EC Merger Regulation.[24] The Commission has exclusive jurisdiction to allow a merger which is of relevance to the whole Community, under Article 21 of the Merger Control Regulation. Member States cannot prevent such a merger by reference to their own national

---

21. *See* MEIKE EEKHOFF, DIE VERBUNDAUFSICHT 15 *passim* (2006), *for extensive discussion of modern control mechanisms.*

22. Regulation 2913/92 (Community Customs Code); Regulation 2454/93 (Implementation Regulation).

23. Art. 88 s. 3 EC; Art. 2 and 3 Regulation 659/99 (detailed rules for the application of Article 93 of the EC Treaty), OJ 1999, No. L 84, p. 1; *see* Markus Ludwigs, *Die Verordnung (EG) Nr. 659/1999 und die neuere Rechtsprechung der Gemeinschaftsgerichte zum Beihilfeverfahrensrecht*, in Jura 2006, 41 *passim.*

24. Regulation 139/2004, OJ 2004, No. L 24, p. 1.

competition law. Nonetheless, Article 21 §4 enables the Member States to place a hold on the merger by reference to other national law, e.g. media law. Since such a hold can effectively prevent the merger, Article 21 § 4 stipulates that the Community will supervise this application of national law. Article 21 § 4(2) acknowledges certain interests as being legitimate: public security, plurality of the media, and prudential rules.[25] If national law intends to prevent the merger for reasons other than those mentioned, the "public interest" in question must be recognized by the Commission according to Article 21 § 4 (3).

b) Continuous Supervision: "Common Administration"

A more intensive form of continuous supervision can be observed in the institution of "shared management" of funds according to EC Financial Regulation Art. 53 §§ 1, 3,[26] by which the Commission controls the proper use of funds in the fields of financing the agricultural market and structural funds.

– *Clearance of Accounts Procedure:* Clearance of accounts is the starting point for this supervision of the European Agricultural Guarantee Fund (EAGF)[27] financing of the agricultural market.[28] In the agricultural common financing framework, measures such as refunds for exportation of agricultural products to third countries and intervention in agricultural markets are financed centrally from the Community budget, Regulation 1290/2005 Article 2 § 2.[29] These measures are implemented by the Member States by means of so-called paying agencies, Article 6 § 1. At first the Member States receive reimburse-

---

25. This refers particularly the provisions about the control of banks, the stock market and insurance companies.

26. Regulation 1605/2002, OJ 2002, No. L 248, p. 1. *See* BETTINA SCHÖNDORF-HAUBOLD, DIE STRUKTURFONDS DER EUROPÄISCHEN GEMEINSCHAFT 143 *passim* (2005); Wolfgang Schenk, *Die Leistungsverwaltung der EG als Herausforderung für den Europäischen Verwaltungsverbund*, in DER EUROPÄISCHE VERWALTUNGSVERBUND 265, 286 *passim* (Eberhard Schmidt-Aßmann & Bettina Schödorf-Haubold eds., 2005).

27. European Agricultural Guarantee Fund (EAGF), before: Guarantee Section of the European Agricultural Guidance and Guarantee Fund.

28. *See* RUDOLF MÖGELE, DIE BEHANDLUNG FEHLERHAFTER AUSGABEN IM FINANZIERUNGSSYSTEM DER GEMEINSAMEN AGRARPOLITIK (1997); WOLFGANG SCHENK, STRUKTUREN UND RECHTSFRAGEN DER GEMEINSCHAFTLICHEN LEISTUNGSVERWALTUNG 242 *passim* (2006).

ments in anticipation of the tasks to be financed under Article 14 § 1. At the time of clearance of accounts at the end of the payment period, the Commission decides which expenditures are to be excluded from Community financing because they are inconsistent with Community law, under Regulation Article 30 et seq. Prior to a decision to exclude certain expenditures, a procedure of negotiation with the Member State takes place.[30] The Commission has no formal authority to give instructions while Member States are actually spending Community reimbursements. Nonetheless, this *ex post* control becomes a continuous supervision since the Commission, during the financing of funds, expresses its view on what expenditures may be financed in non-binding communications. In effect, these communications are close to commands: according to the ECJ,[31] expenditures cannot be regarded as inconsistent with Community law if the Member State abides by these non-binding instructions.[32] Thus, a continuous hierarchy between the Commission and national administrations develops in the area of indirect implementation.[33]

– *Structural Funds (Implementation Period):* using the mechanisms of financial control in the legal framework for structural funds, the Community co-finances national state subsidies from the Community budget.[34] Community funds are passed on to the final beneficiary by the Member States, who make the concrete allocation decision. In a system of "control of control," the Commission controls the administrative systems of the Member States. The Commission can sanction misconduct by the Member States by cutting their share of the funds.[35] In this area the density of administrative instruments has become so intense that we must talk about a "Common Administration" rather than administrative cooperation.[36]

---

29. Regulation 1290/2005 on the financing of the common agricultural policy, OJ 2005, No. L 209, p. 1, replaced on 01/01/2007 by Regulation 1258/1999, OJ 1999, No. L 160, p. 103.

30. Art. 8 § 1 Implementation Regulation 1636/95.

31. *ECJ*, Case 11/76, 245 *passim* European Court Reports 1979, ; *ECJ*, Case 18/76, 343 *passim*, European Court Reports 1979.

32. Ines Härtel, Handbuch Europäische Rechtsetzung, 2006, § 13 MN. 34.

33. *See* Hatje, WIRTSCHAFTSVERWALTUNG 167, *supra* note 4.

34. For further discussion of the planning stage, see *infra* this Part. *See also* SCHÖNDORF-HAUBOLD, *supra* note 27.

35. The legal foundation for cutting Member States' funds is Regulation (EC) 1083/2006, laying down general provisions on the European Regional Development Fund, the European Social Fund and the Cohesion Fund.

36. SCHÖNDORF-HAUBOLD 37 *passim, supra* note 26.

c) Planning in the Composite

The planning procedures in the European Composite Administration are also mostly vertically structured. This vertical structure
presumably occurs because institutions are not yet strong enough to
delegate distributive decisions. The most important example of such
planning takes place in the context of the European Structural
Funds,[37] by which approximately a third of the Community budget
is distributed. The EC has installed a model of "Common Administration"[38] wherein planning is controlled by intense and formal normative development as well as by effective informal instruments.

2. THE COMPOSITE ADMINISTRATION IN COMPETITION LAW AND THE LAW OF REGULATION

An exclusively vertical perspective, with its connected legal concepts, is no longer sufficient where the legal and factual effects of
enforcement of EC law are not limited to one Member State. In an
increasing number of policy areas, the enforcement of Community
Law requires only that administrative decisions of the Member States
are legally valid in one or perhaps a few Member States. However, the
practical effects of most decisions will reach farther, particularly in the
common area of competition. Decisions by national authorities in
competition law or regarding the regulation of telecommunications
have broad effects throughout the Community. Therefore, in addition
to the legal instruments described above, *administrative mechanisms
of standardization* are necessary. Such mechanisms include the right
of the Commission to be informed, to supervise, or even to carry out

---

37. *See* SCHÖNDORF-HAUBOLD, *supra* note 26. *For more recent discussion, see* Christian
Konow, *Europäische Strukturpolitik*, ZG 2005 328 *passim*, p. 328. Further examples of common planning can be found in environmental law, like the sanctuary network "Natura 2000"
based on the FFH Directive (92/93/EEC).

38. This term was coined by Bettina Schöndorf-Haubold.

a measure itself, as well as the issuance of general guidelines and the creation of complicated consolidation procedures, as in the new legal framework for telecommunications.[39]

In the installation of a highly integrated European Composite Administration[40] through Implementation Regulation 1/2003 (regarding EC Articles 81 and 82), the European legislator has chosen a model of application of legal norms in *competition law* which compared to previous mechanisms constitutes a new level of administrative cooperation.[41] The Commission and national authorities are connected in a new style of unified application of competition law,[42] in which national authorities are to an extent made into an administrative substructure of the Commission. They are removed from the national hierarchy and are integrated into a network of information, action, and decision-making.

Parallel developments can be observed in *telecommunications law*. Because of the dynamism of the market, the new legal framework for telecommunications emphasizes more flexible regulation, i.e., greater discretion for national regulation authorities.[43] At the same time, Article 95 EC in general and

---

39. *See infra* note 45.

40. *See* Alec Burnside & Helen Crossley, *Co-operation in Competition: a New Era?*, 30 E.L. REV. 234 (2005); James S. Venit, *Brave New World: the Modernization and Decentralization of Enforcement under Articles 81 and 82 of the EC Treaty*, 40 CMLR 545 (2003); Heike Jochum, *Das Bundeskartellamt auf dem Weg nach Europa*, 94 VERWARCH 512 (2003).

41. The contents are for the most part sketched out in the "White Paper on modernisation of the rules implementing Articles 85 and 86 of the EC Treaty," COM 99 (101) final, OJ 1999, No. C 132, p. 1. The draft of the Commission dates from 27/09/2000, COM (2000) 582 final, OJ 2000, No. C 365 E, p. 284. See Claus Dieter *Ehlermann, The modernization of EC antitrust policy: A legal and cultural revolution*, 37 CMLR 537 (2000).

42. *See* Schmidt-Aßmann, GVwR I, , § 5 MN. 26 f, *supra* note 1, *for further discussion of the development of networks.*

43. Directive 2002/21/EC on a common regulatory framework for electronic communications networks and services, OJ No. L 108 of 24/04/2002, p. 33 (Framework Directive); Directive 2002/19/EC on access to, and interconnection of, electronic communications networks and associated facilities, OJ No. L 108 of 24/04/2002, p. 7 (Access Directive); Directive 20/2002/EC on the authorisation of electronic communications networks and services, OJ No. L 108 of 24/04/2002, p. 21 (Authorisation Directive); Directive 2002/22/EC on universal service and users' rights relating to electronic communications networks and services, OJ No. L 108 of 24/04/2002, p. 51 (Universal Services Directive); Directive 2002/58/EC concerning the processing of personal data and the protection of privacy in the electronic communications sector, OJ No. L 201 of 31/07/2002, p. 37 (Directive on privacy and electronic communications);

the European law of telecommunications in particular seek to establish a level playing field for competition. To avoid conflict with regulation of competition, regulatory decisions which are highly relevant to the Common Market must be increasingly focused on a common European interest. From the European point of view, national administrations, tied to their respective national government, are seen as potentially biased toward national interests. To control bias, the Framework Directive creates the European regulatory composite administration in the guise of European regulatory authorities under the auspices of the Commission, a network of European administrations.[44] In this regulatory composite, we find an independent concept of European law whose task it is to safeguard the uniform application of law and to prevent distortions of competition. A network of administrations designed in this way in the European administrative area evades exclusively national statutory control and judicial review by national administrative courts.

3. COMMUNITY-WIDE ADMINISTRATION

Special links between administrative procedure law and structure are necessary where decisions are supposed to be made uniformly for the whole administrative area. In addition to centralized decision-making procedures, there are increasing contexts in which single national authorities are given community-wide decision-making responsibility.

Directive 2002/77/EC on competition in the markets for electronic communications networks and services; OJ No. L 249 of 17/09/2002, p. 21 (Competition Directive).

44. Karl-Heinz Ladeur & Christoph Möllers, *Der europäische Regulierungsverbund der Telekommunikation im deutschen Verwaltungsrecht,* in DVBl 2005, 525 *passim;* Hans-Heinrich Trute, *Der europäische Regulierungsverbund in der Telekommunikation,* in FS PETER SELMER 565 *passim* (2004). *For analysis distinguishing between other network areas, see* Gabriele Britz, *Vom Europäischen Verwaltungsverbund zum Regulierungsverbund?,* 41 EuR 46 (2006); Felix Arndt, *Vollzugssteuerung im Regulierungsverbund,* 39 DV 100 (2006). *See also* Hans C. Röhl, *Soll das Recht der Regulierungsverwaltung übergreifend geregelt werden?,* JZ 2006, 831, 837.

d) Central Administration

Central administrative competences on the European level exist only in selected fields and to a limited extent. For our purposes, such procedures are of little interest. This is because a procedural ability to explicitly create coherence and legitimize results is not as relevant when the centrally legitimated Commission makes uniform decisions at the end of the procedure.

Some typical examples are the central authorization of medicinal products according to Regulation (EC) 726/2004[45] and the authorization of genetically modified food and feed according to Regulation (EC) 1829/2003.[46] Such central authorization procedures are based on an informal and tight-knit network woven around the central information processing organ, typically a European authority or agency.[47] In close contact with the national administrations and their accumulated expertise, these European authorities contribute to the creation of a European repository of information as a foundation of decisions valid throughout Europe. The core of this informational composite is formed by the particular committee responsible for the decision.[48]

e) Community-Wide Active Administration of the Member States

More interesting from an administrative procedure law perspective are Community-wide administrative competences of national authorities.[49] For decisions which are valid Community-wide, admin-

---

45. *See* BRIGITTE COLLATZ, DIE NEUEN EUROPÄISCHEN ZULASSUNGSVERFAHREN FÜR ARZNEIMITTEL (1996); Oliver Blattner, Europäisches Produktzulassungsverfahren 2003; Sydow, Verwaltungskooperation 223, *supra* note 4.

46. For additional information, *see* Sydow, Verwaltungskooperation 232, *supra* note 4.

47. Bogdandy, GVwR II, § 25, *supra* note 1. A particularly good example is Daniel Riedel, *Die Europäische Agentur für Flugsicherheit im System des Gemeinschaftsrechts*, in DER EUROPÄISCHE VERWALTUNGSVERBUND 103 (Eberhard Schmidt-Aßmann & Bettina Schöndorf-Haubold, eds., 2005)..

48. *See, e.g.*, Art. 61 Regulation 726/2004.

49. *See* Dieter H. Scheuing, Europarechtliche *Impulse für innovative Ansätze im deutschen*

istrative procedure law must ensure the coherent application of law in order to enable widespread acceptance of such decisions as binding on other Member states. Different models are described below:

– *Reference Decisions:* After a medicinal product is authorized in one Member State the product is authorized in the other Member States through a simplified procedure.[50] The original decision, called the reference decision, determines the authorization procedure. Indirectly, it also determines the decision in the other Member States: If divergent outcomes occur, the Commission decides whether other Member States have a duty to authorize the medicinal product. The ability to make an independent national decision is replaced by the opportunity to participate in the comitology procedure.

– *Transnational Decisions with a Duty to Cooperate:* Where there is a duty to cooperate, the decisions of a Member State have Community-wide effect.[51]

Verwaltungsrecht, in INNOVATION UND FLEXIBILITÄT DES VERWALTUNGSHANDELNS, 289, 331 (Hoffmann-Riem & Schmidt-Aßmann, eds., 1994); Eberhard Schmidt-Aßmann, *Verwaltungs-kooperation und Verwaltungskooperationsrecht in der Europäischen Gemeinschaft*, EuR, Vol. 31, 270 *passim* (1996); EBERHARD SCHMIDT-ASSMANN., ORDNUNGSIDEE, Ch. 7 MN. 18 *passim*; Gernot Sydow, *"Jeder für sich" oder "einer für alle,"* in PLURALITÄT DES RECHTS 9 (Bauschke, Gabriele et al. eds., 2003); Gernot Sydow, *Vollzug des europäischen Unionsrechts im Wege der Kooperation nationaler und europäischer Behörden*, DÖV 2006, 66 *passim*; DANIEL RIEDEL, DIE GEMEINSCHAFTSZULASSUNG FÜR LUFTFAHRTGERÄT 152 (2006).

50. For example, a simplified procedure is the rule in cases of the authorization of medicinal products according to art. 28 et seq. Directive 2001/83/EC. *See* Jens Hofmann, RECHTSSCHUTZ UND HAFTUNG IM EUROPÄISCHEN VERWALTUNGSVERBUND 110 *passim* (2004). A similar instance is the recognition of authorizations granted by another Member State according to art. 4 Directive 98/8/EG (Biocidal Products).

51. For discussion based on the Novel Food Regulation 258/97, see Wahl & Groß 2, *supra* note 4,; DETLEF GROSS, DIE PRODUKTZULASSUNG VON NOVEL FOOD 133 (2001); Sydow, Verwaltungskooperation 174 *passim*, *supra* note 4; Hermann Pünder, *Verwaltungsverfahren*, VerwR, § 14 MN. 51 *passim* (Erichsen & Ehlers, eds.) The Regulation (EC) 1829/2003 on genetically modified food and feed has excluded essential areas from the scope of the Novel Food Regulation and has made them subject to a centralized authorization regime. However, the Novel Food Regulation has not been repealed. The Community-wide authorization of the release of genetically modified organisms according to Article 12 *passim* Directive 2001/18/EC is styled like the Novel Food Regulation. *See* Hofmann, Rechtsschutz und Haftung 116 *passim*, *supra* note 50. The same principle is applied to the administrative procedure for the release of dangerous substances according to Directive 67/548/EEC (in the version of 92/32/EEC): Here, only a notification is provided for (art. 5, 7 Directive). However, the competent Member State may prohibit the release (art. 10 Directive) and is under an obligation to

The participation of the other Member States is guaranteed by giving them veto power. In case of a veto there will be a decision by the Commission. The Member States participate through the comitology procedure in the Commission's decision.

– *European Administration:* A third degree of common administration is reached when a national authority can make decisions on the basis of EC law which enjoy Community-wide validity without the external participation of the other Member States. Such an arrangement can so far be found primarily in the field of authorization for the provision of services, and less often in the field of authorization of products. We also find the recent European driving license within this category.

– *Private Community Administration/Notified Bodies:* The so-called Notified Bodies, which act for the EC in the framework for product authorization, constitute an alternative to national administration. Notified Bodies are primarily private persons who have been authorized by the Member States ("accredited") and to product authorizations ("certifications"). The system of Notified Bodies is an administrative solution which can operate without national administrations. By choosing this solution, the EC has created a genuinely European administrative structure.[52]

B. CONCEPTS OF JUDICIAL REVIEW AND MECHANISMS OF LEGITIMATION IN THE COMPOSITE ADMINISTRATION

1. CONCEPTS OF JUDICIAL REVIEW

The diffusion of responsibility in a composite administration leads to problems regarding the principle of the rule of law, because of the

---

do so if, due to an objection of another Member State, the Commission has decided thus (art. 18 Abs. 2, 29 Directive). For more discussion of the transnational administrative act, see *Bumke*, GVwR II, § 35 MN. 119 *passim, supra* note 17.

52. *See* RÖHL, AKKREDITIERUNG UND ZERTIFIZIERUNG IM PRODUKTSICHERHEITSRECHT 22 *passim* (2000); Hermann Pünder, *Zertifizierung und Akkreditierung*, ZHR, Vol. 170, 567 *passim* (2006).

confusing system of judicial review in Community law characterized by the principle of separation. The jurisdiction to review and declare a legal act inapplicable is strictly divided in the judicial review system of the EC Treaty according to the European or national levels of the courts. In the judicial review system of the composite administration, relief is granted either by the European courts or by the national courts acting as Community courts, based on the subject matter of the complaint.

Gaps in legal protection can initially arise due to the requirement of clear jurisdiction of the courts. If the various administrative contributions are not made sufficiently transparent this may hinder judicial review by the competent court.[53] Additionally, there is the requirement of coherent judicial review:[54] Doctrines such as administrative finality and rules of preclusion, acceptable in a one-dimensional law of procedure, may adversely affect effective judicial review of cross-border and multidimensional administrative action.[55] Deficits in legal protection are particularly problematic in the cracks between the connected instruments of judicial review.

2. DEMOCRATIC LEGITIMATION AND THE COMPOSITE ADMINISTRATION

Administrative legitimation in the European Composite Administration is based on the principle of separation as well: National and European contributions are independently legitimized. For this rea-

---

53. See Hofmann, Rechtsschutz und Haftung 241-99, supra note 50. For more discussion of the requirements of transparency, see Schmidt-Aßmann, GVwR I, § 5 MN. 54; V. Bogdandy, GVwR II, § 25 MN. 33; Gerd Winter, Kompetenzverteilung und Legitimation in der Europäischen Mehrebenenverwaltung, 40 EuR 255, 271 (2005).

54. Schmidt-Aßmann, supra note 53.

55. Hofmann, Rechtsschutz und Haftung 266, supra note 50; for further analysis, see David, Inspektionen 338, 350 passim; Wolfgang Weiß, Schnittstellenprobleme des europäischen Mehrebenenverwaltungsrechts, 38 DV 517, 536 (2005).

son, administrative legitimation in the European Composite Administration is necessarily multidimensional. European and national systems of legitimation must be connected.[56]

Therefore, sufficient clarity in decision-making has to be emphasized.[57] As far as possible, the responsibility for respective contributions must be attributable to the individual administrations involved. This enables parliaments and citizens, the sources of democratic legitimacy, to reliably assess the effects of their own administration's contributions. However, the influence, in some areas intense, of other Member States' administrations and particularly of the Commission makes the responsibility of individual administrations indistinct. The interconnections and linking of administrations in Europe makes identification of the way that any given individual contribution affects a particular decision significantly more difficult. In the long run it will be necessary to considerer additional mechanisms of legitimation, in which transparency and participation will have a significant role to play.[58]

---

56. Trute, GVwR I, § 6 MN. 102 *passim*.

57. SCHMIDT-ASSMANN., ORDNUNGSIDEE, chapter 7 38, 43.

58. See also Groß, VVDStRL 66 (2007), at IV 2.

CHAPTER III

RISK MANAGEMENT ADMINISTRATIVE PROCEDURES

Francisco B. López-Jurado*

* Professor of Administrative Law, University of Navarra, Spain.

INDEX

I

INTRODUCTION

S CIENTIFIC and technological progress is often accompanied by
the threat of future harm that cannot be controlled using current
knowledge. In 1980s Europe, an increase in innovation associated
with potential harm that could not be readily assessed by existing science and technology gave rise to the term "society of risk."[1] Although
this term is insufficient on its own to capture the complexity of present-day societies, it does faithfully reflect three phenomena: 1. An
unprecedented acceleration in scientific and technological development, 2. The appearance of negative consequences and possible future
harm stemming from this progress and, therefore, 3. The loss of blind
faith in progress and increased caution with respect to scientific and
technological development. These phenomena influence the legal system in general and Administrative Law in particular, converting the
"society of risk" into one of the most important challenges that 21st
century Administrative Law has to confront.[2]

This paper is not intended to expound on the variety of problems
that risk-related phenomena pose to the legal system in general. This
paper's object is rather: (1) To demonstrate why a fundamental part of
the statutory response to the uncertainties accompanying scientific
and technological advance is the establishment of administrative procedures of risk management, and (2) To define a concept of administrative procedures of risk management, identifying the functions and
structural elements found in such regulation.[3] In this manner, we will

---

1. U. BECK RISIKOGESELLSCHAFT. AUF DEM WEG IN EINER ANDERE MODERNE (1986).

2. E. Schmidt-Aßmann, *El Derecho Administrativo General desde una perspectiva europea*, in
JUSTICIA ADMINISTRATIVA 8 (L. Arroyo, trad., 2001).

3. *See* A. Voßkuhle, *Strukturen und Bauformen neuer Verwaltungsverfahren*, in VERWALTUN-
GSVERFAHREN UND VERWALTUNGSVERFAHRENSGESETZ, 330-43 (W. Hoffmann-Riem & E.
Schmidt-Aßmann eds., 2002).

fill a gap in administrative procedure typologies and deduce some common legal consequences of administrative structural design.[4]

This paper assumes that the ideal conceptualization of administrative procedure is as a structured process of information procurement and processing carried out under the responsibility of administrative authorities that enables the Government to take rational and legal action. That framework best explains the functions and elemental structures present in risk management procedures.

---

4. Some authors offer an explanation of such an "insufficiency" (*Typenarmut*) regarding the German Administrative Procedure Act, the *VwVfG*. *See*, W. Hoffmann-Riem, *Verwaltungsverfahren und Verwaltungsverfahrensgesetz: Einleitende Problemskizze*, in VERWALTUNGSVERFAHREN UND VERWALTUNGSVERFAHRENSGESETZ 29, 30 (W. Hoffmann-Riem & E. Schmidt-Aßmann eds. 2002). *See also* A. Voßkuhle, 285, *supra* note 3 (also explaining such "insufficiency"). That is also the case in the Spanish statutory framework according to the Administrative Procedure Act, Ley 30/1992, of Nov. 26, 1992.

II
PECULIARITIES OF TECHNOLOGICAL RISK REGULATION

A. CHARACTERISTICS OF TECHNOLOGICAL RISK

Technological risk is characterized by three features: 1. Scientific uncertainty, 2. The influence of human behavior, and 3. The influence that cultural and political contexts of different societies have on their capacity to accept risk.[6]

1. In regards to some technological risks, scientific uncertainty reflects a whole series of methodological, epistemological and even ontological problems inherent to the issue of whether the threat exists and, if it does exist, what its nature truly is; there are no sure odds and a better understanding of the threat cannot be reached simply by further investigation.[7]

2. Technological risk is also frequently unascertainable because its existence and nature depend on human behavior. The interaction between technology and the conduct of the people that manage it makes assessing risk exposure difficult, given the unpredictability of human conduct.[8]

3. Whether the risk is acceptable or not depends on its cultural context. An individual will determine whether or not a risk is acceptable not only according to the magnitude and probability of the risk but also according to that individual's underlying social structure and values.[9] The effects of context on legal regulation are clear if we consider that Law cannot be understood as an abstract

---

5. *See* E. Schmidt-Aßmann, *Structures and Functions of Administrative Procedures in German, European and International Law*, in this same book, Ch. I, and *also* LA TEORÍA GENERAL DEL DERECHO ADMINISTRATIVO COMO SISTEMA 358 (2003).

6. E. FISHER, RISK REGULATION AND ADMINISTRATIVE CONSTITUTIONALISM 7-9(2007).

7. E. FISHER, 7 *supra* note 6.

8. E. FISHER, 8 *supra* note 6.

9. In a similar sense, E. FISHER, 9 *supra* note 6.

reality, perfectly interchangeable between different eras and countries.[10] Law does not spin aimlessly in a vacuum, like a cogwheel disconnected from a machine, but rather operates "in a given social context, that conditions its objectives and evolution."[11] The study of various regulatory sectors such as energy, the environment, welfare, food safety, and others confirm the importance of cultural and political context. These regulations act as a mirror of the needs that are perceived in a determinate moment in history and, at the same time, they form a storehouse for remedies and solutions designed to address those needs.[12] Legal regulation has its origin and expression in society, within a cultural tradition; the change in perceptions, values, and fears of the people that form that society are necessarily reflected in legal regulation.

In addition to technological risk, the continual evolution of the sources of risk is of particular legal relevance. Sources of risk change in conjunction with scientific and technological innovation, causing new "regulatory demands" for protection under the application of new technologies. Scientific and technological progress cause classical sources of risk to acquire new and more sophisticated forms, while new sources of risk emerge simultaneously.

Regulation within specific sectors strives for adequate strategies for protection and promotion of legally protected interests, in an attempt to rationally manage risk in the face of the threat of future harm. Common features can be deduced from those regulations, of which perhaps the most relevant is the heavy weight given to administrative procedures and, with this, the important responsibility that is bestowed upon the administrative authorities.

---

10. Legal concepts should not be considered empty vessels, superficially similar and transferable. *See* C. Harlow, *Voices of Difference in a Plural Community*, available at www.jeanmonnetprogram.org/papers/00/000301.html.

11. A. Nieto, *La vocación del Derecho administrativo de nuestro tiempo*, in 76 *Revista de Administración Pública*, 29 (1975).

12. *See* E. Schmidt-Aßmann, LA TEORÍA GENERAL... 11 *supra* note 5. The idea of public administration as the most intimate and complete mirror of a community could be found years before in L. L. JAFFE, JUDICIAL CONTROL OF ADMINISTRATIVE ACTION 332 (1965).

B. REGULATORY CONSEQUENCES OF THE CHARACTERISTICS OF TECHNOLOGICAL RISK.

Scientific uncertainty as a characteristic of technological risk creates an important challenge for the Law. We come across a peculiar paradox here, in that something new, with uncertain consequences, must be regulated, promoted or prevented in the general interest even before the scope of these consequences is known.[13]

The regulation of risk is a particularly significant example of "communication" and "complementarity" between different fields of law, such as the administrative, criminal and civil branches.[14] Yet at the same time it makes apparent the insufficiency of the civil or criminal responses, even though they contribute indispensable regulatory elements. Nor is traditional administrative formal adjudication in itself a satisfactory response to the magnitude of the negative effects the technological risk can produce. Two aspects of the reality of risk serve as proof. On the one hand, the regulated facilities, products or phenomena are, in many instances, capable of producing complex effects on health or the environment for their long-term manifestation or permanence. On the other hand, administrative supervision of a risk-producing activity, facility or product ceases to be a two-way process between the administrative agency and the regulated entity when one factors in the possibility of adverse effects on society or individual.[15]

Traditional regulatory techniques were developed as a reaction to situations in which both the probability and the extent of harm can be

---

13. W. Hoffmann-Riem, *Eigenstädigkeit der Verwaltung*, in GRUNDLAGEN DES VERWALTUNGSRECHTS 705 (W. Hoffmann-Riem et al. eds., 2006).

14. U. di Fabio, *Risikosteuerung im öffentlichen Recht – zwischen hoheitlicher Überwachung und regulierter Freiwilligkeit*, in ÖFFENTLICHES RECHT UND PRIVATRECHT ALS WECHSELSEITIGE AUFFANGORDNUNGEN 165 (W. Hoffmann-Riem & E. Schmidt-Aßmann eds., 1996, p. 165).

15. U. di Fabio, 148 *supra* note 14. In Spanish, *see* J. ESTEVE PARDO, TÉCNICA, RIESGO Y DERECHO: TRATAMIENTO DEL RIESGO TECNOLÓGICO EN EL DERECHO AMBIENTAL 67-70 (1999).

determined with a certain degree of precision.[16] Where the probability and extent of harm is unknown and unascertainable,[17] traditional tools are insufficient,[18] as there are usually risks on both sides: the risks of adopting a decision and the risks of avoiding the adoption of a decision.[19]

The implementation of delegated powers demands that administrators make reasonable decisions between action and inaction, and once a general course of action is decided, between the particular concrete actions possible to implement that general mandate. The task of the regulator and, therefore, also of the public law scholars, consists of devising new methods and procedures that integrate and harmonize innovation and risk.[20]

Uncertainty, the impossibility of predicting outcomes based on previous experience or cause and effect, inevitably limits the substantive content of parliamentary regulation concerning risk. Statutory provisions in these situations concentrate on regulating administrative procedures to compensate to some degree for that limited content and predictability generating at the same time certainty and confidence in those directly concerned and in the public at large.

The appropriate form of regulation in the face of unpredictable phenomena can only be determined through the establishment of objectives for the regulatory scheme, an agency suited to the imple-

---

16. *See* I. Appel, *Methodik des Umgangs mit Ungewissheit*, in METHODEN DER VERWALTUNGSRECHTSWISSENSCHAFT, 338 (E. Schmidt-Aßmann & W. Hoffmann-Riem eds., 2004).

17. In German doctrine such a distinction between known and unknown probability and extent of harm is made explicit with two words, "danger" for the first situation and "risk" for the second. *See* E. SCHMIDT-ASSMANN, DAS ALLGEMEINE VERWALTUNGSRECHT ALS ORDNUNGSIDEE, 161 (2nd ed., 2004),

18. J. ESTEVE PARDO, 59-75 *supra* note 15.

19. Such risk-risk trade-offs are certainly important, as emphasized in C. SUNSTEIN, LAWS OF FEAR: BEYOND THE PRECAUTIONARY PRINCIPLE, 46, 208-209 (2005).

20. J.M. Baño León, *El principio de precaución en el Derecho Público*, in RESPONSABILIDAD PENAL POR DEFECTOS EN PRODUCTOS DESTINADOS A LOS CONSUMIDORES 38 (J. Boix Reig & A. Bernardi, eds., 2005).

mentation of those objectives, and procedures that guarantee a reasonable approximation of the best response to situations unforeseeable at the time of parliamentary regulation. This type of statutory regulation, consisting of open-ended normative programs,[21] are the best legal answer for risk situations, and are frequently used in what are called "thematic statutes."[22]

Since a prudential decision must take into account the circumstances of the case at hand, the uncertainty associated with situations of risk causes reticence and vagueness in parliamentary legislation and an expansion of the sphere of responsibilities of the Public Administration. An attenuation of the legal determination takes place that, nonetheless, should not necessarily be considered deficient from the perspective of the Rule of Law.[23] The administrative agency, when confronted with risk, is called upon to apply general standards and enjoys broad discretion to construe the statutory clauses.[24] The administrative agency ceases to be a mere instrument for the mechanical application of the statute (its conveyor belt),[25] and elaborates decisions only partially anticipated by the statute.[26] This lack of normative predetermination correlates with the difficulty of anticipating

---

21. The difference between "Zweckprogramme" (evolving normative program) and "Konditionalprogramme" (normative program where the outcome is previously stated) comes from N. LUHMANN, RECHT UND AUTOMATION IN DER ÖFFENTLICHEN VERWALTUNG 36 (1966).

22. M. Shapiro, *Administrative Discretion: The Next Stage*, in Y. L. Jour. 1505 (1983), noted that "although the historical dynamic is moving administrative law beyond adjudication and rulemaking, huge areas of discretion remain uncharted. One of the most intransigent consists of circumstances in which agencies are faced with 'thematic' statutory commands to take into account a number of goals or factors but are given no assignment of relative weights to those factors." Risk regulatory statutes could fit into such a description.

23. E. SCHMIDT-ASSMANN, LA TEORÍA... 207 *supra* note 5.

24. E. Schmidt-Aßmann, *Cuestiones fundamentales sobre la reforma de la teoría general del Derecho administrativo: necesidad de la innovación y presupuestos metodológicos*, in, INNOVACIÓN Y REFORMA EN EL DERECHO ADMINISTRATIVO, 128 (J. Barnes ed., 2006).

25. About the crisis of the "transmission belt" model, see R.B. Stewart, *The Reformation of American Administrative Law*, 88 H. L. Rev. 1669 *passim* (1975).

26. This has been called the rational-instrumental paradigm. E. FISHER, 28-35 *supra* note 6.

scientific and technical developments,[27] as well as, even more importantly, with the difficulty of scientific assessment of the consequences of current developments.[28]

C. CHARACTERISTICS OF RISK REGULATION.

The above-mentioned arguments provide risk regulation with some distinguishing features:[29] 1. Flexibility and temporal, 2. Projection towards the future, 3. Increasing generality and parallel proceduralization, and 4. A reduction of the differences between statutory regulation, administrative rule-making and administrative adjudication.

1. Risk regulation, as will be seen in detail in relation to administrative procedures, is characterized by flexibility and temporality. This means, among other things, that administrative adjudication is largely reversible because of changes in circumstances, the appearance of new knowledge or technologies, or changes in the regulations. As the original statutory regulation foresees change in the sources and manifestations of risks, it anticipates actions by administrative agencies that are provisional and reversible.

2. Inherent uncertainty tends to orient the regulation of risk towards early analysis of the possible consequences of risky actions, which can include both

---

27. F. Reimer, *Das Parlamentsgesetz als Steurungsmittel und Kontrollmasstab*, in GRUND-LAGEN DES VERWALTUNGSRECHTS 574 *supra* note 13.

28. Article 59 of EC Regulation 726/2004 and Article 30 of EC Regulation 178/2002, presuppose this difficulty in establishing a procedure to resolve controversies between scientific findings, a not infrequent occurrence. The Regulation (CE) 726/2004 of the European Parliament and of the Council of 31 march, 2004, establishes communitarian procedures for the authorization and control of medications for human and veterinary use, as well as the creation of the European Agency for Medications, OJ 30.4.2004. The Regulation (CE) 178/2002 of the European Parliament and the Council of 28. January, 2002, establishes the principles and general requirements for alimentary legislation, creates the European Authority of Food Safety, and sets procedures relating to food safety, OJ 1,2, 2002.

29. *See* I. Appel, 331, 352-57 *supra* note 16.

assessment of the risk and evaluation of potential regulatory alternatives. This is a tendency towards anticipation by means of early adoption of adequate measures.

3. Uncertainty, in the terms used above in II.1, gives rise to increasing generality in statutes and more stringent procedures for risk regulation. The legislature often refuses to adopt very specific decisions concerning risk situations, establishing only the framework (ends, priorities, and procedures) for these decisions. The task of the parliamentary statute in these matters is not that of foreseeing which decisions the agency will make, as much as it is to establish structures which will shape and give content to the necessary decisions, through, for example, a list of factors which the agency must consider.[30] In this sense, risk regulation can be considered an example of complex decision-making by an agency armed with insufficient normative guidance to make decisions.[31]

4. The less the substantive content of the legislative regulation of risk, the greater the power of the administrative agency regarding risk management. Incomplete or inconclusive legislative and administrative regulations increase the power of administrative adjudication in specific cases as well as erase the traditional distinctions between regulation and adjudication.

The above-mentioned characteristics of risk regulation are present in Regulation (EC) 178/2002, concerning food safety.[32] Its general objectives, the norms from Articles 1 and 5, would be unattainable through fixed statutory directives which directly set standards for private conduct. Instead, the Regulation establishes a series of administrative procedural guarantees to direct decision-making concerning food safety in a manner conforming to the precautionary principle. This appeal to the precautionary principle, explicitly stated in Article 7 of the same Regulation, permits agencies to change their response to evolving technology. The application of the five general factors defining the precautionary principle[33] allows flexibility that can mitigate the consequences of scienti-

---

30. More on this idea in I. Appel, 354-56 *supra* note 16.

31. *See* H-H. Trute, *Methodik der Herstellung und Darstellung verwaltungsrechtlicher Entscheidungen,* in METHODEN DER VERWALTUNGSRECHTSWISSENSCHAFT 317 (E. Schmidt-Aßmann & W. Hoffmann-Riem eds., 2004).

32. *Supra.*note 28.

33. The Communication of the Commission about the course of the precautionary principle, from February 2, 2000, COM (2001) 1 final, mentions these five "priniciples": proportionality, non-discrimination, coherence, cost-benefit analysis of both action and inaction, and study of scientific progress.

fic uncertainty,[34] while giving direction and a certain structure to decisions adopted in situations of extreme uncertainty.[35] The mechanisms of rapid response and the potential adoption of emergency measures set out in Articles 50 and 53 of the Regulation are concrete expressions of planned flexibility and reversibility of risk regulation. The possible establishment of special, non-specific, or provisional measures adequate to address emergencies, as envisaged in Article 53.1 of the Regulation, is also an example of the aforementioned reduction of the differences between functions of rulemaking (both legislative and administrative) and administrative adjudication.

---

34. I. Appel, 344-45 *supra* note 16.

35. *For discussion of the application of the precautionary principle to the different levels of decision-making and policy-making, see Our "Public Health, Environmental Protection and Trade Restrictions: the Precautionary Principle as Applied in EC Law, in* CARL HEYMANNS, WIRTSCHAFT UND GESELLSCHAFT IM STAAT DER GEGENWART: GEDÄCHTNISSCHRIFT FÜR PETER J. TETTINGER 731-46 (2007).

III
RISK MANAGEMENT ADMINISTRATIVE PROCEDURES

A. CONCEPT

Given the above peculiar characteristics of risk regulation, the question is whether a definitive category of administrative procedures with common characteristics is identifiable. These characteristics can be identified in reference to a series of circumstances in which these procedures operate, inasmuch as these circumstances determine the type of functions that the procedures are destined to carry out and the existence of common structural elements.

In order to establish the category of administrative procedures, different criteria can be applied. Among others, the traditional criteria are:[36] the method used to set the procedure in motion following administrative or private initiative, the number of interested parties, the homogeneity or heterogeneity of the interests at stake, the participation of one or several subcomponents of one or several administrative agencies, the primary or secondary nature of the procedure (in the sense that it may or may not influence a previous procedure), and the objective or result to which the procedures are oriented (procedures concerning contracting, the granting of funds, expropriation, imposition of sanctions, etc). These classification criteria continue to be useful. Nevertheless, they do not exhaust the possibilities for the construction of typologies.

The classification criterion used to identify the administrative procedures of risk management in this paper is that of the conditions under which those procedures are developed. In short, we understand administrative procedures of risk management to be those decision-making processes of the administrative agency that take place in con-

---

36. A. Voßkuhle, *Strukturen und Bauformen...* 285-86 *supra* note 3.

ditions of elevated complexity and cognitive uncertainty, in relation to scientific or technological innovation (products, facilities, actions, etc.) that entail risk, and whose objective consists of finding a reasonable response among the set of legally possible responses in light of affected, legally protected assets. Identification of the conditions of initial regulation partially determines, as we shall see, the ordering of mandated functions of the agency and their structural elements.

B. FUNCTIONS PERFORMED

Administrative procedures fulfill several functions;[37] particularly relevant is the assurance of the lawfulness of administrative activities.[38] Such assurance is even more crucial in risk management procedures due to the openness of the statutory framework regulating administrative control of risk. The discretion enjoyed by the administrative authorities finds a balance in the required procedure and potential judicial review of administrative procedure requirements. The more intense procedural requirements compensate to a certain extent for the openness of the statutory regulations.[39]

Administrative procedures perform, nevertheless, other important functions besides controlling agency actions.[40] The regulation of administrative procedures guides administrative agencies in the sense that it determines *how* the agencies and other parties involved in the procedure operate.[41] This is especially important in risk management

---

37. E. Schmidt-Aßmann, *Strutures and Functions of Administrative Procedures...supra* note 5.

38. W. Hoffmann-Riem 13, 28 *supra* note 4.

39. W. Hoffmann-Riem 22 *supra* note 4.

40. *With reference to Spain see,* J. Tornos Mas, *La simplificación procedimental en el ordenamiento español,* 151 REVISTA DE ADMINISTRACIÓN PÚBLICA, 45 (2000), and J. PONCE SOLE, DEBER DE BUENA ADMINISTRACIÓN Y DERECHO AL PROCEDIMIENTO ADMINISTRATIVO DEBIDO (2001). *Recently,* J. Barnes, *Sobre el procedimiento administrativo: evolución y perspectivas,* in INNOVACIÓN Y REFORMA EN EL DERECHO ADMINISTRATIVO 270 *supra* note 24.

41. W. Hoffmann-Riem 27, 39 *supra* note 4.

procedures because there are usually diverse interests at stake, high levels of uncertainty, and a variety of complex factors that should be taken into account, as previously noted.

The steering function of administrative procedures can be specified through several more detailed functions such as: allowing broad participation, providing for interest-balancing, promoting administrative transparency and clarity, making cooperation among disparate agencies possible, and enhancing administrative efficiency.[42]

Thus, the statutory content of risk regulation often focuses on administrative procedural requirements in order to assure that those procedures fulfill the desired functions of controlling risk.

C. STRUCTURAL ELEMENTS

Some patterns can be perceived as common structural elements of the risk regulation statutes imposing administrative procedure requirements. Most of them do not add innovations to the previous administrative procedure requirements already well established in other fields of administrative regulation. What could be considered peculiar is the correlation between the presence of the elements of risk and the intensity with which administrative procedural requirements are applied.[43] The list of these common structural elements would include the following points.

1. THE REINFORCEMENT OF COOPERATIVE OBLIGATIONS THAT FALL ON THE APPLICANTS

The regulations regarding risk management procedures impose very strict cooperative obligations on the part of the promoter of the

---

42. E. Schmidt-Aßmann, *supra* note 5. *See also*, W. Hoffmann-Riem 28 *supra* note 4.

43. A. Voßkuhle 340 *supra* note 3.

product, facility or activity likely to cause risks.[44] Among other reasons for this imposition, the scarcity of resources and of specialized personnel within the administrative agency are usually mentioned.[45] The high costs of risk assessment, and the fact that the knowledge needed can often only be found in the private sector are also important factors in this cooperation requirement.[46] Nevertheless, the underlying questions are: who is to bear the costs, and how deal with other interested parties that cannot afford the high costs involved in obtaining second opinions or alternative analysis of risk assessment. Dealing with the variety of interests with diverse economic situations and varying stages of technological development is one of the greatest challenges faced by the regulation of risk management procedures.

Reinforcement of cooperative obligations, specific to risk management procedures, tends to allow access by parties with different levels of resources in order to make sure that different private interests are equally represented.[47] The establishment of generalized obligations of documentation, investigation and information for the regulated entity expands public-private collaboration within risk management procedures. That requirement of cooperation is higher than what is usual in other more traditional administrative procedure modes.

2. INTENSIFIED INFORMATION ON RISK

One of the functions performed by administrative procedures that is particularly necessary in risk regulation is the facilitation of acceptance of regulation by the different parties involved as well as accep-

---

44. *In similar terms, Id.*

45. *See Id.*

46. For example, toxicological exams and trials previous to grant a license to commercialize medicines.

47. *See,* H-H. Trute, *Die demokratische Legitimation der Verwaltung* 372 *supra* note 31.

tance by the public in general.[48] In risk management, therefore, information and communication with all those possibly affected is not limited to an isolated act in the midst of the agency procedure. In the initial proceedings of risk management, there is a general tendency to augment communication between the interested parties.[49] Moreover, the communication of risk is configured as a continuing obligation, whenever reportable incidents arise. Present in the initial decision-making process, provision of information on risk goes beyond the initial phase and becomes a continuous component of the ongoing relationship between those that generate the risk-generating phenomenon (product, installation or activity), the administrative agency, those possibly affected and the general public.

Another dimension of communication of risk is the obligation to inform the public about the nature of risk, specifying the origin and the measures that should be adopted to prevent, minimize or eliminate such risk. The duty often lies with administrative authorities.[50] The statutory clauses detailing such obligations emphasize the right to get accurate information. Infringement of those rights could be considered a statutory violation and in some legal systems also a constitutional violation.[51]

---

48. The need to look after the acceptance of the involved individuals or companies is considered by W. Hoffmann-Riem as one of the criteria of governance that should characterize a good administrative practice. *See* W. Hoffmann-Riem, *Methoden einer anwendungsorientierten Verwaltungsrechtswissenschaft* in METHODEN DER VERWALTUNGSRECHTSWISSENSCHAFT 49-50 (E. Schmidt-Aßmann & W. Hoffmann-Riem eds., 2004).

49. A. Voßkuhle 334 *supra* note 3.

50. *See, for example,* Article 10 of the EC Regulation n° 178/2002, cit. note 35, for the health authorities regarding food or feed, when there is reasonable cause to suspect that it could represent a risk for human or animal health.

51. Thus, in Spain it could be considered a violation of Article 20.1.d) of the Spanish Constitución 1978. *See,* F. VELASCO CABALLERO, LA INFORMACIÓN ADMINISTRATIVA AL PÚBLICO 126, 134 (1998).

3. The Importance of Expert Opinion

Knowledge is simultaneously a factor in the production of risk and a decisive means of risk prevention.[52] Knowledge is necessary to understand the extent of the risk, and shapes the plan of action in the face of risk situations. The assessment of the risks entailed by a new product, facility or activity usually requires advanced technical and scientific knowledge, which are not always available within the agency empowered to license such innovations. The limited information available within the agency frequently brings about dependence on external expert opinion as a central element in the decision-making process.[53] The appeal to experts, whether individuals or commissions, plays a decisive role in the evaluation of risk and, therefore, in the decisions taken regarding its management.

Several administrative procedural safeguards are related to dependence on expert knowledge, among others:[54] the choice of experts, the transparency of the designation process, and the commitment of the agency to following the opinions of the experts. Those who evaluate agency action may also wish to examine the use of any professional expertise obtained outside the original procedure, the method of communication of the results, the consequences of dissension among the designated experts, and the way to proceed in the face of inconclusive results or in cases when no consistent or accurate results regarding the risk assessment are available.

The above issues demonstrate that risk-assessment and risk-management are and should be regarded as closely related but slightly different activities, each of them with its specific features. The first confronts factual reality and its ultimate objective is to find the best possible understanding of the situation at hand. The second concerns the adoption of a decision and attempts to find the most appropriate solution.

---

52. *See* I. Appel 328 *supra* note 16.

53. W. Hoffmann-Riem 58 *supra* note 4, and A. Voßkuhle 341 *supra* note 3.

54. *See* W. Hoffmann-Riem 58 *supra* note 4.

This creates two "powers," the scientific, charged with the assessment of the risk, and the administrative, orientated towards decision-making, each of them often confined to different departments, agencies or commissions. The "scientific power" is often conferred on committees created *ex profeso* to act autonomously towards the completion of their assignment; the "political-regulatory power" lies with already existent political or institutional authorities.[55] The functions of the scientific power are information, determination, and, essentially, evaluation of risk, but not that of decision-making or adjudication. The administrative authorities must decide each case by following specified procedures for adjudication and giving consideration to scientific findings, at the same time taking into account whether a determined risk can or cannot be assumed and if it is acceptable to society.[56]

Along with the necessity to turn to expert advice, there is the need to develop rules to determine when this advice is considered adequate. These are rules that facilitate the decision on when the amount of knowledge and expertise acquired through a specific procedure is sufficient. In general, the uncertainty involved in the understanding of risk situations requires the creation of these types of rules, without which the investigative process would carry on indefinitely. These rules are concerned with the termination of administrative procedure (known in German as "*Stopregeln*").[57] Such rules play an important role in judicial review of administrative decision-making regarding risk, as well as providing an instrument for the determination of possible administrative liability when the regulated entity is damaged by defective risk-assessment.

---

55. *See* J. Esteve Pardo, *Ciencia y Derecho ante los riesgos para la salud. Evaluación, decisión y gestión*, 142, 144 (2003). This author refers to the "institutionalisation of scientific assessment and evaluation" by the creation of those agencies and committees.

56. *For Spanish scholarly legal doctrine about the acceptability of risk and its limits, see* M. Rebollo Puig &, M. Izquierdo Carrasco, *El principio de precaución y la defensa de los consumidores*, 265-266 Documentación Administrativa 228 and *passim*.

57. W Hoffmann-Riem, *Methoden einer anwendungsorientierten Verwaltungsrechtswissenschaft* in Methoden der Verwaltungsrechtswissenschaft, 64 (E. Schmidt-Aßmann & W. Hoffmann-Riem eds., 2004).

4. The Temporary Nature of the Adjudicative Decisions Taken by the Administrative Agency

It is generally understood that the connection between the administrative agency and the interested parties during administrative procedures is provisional, while the adjudicative decision that ends the procedure carries with it a series of guarantees of stability and permanence. In risk management procedures, this rule is inverted; the decisions made in situations of uncertainty should be considered provisional, as moments in a linear representation of a procedural relation that continues in time.[58]

In risk management procedures the decisions is more likely to be modified than in traditional administrative decisions. This is apparent in the frequently employed temporary limitation of authorizations, in the increased possibilities for changing or refining decision due to changing circumstances, the acceptance of conditions imposed *a posteriori,* and in the ample stipulations concerning the suspensive effects of decisions.[59]

Moreover, risk management procedures extend beyond the adjudicatory decision, creating a lasting relationship between the administrative agency and the regulated entity. In this sense, the procedures of risk management are a manifestation of the generalized tendency of administrative "procedural perpetuation,"[60] a consequence of more intense informative and communicative connections, the existence of permanent controls and inspections, as well as the obligation to submit periodical reports. In this sense, risk management procedures never come to a true end,[61] and generate permanent obligations of surveillance.[62]

---

58. *See*, A. V, 341 *supra note 3.*

59. *Id.*

60. The idea can be seen in A. Voßkuhle 345 *supra* note 3.

61. A. Voßkuhle, 34 *supra* note 3.

62. G. Doménech Pascual, *El seguimiento de normas y actos jurídicos* in 98-100 (May-August 2005).

5. The Importance of the Interim Administrative Decisions

Risk caused by products, facilities or activities frequently requires a rapid response by an administration. Administrative procedure, while ostensibly guaranteeing legality and rationality, is one more delay in regulation. Provisional response in the face of risk, including decisions adopted before the corresponding legal procedures are complied with, is made possible by the inclusion in the statutory mandate of provisional administrative measures. The adoption of interim relief gives rise to a decision, a declaration or a disposition in a given matter, that is to say, it gives rise to an adjudicatory decision of the administrative agency. The adoption of such measures is unilateral and implies the use of public power having a positive or negative effect on the legal situation of those affected. The administrative agency adjudicates a concrete case, although it does so subject to the later imposition of the formal procedure to which this provisional measure is ancillary.

The regulation of administrative procedures of risk management is characterized by the authorization of the administrative agency to adopt interim measures when they are adequate, necessary, and proportionate to the end pursued. In a field where administrative procedure guarantees play as important a role as previously stated, statutory regulation empowers the administrative authorities to adopt provisional decisions with very little or no procedure at all.

IV
CONCLUSION

THERE are few areas that demonstrate such an intense interaction between law and reality as does that of risk regulation. The characteristics of risk regulation place strict conditions on regulation designed to realistically minimize future harm arising from situations of risk. Because of the complexity and multiplicity of the sources of risk, the connection between law and risk is subject to constant change.

An analysis of the regulations designed to control risk makes two phenomena clear: the reliance of risk regulation on corresponding administrative procedures which take risk into account and, closely related to this reliance, the great discretion given to the administrative authorities in risk management. These phenomena affect the position that the administrative agency occupies in relation to statutory law in these sectors, and emphasize the importance of the analysis of specific risk management administrative procedures.

This category is composed of a wide variety of institutions associated with the performance of an important series of functions and the presence of common structural elements. The functions and structural elements characterizing these procedures are also present in other administrative procedures found in a wide range of fields. But specific to these procedures are the concentration and importance of the functions and structural elements used to organize in an innovative manner the role of scientific and technological experts, the position of the regulated entity, and the administrative agency's responsibilities.

Contrasting the elements common to administrative procedures for management of risk and the common elements established in statutes regarding general administrative procedures makes their difference apparent. More general statutory regulations were created with specific situations in mind. In today's legal regime, these statutory regulations, particularly regulations regarding risk, should be consistent with the multiplicity of functions that contemporary administrative procedures must carry out, keeping in mind that the peculiarities arising from the specific characteristics of the different regulatory sectors exert a very important influence over projected procedures.

CHAPTER IV

ADMINISTRATIVE PROCEDURE AND THE INFORMATION AND KNOWLEDGE SOCIETY

Ricardo García Macho*

* Professor of Administrative Law, University Jaume I, Castellón, Spain.

INDEX

THIS paper will lay out the effects that the information and knowledge society has on administrative procedure and the current process of administrative procedure restructuring under the aegis of the reform of administrative law. In effect, the structure of traditional administrative procedure is insufficient to meet the demands that the information society places on the exchange of information between the citizen and public administration. Administrative procedure therefore must be reoriented and adapted to the challenges of public participation in specific areas—for example, those concerning the environment and urban planning. Such reorientation of procedure is the focus of this article, which will lay out the inadequate nature of traditional administrative procedure and will propose particular processes for adaptation to the changes that have come about in modern society.

I
THE INFORMATION AND KNOWLEDGE SOCIETY

A. THE CONCEPT OF AN INFORMATION AND KNOWLEDGE SOCIETY

The idea of an "information society" arose in the 1960s as a means of characterizing fundamental changes in industrial society from a political, economic, and scientific perspective.[1] In Spain, the concept has expanded rapidly, not only into the field of law,[2] but also into other diverse areas of study, among which are the fields of economics, politics, and sociology. Although now accepted as a scholarly term, its definition

---

1. See J. Tauss et al., *Einfürung: Wege in der Informationsgesellschaft,* in DEUTSCHLANDS WEG IN DER INFORMATIONSGESELLSCHAFT 18 (J. Tauss et al., eds., 1996).

2. See J.L. Piñar Mañas, *Revolución tecnológica, Derecho Administrativo y Administración Pública. Notas provisionales para una reflexión,* in PUBLICACIONES DE LA ASOCIACIÓN ESPAÑOLA DE PROFESORES DE DERECHO ADMINISTRATIVO (ACTAS DEL I CONGRESO DE LA ASOCIACIÓN ESPAÑOLA DE PROFESORES DE DERECHO ADMINISTRATIVO) 54 (2007) [hereinafter ACTAS DEL I CONGRESO DE LA ASOCIACIÓN].

and scope of application are nonetheless murky, given that it can be applied to a wide variety of concepts and is used to fix the boundaries of a multitude of differing criteria.[3] An important starting point from which to understand the profound changes in society is to assert that the industrial society has been replaced by the information society.

A first step in the interpretation and characterization of the information society is to consider it from the standpoint of the economics of information. Two major indicators demonstrating the vigorous impulse increased information has given to the economy are the process of wealth-creation and the growing number of employees in sectors related to information-processing. A second consideration is that the concept of an information society implies the existence of a post-industrial society, in which structures designed to produce and distribute massive amounts of goods have given way progressively to a service-based society dealing in information. Finally, a third way of defining the information society is to consider it as a digital society built on the twin foundations of communication and information, through interconnection and the velocity of diffusion.[4]

These changes demonstrate how the information society is characterized by the intensive use of *information*, which acquires economic as well as cultural and educational value.[5] This process has significant political ramifications beyond the scope of this study.[6] The increasing

---

3. *See* W. Hoffmann-Riem, *Verwaltungsrecht in der Informationsgesellschaft-Einleitende Problemskizze, in* VERWALTUNGSRECHT IN DER INFORMATIONSGESELLSCHAFT 10 (W. Hoffmann-Riem & E. Schmidt-Aßmann, eds., 2000).

4. *For an in-depth study, see* Tauss et al. 19, *supra* note 1.

5. As N. Luhmann has pointed out, the information society in this sense has, above all, economic value, with its foundations in the binary of production and consumption, and so more and more time is spent on the production of information, and more and more work and free time is needed for its consumption. Information becomes a type of merchandise that is produced, transmitted and consumed; in other words, a disposable product. This of course opens up new questions on the way we conceptualise information. N. LUHMANN, II DIE GESELLSCHAFT DER GESELLSCHAFT Ch. 4-5, 1088 *passim* (1997).

6. *For a critical point of view on the use of information, see* W. Gellner, *Individualisierung und Globalisierung. Die Privatisierung der Öffentlichkeit?, in* POLITIK UND DEMOKRATIE IN DER INFORMATIONSGESELLSCHAFT 25 (1997).

importance of information leads to the focus on another basic concept, its *transmission*, carried out today on a massive scale through existing technologies. The fact that information is transmitted with the intention that it be made available to public and private institutions, companies, social groups etc, leads us to a third fundamental concept, *knowledge*,[7] through which we acquire an understanding and interpretation of information as the basic foundation for decision-making.[8] Knowledge is elaborated information, and is created when information is made comprehensible.[9]

1. LAW AND INFORMATION SOCIETY

The information society cannot be fully implemented unless a corresponding discipline of Information Law is developed systematically, extending into both the domains of public and private law.[10] We limit our study in this article to the manner in which the information society influences administrative procedure within the framework of an "Administrative Law of Information," taking as a given that information is an essential element of administrative law.[11] This point has been underlined by R. Pitschas,[12] who points out that an administrative law

---

7. *See* M. Castells, I LA ERA DE LA INFORMACIÓN, 43, 94 ,(2005).

8. The difference between information and knowledge has been explained clearly by N. Stehr, underlining the fact that knowledge is a deeper concept, requiring intellectual capacity, and thus is restrictive; while information is a more general concept, whose reception does not need great intellectual capacity. Information is not on the same level as knowledge, but the first is a requirement for using the second. N. STEHR, THE FRAGILITY OF MODERN SOCIETIES: KNOWLEDGE AND RISK IN THE INFORMATION AGE 41 (2001).

9. *See* Hoffman-Riem 12, *supra* note 3 and A. Scherzberg, "Die öffentliche Verwaltung als informationelle Organisation," in VERWALTUNGSRECHT IN DER INFORMATIONSGESELLSCHAFT 2000, *supra* note 3.

10. *For a comprehensive discussion of "Information Law," see* M. KLOEPFER, INFORMATIONS-RECHT (2002).

11. The bibliography on the crucial theme of information and administrative law from different perspectives is extensive, and in part has been included by L.A. BALLESTEROS MOFFA, LA PRIVACIDAD ELECTRÓNICA 25-27 n.1 (2005).

of information will include all those norms and laws in the juridical-public domain regulating the state's relationships within the areas of communications and information, and which regulate proper conduct in the interaction among public employees themselves, and in their communications with the citizen. This description of an administrative law of information has been restructured and widened in Pitschas' later works,[13] which include analysis of both the general category (describing those norms and laws that regulate information and communication technology, the basic supply of information to citizens, and the various options open to the state regarding data protection and the right to information), and the specific administrative provisions (norms and laws dealing with information exchange between state and citizen, between differing public authorities, or as used to regulate specific areas, such as telecommunications). This area of law also fulfills the role of leadership or governance of the State, in tandem with a Constitutional Law of Information, and, furthermore, includes specific regulatory models for communication in high risk areas (among others genetic engineering, chemical products and nuclear energy).

Javier Barnes takes a wider perspective, finding that an administrative law of information should be broad enough to encompass more than the implementation of new information technologies, and should incorporate areas such as knowledge development, information and communication (the global economy, the risk society, and so on), and the effects or consequences of the information society (new regulatory methods or forms of public administration), from a point of view that emphasizes the "nature" of information.[14]

---

12. *Allgemeines Verwaltungsrecht als Teil der öffentlichen Informationsordnung*, in REFORM DES ALLGEMEINES VERWALTUNGSRECHT 241 *passim* (W. Hoffdman-Riem et al. eds., Baden-Baden, 1993).

13. Here, I refer the reader to a Spanish translation of the author's work, which includes a bibliography of his other studies. Pitschas, *El Derecho Administrativo de la Información: La regulación de la autodeterminación informativa y el gobierno electrónico, in* INNOVACIÓN Y REFORMA EN EL DERECHO ADMINISTRATIVO 237 (J. Barnes, ed., 2006).

14. Javier Barnes, *Sobre el Derecho Administrativo de la Información*, 35 REVISTA CATALANA DE DRET PÚBLIC 5 (2007).

B. THE SIGNIFICANCE OF INFORMATION IN ADMINISTRATIVE LAW

Describing the information society requires referral to the concept of "information" (in spite of conceptual difficulties)[15] in the context of its association with public administration. Information has become an object of law,[16] and in fact "Information Law" is now an accepted concept and has become a legal discipline applied to the information society.[17] It is evident that the development of information and communications technologies (ICT) has had crucial effects on public administration, evidenced by the growing automation of administrative actions and the development of electronic administration.

An example of this phenomenon is Law 11/2007 (June 22),[18] dealing with the electronic access by citizens to public services. This Law represents a first important step in the development of electronic administration, within the context of how public administration relates to the citizen, and only superficially regulates information exchange between different public administrations.[19]

---

15. Developing this argument, Hoeren emphasizes that no one really knows what "information" is, although everybody uses the term without fully defining its meaning. Hoeren, *Zur Einführung: Informationsrecht*, JuS 947 (2002).

16. *On the significance of information for law, see* M. Albers, *Information als Neue Dimension im Recht, in* RECHTSTHEORIE 61, 77 (2002).

17. This is how M. Kloepfer understands it. *See* Kloepfer Prologue (Vorwort) v, vii, *supra* note 10. *See also* K. Stohrer, *Informationspflichten Privater gegenüber dem Staat in Zeiten von Privatisierung, Liberalisierung und Deregulierung, Berlin, 200," 44 passim.*

18. Unless otherwise noted, the Laws cited are those of Spain.

19. It is law that is restrictive from the viewpoint of the information society, referring in essence to the bilateral relationship between the citizen and the administration, without including significant innovations in administrative procedure that would create a public administration capable of transmitting and generating information, appropriate to the information society. It is anchored in traditional administrative procedure, stated out in law 30/1992. A profound study of the law is to be found in J. Barnes, *Sobre el Derecho Administrativo de la Información* 9, *supra* note 14.

At present, the tendency is not so much towards an electronic administration, but rather a electronic government, where all public administration's internal business, as well as its interactions with the citizen, are carried out electronically. The long-term goal of electronic government is to establish non-hierarchical relationships between institutions where public authorities function using a fully computerized management system, as yet an ideal far from achieved in daily administrative activities.[20]

It seems clear that both the qualitative and quantitative increases in available information influences both the way that public administration functions and the legal regulation of administration, making it imperative to find solutions for the new and unexpected problems arising from this increase. For example, Information Law cannot be limited to protecting personal information, but must instead be understood in a broader context as creating a framework within which public authorities carry out new tasks and execute new responsibilities. While a defensive perspective on protecting fundamental rights against the state and safeguarding personal privacy remains important, the right to possess and receive information, in whose provision public authorities play a vital role,[21] must also be considered, given that it is this information that allows the citizen to participate effectively in decision making. Public administrations, and therefore administrative law, are facing new challenges which are changing their objectives and the way in which they carry out their functions.[22]

Within this context, there must be a restructuring of public administrative objectives. Information gathering must be a primary objective, not only because information has to be made available to the

---

20. *See* G. Britz, *Elektronische Verwaltung, in* II GRUNDLAGEN DES VERWALTUNGSRECHTS 410 (Hoffmann-Riem et al., eds., 2008).

21. The information necessary for an informed public capable of actively influencing social and political life is, of course, not only transmitted by public administrations, but also involves the media in its widest sense, as well as different types of association, forums, and so on. These facets of an information society create a communication flux that molds informed public opinion and gives it decision and control capacity. *See* J. HABERMAS, FACTICIDAD Y VALIDEZ 439 (1998).

22. *See* E. SCHMIDT-ASSMANN, LA TEORÍA GENERAL DEL DERECHO ADMINISTRATIVO COMO SISTEMA 288 (2003).

citizen, but also because its availability improves the public administration's efficiency and capacity. In specific areas, such as environmental or urban planning law, strategic planning, and telecommunications, where "complex administrative decisions"[23] have to be made, it is unlikely that public administration can be used as a primary information source. In these areas, it is necessary to resort to private sources of information, reinforcing the need for strong cooperation between the state and its citizens.

Examining all of the above considerations, it is clear that both information and knowledge, as well as their transmission, play vital roles in the workings of public administration, thus underlining the need for the specific legal regulation of Information in Public law. This conclusion has led Voßkuhle[24] to establish a system of classification that includes four areas of regulation. First, a law of administrative communication, regulating information and communication flows between public administration and the citizen,[25] ensures that the former efficiently fulfills its obligations in collaboration with the latter, creating a system of administrative procedure and action. Secondly, legal regulation of the administrative organization of information, allowing for the internal structural reorganization of public administration in line with the new tasks that now face it, requires an essential

---

23. *See* E. Schmidt-Aßmann, *Verwaltungsverarwortung und Verwaltungsgerichtsbarkeit, in* VVDStRL, Bd. 34. 222 (1976).

24. *Schmidt-Aßmann Der Wandel von Verwaltungsrecht und Verwaltungsprozessrecht in der Informationsgesellschaft* 355, *supra* note 3. Similarly, Schmidt-Aßmann accepts the division established by Vosskuhle regarding these four areas of regulation defining the existence of the discipline administrative law of information, in E. SCHMIDT-ASSMANN, DAS ALLGEMEINE VERWALTUNGSRECHT ALS ORDNUNGSIDEE 280 (2nd ed., 2006).

25. Beyond the mere provision of news and data by the administration, information and communication between public administrations and the citizen can be improved by allowing for access without restrictions to files, proceedings and administrative documents, or by reinforcing the obligation to cooperate in the administrative procedure. The strengthening and development of article 105 Spanish Constitution from an administrative law perspective, where information plays a primary role, would also improve information and communication between public administration and the citizen. Current steps in this direction do not go far enough, and in fact the lawmaker in Spain has restricted the potential of this article.

shift in the manner that the administration communicates information and in the way that it compiles knowledge in order to make it available to the citizen. This second area refers to the challenges presented by the intertwining of data and information in the European or international sphere,[26] and the difficulties of publicizing the large quantity of data that is produced as a consequence of new Information and Communications Technologies (ICT) and the change predicated on these technologies.

As problems arise, they must be resolved; particular areas creating legal problems include data security and control, joint projects within the administration or with private entities, and data and information management.[27]

The third area of regulation is the use of information in the private sector, where relations between private individuals are regulated and where access to sources of information is permitted on a private basis to all requesting parties.

In this regard, Directive 2000/31/CE (June 8) on electronic commerce is relevant. The Directive aims to develop information society services within Europe without internal frontiers, thus increasing the competitiveness of European companies - particularly in small and medium-sized enterprises. Developing this Directive, Law 34/2002 (July 11) on information society services and electronic commerce[28] has as its main aim the establishment of a type of free market model based on competitive criteria (Art. 1), with certain restrictive exceptions involving public order, public health, and the protection of minors (Art. 8). Other laws, such as Law 32/2003 (Nov. 3) on Telecommunications, have

---

26. *E.g.*, the Schengen Information System in the European Union.

27. *For a general study on this matter, see* M. Gómez Puente, La Administración Electrónica, in Actas del I Congreso de la Asociación 116, *supra* note 2.

28. There is a proposed law on measures to give impetus to the information society, included in the 2006-2010 Plan to develop the information society, which would introduce important changes in Law 34/2002 and in other laws such as the laws on telecommunications and electronic signatures. This proposed law seeks to promote information technology and guarantee citizen rights in the information society.

dealt with the provision of information (art. 9)[29] in the information society, fostering effective competition in the telecommunication market (Art. 3-a).[30] Law 26/2003, regulating stock market Public Limited Companies, has an objective of increased transparency in Public Limited Companies, and so reinforces duties relative to information and transparency.[31]

Finally, the fourth area of regulation involves laws on the transmission of information, and is intertwined with the other three areas, although in a wider sense it is concerned with the protection of individuals in an information society that can generate and transmit data on a global scale. Within this fourth area of regulation there is a balance between an individual's fundamental right to have his personal information protected (Art. 18.4 CE)[32] and the right to participate directly in public affairs and to receive and to communicate information (arts. 20.1-d and 23.1 CE)[33], in which the first, a right to individual freedom, does not necessarily prevail over the other two, which are rights to receive a service.

---

29. The supply of this information is subject to specific limits, and infringement of rights implies a very serious administrative infraction. *See* J.J. Lavilla Rubira, *Comentario al artículo 9*, in COMENTARIOS A LA LEY GENERAL DE TELECOMUNICACIONES,139 (E. García de Enterría & T. de la Cuadra-Salcedo, eds., 2004).

30. *See* J.F. Mestre Delgado, *Comentario al artículo 3, in* COMENTARIOS A LA LEY GENERAL DE TELECOMUNICACIONES, 70 (E. García de Enterría & T. de la Cuadra-Salcedo, eds., 2004).

31. Article 16 guarantees information within listed limited companies, while in the Law of Public Limited Companies article 112 establishes the right of information of shareholders from company administrators. Along these lines, S. Muñoz Machado has referred to the importance of information and transparency in corporate culture, as in the American model. S. MUÑOZ MACHADO, I TRATADO DE DERECHO ADMINISTRATIVO Y DERECHO PÚBLICO GENERAL 1217 (2nd. ed., 2006).

32. Art. 18.4 CE: The law shall limit the use of information, to guarantee personal and family honor, the privacy of citizens, and the full exercise of their rights.

33. Art. 20.1.d CE: The following rights are recognized and protected: d). To communicate or receive freely truthful information through any means of dissemination. The law shall regulate the right to the protection of the clause on conscience and professional secrecy in the exercise of these freedoms; Art. 23.1 CE: Citizens have the right to participate in public affairs, directly or through representatives freely elected in periodic elections by universal suffrage.

C. TRANSFORMING ADMINISTRATIVE PROCEDURE

The significant growth in electronic media and the permanent generation of information, in which we can find the origins of an electronic administration, have crucially important consequences for administrative law. These changes are so crucial that today terms such as "information," "communication" or "knowledge" are as equally important for the science of administrative law, and, of course, for administrative procedure, as terms such as "Administrative activity" or "Administrative resolution"[34] once were. What should be underlined here is that we are not only dealing with the construction of an electronic administration, as discussed above in Part I.2,[35] but also with the fact that, during an administrative procedure, under the auspices of an employee of the public administration,[36] information can be created and elaborated. This is a new direction insofar as the objectives of administrative procedure go, given that the final product of administrative procedure has always been an administrative decision, and not the generation of information.

The development of an administrative procedure capable of elaborating and transmitting information so as to make it widely available has been strongly promoted by European Community law, by the Charter of Fundamental Rights of the European Union and by the Spanish Constitution.

---

34. See T. Vesting, *Die Bedeutung von Information und Kommunikation für die verwaltungsrechtliche Systembildung*, in II GRUNDLAGEN DES VERWALTUNGSRECHTS 4, *supra* note 19.

35. *See* J. Barnes, *Sobre el procedimiento administrativo: evolución y perspectivas*, in INNOVACIÓN Y REFORMA EN EL DERECHO ADMINISTRATIVO 302, *supra* note 13.

36. Along these lines, see E. Schmidt-Aßmann, *Structures and Functions of Administrative Procedure in German, European and International Law*, *supra* Ch. I (Part I.1).

1. References to Administrative Procedure and Information Included in European Constitutional Texts

Access to public documents is regulated in article 255 of the Treaty Establishing the European Community (TEC), where reference is made to access to European Parliament, Council and Commission documents (art. 255.1), as well as to general principles, subject to the provisions of the procedure laid out in article 251 (art. 255.2). It is not until Regulation 1049/2001 (May 30) that the effective exercise of this right is regulated, as mentioned in its preamble. This regulation has become the general framework for access to public documents within European institutions, with its main aim being the widest possible access to documents while promoting good administrative practice (arts. 1-a and b). The TEC also refers to the factors underlying regulations and administrative acts (art. 253), one of which is access to information. The fact that public administrations must make publicly available the reasons behind their acts has a profound impact on their motivations and behavior. These regulations are binding on Spanish administrative procedure law insofar as they affect national law. Regulation 1049/2001 is also directly applicable.

Article 41 of the Charter of Fundamental Rights of the European Union, referring to the right to good administration, strengthens the right to information in administrative procedure, given that its second paragraph lays out: the right of every person to be given a hearing before the taking of any individual measure which would affect him or her adversely (art. 41.2), the right to access his or her files, with some restrictions to protect legitimate interests in confidentiality and in professional and business secrecy (art. 41.2), and the obligation of the administration to give reasons for its decisions (art. 41.2). Likewise, promoting information access is a fundamental rule laid out in article 42, which regulates the right of access to European Parliament, Council and Commission documents. Article 42 has the same content as article 255.1 TCE, reinforcing its effectiveness.

2. Effects of the Spanish Constitution on Administrative Procedure of Information

There are various Constitutional provisions that have brought about the creation and development of an administrative procedure whereby information is generated and transmitted to the citizen, and have built the foundations for a more transparent public administration. This trend toward an increasingly transparent administration continues.

The fundamental right provided for in article 20.1-d of the Constitution, which should be understood as the right to receive information and, consequently, to be informed,[37] is connected with the right of access to public documents (art. 105-b CE).[38] The individual's right to be informed is not limited to relations with the media, but extends to information held by public bodies, including public administrations. This provision strengthens both access to information and the process of the distribution of information by public administrations to citizens, channeled through administrative procedures.

A citizen's right to participate directly in public affairs (art. 23.1) is a fundamental right linked to participation in administrative procedure,[39] presupposing the existence of effective measures that permit citizen participation in the public domain. With overtones of the general and common good, it has as its counterpoint those kept "private" or "secret."[40] Its recognition as a fundamental right acts as a deci-

---

37. *See* I. VILLAVERDE MENÉNDEZ, ESTADO DEMOCRÁTICO E INFORMACIÓN: EL DERECHO A SER INFORMADO 49 (1994).

38. Art. 105b CE: The law shall regulate: b) access by the citizens to the administrative archives and registers except where it affects the security and defense of the state, the investigation of crimes, and the privacy of persons. *On the relationship between these two juridical concepts, see* F. Garrido Falla, *Comentario al artículo 105, in* COMENTARIOS A LA CONSTITUCIÓN 1453, (F. Garrido Falla, ed., 1985); J.M. Castells Arreche, *El derecho de acceso a la documentación de la Administración Pública, in* CUESTIONES FINISECULARES DE LAS ADMINISTRACIONES PÚBLICAS 200 (1991); J. Bermejo Vera, *El secreto en las Administraciones Públicas: Principios básicos y regulaciones específicas del Ordenamiento jurídico español, in* 57 REDA 22(1988); J.R. Parada Vázquez, M. Bacigalupo Saggese, *Comentario al artículo 105 CE, tomo VIII, in* COMENTARIOS A LA CONSTITUCIÓN DE 1978 535 (O. Alzaga Villamil, ed., 1998); F. VELASCO CABALLERO, LA INFORMACIÓN ADMINISTRATIVA AL PÚBLICO 126 (1998).

39. E. García de Enterría and T.-R. Fernández feel that article 23 CE not only refers to citizen participation through representatives, but "directly" in public affairs, which links it to participation in administrative procedure. E. GARCÍA DE ENTERRÍA & T.-R. FERNÁNDEZ, CURSO DE DERECHO ADMINISTRATIVO II 456 (9th ed., 2004).

40. *See* E. Schmidt-Aßmann, *La teoría general del Derecho Administrativo como sistema* 122, *supra* note 22.

sive stimulus for increased public participation in matters which are of concern to the citizen in general, and eases restrictions on access to public documents while facilitating information transmission by public administrations, making it easier for public opinion to hold administrations accountable, thereby creating greater administrative transparency. This fundamental right should also broaden criteria for participation in administrative procedures: Instead of limiting participation to those with direct interests, it should extend participation to the public in general - as is the case, for example, in environmental matters and in urban and territorial planning law.[41]

When enacted, article 105 of the Constitution was an important first step towards opening participation in administrative procedure to the general public, rather than just the interested parties, and establishing the foundations of a drive towards an "Administrative Law of Information."[42] The fact that hearings should be given to citizens "directly" in the elaboration of administrative norms that "affect" them means that administrative procedure must allow the participation, using the broadest possible interpretation, of any citizen that may feel affected, not only in those cases where the norm "affects the legitimate rights and interests of citizens,"[43] given that the terms "legitimate interest,"[44] as well as "rights," are more restrictive expressions than the wording used in article 105-a CE.

---

41. The new land use law (8/2007) recognizes, on the one hand, the right of the citizen to access to information on territorial and urban planning and the environment (art. 4-c), and, on the other hand, the right to be informed on urban planning matters by public administration (Art.4-d).

42. Art.105a CE: The law shall regulate: a) The hearing of citizens, directly or through the organizations and associations recognizes by the law, in the process of elaborating the administrative decisions which affect them.

43. Article 24-c of law 50/1997 (Nov. 27), on the Organization, Duties and Functioning of the Government uses this expression when referring to the hearings granted to citizens in the national government's rulemaking procedure.

44. These arguments are also valid for organizations and associations recognized by law, given that their access to information is also restricted by this rule.

For example, when the government elaborates an environmental or urban planning law, according to this provision any citizen should be able to accede to the information concerning its elaboration. However, according to the provisions laid out in article 24.1 of Law 50/1997, this right applies only to those who have a legitimate interest. The time period for a public hearing, established in article 24.1, is also very short– less than 15 working days. Article 35-a of Law 30/1992 on the rules governing the public authorities and the common administrative procedure (LRJ-PAC) should also be kept in mind, due to the limits placed on cognizance of the procedure to "interested parties," creating a restrictive interpretation of article 105, which recognizes this right for all citizens.

Article 105-b of the Constitution signified at the time of ratification a transcendental change in the workings of public administrations. It demanded greater transparency. The right of general access by citizens to administrative records and registries, with three well-defined exceptions,[45] meant that it was possible for them to obtain information possessed by public authorities. This was an important step towards the information society and a public administration open to the citizen. Article 105-b) also made significant changes in administrative procedure, and so Act 30/1992, developing the provision included in 105-b, included various rules (article 35 *passim*) regulating access to administrative records and registries.

While not pausing to analyze how article 37 of the Law of Administrative Procedure develops this constitutional command, it is worth pointing out that it is, in practice, more restrictive than article 105-b of the Spanish Constitution. For example, the first paragraph of article 37 allows access only to "finished" proceedings, a requirement not included in the Constitution, which draws no distinction between finished or unfinished proceedings.

---

45. *See supra*, note 38.

II
INADEQUACY OF THE CURRENT RULES ON GENERAL ADMINISTRATIVE PROCEDURE FOR THE INFORMATION SOCIETY

A. ADMINISTRATIVE ACTION AND THE MULTIFUNCTIONA-LITY OF THE ADMINISTRATIVE PROCESS

WHEN a regulation is significantly out of step with day-to-day reality, it loses effectiveness, and such is the case in the administrative process. The administrative process must adapt to changing needs and thus be suitable for public administrations efficiently carrying out their duties in real-life situations, something that does not appear to be the case in the general administrative procedure regulated in Law 30/1992. As solutions do not exist for public administrations which act in widely differing areas,[46] this does seem to give rise to certain problems.

The transcendental changes unleashed in society, which affect at their core the state itself, include informal administrative action, privatization, deregulation, Europeanization, and cooperation.[47] Placing new challenges before public administrations requires that they afford guidance to resolve real life problems, and gives a central role to administrative procedure, as a means to give structure to new forms of administrative action.

---

46. Today, public administrative activity goes far beyond the classic definition used by Jordana de Pozas (policing, economic stimulation, and public service), or that used by Garrido Falla (*coacción*, economic stimulation, and service), which describe the typical activities of the administration with slightly differing terminology.

47. R. Schmidt, *Die Reform von Verwaltung und Verwaltungsrecht, in* VERWALTUNS-ARCHIV 150 (2000); A. Vosskuhle, *Schlüsselbegriffe der Verwaltungsrechtsreform, in* VERWALTUNGS-ARCHIV 203 (2001).

The increasing importance of administrative procedure, as seen within the context of new developments in administrative law, means that procedure must incorporate diverse new functions, especially in the areas of information, the protection of individual and collective rights, and the pursuit of consensus, balance, control, and legitimacy.[48] As Schmidt-Aßmann[49] has pointed out, there is an increasing administrative proceduralization of functions previously considered within the sphere of substantive law. It is worth emphasizing that administrative procedure can be a means of democratic legitimation: Certain complex administrative procedures, such as environmental regulation and urban planning, can be seen as political processes in the sense that the development of regulation through an administrative procedure in these areas has clear political overtones and is stimulated by the generation of information, and the acceptance of decisions through the procedure.

As a multiplicity of administrative activities has resulted from changing social and economic conditions, a substantial broadening of the role of administrative procedures has been necessary. The diverse scope of administrative action must be understood within the context of the relative autonomy enjoyed by public administrations,[50] which gives the administration flexibility to adapt its action to a wide variety of contexts.[51] Any understanding of administrative activity must include the different social and economic spheres within which public administrations must carry out their duties with effective leadership

---

48. *See* W. Hoffmann-Riem, *Verwaltungsverfahren und Verwaltungsverfahrensgesetz, in* VER-WALTUNGSVERFAHREN UND VERWALTUNGSVERFAHRENSGESETZ 28 (W. Hoffmann-Riem/E. Schmidt-Aßmann, ed., 2002); E. Schmidt-Aßmann, *Der Verfahrensgedanke im deutschen und europäischen Verwaltungsrecht, in* II GRUNDLAGEN DES VERWALTUNGSRECHTS 487 (Hoffmann-Riem et al., eds., 2008).

49. E. Schmidt-Aßmann 491, *supra* note 22.

50. Here reference is made to the Administration's autonomy from other powers, in the sense that it can choose and decide between various options, or to the limits on Administrative action, given that the power to administrate stems from underlying legislation.

51. *See, for example,* Parejo Alfonso's *classification of administrative activity.* L. PAREJO ALFONSO, DERECHO ADMINISTRATIVO 633 (2003).

capacities. Below, we will follow a conventional understanding model;[52] although the first two categories are not new, the important factor is that overall this classification system responds more adequately than traditional models to the challenges faced by public administration today.

The first category is command-and-control administrative action or policing, a traditional concept characterized by the placing of obligations upon citizens. The agency sanctions those who do not comply with administrative rules and acts. This type of administrative action is widespread, not only in areas traditionally subject to administrative action, but also in more modern areas of law, such as the environment, urban planning, and telecommunications, areas where policing has been proven to be absolutely necessary. A second traditional area of administrative action is promotion, which promotes voluntary action rather than providing mandatory rules. Promotion involves incentives such as grants to private individuals with predetermined procedural requirements, which have as an object the stimulation of the economy, culture, or science. The third area of administrative activity is change or innovation, produced in social or economic domains through the guidance of public administrations. Innovation can take place through grants to entities which act in the common good, be they companies, social institutions, or even private individuals: an example of this would be the use of flexible administrative procedures to facilitate investigation, or grants to companies working in new fields such as advanced areas of technology, or grants to help introduce a new product into the market. We could also include under the umbrella of innovation the concept of "competitive dialogue" in public tendering, with procedures that expedite dialogue between the administration and bidders, and which serve as a foundation for the subsequent presentation of offers.[53] Flexibility and an innovative character are characteristics of this type of administrative activity.

---

52. The division established by W. Hofmann-Riem is followed; *Eigenständigkeit der Verwaltung*, in I GRUNDLAGEN DES VERWALTUNGSRECHTS 702 *passim* (2006).

53. *On this point, see* M. OLLER RUBERT, SANEAMIENTO DE AGUAS RESIDUALES Y REFORMA DEL DERECHO ADMINISTRATIVO 315 *passim* (2008).

The last field of influence for the administration, articulated by Hofmann-Riem,[54] is the preparation and transmission of information, which signifies a challenge for the new science of administrative law. In the information and knowledge society, as laid out in Parts I.1 and I.2, supplying essential information to citizens is increasingly important, as information takes on a legal significance. The administration's role in the preparation and transmission of information becomes fundamental. The need for procedural capacity to elaborate information[55] and specific infrastructure for transmission of information leads to the birth of administrative law of information.

Access to adequate information is essential in any decision making context, not only for public administration, but also for the citizen. A new legal regime must be created to regulate the flow of information between public administrative agencies and citizens, between different administrative bodies, and within any one particular administrative agency.

B. PRINCIPLE OF INVESTIGATION

The administrative procedure, as specified in Act 30/1992 on administrative procedure (article 68 *passim*), has always been designed, from its enactment and throughout a series modifications,

---

54. We have followed this author's classification principally because of the last category included, which is very useful for the purposes of this article.

55. We are not here referring to data, given that the term "information" implies that data has been interpreted and given sense and form. In the same sense, where we talk about "communication," we are not only referring to the transfer of information but rather of the selection of particular information as relevant. This interpretation should be born in mind when discussing information elaboration. *See* T. Vesting, *Die Bedeutung von Information und Kommunikation für die verwaltungsrechtliche Systembildung, in* II GRUNDLAGEN DES VERWALTUNGSRECHTS 17 (Hoffmann-Riem et al., eds., 2008).

56. Legal scholars are practically unanimous on this point. *See, e.g.*, GARCÍA DE ENTERRÍA & FERNÁNDEZ 453, *supra* note 39. and PAREJO ALFONSO 708, *supra* note 51.

to reach a final administrative decision.[56] It is of markedly *formal* character. Its main goal is the balancing of individual demands with the public interest.

The importance of this type of administrative procedure should not be underestimated: a large part of administrative activity involves adjudicative and regulatory decision making. However, if public administrations are to adapt to multifunctionality, the simple use of standard administrative procedure essentially designed to resolve a particular question of legal rights or specific legal interests will not suffice.[57] Many other circumstances exist wherein the public administration's role is not, at least in the first instance, to produce a final administrative decision. These are situations in which the public administration's role is to reach negotiated solutions, to consider and balance different interests, to elaborate or transmit information, or to act using the techniques of private law.[58] This now constitutes an important part of a public administration's functions, and is not adequately served by the general administrative procedure laid out in Law 30/1992.

The *judicial* character of standard administrative procedure, seen from the perspective of a succession of procedural requirements,[59] does not easily adapt to regulation of the information society, particularly with regard to the investigation phase of administrative procedure (Act 30/1992 art. 78). The rules laid out in Act 30/1992 are suffused with the idea of resolution of individual goals. This individualist perspective causes the restriction of the investigative phase of

---

57. In this sense E. García de Enterría and T.-R. Fernández point out that the administrative procedure is the method by which administrative acts are produced, with a specific objective, the administrative resolution/decision. García de Enterría & Fernández 452, *supra* note 39.

58. *For an in-depth study of this point from an untraditional perspective, see* Barnes 295, *supra* note 35.

59. There are important material differences between the administrative and judicial procedure, among which is that in the first, the Administration is both judge and interested party, while in the second, the judge is independent. There are other differences that have been caricaturized, and are only partially true. *See* F. Garrido Falla & J.M. Fernández Pastrana, Régimen Jurídico y Procedimiento de las Administraciones Públicas, 304 (3d ed., 2000).

the procedure to only the interested parties. This factor limits the possibility of receiving a reply from the administration when the course of action involves someone who does not reach the status of a directly interested party.[60] This procedural phase is directed first and foremost at guaranteeing private individual rights[61] and liberties, and leads eventually to a unique administrative decision. This type of procedure is not open to the investigation phase used in other fields such as the environment, urban planning and food safety, where a great number of citizens may have an interest in the proceedings.

The final goal of traditional administrative procedure is to make an administrative decision, and not the production of information.[62] Nevertheless, information does play a central supporting role sustaining this final decision. In other words, while information does not constitute the primary object of administrative procedure, the procedure itself is based on information and on its communication. The reasoning behind the final administrative decision would be greatly improved if, during the instruction phase of administrative procedure, a constant interchange of information between the public administration and interested parties were to take place, with the default inclusion of the general public subject only to limited, specified exceptions.[63] Indeed, information also rationalizes the decision, especially where the final decision cannot be fully determined *a priori*, as the outcome depends on information that flows from new evidence or from claims

---

60. *See* A. Fanlo, *Disposiciones generales sobre los procedimientos administrativos: iniciación, ordenación e instrucción, in* LA NUEVA LEY DE RÉGIMEN JURÍDICO DE LAS ADMINISTRACIONES PÚBLICAS Y DEL PROCEDIMIENTO ADMINISTRATIVO COMÚN 242 (J. Leguina Villa & M. Sanchez Morón eds., 1993).

61. The fact that the instruction procedure refers to the participation of interested parties, and not of citizens in general, reveals its restrictive and inflexible character, which does not facilitate the widespread interchange of information between the citizen and a public administration.

62. *See* H. ROSSEN, VOLLZUG UND VERHANDLUNG: DIE MODERNISIERUNG DES VERWALTUNGSVOLLZUGS 112 (1999).

63. For example, the exemptions can involve the three situations where access to administrative files is restricted in article 105-b) of the Constitution, limiting the margins of discretion to the maximum extent possible.

made by interested parties or the general public. Only with a greater inclusiveness and openness to information will the final administrative decision be balanced and fair. Similarly, increased information may hasten a final decision, avoiding the need to open subsequent administrative procedures. Indeed, increased communication between the parties involved in the procedure may make negotiated settlements more likely through a broader framework for information exchange.[64]

C. NEW PERSPECTIVES ON ADMINISTRATIVE PROCEDURE IN THE REALM OF AN ADMINISTRATIVE LAW OF INFORMATION

The new perspectives and challenges that the information society creates for administrative law are barely dealt with in the administrative procedure laid out in Law 30/1992. In this law, the procedures for the elaboration and interchange of information between administrators and the citizen are limited and insufficient. General administrative procedure is designed to regulate the relationship between the administration and interested parties, rather than between the administration and the public.

As for the interchange of information between different public administrations, it is regulated by article 4.1-c Act 30/1992[65] and article 55-c of Law 7/1985 (Apr. 7)[66] on local government rules (LBRL), among other provisions.

---

64. *For an ample and detailed study of this point, see* E.Schmidt-Aßmann, *Verwaltungsrecht in der Informationsgesellschaf-Perspektiven der Systembildung* 421 *passim, supra* note 3, and Ch. Gusy, *Die Informationsbeziehung zwischen Staat und Bürger, en Grudlagen des Verwaltungsrechts* 246 *passim, supra* note 19.

65. Article 4.1 c) states: Principles of dealings between administrations:…c) provide that information to other administrations that they need on acts that they carry out while exercising their attributed functions.

66. Article 55-c states that: In order to ensure effective coordination and administrative efficiency, the State administration and Autonomous Communities on the one hand, and Local autho-

Two questions are raised by this regulation: what the practical consequences of this law are, and what effects the exchange of information between agencies has on the flow of information to the public as the principal recipient of agency action.

1. THE RELATIONSHIP BETWEEN THE PUBLIC ADMINISTRATION AND THE CITIZENS

In an Information and Knowledge Society, administrative procedure should be open not only to directly interested parties, but to the public, because those citizens who are excluded from any particular administrative procedure are also excluded from the process of information exchange with public administrations. Therefore they can neither enjoy access to information, nor demand information from the public administration. The "information blackout" in which they find themselves has enormous implications with respect to their ability to make reasoned decisions.

The administrative procedure laid out in Law 30/1992 is substantially open to the interested parties, while access by the general public faces severe restrictions. If administrative procedure implies a process of communication between the administration and the citizen, this process must be carried out according to the principles provided in article 3 of the Law: the principles of efficiency and service to the citizen (art. 3.2) and the principles of transparency and public participation (art. 3.5). The process of communication cannot be carried out (or must be deemed insufficient) within a framework of restrictions in place during the instruction phase, or during any phase of the administrative procedure as a whole. These restrictions on information and public participation also limit the principle of participation established in article 9.2 of the Constitution: "facilitate participation of all citizens

---

rities on the other hand, should conduct their reciprocal relationships in a way that:....c) Provides to the other administrative body that information on their own activities which is necessary for the correct fulfillment of their functions.

in the political, economic, cultural, and social life."[67] The manner in which citizen access to information is regulated by articles 35 and 37 of the Act 30/1992 embodies a restrictive alternative to the permissive structure of the Constitution, as discussed above.

Administrative procedure is, in essence, a communication process between administrators and citizens. This communication is the prime objective of Law 11/2007 (June 22) on electronic access by citizens to public services,[68] according to the law's heading and preamble.

The text says, for example, that the law "takes on the responsibility of making the information society a reality." Nevertheless, when dealing with an individual citizen's right to participation in administrative procedure, the law limits access to interested parties only (art. 6.2 d).

It should be remembered that articles 6, 35 and 37.1 of Law 11/2007 are "basic" rules, which means that these rules are also binding to all administrations in Spain. As underlined by Barnes, this Law 11/2007, on electronic access by citizens to public services, essentially runs parallel to the administrative procedure laid down in Law 30/1992, with only minimal improvements if, in fact, there are any improvements at all.[69] Although article 3, when laying out the purpose and intent of the law, mentions a citizen's electronic access to information, the close relationship between the administration and the citizen, and the need for administrative transparency,[70] these principles are severely limited when the law specifies the administrative procedure that guarantess a citizen's right to information.

---

67. *See* M. SÁNCHEZ MORÓN, DERECHO ADMINISTRATIVO (PARTE GENERAL) 77 (3d ed., 2007).

68. Article 45 LRJ-PAC encourages e-administration, as do other norms passed previous to law 11/2007. *See* R. RIVERO ORTEGA, EL EXPEDIENTE ADMINISTRATIVO (DE LOS LEGAJOS A LOS SOPORTES ELECTRÓNICOS) 155 (2007).

69. Barnes 307, *supra* note 35.

70. *See* J.L. Blasco Díaz, *Los derechos de los ciudadanos en su relación electrónica con la Administración in* HOMENAJE A L. MARTÍN-RETORTILLO (*forthcoming*).

2. Inter-administrative Relationships

In order to make decisions, public administrations need information. Therefore, information collection and the right to obtain information are crucial in decision making procedures. The civil servant or relevant public body may often lack the necessary information; steps to mitigate this absence should include communication with other individuals within the same agency or with other public bodies.[71]

Law 30/1992 introduces the principles of cooperation and collaboration as general rules for inter-administrative relationships (art. 3.2). The inclusion of these principles in the Constitution of 1978 would probably have given such cooperation greater legal force.[72] Nevertheless, the embodiment of these principles into a law on common administrative procedure should facilitate the interchange of information by mandating inter-administrative cooperation.

Article 4.1-c of Act 30/1992 establishes a legal obligation, based on principles of governmental unity, to make available to other agencies any information necessary to fulfill their responsibilities. The duty is reinforced by the obligation of the agency receiving the request to hand over the information without reservation (article 4.2), even though article 4.3 does introduce some limits on that obligation.[73]

---

71. Communication within a single agency is an area of great interest, as information exchange within a public administration itself is of vital importance to administrative efficiency and expertise. The internal regulations of public administration (orders, instructions, ordinances etc), are also relevant here, as is the method of regulating information and communication between administrative organisms with different jurisdictions (horizontal relations) or between organisms with hierarchical relationships (vertical relations).

72. One example is article 35.1 of the Fundamental Law, which mentions mutual administrative assistance between the Federal and Länder administrative authorities. This administrative cooperation between administrations and functionaries of different administrations implies a building of bridges as opposed to the growing tendency of compartmentalization. It also implies that the information held by a public administration is not exclusively its own, but rather must be shared with others. *See* B. Holznagel, *Informationsbeziehungen in und zwischen Behörden*, *in* II Grundlagen des Verwaltunsrechts 314 (Hoffmann-Riem et al., eds., 2008).

73. Specifically, the exceptions include where there is a lack of means to hand over the information, or where handing it over would gravely prejudice the interests of the administration supplying the information (art. 4.3).

Article 55-c of Law 7/1985 on municipalities also refers to the exchange of information between different State, Autonomous Community, and local administrations. In so doing, the law draws a connection between the interchange of information and the principles of efficiency and coordination, and points out that sufficient information improves the proper functioning of the administration and also its *esprit de corps*. This obligation is given form in articles 56.1 and 56.2, which force local government, when so requested by autonomous and central administrations, to provide information about municipal agency action, including the obligation to hand over administrative records and to prepare relevant reports.

Law 6/1997 (April 14), on the Organization and Functioning of the Central Administration (LOFAGE), deals with the principles behind the organization and function of central ("federal") administration in article 3, introducing and linking the principles of coordination and cooperation (art. 3.2(h)). Coordination, cooperation and collaboration are absolutely necessary for the achievement of efficient inter-administrative functioning;[74] the recently approved modification of the Statute (or "Constitution") of the Autonomous Community of Valencia[75] introduces these principles when regulating local administration and its relationship with the autonomous regional government – the *Generalitat* (art. 62.2-.3). Legal scholars[76] view the introduction of these principles as a strengthening of cooperation between the *Generalitat* and local government.

The relevant question is whether this information exchange is effectively taking place and whether it has been incorporated into administrative procedure. This does not seem to be the case, insofar as the provisions mentioned above are all considered general principles, without solid regulation or concrete procedural requirements. A true incorporation of information exchange would establish effective channels for inter-administrative communication. In order for information exchange to be effective, state and regional laws of administrative procedure must make it obligatory for different administrations to communicate informa-

---

74. *For further analysis of the relationship between these different principles, see* PAREJO ALFONSO 413, *supra* note 51.

75. The original statute was modified by Ley Orgánica 1/2006 of 10 April 2006.

76. *See* R. Martín Mateo & J. Rosa Moreno, *La Administración Local: Planteamiento General, in* COMENTARIOS AL ESTATUTO DE AUTONOMÍA DE LA COMUNIDAD VALENCIANA 510 (J.M. Baño León ed., 2007).

tion. This would include, for example, an obligation between administrations: 1) to prepare oral or written reports on factual information within the administration itself, 2) to establish specific mechanisms providing for permanent information exchange between administrations, regardless of whether specific information requests have been made, and 3) to send periodical reports on certain activities which are of interest to multiple agencies. Without a fluid cooperation between agencies a sense of "ownership" of information grows within public administrations, which jealously guard their information and do not readily share it other administrative bodies. This jealousy is to the grave detriment of those basic principles that sustain the modern state (such as governmental loyalty, cooperation, coordination, and serving the public interest).

III

IMPETUS GIVEN BY COMMUNITY LAW TO ADMINISTRATIVE PROCEDURE

As Schmidt-Aßmann[77] has pointed out, administrative procedure is one of the areas most heavily influenced by Community Law. This influence is most strongly apparent in the area of environmental law, understood in its broadest meaning as defined by the second generation of European directives, such as Directive 2003/4/EC or 2003/35/EC. As a consequence of this broad definition, the influence is also readily apparent in areas with a distinct environmental impact, such as urban and territorial planning. In these latter areas, which directly affect individual quality of life, procedural channels for administrative information have been strengthened.

A. ACCESS OF THE GENERAL PUBLIC TO INFORMATION THROUGH ADMINISTRATIVE PROCEDURE

European Directive 1985/337[78] undeniably strengthens administrative procedure.[79] It establishes that certain public and private pro-

---

77. Schmidt-Aßmann 368, *supra* note 24.

78. Council Directive 85/337/EEC (June 27) on the assessment of the effects of certain public and private projects on the environment, modified regarding public participation in respect of the drawing up of certain plans and programs relating to the environment by Directive 2003/35/CE (May 26).

79. The procedural importance of Directive 1985/337 has been underlined by scholarly opinion that has emphasized three underlying obligations within the text: the need to inform the public about the projected activity, consultation with the public on the projected activity and making information public about the final decision taken. *See* J.A. RAZQUIN LIZARRAGA & A. RUIZ DE APODACA ESPINOSA, INFORMACIÓN, PARTICIPACIÓN Y JUSTICIA EN MATERIA DE MEDIO AMBIENTE (COMENTARIO SISTEMÁTICO A LA LEY 27/2006, DE 18 DE JULIO) 58 (2007).

jects[80] should be subject to environmental impact assessment (art. 4.2). It also introduces into the procedure the obligation to facilitate information to the general public (including natural and legal persons, groups, and associations) and, therefore, all those affected by, likely to be affected by, or merely interested in environmental decision making procedures. The obligation placed on public authorities or private individuals to provide information extends, as in all cases, to the interested parties, but also to the public in general. At the time the directive was passed, this obligation represented a significant change in thinking and significantly broadened public participation in the decision making process. Directive 1985/337 was modified by article 3 of Directive 2003/35, deepening a citizen's rights to information and participation, extending information to the general public and interested parties[81] at an early stage in the procedure, and ensuring full, effective participation at various stages in the administrative procedure.

European Directive 1990/313 (June 7)[82] established channels to relay information to the public, thereby creating a public with an informed opinion and also with the capacity to hold public and private actors accountable. This directive was a milestone, establishing a procedure through which any natural or legal person could gain access to information on the environment, in spite of some vague limitations (art. 3.2) and other failings.[83] This broad access extends only to environmental information, given here a narrow interpretation (art. 2-a). Directive 2003/4, which repeals the previous directive, develops the right to access to information, strengthened by changes to the founda-

---

80. Annex II of the Directive refers to different types of projects, such as agriculture, the extractive industries, energy industries, chemical industries, food industries, infrastructure projects (among which are urban-development projects), and other projects (among others: hotel complexes, installations for the disposal of industrial and domestic waste and wastewater treatment plants).

81. The directive begins by defining "public" and "interested public," adding these definitions in article 1, paragraph 2, which clarifies and limits the content of each one of these concepts.

82. Directive 90/313 has been abolished by Directive 2003/4/CE (Jan 28) on the assessment of the effects of certain public and private projects on the environment.

83. See RAZQUÍN LIZARRAGA & RUÍZ DE APODACA ESPINOSA 59, *supra* note 79.

tional treaties.[84] For example, the exceptions established to the right of access are clearer than in the previous directive, and the concept of "environmental information" is extensive, and extends into other fields (article 2.1).

Public information in turn facilitates the existence of public opinion with decision making capabilities. This permits public participation in decisions of concern to the general public. On the one hand, these norms strengthen the fundamental right of access to information in Spanish law, anchored in articles 20-1-d and 23.1 of the Spanish Constitution.[85] On the other hand, this body of law has laid the foundations for further statutory development of administrative procedure, understood as a regulatory model which can realize the general principles of efficiency, service, transparency and participation included in article 3 of Law 30/1992 —a law applicable to all public administrations. Insofar as the administration is concerned, Law 6/97 (April 14) on the Organization and Functioning of the Central or State Administration, introduces a series of organizational and functional principles (proximity to citizens, the rationalization and flexibility of administrative procedures, and the objectivity and transparency of administrative acts) which, taken together, set up an administrative procedure providing public access to information.

B. EFFECTS OF LEGISLATIVE DEVELOPMENTS ON SPANISH ADMINISTRATIVE PROCEDURE

Substantial changes in administrative procedure in environmental legislation have been accomplished as a consequence of the incorporation of Community law, and in the procedural process, access to infor-

---

84. Article 85 of the Treaty Establishing the European Community recognizes the right of access to European Parliament, Council, and Commission documents (art. 255.1 TEC).

85. R. García Macho, *Derecho de acceso a la información y protección de datos en la sociedad de la información, in* HOMENAJE A L. MARTÍN-RETORTILLO, apartado III.1. (*forthcoming*).

mation held by the administration has been given to the general public. The right to intervene in the procedure now extends well beyond the realm of the directly interested parties. We must take into account that there are individuals and associations, that, while not being directly interested or having a personal stake in the procedure, are able to participate nonetheless.

These changes are seen, for example, in Law 27/2006,[86] which differentiates between the public in general and interested parties in the preamble, taking as "general public" any natural or legal person, as well as associations and organizations (art. 2.1).[87] Furthermore, the law states that "everyone" can exercise the legal right to demand a safe environment (art. 3).[88] This innovative approach means that, within the administrative procedure, part of the public administration's duty is the collection and elaboration of information, which it must then make available to all requesting parties. Law 27/2006 also interprets "environmental information" broadly (art. 3), defining "environmental" to include such diverse areas as: health, water, territorial planning, housing, and energy. The expansion of public participation succeeds in reforming administrative procedure and law, and goes well beyond the traditional goal of administrative procedure of reaching a decision in the context of a limited adversarial process.

The meaning given to environmental information in Law 27/2006 includes land use, and thus extends into the areas of territorial planning, urban planning, and housing. Closely related to Law 27/2006, RD 2/2008 (June 20), approving the consolidated text of the Land Use Law, has come into force. The law effectively takes as a starting point that the right to an adequate environment is a fundamental principle to be taken into account when dealing with land use. This principle is stated in the preamble and in the main text (for example, in articles 1 and 2). The basis for this assertion appears in the Community Directives previously discussed (III.1), and in the Spanish Constitution (arts. 45 and 47).

---

86. Law 27/2006, of the 18th of July, regulating the right to access information, public participation and access to justice in environmental matters (incorporating Directives 2003/4/CE and 2003/35/CE).

87. *On the meaning and extension of the definition of "general public," see* RAZQUIN LIZZARRAGA & RUIZ DE APODACA ESPINOSA 116, *supra* note 79.

88. While article 13 does include a wide variety of exceptions, they should this be *particularly* understood (article 13.4), in order to be consistent with the law's intent.

Finally, this assertion is a response to the deteriorating environmental situation in Spain as a consequence of urban development based only on economic considerations. The current condition of the Spanish environment makes it absolutely necessary that sustainable development become a main reference point in future land use policies.[89]

Land use policies have a vital effect on the general public's quality of life, and so public participation in the regulation of land development becomes absolutely necessary as a basic, democratic principle. The recognition of the public's right to information contained in article 3.2.c of the Land Use Law means that citizens must be informed by the relevant agency about administrative procedures that affect territorial and urban planning. This recognition of the right to information as a general principle is given shape in two different ways in article 4-c and d) of the consolidated text of the Land Use Law. On the one hand, it is expressed as the right to access information on territorial and urban planning and related environmental impact assessments already in the hands of a public administration, as well as the right to obtain copies or certificates of administrative decisions or activities All this solidifies, completes, and broadens the scope of the provisions included in articles 35 and 37 Act 30/1992, taking into account the restrictive nature of article 37.[90] On the other hand, paragraph d) looks at the right to information from the point of view of a "right of service," obliging the administration to inform the public in writing about the legal regime governing the planning phases of a new building. It is also established a public system of information on land-use and urban planning which the government must use in collaboration with the autonomous communities and within the ambit of the relevant administrative procedure.[91]

---

89. *For an in-depth study, see* L. Parejo Alfonso, *Condiciones básicas de igualdad de los ciudadanos y régimen básico del suelo en la LS, in* CIUDAD Y TERRITORIO (ESTUDIOS TERRITORIALES) 313, Ministerio de Vivienda, nº152-153 (2007); M. Vaquer Caballería, *Estudio preliminar: Constitución, ley de suelo y ordenamiento territorial y urbanístico, in* COMENTARIOS A LA LEY DE SUELO (LEY 8/2007, DE 28 DE MAYO) 28 (L. Parejo Alfonso & G. Roger Fernández, eds., 2007); R. García Macho, *Ordenación del territorio y urbanismo en el Estatuto de Autonomía Valenciano, in* COMENTARIO AL ESTATUTO DE AUTONOMÍA VALENCIANO 674 (J.M. Baño León, ed., 2007).

90. On the restrictive nature of this provision compared to article 105 of the Constitution, see supra part I.3-b.

91. *See* COMENTARIOS A LA LEY DE SUELO (LEY 8/2007, DE 28 DE MAYO) 103, 389 (L. Parejo Alfonso & G. Roger Fernández, eds., 2007).

IV
CONCLUSION

THE information and knowledge society highlights the vital importance the access to information has in the development of the individual's decision making capacity. Without adequate information, individual citizens find themselves subject to an "information blackout," which makes them vulnerable and easily manipulated. Within this context, public administration has a primarily two-fold role to play: to permit public access to information held by the administration, and to publicize particularly important information even when it is not requested.

The European Community Directives and Spanish law examined in Parts III, 1 and 2, take as their starting point an administrative procedure that includes among its aims the search for and elaboration of information by public administrative bodies with the ultimate goal of its diffusion to the population. These objectives differentiate this type of administrative procedure from the narrower traditional model, in which the only reason for an administrative procedure was the ultimate adoption of a decision. This traditional idea, as laid out in the procedure envisaged in Law 30/1992, must be broadened in order to respond to the new challenges presented by the ever-evolving information and knowledge society. The current social and technological context demands a profound reform of Law 30/1992, starting with articles 35 and 37, and continuing with reforms to the general rules on administrative procedures (Title VI- Art. 68 and following), compatible with the relevant general principles (namely, art. 3).

CHAPTER V

COLLABORATION AMONG PUBLIC ADMINISTRATIONS THROUGH DOMESTIC ADMINISTRATIVE PROCEDURE

Javier Barnes*

* Professor of Adminisrative Law, University of Huelva, Spain.

INDEX

*An earlier and more reduced version of this article was published in the book *ALLGEMEINES VERWALTUNGSRECHT – ZUR TRAGFÄHIGKEIT EINES KONZEPTS* 255 *passim* (H.-H. Trute et al. eds., 2008).

My thanks to Professor Michael Nimetz for reading the first draft of this article.

THIS chapter deals with the ongoing collaboration among public administrations at the domestic level, under the influence of the European Union. It is based on the premise of a broad concept of administrative procedure understood as a system for communication,[1] and not merely as a decision making process or as a tool for applying and enforcing the law in a manner resembling judicial process. First, this chapter evaluates the link between the method of regulation or governance and administrative procedure and emphasizes that cooperative procedure is a hallmark of new forms of regulation and governance. Secondly, it holds that this cooperation between networked administrations in Europe should begin on the domestic level. Finally, it summarizes some elements of this collaboration. Beyond these questions lie two more far-reaching issues: collaboration strategy has important consequences for the design of administrative law and procedures. Furthermore, the new national-level procedural collaboration requires techniques that are much more modern, flexible and open than those now in use in traditional methods of regulation.

In this chapter I will not assess the emerging new methods to achieve regulatory goals and the implications of these new methods in administrative law. Instead, I will briefly summarize some elements of the collaboration between administrations through formal and informal administrative procedures at the national level under the influence of the European Union.

I
INTRODUCTION.
THE CONNECTION BETWEEN ADMINISTRATIVE
PROCEDURE AND METHODS OF REGULATION AND
GOVERNANCE: COOPERATIVE PROCEDURE AS A
MEANS OF ACHIEVING A NEW REGULATION STRATEGY

As Richard Stewart writes, "Our existing models of administrative law have largely developed in response to a single method of regula-

---

1. "Administrative procedures are structured processes of information procurement and information processing carried out under the responsibility of administrative authorities. They are

tion: the command method. The adoption of entirely different methods of regulation and governance will invite and require the development of new approaches to administrative law."[2] This statement is doubly true when the premises of the traditional system of "command-and-control regulation" are questioned or challenged. I refer for example to the capacity of the law to control and steer a sector using material programs of rules that are comprehensive, general, and intended to be permanent.[3] In any debate over the new forms of regulation and governance necessary to cope with a world undergoing rapid and profound changes, one must pay attention to the many adjustments to, consequences for, and effects on the traditional tools of administrative law. In this context, I want to highlight the close connection between diverse methods of regulation and governance on the one hand, and administrative procedures on the other.

"Administrative procedures" and "methods of government and regulation" are closely related questions. In fact, an analysis of administrative procedure would be incomprehensible, if various forms of regulation were not taken into consideration at the same time.

---

designed to enable the administration to act rationally. Such procedures do not always result in a concrete legally binding decision. Direct administrative action, internal administrative coordination and (periodic) reporting duties independent of particular occasions can also be the object and aim of administrative procedures." *See* Eberhard Schmidt-Aßmann, *Structures and Functions of Administrative Procedures in German, European and International Law*, in THE REFORM OF ADMINISTRATIVE PROCEDURE (Javier Barnes ed., forthcoming 2008) . *See* SCHMIDT-ASSMANN, *DAS ALLGEMEINE VERWALTUNGSRECHT ALS ORDNUNGSIDEE*, 305 (2nd ed. 2004).

See also Schmidt-Aßmann, *El procedimiento administrativo entre el principio del Estado de Derecho y el principio democrático* in EL PROCEDIMIENTO ADMINISTRATIVO EN EL DERECHO COMPARADO 317 (Javier Barnes ed., 1993); SCHMIDT-ASSMANN, *LA TEORÍA GENERAL DEL DERECHO ADMINISTRATIVO COMO SISTEMA* 358 (2003); Javier Barnes, *Sobre el procedimiento administrativo: evolución y perspectivas,* in INNOVACIÓN Y REFORMA EN EL DERECHO ADMINISTRATIVO 267 (Javier Barnes ed., 2006).

2. Richard B. Stewart, *Administrative Law in the Twenty-First Century* 78 N. Y. U. L. Rev. 437, 454 (2003).

3. *See the series of books on the reform of administrative law* SCHRIFTEN ZUR REFORM DES VERWALTUNGSRECHTS (Eberhard Schmidt-Aßmann & Wolfgang Hoffmann-Riem eds., 1993–2000).

At first view, the relationship between the two seems obvious, since administrative procedure is *present in and forms an integral part of* regulation and governance, not only in the traditional model (i.e., the command-and-control system which uses regulations, permits, or licensing authorizations), but also in alternative or additional methods (e.g., administrative governance in the EU, such as the comitology system or the open method of coordination).[4] Diverse systems of regulation come into being through suitable rules of procedure.[5]

There are profound implications that follow from the relationship between methods of regulation and administrative procedure, since each method of regulation (command regulation and formal adjudication; negotiated rulemaking, agreements or "negotiated command and control"; self-regulation in privatized sectors; economic incentive systems; etc.) *describes and colors* the structure, nature, and function of the procedures that underlie each regulatory model.[6] *Procedures*

---

4. *See* ALEXANDRA GATTO *Governance in the European Union: a Legal Perspective*, 12 Colum. J. Eur. L. 487 (2006) *for more discussion of these regulation methods. See also* EU ADMINISTRATIVE GOVERNANCE (H.C.H. Hofmann & A. H. Türk eds., 2007).

The European open method of coordination employs non-binding guidelines, which are developed by both the public and stakeholders as well as member states. The planning process is iterative as plans are revised periodically to take advantage of new knowledge. *See also* Jonathan Zeitlin, *Introduction: The Open Method of Co-ordination in Question, in* THE OPEN METHOD OF CO-ORDINATION IN ACTION: THE EUROPEAN EMPLOYMENT AND SOCIAL INCLUSION STRATEGIES (Philippe Pochet & Jonathan Zeitlin eds., with Lars Magnusson, 2005); DAVID M. TRUBEK & LOUISE G. TRUBEK, *New Governance & Legal Regulation: Complementarity, Rivalry, and Transformation*, 13 COLUM. J. EUR. L. 551.

5. Take as an example the new methods of governance in the EU: comitology and the open method of coordination. Comitology itself is a procedure. The open method of coordination includes informal cooperation such as non-binding guidelines, horizontal networking, iterative planning, benchmarking, league tables, deliberative fora, mandated participation, and peer review. These techniques need informal procedural rules (see *supra* note 4).

Another example is the application of regulatory choice methods, carried out through special procedures. *See e.g.*, MARTIN EIFERT *Regulierungsstrategien* in GRUNDLAGEN DES VERWAL-TUNGSRECHTS, BAND I 1309 (Hoffmann-Riem et al. eds., 2006).

6. For example, in order to achieve an environmental agreement, the government establishes a process of informal negotiation with the aim of securing agreements on individualized, hand-tailored rules or orders that are substitutes for those generally applicable. *See* RICHARD B. STEWART *A New Generation of Environmental Regulation?*, 29 CAP. U. L. REV. 21, 61 (2001).

should be adapted to reflect the requirements of each system or method of regulation and governance. For example, the design of new or revised procedures will be very different if the idea is to delegate decision making to systems of governance with the ability to respond to legal diversity within the EU, such as comitology and the "open method of collaboration,"[7] or if the aim is to make greater use of regulatory negotiation and other collaborative processes.[8]

Many of the outstanding trends in administrative procedures on a regional, national or global level can only be explained within the framework of different regulatory methods.[9] This relationship of *instrumentality* or *subordination* is prominent in many cases. For example, the trend towards regulatory negotiation (including negotiation with external actors within rulemaking) that characterizes negotiated rulemaking (an increasingly utilized process) requires greater cooperation. Agency decision making has to become more inclusive and less adversarial towards regulated parties and other stakeholders, such as environmental organizations and community groups.[10] In other cases, the regulatory system's influence on administrative procedure design may not be easily apparent, but this does not mean that it is less important.[11] From this perspective, the ability of administrative

----

7. *On administrative governance issues see, e.g.,* Hofmann & Türk 579, *supra* note 4.

8. *See, e.g.,* C. M. Ryan, *Leadership in collaborative policy-making: an analysis of agency roles in regulatory negotiations,* in POLICY SCIENCE 34 221 *passim* (2001), (regarding the implications of the new regulatory negotiations method for the contemporary US APA).

9. For instance, public participation in SEA procedures (see III.1) must be understood in the context of a method of regulation based on public-private cooperation.

10. For example, a core principle of the transformation of U.S. Administrative Law beginning in the U.S. post-war order was that new grants of governmental regulatory power should be accompanied by the extension of procedural, participatory rights to the relevant stakeholders – both the objects of regulation and the beneficiaries. *See* Richard Stewart, *The Reformation of American Administrative Law,* 88 HARV. L. REV. 1669, 1670 (1975).

11. One example is the extension of procedural rules into the private sector, when regulatory techniques consist of so-called "public bodies-supervised industry self-regulation," in fields such as telecommunication or energy. This technique responds to a regulatory strategy based on cooperation between the State and society; the state ensures a final result, although it does not itself carry out the activity or service. The provision of services is delegated to the private

procedure to promote cooperation between different public bodies will be better understood when examined within the context of the new methods of regulation and governance in Europe today.[12]

One basic consequence of this approach is the need to apply administrative procedural rules and instruments considered to be the most suitable for each case *according to the model of regulation* governing the case. Without suitable administrative procedure instruments, regulation cannot accurately respond to changing fact patterns and paradigms. The features and techniques that characterize procedures in a "command regulation model" cannot be applied without significant adjustments and adaptations to procedures meant to informally coordinate administrative action in areas of new forms of governance, where the purpose is to increase flexibility, improve participation, and accommodate regulation and implementation by multiple levels of government (e.g. the 2000 EU Water Framework Directive[13]).[14]

Administrative procedure, however, is not only a tool in the hands of administrations within every method of regulation and governance. Administrative procedure may be at the same time an instrument of

---

sector, and carried out by means of government-industry cooperation. To this end, procedural rules must be established for the private operators which will ensure transparency, accountability, impartiality, the participation of experts and the public, and proper conflict resolution methods, along with other important public goods.

12. For example, collaboration is less important when the goal of the procedure is to make a particular decision (adjudication), the result of which is dictated by one particular statute and the scope of which is limited to a single Administration or agency (e.g., a municipal authorization to open a small business). On the contrary, collaboration is an essential part of the open method of cooperation, inasmuch as it deals with cyclical benchmarking that is used to coordinate national policy, providing guidance and assessment at the European level. As agency discretion increases, and the application of the law will be governed by two or more agencies, cooperation becomes increasingly essential.

13. *See, e.g.,* TRUBEK & TRUBEK, *supra* note 4, 539, 550.

14. The techniques of collaboration developed for procedures of command regulation (e.g., the delivery of non-binding statements or reports by one administration to another concerning territorial planning regulations) often prove to be inferior or deficient in many other cases in which the collaboration is not limited to a specific and occasional connection based on some hierarchical relationship, or founded on the premise of an isolating barrier between administrations. E.g. eGovernment. *See infra III.*

political control[15] and a way to direct a given administration.[16] In other words, administrative procedures can be used as strategic and structural regulations by statutes establishing, for example, *how* the decision making process is to be carried out (e.g., SEA procedure).[17]

First of all, however, we must briefly explore the metaphor of a "networked" administration in order to emphasize that the need for collaboration is not a phenomenon that only occurs outside national borders.

---

15. *See* Matthew D. Mc Cubbins et al., *Administrative Procedures as Instrument of Political Control,* 3 J. INT'L L. ECON. & ORG. 243 (1987) (from the point of view of *positive political theory*).

16. *For further discussion from the point of view* of administrative law, *see* Schmidt-Aßmann, *Das allgemeine Verwaltungsrecht als Ordnungsidee* 203, 305, *supra* note 1.

17. *See infra* Part III.1. *See also* Barnes, *Sobre el procedimiento administrativo: evolución y perspectivas* 267, 287-88, *supra* note 1. The law does not establish what is to be the best solution, but rather how that solution is to be found. This all remits to the procedure when understood to be a forum to promote convergence.

II
THE IMAGE OF THE "NETWORKED" ADMINISTRATION

A. "NETWORKED" ADMINISTRATION

COLLABORATION among public bodies has become a necessity. It could be argued that the future of any administration depends on improved patterns of collaboration. The image of a network is helpful when attempting to illustrate this phenomenon: a modern administration must be perceived as a network of administrative agencies acting in cooperation with the citizenry and with business interests.

Public administration is now less hierarchical and isolated than before. It is increasingly networked. The distinction between hierarchy and network refers to the structure and mode of coordination within or between organizations. In a hierarchical organization, coordination is achieved through vertical chains-of- command, with higher-level units directing the behavior of units below them. In contrast, network forms of organization operate horizontally as well as vertically and achieve coordination through mutual cooperation rather than through a command structure.[18]

In the social sciences, networks have become a powerful metaphor for explaining the social, economic, technological, and political realities of our times. A network, defined minimally, is a system of interconnected elements or nodes, where each node represents an intersection of flows within the network. What a node is, M. Castells says, depends on the kind of concrete networks of which we speak.[19] Each

---

18. *See, e.g.,* Chris Ansell, T*he Networked Polity: Regional Development, in* 13 WESTERN EUROPE GOVERNANCE: AN INTERNATIONAL JOURNAL OF POLICY AND ADMINISTRATION, No 3, 303-333 (July 2000).

19. *E.g.,* MANUEL CASTELLS, THE RISE OF THE NETWORK SOCIETY 501(2nd ed., 2000). According to Castells, flows within a given network have no distance, or the same distance,

node is connected to other nodes through some kind of exchange process.[20]   A bridge does not simply join two independent villages across a river; it creates a new city. From the viewpoint of an administrative lawyer, a network of flows is a process that connects administrative units in order to make decisions, deliver services, share information, and so on. Through this lens, administrative procedure is a tool of interconnection or interagency partnership. Cooperative procedure may be understood as a key part of any networked public administration.

B. EUROPEAN AND NATIONAL NETWORKS

Administrative procedure is thus not only a means of enabling the protection of the individual, the participation of the citizenry, or the implementation of greater efficiency in the decision making process. It is also a tool for collaboration between public bodies.

Although the idea of a "networked Administration" and the cooperation principle comes close to describing the European system, the network begins at the national level. On the one hand, national public administrations must participate in the formulation, development, and implementation of EU Law. On the other hand, a network constitutes a unit, and the European administrative network includes all public bodies, even though these only operate on a limited national level. In addition, a variety of national administrative proceedings exist under international and European influence with a strong collaborative bent

---

between nodes. Thus, the distance (physical, social, economic, political, cultural) to a given point or position varies between zero (for any node in the same network) and infinity (for any point external to the network). On the other hand, networks to Castells are open structures, able to expand without limits, integrating new nodes as long as they are able to communicate with the network.

20. The topology defined by networks means that the distance - or intensity and frequency of the interaction between two points or social positions - is shorter or more frequent or more intense, if both points are nodes in a network than if they do not belong to the same network.

(e.g., strategic environmental assessment procedure, eGovernment procedures, and regulatory or legislative impact assessments), in which the horizontal and vertical relations between local, regional, and national administrations *within* each member state are deeply influenced by the EU/EC system as well.

Domestic collaboration is also needed when a national administration does not act as "indirect administration" of EC Law (which is already ruled by the basic principle of effective cooperation).[21] Harmonized national administrative legislation provides many examples of cooperation within the state. In some cases, cooperation is even required between specific authorities at the national level.[22] The smooth operation of the market requires not only legal rules, but also close and consistent cooperation. The same can be said of environmental issues and other areas of public regulation.

In this context, domestic administrative procedure is setting new patterns of collaboration under European guidance. *Domestic* administrative procedure is silently and progressively acquiring a growing importance.

21. *See, for example,* Directive 2006/123/EC, of the European Parliament and of the Council of 12 December 2006, on services in the internal market, number 6, 7, 32, 74, 104, 105, 111–113; and Chapter VI: Administrative Cooperation.

22. *See, for example,* the Proposal for a Directive of the European Parliament and of the Council amending Directive 97/67/EC concerning the full achievement of the internal market of Community postal services, Brussels, 18. 10. 2006, COM(2006) 594 final: the proposed amendment to Article 22, establishes the requirement for cooperation between national regulatory authorities and consumer protection bodies.

III
DOMESTIC COOPERATIVE ADMINISTRATIVE PROCEDURES UNDER EU INFLUENCE. TWO EXAMPLES

A. NATIONAL COOPERATIVE PROCEDURE: THE CASE OF STRATEGIC ENVIRONMENTAL ASSESSMENT (SEA)

1. INTRODUCTION: THE SIGNIFICANCE OF STRATEGIC ENVIRONMENTAL ASSESSMENT FOR NATIONAL ADMINISTRATIVE LAW

ACCORDING to the European model,[23] the administrative network for Strategic Environmental Assessment is fundamentally *domestic*, although in some cases it could have a transboundary effect.[24] A distinguishing characteristic of environmental problems – their correlation with ecosystems and geographic features rather than political boundaries – often renders isolated actions ineffective, and frequently demands cooperation at various levels. The adoption of environmental assessment procedures at the planning and programming level should benefit agency decision making by providing a more consistent framework that includes relevant environmental information in the decision making process.[25] The European Directive is of an administrative *procedural* nature, and its requirements should either be integrated into existing procedures in member states or incorporated into specifically established procedures.[26]

The term "strategic environmental assessment" (SEA) is now widely used to refer to a systematic process for analyzing the environ-

---

23. Directive 2001/42/EC of the European Parliament and of the Council of 27 June 2001 on the assessment of the effects of certain plans and programs on the environment.

24. Id. art. 7.

25. (5) Directive 2001/42/EC.

26. Id. at (9), art. 4.2.

mental effects of policies, plans and programs. Increasingly, SEA is seen in the international arena as an entry point or stepping stone toward integrated assessment or sustainability appraisal. It is a holistic, cross-sectional approach to the implementation of sustainable development.[27] SEA promotes an integrated approach, taking into account economic, social, and environmental dimensions of sustainable development.[28]

The mandate, institutional arrangements, and scope of application of SEA vary, in some cases significantly. Many SEA systems were instituted during the 1990s, or earlier in the case of the United States. Often, this process is equated with a formal administrative procedure based on an environmental impact assessment (EIA), as set forth by the European Union[29] and in the Kiev Protocol.[30] However, the SEA administrative procedure is much more complex and interesting, particularly from the point of view of administrative collaboration.[31]

---

27. BARRY DALAL-CLAYTON &BARRY SADLER, STRATEGIC ENVIRONMENTAL ASSESSMENT: A SOURCEBOOK AND REFERENCE GUIDE TO INTERNATIONAL EXPERIENCE 1, 4 (2005).

28. According to the Preamble of the Directive 2001/42/EC of the European Parliament and the Council of 27 June 2001 on the assessment of the effects of certain plans and programs on the environment, environmental assessment is an important tool for integrating environmental considerations into the preparation and adoption of certain plans and programs which are likely to have significant effects on the environment in Member States, because it ensures that the effects of implementing such plans and programs are taken into account during their preparation and before their adoption. The adoption of environmental assessment procedures at the planning and programming level should benefit administrative action by providing a more consistent framework, including the relevant environmental information for decision making. The inclusion of a wider set of factors in the decision making process should contribute to more sustainable and effective solutions.

29. Directive 2001/42/EC.

30. SEA Protocol to the UN Economic Commission for Europe, UNECE Convention on EIA in a Transboundary Context, agreed in 2003. Both instruments prescribe an EIA-based procedure for SEA. See DALAL-CLAYTON & SADLER, supra note 28, at 1, 4, 36, 37.

31. See PERSPECTIVES ON STRATEGIC ENVIRONMENTAL ASSESSMENT 4 (Maria Rosário Partidário & Ray Clark eds., 2000). To better understand these wider consequences in different cases, one must bear in mind that SEA entails a systematic, on-going process for evaluating, at the earliest appropriate stage of publicly accountable decision making, the environmental quality and effects of alternative visions and development intentions incorporated on policy, planning, or program initiatives, ensuring full integration of relevant biophysical, economic, social, and political considerations.

Each policymaker must empower the appropriate analyst to study alternatives that may be *broader* than the policymaker's authority, i.e., to begin coordination with the public and other agencies before a firm proposal is made. This requires efficient collaboration. The complexity of the processes associated with SEA may be one of the difficulties standing in the way of its application in some domestic systems. Some achievements integral to the SEA but extremely difficult to achieve include: integrated views of the main policy goals within the same administration or agency; horizontal and vertical collaboration between different public bodies; transboundary cooperation; effective dialogue between administrations and the public; etc.

The dynamic nature of strategic decision making means that no decision is ever *definitive*. In the case of plans or programs approved by *agencies* or by *statutes*, this implies amending or reforming administrative plans, programs and statutes that are not achieving their intended effect or are having an unintended environmental impact. The SEA system is changing the traditional *static* concept of plans and programs. They become a process in constant change, a "moving picture" rather than a snapshot. The dynamic concept of both plan and program is based on the recognition that any policy and planning decision is bound to be characterized by uncertainty and openness to change. Cooperation also has a strong *temporal* dimension; administrative procedure must also establish permanent collaboration between administrations in order to monitor their efficiency.

Environmental policy-making must be based on the best available scientific and economic assessment, and on a deep knowledge of the state of environmental trends.[32] However, many decisions are actually made on the basis of imperfect information, despite the effort and resources spent on gathering data and information. The SEA system calls for good communication mechanisms to ensure that all partners in the SEA process are adequately involved and their perspectives are

---

32. Decision No 1600/2002/EC of the European Parliament and of the Council of 22 July 2002 laying down the Sixth Community Environment Action Program.

taken into account, i.e., that there is an effective dialogue. Good communication is also needed to establish an articulation across sectoral policies and institutional contexts and to find credible and feasible alternatives that allow for an evaluation of any given decision based on comparable rather than absolute values. Communication is seen as a tool to achieve effective integration and influence. The best information can also provide the basis for policy decisions about the environment and sustainable development – the follow-up and review of sector integration strategies as well as of sustainable development strategy – and to share information with the wider public.

Better planning and policymaking practices also entail flexibility. SEA is a decision-aiding process that can and should be applied flexibly to the decision cycle, recognizing that these terms mean different things and often cover different types of decision making processes. SEA must be absolutely tailored to the kind of decision at stake and the nature of the decision making process in place.[33] Every policy, plan, and program is different.

As a result, the methods of cooperation through procedure should also be *elastic* and *custom-made, experimental* and *revisable, participatory* and *open-ended.*

2. ADMINISTRATIVE PROCEDURE IS USED FOR BALANCING DIVERSE INTERESTS, AND GUIDING AND PILOTING THE ADMINISTRATION ITSELF IN ITS DECISION MAKING PROCESS

The SEA Directive is a framework law that establishes a minimum common procedure[34] for major official plans and programs prepared for agriculture, forestry, fisheries, energy, industry, transport, waste

---

33. Perspectives on Strategic Environmental Assessment 7, 19, *supra* note 31.

34. According to the Directive, the different environmental assessment systems operating within member states should contain a set of common procedural requirements necessary to contribute to a high level of protection of the environment.

management, water management, telecommunications, tourism, town and country planning, or land use.[35]

According to one traditional point of view, administrative procedure focuses mainly on the outcome, and on judicial review of that outcome, disregarding the decision making process. Administrative procedure is associated with the implementation of policies defined in laws or other government programs. However, new administrative procedures, such as those concerning the SEA, focus much more on internal structure than the ultimate outcome. It is not a question of implementation. Here there is little to be implemented. The key role of the procedure lies in its internal phases (participation of the citizenry, inter-agency collaboration, balancing of diverse interests, etc.). In the SEA system, intensive administrative cooperation and interaction does not take place only in the implementation phase, but, more strikingly, in the preparatory one, that is, in the phases of agenda setting and policy formulation.

The SEA Directive imposes a model of administrative procedure that goes well beyond the traditional conception of adjudication or application procedures of general statutes. The traditional approach views administrative procedure as the application and enforcement of the law in concrete circumstances, *i.e.*, as akin to courtroom proceedings, and does not take into account other relevant approaches to procedure: administrative procedure as a way of controlling and steering public bodies,[36] or as a system of information exchange and information regulation,[37] and so on.

The SEA procedure, on the other hand, encompasses these relevant issues. The implementation of this kind of procedure is not easy at all, if judged (1) by the delayed incorporation of the SEA Directive on the part of many member states,[38] and (2) by the scant updates to

---

35. Sec. 3 Directive 2001/42/EC.

36. See *supra* Introduction.

37. *Id.*

38. *See, e.g.,* SIXTH ANNUAL SURVEY ON THE IMPLEMENTATION AND ENFORCEMENT OF COMMUNITY ENVIRONMENTAL LAW 2004, COMMISSION OF THE EUROPEAN COMMUNITIES, Brussels, 1055, (17. 8. 2005, SEC(2005)).

traditional techniques and tools, updates whose purpose would be to ensure public consultation, and collaboration between administrations.

3. SEA AS A COLLABORATIVE ADMINISTRATIVE PROCEDURE

The strategic environmental evaluation system implies, as noted, thorough collaboration and cooperation between public bodies. Obviously, this must first take place within each individual administration on a local, regional, or national level, as with intra-agency cooperation between the different organs and units that make up a local government.

Secondly, the SEA procedures must involve the public bodies that will be affected by the proposed plan or program, on both a horizontal and a vertical level.[39] Finally, collaboration with the administration or agency responsible for environmental issues (or "consultant administration") must be on a much more specific level, since that administration has particular formal functions at various stages in the assessment procedure.[40]

Collaboration is thus needed during all administrative procedure stages:

– *Screening of plans and programs*, to ensure that their overall characteristics fall within the requirements of the SEA Directive, and to assess their environmental significance. The first output is the *screening statement*. Environmental authorities must be consulted when undertaking case-by-case screening or when specifying certain types of plans and programs.[41]

---

39. The Directive refers only to consultation with the Consultation Bodies and with the public. Responsible authorities will, however, normally consult a range of other bodies in the course of preparing their plans and programs (e.g. Local, Regional and National Authorities, Agencies, etc.) and information from these may be useful in SEA. Some statutes implementing the SEA Directive into national law have not taken into account this point of view. *See, e.g.,* Spanish Statute on SEA, number 9/2006, April, 28th.

40. *See* SEA Directive, sec. 5 and 6.

41. Sec. 3.6 Directive SEA. The intention behind the screening provisions is to ensure that due and transparent consideration be given as to whether an environmental assessment is required.

– *Scoping the SEA*, to choose the key elements of the plans and programs at stake; highlight those environmental issues which are vital; collect and report on relevant international, national, and local plans, objectives, and environmental standards (existing and emerging) that may influence or impact on the plans or programs; develop draft environmental objectives, indicators, and targets to allow the evaluation of impacts based upon the findings; identify reasonable alternative means of achieving the strategic goals of the plans and programs; etc. These main points can only be identified through discussion and consultation at this stage.[42] The second output is the scoping report. Environmental authorities must be consulted as to the scope and level of detail to be covered by the SEA.[43]

– *Identification, prediction, evaluation, and mitigation of the potential environmental impact.* The purpose of this stage of the procedure is to identify and address the likely environmental impact of the plans and programs in question, establishing the environmental baseline (existing and future trends), predicting, evaluating and mitigating this impact, and justifying selected alternatives. The *SEA report* is the main output of the SEA procedure and will be the document that most stakeholders will review. An independent quality review of the pertinent draft SEA report is necessary as well. Environmental authorities (the responsible agencies) must be given an opportunity to comment on the report.[44]

– *Consultation, revision, and post-adoption activities.* The procedural tasks here are: to review comments for applicability of SEA to plans and programs; to undertake "fast-track" SEA on significant changes in plans and programs; to

---

Moreover, these screening provisions are designed to ensure that the environmental assessment requirements of the Act are targeted effectively at plans and programs likely to have significant environmental effects. *See, e.g.,* sec. 9 (31), Explanatory Notes to Environmental Assessment (Scotland) Act 2005.

42. Much baseline information will be generic to an area or sector, rather than specific to the particular plan or program on which SEA is being carried out. This information could therefore be used to support assessments for a range of plans or programs prepared by one or more authorities. There are potential opportunities for sharing information and collaborating when information is collected. To best exploit baseline information, one must update it constantly and regularly. To get the best value from baseline information, it is desirable to keep it up to date rather than leave it as a frozen snapshot of the situation at a particular time. *See* PRACTICAL GUIDANCE ON APPLYING EUROPEAN DIRECTIVE 2001/42/EC "ON THE ASSESSMENT OF THE EFFECTS OF CERTAIN PLANS AND PROGRAMMES ON THE ENVIRONMENT" 26 (Office of the Deputy Prime Minister, London, 2005).

43. Article 5.4 Directive SEA.

44. *See* art. 6.5 Directive SEA. *See also* art. 7 (Transboundary consultations).

elaborate a *SEA statement*; to commence environmental checks regarding the implementation of the plans and programs; to revise the monitoring program periodically; and to report regularly on monitoring results.[45] The SEA statement must be made available to the relevant authorities.[46]

4. SEA PROCEDURE: SOME FEATURES

The emphasis here is on the processes of reasoned decision making in relation to competing interests and values as well as relevant options, information and evidence. An integrated view of the process of making significant choices implies an integrated administration and cooperative procedure. Collaboration between administrations during the assessment procedure is inherently permanent and systematic:

– Its style of cooperation unifies procedurally all administrative units and levels involved (responsible authorities, environmental or consultant bodies, other affected administrations); it presumes an internal collaboration within the responsible authority.

– It covers all administrative procedure stages from screening and staging to monitoring; collaboration is ongoing throughout all stages of the plan or program. The collaboration among domestic public bodies expands to encompass agenda-setting, policy-making, and policy implementation.

– It covers multiple tasks, such as the handling of information (the gathering of the best information available, the exchange of information, the processing of information). In addition, it takes into account the choice of alternatives and methods of monitoring.

Collaborative functions can be carried out in two major ways. First, they can be developed through formal and traditional adminis-

---

45. P. Scott & P. Marsden, Development of SEA Methodologies for Plans and Programmes in Ireland, (Environmental Protection Agency, Ireland, 2003).
46. *See* article 9.1.

trative procedural rules subject to a detailed regulation of a sequential nature. Secondly, and more importantly, collaboration can be realized through informal and modernized administrative procedure rules, which are implemented in a more flexible and open manner. In this case, statutes set the ends and guarantees that administrations should attain, and allowing them a greater leeway and discretion regarding the choice of means and techniques (such as focus groups, public meetings, intergovernmental fora, consensus conferences, advisory committees, and steering groups).[47]

In cases where domestic law lacks a previous SEA tradition, the transposition of the SEA Directive has been much more difficult. The problem has been that antiquated procedural tools, useful for other ends, do not meet the challenges of the SEA system.[48] However, there are many examples of best practices from countries with an SEA tradition; many scholars have offered innovative proposals in this area.[49]

---

47. The evaluation of many of these procedural stages, tasks, and tools is not a formal requirement of the SEA Directive, but is recommended as good practice and guidance (*e.g,*. the scoping report at the second procedural step). *See* SCOTT & MARSDEN, *supra* note 45. The purpose of the scoping report is to *inform* stakeholders about key environmental issues, core elements of plans and programs, as well as alternatives within these plans and programs. It also aims to generate comment from stakeholders on the scope of, and approaches to SEA, and on proposed plans and programs. Therefore, it should be freely available to the public along with any parallel documents such as Issues Papers or Discussion Papers that describe the plans and programs in question.

Regarding the implementation of the SEA system, there are also many available tools: information sharing, guidance on technical issues, information and data management, testing and validation, etc.

48. Regarding proposed methods and tools for consultation and participation in the SEA procedure, *see, e.g.,* SCOTT & MARSDEN, *supra* note 45, at 31. Furthermore, it should be noted that there are many informal procedural tools for achieving collaboration and cooperation. *See supra* note 47 and accompanying text.

49. *See, e.g.,* SCOTT & MARSDEN, *supra* note 45.

B. REGARDING THE COLLABORATIVE ESSENCE
OF EGOVERNMENT

1. EGOVERNMENT AND ADMINISTRATIVE LAW

The organizational model of classical Administration can be profoundly changed as a result of a collaborative network of public bodies. eGovernment will challenge conventional perspectives.[50] Both the European Union and its member states hold that a citizen-focused public administration should be built on close cooperation between different government authorities and levels of government.[51]

The notion of "eGovernment" or "electronic Public Administration" encompasses much more than simply offering better services to citizens and/or enterprises through new electronic channels for information and service delivery.[52] It includes the ideal of strengthening democratic legitimacy through enhanced transparency and citizen participation in the policymaking and decision making processes.[53] One of the aims of eGovernment is to improve the efficiency of the administration and to better serve the citizenry.[54]

---

50. eGovernment may force an administration to move from a closed administrative organization to an open network public administration, or from a strict duality norm-application system to new models. From a more practical point of view, it must be noted that the on-line provision of services to citizens presupposes, among other considerations, the reorganization of existing administrative procedures and the creation of new procedures.

51. Many national reports on eGovernment are available. *EU: eGovernment in the European Countries*, in http://www.epractice.eu/document/3090, (October 2007); also particularly *Id.*, *eGovernment in Sweden* 10 (September 2007). Although these reports center on Europe, their substance can be shared by many other countries. *See, e.g., US E-Government Act of 2002, UN Global E-government Readiness Reports*, in http://www2.unpan.org/egovkb/global_reports/05report.htm (2004, 2005).

52. According to the European Commission, "eGovernment" means the use of information and communication technologies (ICT) in public administrations combined with organizational changes and new skills: the objective is to improve public services, democratic processes and public policies. *See The Role of eGovernment for Europe's future*, in COM(2003)567 final (2003).

53. *See, e.g., eGovernment in Sweden, supra* note 51.

54. Some countries have found that eGovernment makes government more focused on citizens and results. *See, e.g., US E-Government Act of 2002, supra* note 51.

Technology in and of itself is not the savior of these values. Nonetheless, technological development is generating new challenges and opportunities.[55]

eGovernment holds enormous potential for transforming the face of modern administration; it is capable of not only changing its own structure and organization but also assuming new responsibilities with respect to other public authorities and society at large.

The term "eGovernment" actually covers a broad field with rather uncertain contours. Here, we will only focus on administrative procedure as a mechanism for *collaboration* and *dialogue* among responsible public bodies within the state.[56]

2. EGOVERNMENT AND ADMINISTRATIVE PROCEDURE

Administrative procedure constitutes a core element of the "legal infrastructure" necessary to support relations between administrations, and with citizens and businesses as well. In the long run, a well-established collaborative administrative procedure is a basic legal

---

55. For example, to reach the EU policy aims for 2010 in regard to social inclusion and regional cohesion, more research must be done on outward-facing aspects of eGovernment and the interface between government and citizens. The focus should be on the development and delivery of appropriate content and services, and networked, coordinated and joined-up governments. *See* BRINGING TOGETHER AND ACCELERATING EGOVERNMENT RESEARCH IN EU, FP6 PROJECTS REPORTS (PREPARED FOR THE EGOVERNMENT AND CIP OPERATIONS UNIT DG INFORMATION SOCIETY AND MEDIA EUROPEAN COMMISSION) [HEREINAFTER BRINGING TOGETHER] A-116 (2007), *available at* http://ec.europa.eu/information_society/activities/egovernment/studies/trendswatch/docs/20080804-01-d02-egovr-id1-2-4_2_2_2-analysis_of_egov_research_projects-annual_reports.10-online.pdf.

56. Collaboration is needed, for example, to handle single and multiple integrated transactions and developing intergovernmental projects, electronic rulemaking participation, etc. At the same time, collaboration may not be so necessary if eGovernment is reduced to less evolved stages, such as the stage of simply providing information and on-line forms to citizens, or accepting completed online forms. eGovernment services supporting everyday life (related to work, housing, education, culture, transport, etc.) are today popularly utilized. *See* BRINGING TOGETHER A-8, *supra* note 55. Much of this is about access to information.

tool.[57] Procedure, broadly understood, gives structure to many of the rules that derive from the diverse legal sectors involved (data protection, the right to access information, e-Procurement, etc.), and, more specifically, to the function of collaboration between administrations (ways and means in which collaboration is to be carried out, its effects and consequences, etc.).

In my opinion, procedure should give form to many of the questions raised here,[58] particularly those concerning mutual tasks approached jointly by various administrations.[59] In short, this requires not merely the addition of new sections or provisions to existing legislation,[60] but rather the implementation of an entirely new approach.[61] Legal answers and solutions have been for the most part of a *sectorial character* (e.g., data protection, e-procurement, e-signature, etc.).

---

57. The legal framework of eGovernment is not limited to procedural rules alone. In fact, there are manifold aspects and dimensions as well as different sectors and branches of the law that must be considered and satisfactorily interlaced. It is also obvious that not every question relating to the procedure may necessarily refer to aspects of coordination and collaboration.

58. If we take administrative procedure in its broadest sense, *see supra* note 1, and not merely as a sequence of acts organized according to a model of legal process, then the legislation for the procedure would suffice to explain and to provide: the architecture and infrastructure of eGovernment (e.g., organizational, technical and semantic interoperability); the software necessary for that purpose (for example, the decision to adopt open source software and open standards, given its openness and cross-platform compatibility for the provision of eGovernment services); the methods required to guarantee rights relating to data access and free access to information, and the permanence of public data. It also should contain the rights of every beneficiary of eServices.

Moreover, the procedure must take into account the regulatory powers inherent in software itself, both those concerning the actual design of rights as well as those concerning the embodiment of the political values at stake (democracy, separation of powers, protection of rights, etc.). Such design and embodiment must be determined by each parliament, and not only by software engineers. Because of this, the statutes on procedure must establish precise provisions, at least where objectives and guarantees are concerned.

59. In other words, the manner in which different administrations participate and intervene in processes run by other administrations from a technical, material, as well as judicial standpoint.

60. Administrative procedure legislation should integrate many elements of these new phenomena in a systematic and coherent manner.

61. Barnes, *Sobre el procedimiento administrativo: evolución y perspectivas*, 267, 333. *supra* note 1.

Legislation must pursue *specific objectives* (e.g., digitalization of some processes; digital inclusion; etc.), which often are implemented in *fixed stages* or *time periods.*[62]

Still lacking is a proper and innovative system of procedure and, as a consequence, both a modern model of administration (including new systems of working in common) and of governance (including new regulatory methods, inter-agency partnerships, and public-private collaboration). For example, administrations will need to share and distribute information between themselves in a new way. The traditional structure of national administrative procedure does not encourage sharing and exchanging information between authorities, nor does it encourage participation in the administrative procedures carried out by other public bodies. If we look at the basic public services that the European Commission has defined as *reference services* in order to gage the evolution of eGovernment in member states, as adopted by the Council of the EU in March 2001,[63] it is easy to understand the need for intercommunication and collaboration between different administrative bodies.[64] The stumbling blocks in the way of collabo-

---

62. *See* Spanish Act 11/2007, on Access to ePublic Services; for an example at the European level, also *see* OLUF NIELSON, i2010 – A EUROPEAN INFORMATION SOCIETY FOR GROWTH AND EMPLOYMENT (2005), both available at http://info.worldbank.org/etools/docs/library/145274/i2010.pdf.

Many member states have foreseen various requirements involving digital administrative procedures between administrations and citizens. Frequently, the first national laws concerning electronic administrative procedure are restricted to the opening of new channels of communication with any given administration, that is, to merely incorporate new technologies in administrative relations and resolve any problems of adaptation arising naturally in the new situation (digital signatures, electronic notification, personal data protection, etc).

63. For citizens: income tax declaration, job searches by labor offices, social security contributions, personal documents, car registration, application for building permits, declarations to the police, public libraries, marriage and birth certificates, request and delivery, enrollment in higher education, moving announcements (changes of address), health-related services (e.g. hospital appointments). For businesses: social security contributions for employees, corporate taxes, VAT declarations, registration of new companies, submission of data to statistical offices, customs declarations, environment-related permits, public procurement, etc.

64. For example, in Spain, most of these services have some component requiring the intervention of the central administration, autonomous government bodies and/or local governments.

rative transactional cross-agency services—technological, political, and legal difficulties in working together—keep contemporary administrations away from a comprehensive solution.

3. SCOPE OF THE COLLABORATION

eGovernment is a long-term project, which must be planned and developed in a coordinated and mutually agreeable manner.[65] A more coordinated effort is needed to establish common rules, main infrastructure components,[66] and knowledge transfer systems between all administrative levels. These basic functions are necessary for joint services based on networked public bodies, which is the first goal of a citizen-focused and efficient administration.[67] Cooperation is clearly necessary at all levels: political,[68] legal,[69] technical,[70] economical,[71] etc.[72]

In any case, these services are only some of many examples of this incipient phenomenon. The list must be extended to other activities and to more complex and interrelated administrative services.

65. BRINGING TOGETHER A-24, *supra* note 55.

66. *E.g.*, portal, eAuthentication infrastructure, networks, e-procurement infrastructure, eInvoicing, knowledge management infrastructure, etc. Joint eGovernment infrastructures must be established and developed in order to facilitate the exchange of data and to avoid parallel developments.

67. *I.e.*, the development of integrated eServices for citizens and businesses in order to make available on-line the most important cross-level administrative services (such as unemployment, social, and welfare assistance). *See eGovernment in Sweden* 11–12, *supra* note 51. It also means, for example, that the parliaments must decide on basic guidelines for organizational development (new networked administrative structures); coordination of public procurement in the areas of information and communication technology; training and education; creating knowledge about best practices; the creation of an internal strategic coordination function in government offices for an IT society from a holistic perspective; and the creation of coordination channels between public bodies at a national level and the business sector with the support of public eServices.

68. It is necessary to design a cooperative administrative architecture. To this end, design must take into account very diverse questions relating to collaboration and joint-effort tasks. For example: how to integrate local government with centralized eGovernment processes and services; whether a local government acts as a front office for delivering eGovernment services regardless of the administrations actually involved (back-office); the creation of new organizations (such as a centralized Data Handling Service); certain inter- and intra-enterprise organi-

Therefore, fundamental changes, such as the replacement of a manual procedure by an electronic one, should ideally integrate all available levels (legal framework, ICTs, processes, re-organization, human capital, etc.) within a context of heightened coordination at central, regional and local levels. To achieve an eGovernment infrastructure, it is necessary to increase collaboration and interoperability among the information systems of agencies and public administrations.[73] Modern public administration must be built upon sophisticated ICT infrastructures and streamlined eGovernment processes. However, eGovernment is not only a technological issue; it is more importantly a conceptual one.[74] The most basic problem is not that of deciding how administrative procedure rules have to be modified for efficient and practical computer and Internet use.[75]

---

zational aspects; how to respect the security, privacy protection and autonomy of each institution involved in the process; etc. *See, e.g.*, BRINGING TOGETHER 23–24, *supra* note 55.

69. *See infra* Part III.2.d.

70. Technical interoperability covers the technical issues of linking computer systems and services, interfacing heterogeneous existing IT systems, and information as a strategic resource, also known as information modeling. *See, e.g.*, Communication from the Commission to the Council and the European Parliament – Interoperability for Pan-European eGovernment Services, COM(2006)0045 final.

71. The scope of the eGovernment program with the large number of public authorities involved, the large number of eGovernment services to be expanded and, last but by no means least, the scope of investment required to implement goals, call for an efficient organization and cost-effective implementation of pertinent measures. The cost-effective implementation of an eGovernment program comprises, as a sine qua non, closer cooperation between all public authorities, as well as the provision and use of joint solutions for similar tasks and the safeguarding of existing investments made by a government in eGovernment services. *See, e.g.*, *Focused on the Future: Innovations for Administration, The Government's Programme* (Federal Ministry of the Interior, Germany, 1st ed., November 2006) *available at* www.bmi.bund.de/ Pogramm_ Zukunftsorientierte_Verwaltung_en.pdf.

72. In different and extralegal terms, it can be said that the prerequisites for an c-Government enactment strategy are the achievement of technological interoperability of platforms and a deeper cooperation at an organizational level. *See* M. CONTENTI ET AL., A DISTRIBUTED ARCHITECTURE FOR SUPPORTING E-GOVERNMENT COOPERATIVE PROCESSES 181–92, 182 (2005).

73. *See, e.g.*, *KBSt, Bundesministerium des Innern*, in *IT-Architekturkonzept für die Bundesverwaltung*, (24 July 2007), available at http://www.epractice.eu/document/3727.

74. *See* Barnes, *Sobre el Derecho Administrativo de la Información*, in 35 REVISTA CATALANA DE DRET PUBLIC, 121 (2007); *see also* BARNES, *Sobre el procedimiento administrativo: evolución y perspectivas* 302, *supra* note 1.

75. For example, how should traditional rules to solicit and consider public comments before

The most basic problem is the previous question of political design.[76] What type of administration do we want to set up? Once that is decided, what model of electronic procedure should we choose, and what guidelines for collaboration among various public administrations should we establish?[77] As noted before, it is not a question of translating or simply transferring the paper-based administration's pattern to the ethereal world of bits and bytes.[78] Whatever shape the technical architecture is to take must be decided beforehand. A new concept of networked public administration is thus needed. A policy of "rethinking things before automating them" must be implemented. The influence of the principles of the *rule of law*, of *democracy* and of *efficiency* must be taken into account when establishing new eGovernment procedures.

---

promulgating rules of general applicability be adapted to the new media of electronic communication? How should polities redesign administrative rulemaking as "e-rulemaking"?

76. The integration of information technologies in general, and the Internet in particular, into the rulemaking process could take myriad forms. Even among technologies designed to enhance participation by any and all interested citizens, there are many possible variations. *See, e.g.*, Stuart Minor Benjamin, *Evaluating E-Rulemaking: Public Participation and Political Institutions*, 55 DUKE L. J. 893, 898 (2006). Integration of technology necessarily entails a political debate.

To ensure a more deliberative and democratic process and create deliberative dialogues between citizens and public bodies for their mutual benefit will also require more than finding the right tools and the right methods of discussion. We must connect the deliberative processes to real-world decision making. Citizen participation processes should be reviewed in various political contexts, including rulemaking, government enforcement functions, and wherever authorities provide information, planning and review procedures. *See* BETH SIMONE NOVECK, *Designing Deliberative Democracy in Cyberspace: The Role of the Cyber-lawyer*, 9 B. U. J. SCI. & TECH. L. 1, 89 (2003).

77. *See, e.g.*, Barnes, *Sobre el procedimiento administrativo: evolución y perspectives* 302-10, *supra* note 1.

78. *Id. See also* Barnes, *Sobre el Derecho Administrativo de la Información* 149, *supra* note 74.

4. Perspectives Derived from the Principles of Rule of Law, Democracy, and Efficiency

A multiorganizational model of cooperation needs rules on administrative procedure to develop a framework for new working processes, both inside and outside the organization concerned; that is, not only an interdepartmental and interadministrative or interagency partnership, but also cooperation with the private sector.

eGovernment demands structural reform of the work process—the way in which agencies gather information and take action. The approval of new procedures within the framework of eGovernment must come about based on the principles of rule of law, democracy, and efficiency.

From the viewpoint of the *rule of law*, some requirements to be met by new collaborative administrative procedures include:

- The *identification* of responsibilities and duties of all participating administrations within every administrative procedure (for the purposes of the sharing of responsibility, liability and accountability, even in a judicial review process);[79]

- The implantation of greater *transparency* in all administrative procedures, regardless of the administrative level involved;

- The application of common rules and standards of procedure (such as infringement of procedural rules, liability claims in case of violations, and equal treatment of all citizens);

- The encouragement of interoperable, inclusive, and transparent ICT solutions, and of initiatives relating to collaborative management and development at central, regional, and local levels;

- The achievement through administrative procedural rules of an appropriate balance between individual privacy and the government's need to gather information, so as to avoid the risk that government itself will abuse its data collection powers in the exercise of e-surveillance;

---

79. Indeed, an important requirement is the need for each public administration involved to maintain not only its autonomy but also a well-defined jurisdiction and responsibility governing the steps and sub-processes that each public agency is required to follow.

– The recognition that the highly networked nature of the current computing environment involves providing effective government-wide management and oversight of related information security risks, including coordination of information security efforts throughout civilian, national security, and law enforcement communities;

– The establishment of an equilibrium between the automation of existing manual procedures and the recognition of certain discretionary powers for the individualization of special circumstances in each case (a serialized or automatic response can be unjust in concrete cases).

eGovernment allows the use of administrative procedure as a tool to strengthen the *democratic legitimacy* of the regulatory State.[80] From the standpoint of the *principle of democracy*, the law must make use of new technologies to set up more transparent procedures (available information, monitoring, tracking, etc.) and more intense, fluid, and effective channels of citizen participation.

As to the *principle of efficiency*, we can highlight other requirements:

– Simplification of administrative procedures for quicker results, in order to lighten the weight borne by citizens and businesses; this requires a global revision of the public administration's work processes, based on a cooperative model within which each internal service delivered by each sub-administration is clearly defined;

– Effective procedures for reaching consensus rapidly;

– Compatibility of procedures;

– Reduction of the costs of administrative procedures;

– Identification of respective competencies and activities for working collaboratively and avoiding overlaps;

---

80. In the field of administrative governance, some of the central challenges facing national and European administrative law involve the control of heterarchic structures. "These heterarchic structures arise when Administrations are required to merge the input from administrative agencies and the private sector as well as scientific expertise from multiple levels into one single administrative procedure." *See* HOFMANN & TÜRK 580-81, *supra* note 4.

– Reciprocal access to administrative information among administrations, based on shared rules and standard modalities;

– Surveillance of the quality of those internal administrative procedures aimed at supplying services;

– Design of end-to-end electronic procedures which link up all the administrative levels involved.

Collaboration begins, in other words, at the *legislative level.* Statutes governing administrations must be coordinated, in order to establish the necessary rules of acceptable procedures.

5. SOME FEATURES OF eGOVERNMENT PROCEDURES

We return to our initial considerations to emphasize two points. First, eGovernment makes it clear, as do many other aspects of administration,[81] that networking begins at a domestic level, as a part of a whole.[82] Second, as an instrument of new methods of regulation and

---

81. Consider, for example, administrative procedures for scrutinizing regulatory policy, in particular EU policy on better regulation, regulatory management, regulatory impact assessments, policy planning systems, and other variables. *See* European Commission Staff, Working Paper on Impact Assessment and Ex Ante Evaluation, COM (2005)119 final, (2005). *See also Regulatory Management Capacities of Member States of the European Union that Joined the Union on 1 may 2004, Sustaining regulatory management improvements through a Better Regulation Policy, in* Sigma Paper no. 42, 26–29, available at *http://www.ec.europa.eu/enterprise/regulation/better_regulation/docs/final_synthesis_report_ sigma.pdf.*

We need effective structures to coordinate policy planning and procedures, to resolve conflicts between priorities, to identify problems, and to ensure consultation and cooperation.

82. Naturally, if it is intended that eGovernment services be delivered at all levels of government, the network must extend to both the European and global levels,.

"Interoperability must be ensured between local, regional, national and European administrations to provide seamless service" Communication from the Commission to the Council and the European Parliament – Interoperability for Pan-European eGovernment Services, COM(2006)0045 final, 1.2. Cooperation is required to develop pan-European services; it relies to a greater extent on the interoperability of information and communication systems used at all levels of government. *Id.* at I.1.

governance, eGovernment demands the design of appropriate cooperative procedures adapted to new needs.[83]

The underlying concept of eGovernment and the user-centered on-line public services approach permits collaboration to increase exponentially in both intensity and extension to limits unknown until now. Keep in mind that cooperation, in any of its aspects, can be:

- Horizontal and vertical at the same time;
- "Ad intra" (within the same public body) and "ad extra" (allowing for an interagency partnership);[84]
- Local, regional, national, and supranational;
- Systematic, comprehensive, and permanent, or specific and sporadic;
- oriented towards both citizens, and other administrations;[85]
- Of both a sectoral and a transverse character;[86] and
- Geared towards the provision of government services,[87] strengthened participation, and representation of interests.[88]

---

83. Collaboration thus becomes a key element of new regulatory strategies. *See supra* Part I.

84. For example, governments can facilitate the announcement of a change of address by offering an on-line interface that will enable the citizen to provide the needed information only once. The system will propagate this information to all concerned agencies.

85. eGovernment makes many government processes available to other administrations as eGovernment services, such as access to existing legacy information systems and databases from multiple administrations. *See Report on the Impact of eGovernment on Territorial Government Services,* http://www.terregov.eupm.net/my_spip/index.php (last visited July 2008).

86. The delivery of cross-border public sector services constitutes a more advanced stage of eGovernment.

87. *See, e.g.,* Directive 2006/123/EC of the European Parliament and of the Council, 12 December 2006, articles 6, 7.3, 7.4, 8, 34.1 (providing procedures for services in the internal market).

88. The providing of government e-services is not the only objective of eGovernment, EU insistence in this area notwithstanding, although as a consequence of its presently limited competences in the material this belief is easily understandable. The competencies of the EU/EC are based on two fundamental freedoms (freedom of establishment and freedom to provide services) enshrined in the EC Treaty. Apart from this area, eGovernment can serve to reinforce the citizen's participation in administrative procedures concerning government regulation, town planning, environmental issues, and, in general, procedures set up for policy-making.

eGovernment is therefore not limited to a particular type of administrative action or a specific sector, but, on the contrary, extends its scope to the entire range of actions undertaken by all administrations.

The reticular architecture that must be formed in conjunction with multiple administrations via eGovernment is not *ephemeral*. This governmental architecture has relevant administrative procedure aspects, not just organizational, technical or operational aspects.

Any joint effort carried out through eGovernment requires the redefinition or remodeling of numerous paper-based administrative procedures, in order to use new technologies to greater advantage. It also compels the agencies or administrations to improve collaboration and to meet the objectives each procedure requires.[89] To simplify administrative procedures for citizens presupposes much more sophisticated and collaborative administrative procedures at the interagency level.

The participation of various administrations can be carried out through staggered and formal procedures. Nevertheless, this collaboration does not necessarily entail the transformation of the procedure into a "composite" administrative procedure with formal administrative procedure stages and input during specific phases from several different administrations.[90] For example, cooperation, within the framework of eGovernment, can consist of the simple rendering of information services to another administration[91] or the use of a com-

---

89. One example is the depiction of the various phases of the public eProcurement lifecycle, in order to create more open competition. *See, e.g.,* European Commission, STATE OF THE ART REPORT I, CASE STUDIES ON EUROPEAN ELECTRONIC PUBLIC PROCUREMENT PROJECTS 26 (July 2004). In this sector, procedural eProcurement practices should strengthen equal treatment, transparency, effectiveness, interoperability, security, general availability, and confidentiality (*Id.* p. 47).

90. *See* Sabino Cassese, *European Administrative Proceedings,* in 68 LAW & CONTEMP. PROBS. 21 (2004), for discussion of this theme on a European level,

91. Collaboration can be limited to providing information to other Administrations, as a government eService, using agreed-upon procedures for exchanging information, and without taking part in the final outcome or in the decision making process at all.

Each cooperating public body can act both as a provider of its own services and as a petitioner of services available in other organizations.

mon-knowledge management infrastructure.[92] "Cooperative procedures" does not necessarily mean "composite procedures," nor does it imply establishing standardized and *formalized* procedures. They also may have a non-linear structure.

In summary, it can be said that administrative procedure, broadly understood,[93] and within the framework of eGovernment, comprises a particularly useful instrument to set up the legal dimensions of new work processes;[94] to rationalize the system of both intra- and inter-administrative relations and communications,[95] as well as those between an administration and the citizenry (information exchange systems, rights and duties, sharing of responsibilities, etc.); and, finally, to establish principles of collaboration between public authorities at all levels.

---

92. The ICT also allows the simultaneous participation of different administrations and of the public in the information-gathering process required by each case. Here the rigid order of procedure, common in judicial processes, is not followed.

93. *See supra* note 1.

94. The delivery of eGovernment services "requires the availability of efficient, effective and interoperable information and communication systems between public administrations as well as interoperable administrative front and back office processes in order to exchange in a secure manner, understand and process public sector information." Decision 2004/387/EC of the European Parliament and of the Council, 21 April 2004, on interoperable delivery of pan-European eGovernment services to public administrations, businesses and citizens (IDABC), 14.

95. For example, administrative procedure should be able to provide support in the management of semantic inconsistencies that may occur in cross-border exchanges of data, terms, and concepts.

IV
FINAL REMARKS

THE increasing need for collaboration among public administrations reflects a shift to principles and procedures at odds with traditional or standard systems. A greater emphasis on flexibility, informal approaches, and cooperation in procedure is necessary.

The above examples, SEA procedure and eGovernment, suggest that domestic administrative law is likely to be strongly transformed through European influences on administrative procedure's functions, scope, and structure. The functions of administrative procedure in the European sphere – among others, efficiency, collaboration, and political control of the administration– are already reflected in the internal features of some incipient domestic procedures.

The European Union itself extends this formula to the national level, either *directly* (as in SEA procedures),[96] or *implicitly* (as in the simplification of procedures regarding services in the internal market),[97] or via other non-binding means of influence (e.g. eGovernment procedures).[98] All of these are beyond the scope of the "indirect administration" of Communitarian Law. This being said, the cooperation necessary at a national level far exceeds the cooperation the European Union can demand or promote, given the limited competencies it has been endowed with.[99] Collaboration is, first and foremost, an obligatory response to globalization and to new methods of

---

96. *See supra* Part III.1.

97. Directive 2006/123/EC on services does not call into question the allocation of competencies at the local or regional level. *See* Directive 2006/123/EC, article 10.7 Nonetheless, it implicitly requires strong internal coordination and cooperation at all levels between the administrations involved. *See, e.g., Id.,* articles 6, 7.3, 7.4, 8, 34.1.

98. *See supra* Part III.2.

99. *Id.*

regulation and governance. "New governance mechanisms are designed to increase flexibility, improve participation, foster experimentation and deliberation, and accommodate regulation by multiple levels of government."[100]

The characteristic European administrative model of *separation* of different administrations on the organizational level and *cooperation* among all of them on a functional level[101] can also be reproduced domestically in local, regional, and national administrations. This must happen in accordance with the respective constitutional structures. Public bodies become more dependent on each other by setting common goals for their partnerships. Administrative procedural rules must reflect the multiple aspects of *functional* cooperation.

Each form of cooperation generates specific problems. In fact, every kind of cooperation provides an *interface* or functional connection between the different areas or spaces in which different actors play out their roles. "One effect of a more flexible attitude toward reaching decisions is that it allows more integration between stages of the legal process. Unlike the regulatory model, the governance model does not insist that legislation, implementation, enforcement, and adjudication are separate stages, but rather seeks to form dynamic interactions among these processes."[102]

The requirement of collaboration among local, regional and general public bodies in domestic administrative procedure is not always sufficiently or adequately understood and developed by member states.[103] On the one hand, the cooperation techniques ordinarily contained in

---

100. *See* TRUBEK & TRUBEK, *supra* note 4, at 539.

101. *See* Schmidt-Aßmann, *Das allgemeine Verwaltungsrecht, supra* note 1, at 381–84.

102. Orly Lobel, *The Renew Deal: The Fall of Regulation And The Rise of Governance in Contemporary Legal Thought*, 89 MINN. L. REV. 342, 391 (2004).

103. In some cases, as in Spain, the general collaborative approach among public administrations is surprisingly narrow as a result of cumulative effects of: 1) the decentralization process of the State begun in 1978 (the Constitution of 1978, Statutes of Autonomy, laws, regulations and practices) which still, in some ways, focuses on the "isolated" or individual action of public administration at the local and regional level; and 2) a misunderstanding of Constitutional case-

the general rules of national administrative procedure are outdated and meager. On the other hand, national statutes show an excessive dependence on European Union initiatives and, as a consequence, little autonomy or creativity when it comes to establishing new cooperative procedures in other areas.

This article argues for a paradigmatic shift away from *traditional*, that is to say sporadic and non-systematic, cooperation among administrations now dependent on written quasi-judicial procedures, towards *new collaborative practices*, and new *formal* and *informal procedural rules*, understood as flexible and fluent communication systems designed to promote less hierarchical, more sustained forms of participation and cooperation among all public bodies involved at the domestic level. The use of information and communication technology can make this model more effective.

The traditional core of administrative law has focused on securing the rule of law and protecting our liberties by ensuring that public bodies follow fair and impartial decision making procedures, that they act within the bounds of the statutory authority delegated by the legislature, and that they respect the rights of the individual. Here the function of administrative law is primarily *negative*: to prevent the unlawful or arbitrary administrative exercise of power.[104]

In recent decades, administrative law has also assumed *affirmative* tasks. Through new procedure requirements, among other approaches, it ensures that administrations exercise their policymaking discretion in a manner that is well-reasoned and responsive to the wide range of social and economic interests affected by their decisions.[105] It is appropriate to develop an administrative law for these new scenarios

---

law concerning this issue (cooperation and coordination doctrine), frequently interpreted out of context. This case-law must be viewed in historical context: It was produced during the first post-1978 constitutional years for the purposes of promoting the decentralization process, without taking into account the construction of the State as a whole.

104. *See* Stewart 439, *supra* note 2.

105. *Id. See also* Barnes, *Sobre el procedimiento administrativo: evolución y perspectivas 267*, *supra* note 1.

that will serve both the *negative* (power-checking) and *affirmative* (power-directing) functions of administrative law.[106]

The collaboration principle among administrations belongs to the positive or affirmative dimension of administrative procedure: Its primary objective is, first, the guarantee of efficiency and quality in the final "product" (e.g., decisions, regulations, and services), and second, better representation, participation, and cooperation of civil society in administrative decision making. The affirmative side of administrative law, when structuring discretionary lawmaking, will increasingly rely on structures that do not require court participation and thus will conserve scarce judicial resources.[107]

In general terms it can be said that many national administrative procedure laws are out of date, because they fail to recognize the new modes and methods of governance that characterize the administrative state, such as the setting of priorities, resource allocation, research, planning, targeting, guidance, and strategic enforcement.[108] These superannuated statutes fail to craft requirements that are appropriate to these activities, either leaving them essentially unregulated or subjecting them to inappropriate administrative procedure rigidities.[109] In this context, the new features of modern administrative cooperation, beginning at the domestic level, must establish new national statutes of administrative procedure. Among other tasks, these statutes should

---

106. Stewart 457, *supra* note 2. *See also* Schmidt-Aßmann, *Das allgemeine Verwaltungsrecht als Ordnungsidee* 16–26, *supra* note 1.

107. *See Stewart* 454, *supra* note 2.

108. *See* E. Rubin, *It's Time to Make the Administrative Procedure Act Administrative*, in *Public Legal and Legal Theory Research Paper No. 30*, 89 Cornell L. Rev. 2 (2002), regarding the US APA. This remark referred by the author to the US APA may be extended to many other national statutes. For discussion of this issue from a continental-European perspective, see W. HOFFMANN-RIEM & E. SCHMIDT-ASSMANN, VERWALTUNGSVERFAHREN UND VERWALTUNGSVERFAHRENSGESETZ (2002); Barnes, *Sobre el procedimiento administrativo: evolución y perspectivas* 333-41, *supra* note 1; Barnes, *The Reform of Administrative Procedure*, *supra* note 1. *See also* text, *supra* note 47.

109. *See* Rubin 2, *supra* note 108. This consideration may be extended to many other national statutes.

address the administrative process itself, and the distinctive mode of governmental action that arises from new methods of regulation and governance. Understanding the range and complexity of interdependent relationships to which administrative law must respond is the first step towards developing a new collaborative administrative procedure among public bodies.

CHAPTER VI

TOWARDS A NEW CONCEPT OF ADMINISTRATIVE PROCEDURE:
THE PROVISION OF HEALTH SERVICES

José María Rodríguez de Santiago*

* Professor of Administrative Law, Universidad Autónoma de Madrid, Spain.

INDEX

I
THE CONCEPT OF
"ADMINISTRATIVE PROCEDURE"

S OCIAL administrative law can contribute to a broader conception of administrative procedure.[1] Traditionally, "administrative procedure" has been thought of as an orderly succession of agency action or proceedings that leads to an administrative, binding decision, usually in the form of an "administrative act" (formal decision or adjudication). This conception of procedure draws its inspiration from administrative activity in the liberal State in the 19th Century based on monitoring and control, including limitation of freedoms or rights when necessary ("police administration").[2] It is not useful for explaining vast sectors of the modern welfare state, particularly the provision of personal services by public authorities. Alongside this "decision-making procedure," it is therefore necessary to define a new model of administrative procedure: the "provision of services procedure."[3]

---

1. E. SCHMIDT-ASSMANN, *Zur Reform des Allgemeinen Verwaltungsrechts – Reformbedarf und Reformansätze, in* REFORM DES ALLGEMEINEN VERWALTUNGSRECHTS. GRUNDFRAGEN, SCHRIFTEN ZUR REFORM DES VERWALTUNGSRECHTS 33 (Hoffmann-Riem et al, eds, 1993). Schmidt-Aßmann argues that general administrative law becomes a system as result of an inductive and deductive process, in the course of which general administrative law draws its concepts from various "reference sectors." One of these sectors is precisely that of social administrative law. *See also* E. SCHMIDT-ASSMANN, DAS ALLGEMEINE VERWALTUNGSRECHT ALS ORDNUNGSIDEE. GRUNDLAGEN UND AUFGABEN DER VERWALTUNGSRECHTLICHEN SYSTEMBILDUNG (1998) [hereinafter *Ordnungsidee*]. The same idea is developed by Javier Barnes, *Sobre el procedimiento administrativo: evolución y perspectivas in* INNOVACIÓN Y REFORMA EN EL DERECHO ADMINISTRATIVO 319-21 (Javier Barnes ed., 2006) .

2. A police administration is the administration entrusted with controlling and protecting functions.

3. SCHMIDT-ASSMANN, *Ordnungsidee*, *supra* note 1, at 288-289. *See also* Peter J. TETTINGER, *Verwaltungsrechtliche Instrumente des Sozialstaates*, 64 VERÖFFENTLICHUNGEN DER VEREINIGUNG DER DEUTSCHEN STAATSRECHTSLEHRER 213 (2005).

Theoretically, it is difficult to define the boundaries of the "social or welfare administration." For our present purpose, we shall not tackle this issue, which we have dealt with elsewhere in depth.[4] Let us just say that welfare administration includes social security, health care, and social aid.[5] We are therefore dealing with an extensive concept, to which a wide range of functions is attached.

The administrative activity used to perform these functions can be divided into two basic actions: the disbursement of payments and the provision of personal services. The welfare administration makes payments—compensation for accidents, temporary or permanent disability, maternity leave, retirement, unemployment, and so on, but it also provides personal services—such as medical care and social assistance for the elderly or the homebound. We are thus confronted with two different types of *social* administrative activity, each of which has a different structure and requires a different legal regime.

Following the same reasoning, one may say that a welfare administration has two branches: the *paying branch*, which makes or executes payments, and the *provider branch*, which provides personal services. Activities carried out by the *executive branch* fit into the traditional scheme of administrative activity: They implement conditional rules.[6] Activities carried out by the *provider branch*, in contrast, do not fit into this scheme: they implement programs that cannot be reduced to conditional rules, because their execution requires complex decisions concerning the exact content of the service provided in each case.[7]

---

4. José María Rodríguez De Santiago, La Administración del Estado social (2007).

5. These tasks were assigned to the public administration by the 1978 Spanish Constitution. *See* constitutional articles 41 and 149.1.17 (social security); 43 and 149.1.16 (health), and 148.1.20 (social aid).

6. Granting payments is a typical *conditional program*: The administration must simply implement norms, checking that the beneficiary meets the legally established requirements. Administrative action can also respond to an *outcome-oriented program*, wherein the administration must reach general objectives set by law; this might require complex administrative decisions. A third hypothesis is conceivable: Administrative law can limit itself to delineating the organizational framework of a public body and its general procedural rules, without using conditional or outcome-oriented norms.

The work of the *executive branch* basically responds to the traditional "decision-making procedure," as a formalized procedure leading to a binding decision. We are not concerned with this *social* administrative procedure, even though it has unique characteristics worthy of future study.

The activity of the *provider branch* does not correspond to traditional "decision-making procedure." The provision of personal services such as health assistance or education cannot be reduced to a formalized procedure, where every stage is legally preordained. For this reason, administrative lawyers seldom use the concept of "administrative procedure" to explain the provision of personal services by the state.

The provision of personal services by the state is usually studied in Spain within the framework of French "public services theory."[8] This approach is valid, but it tends to focus on general issues such as the organizational structure of the service, its management, and the conditions that entitle the citizenry to its benefits. Besides, this approach tends to emphasize the legal relationship between the public authorities and the public or private provider, while the ultimate beneficiary of the service is generally considered a third party.

The provision of personal services by the state can certainly be conceptualized as an "administrative procedure." The use of the concept of "administrative procedure" offers important advantages. First, the procedural approach highlights the dynamics of the process that

---

7. RAINER WAHL, *Die Aufgabenabhängigkeit von Verwaltung und Verwaltungsrecht, in* REFORM DES ALLGEMEINEN VERWALTUNGSRECHTS. GRUNDFRAGEN, SCHRIFTEN ZUR REFORM DES VERWALTUNGSRECHTS 203-08 (Hoffmann-Riem et al, eds., 1993).

8. *See, e.g.,* SANTIAGO MUÑOZ MACHADO, I TRATADO DE DERECHO ADMINISTRATIVO Y DERECHO PÚBLICO GENERAL 980-95 (1ª ed., 2004); JUAN ALFONSO SANTAMARÍA PASTOR, II PRINCIPIOS DE DERECHO ADMINISTRATIVO 328-36 (1999); EDUARDO GARCÍA DE ENTERRÍA & TOMÁS-RAMÓN FERNÁNDEZ, CURSO DE DERECHO ADMINISTRATIVO II 67-83 (10th ed., 2006); RAMÓN PARADA, DERECHO ADMINISTRATIVO I 390-93 (16th ed., 2007); LUCIANO PAREJO ALFONSO, ANTONIO JIMÉNEZ BLANCO, & LUIS ORTEGA ÁLVAREZ, MANUAL DE DERECHO ADMINISTRATIVO 423-27 (3th ed., 1994); LUIS MORELL OCAÑA, II CURSO DE DERECHO ADMINISTRATIVO 119-45 (1996).

leads to the provision of the service, paying particular attention to its different stages. Also, the administrative procedural approach emphasizes the ultimate beneficiary of the service - the citizen - rather than the relationship between the various entities involved in the process. Finally, the administrative procedure approach can focus on the outcome of the process and thus determine whether its goal has been fulfilled.

This essay argues that the concept of "administrative procedure" should be widened so as to cover activities carried out by the provider administration. In order to elaborate a new concept of administrative procedure, the essay will focus on a specific service, namely the provision of medical care by the state. As it is thoroughly regulated in Spain and other European countries, provision of medical service should constitute a solid basis for this theoretical enterprise. At a later stage, the essay will use the concept of "administrative procedure" to explain health system regulation.

II
THE DECISION-MAKING PROCEDURE AND
THE PROVISION OF SERVICES PROCEDURE

FROM a doctrinal perspective, there is no reason why the concept of "administrative procedure" should refer solely to the traditional "decision-making procedure." As far as outcome is concerned, there is no doubt that the "decision-making procedure" and the "provision of services procedure" are completely different: The former typically results in the adoption of a formalized decision by an administrative organ, while the latter results in the provision of a personal service to a citizen. Nonetheless, these types of procedure have one thing in common: They can be seen as an "orderly succession of actions, aimed at obtaining and handling information, which takes place under the responsibility of an administrative body."[9] Thus defined, the concept of "administrative procedure" seems broad enough to be applied to the provision of services.

In addition to this, the adoption of formalized decisions by the state poses the same regulatory problems as the provision of services. One must remember at this point that the concept of "administrative procedure" serves three basic purposes. First, it unifies the multiple contacts that the administration may have with a citizen, or with another legal entity,[10] in order to achieve a single goal. Second, it protects citizens' rights and interests, as the concept of administrative procedure can be viewed as a guarantee arising from the principles of the Rule of Law.[11] Finally, it structures the gathering and processing of information, and hence the process of decision-making: what personal

---

9. The definition is taken from SCHMIDT-ASSMANN, *Ordnungsidee, supra* note 1.

10. SCHMIDT-ASSMANN, *Ordnungsidee* 288, *supra* note 1.

11. THOMAS SIMONS, VERFAHREN UND VERFAHRENSÄQUIVALENTE RECHTSFORMEN IM SOZIALRECHT 48 (1985).

data to use at each stage and under what conditions, who must supply the data, who must bear the burden of proof under particular conditions, who is in charge of evaluating the information provided, and what information must be offered to the citizen.

These issues also come into play when dealing with the provision of services by a public entity. In order to build a coherent legal regime, it is necessary to unify the multiple contacts that the service provider may have with the citizen. It is obvious that the activity carried out by the *provider branch* necessarily invades the private sphere of individuals. It is therefore especially important to guarantee the citizens' rights in this field. Information-gathering and processing must also be regulated in this field. If the provision of services by the state poses the same regulatory problems as the adoption of formalized decisions, there is no reason why this sort of administrative activity should be excluded from the concept of "administrative procedure."

The concept of administrative procedure embodies three different sets of rules, which in turn raise three different issues:

1) Different administrative procedure stages. By definition, any procedure implies an orderly succession of actions through time. Consequently, the different stages that form the procedure need to be defined and regulated. In general, however, the regulation of the different steps of the "provision of services procedure" will be more flexible than in the "decision-making procedure," because one cannot apply the same pattern in all cases.[12] In particular, while in some cases the administrative procedure will be initiated following a formal decision adopted by a public entity, in others it will simply be initiated when the patient visits his or her doctor. The main phases of the procedure will then typically be: diagnosis, informing the patient of treatment options and consequences, patient's consent, and treatment. The discharge of the patient who has undergone treatment will normally end the procedure; however, the procedure can end in other ways, for instance, with a voluntary or compulsory discharge issued before completion of treatment.

---

12. *See* SIMONS 63, *supra* note 11, who argues that "cooperative procedures" are not usually subject to a strict pattern: They lay down guarantees, but the actual deployment of the procedure depends on the parties involved.

2) The rights and duties of the different parties involved. The concept of "administrative procedure" can be seen as a guarantee arising from the principle of the Rule of Law. A wide range of rights and duties are implicit in this concept. The provision of medical services raises a specific problem—how to bridge the gap in knowledge and power between the parties.[13] The specialized knowledge of the professional undoubtedly places him in a powerful position in relation to the patient. The law must compensate for this inequality, making it possible for both parties to interact and for the patient to intervene in the process in an informed manner.

3) The resolution of conflicts throughout the process. Nothing prevents the parties involved in an administrative procedure from having recourse to the courts. It is nevertheless convenient to adopt flexible formulas that make it possible to resolve conflicts without administrative procedure interruption or delay. This is especially true in the field of medical services, where excessive delays or interruptions may jeopardize a satisfactory outcome.

---

13. SIMONS 48-64, *supra* note 11.

III

THE CONCEPT OF "ADMINISTRATIVE ACT" (DECISION OR ADJUDICATION): ITS ROLE WITHIN THE "PROVISION OF SERVICES PROCEDURE"

THE concepts of a formal and binding decision taken by the administration—the so called "administrative act"—and "administrative procedure" are closely connected. This connection is problematic, because the concept of "administrative act" plays a limited role within the "provision of services procedure." At first blush, this may seem paradoxical: administrative acts are meant to apply abstract regulations to specific situations. Developing and applying specific norms is particularly necessary within the context of services, where the regulatory framework tends to be especially indeterminate.

However, the truth is that the "provision of services procedure" is normally completed without issuing a single administrative act. The initiation of the process does not require a formal adjudication, since it normally begins with the patient simply visiting the doctor. The development and termination of the process also do not require adjudication. An administrative act may be issued in some cases—for example, in order to declare someone entitled to treatment—but this is far from being the general rule.

Of course, "administrative acts" are not completely absent in this context. For instance, some benefits require a formal administrative decision declaring that the beneficiary is entitled to them. But even when an administrative act is issued, its regulatory content is limited, because it will rarely determine the exact content of the service appropriate for each case. The act will normally declare that the service must be provided, but the exact content and duration of the treatment will be decided during the procedure itself by professionals acting "on the ground." Medical professionals are thus given important leeway—

a logical step, since one cannot foresee the issues that may arise in the course of medical treatment.

At this point, it might be useful to distinguish two different relationships: the *basic* relationship linking the patient to the public entity in charge of medical services, and the *direct* relationship linking the patient to his doctor or surgeon. Administrative acts will often be issued under the framework of the basic relationship, but not under the direct one. Crucial decisions concerning his treatment will normally be made informally in the context of the direct relationship.

One might well wonder whether medical decisions can also qualify as administrative acts. From a legal or administrative perspective, these decisions are far from being irrelevant: The doctor belongs to a public organization which is ultimately responsible for his actions. Strictly speaking, however, medical decisions are not administrative acts: The doctor cannot adopt *legal* decisions on behalf of the public organization, even though his medical decisions can be *legally* attributed to it. In addition, the strict legal regime to which administrative acts are subject is inadequate for medical decisions. Medical procedures would be seriously hindered if the strict conditions required to revise administrative acts were applied to them.

IV
PROFESSIONAL CONDITIONS REQUIRED FOR THE SERVICE PROVIDER: STEERING ADMINISTRATIVE ACTIVITY THROUGH PROFESSIONAL TRAINING

ADMINISTRATIVE law is concerned with administrative activity, that is, with activity carried out by a public administration. Modern administrative law relies heavily on the idea that public officers act on behalf of the public organization that they belong to. Actions *actually* performed by public officers are, for all purposes, *legally* attributed to the organization. Consequently, administrative law tends to focus on the *office* rather than on the *office-holder*. Little attention is normally paid to the individuals that actually carry out administrative actions.

The personal qualities of the individual are of the utmost importance, however, when dealing with the provision of personal services, particularly medical services. Indeed, there are few administrative sectors where the individual occupies such a prominent position. This consideration calls for a thorough regulation of the personal and professional requirements for medical professionals within a public organization. But it also calls for regulation of the doctor-patient relationship.

Regulating such a personal and private relationship is not an easy task. The law-maker must not forget that the doctor-patient relationship is ultimately based on trust and that the success of the procedure partially depends on that. Trustworthiness, however, cannot be imposed by law;[14] there remains a need to adopt measures such as the recognition of the right to choose—and change—one's doctor.

---

14. SIMONS 529-30, *supra* note 11.

Both rights can be exercised without having to justify one's decision: There is no need to prove that a doctor has been negligent, or has otherwise breached his duties, in order to request the services of a different one. The ability to fire your doctor is only an example, but it proves to what extent the personal qualities of the officeholder matter in this field.

Needless to say, these considerations do not compromise the organic relationship between the professional and the public organization to which he belongs, and to which all his actions are ultimately attributed. This implies that medical decisions taken within a public organization are a genuine form of administrative activity. Yet, unlike other forms of administrative activity, medical decisions are difficult to guide and control. This is due to the central position occupied by the doctor or practitioner within the medical administrative procedure.[15] There are three reasons why the relationship is pivotal and difficult to regulate. First, medical services can only be provided by qualified professionals whose technical knowledge places them in a prominent position. Second, as mentioned above, the provision of medical services cannot be subject to rigid and predetermined procedures, giving medical professionals a certain leeway. Third, doctors and practitioners do not only conduct the medical procedure itself: They may also prescribe medicines or orthopedic devices, thus extending their influence and authority to other professionals such as pharmacists and orthopedists.

For all these reasons, it is difficult to subject the provision of medical services to strict control. The law can only set general guidelines and fix the organizational and administrative procedure framework under which the service will be provided. In the end, the most effective means for controlling performance is professional training.[16]

---

15. See DAGMAR FELIX, *Verwaltungsrechtliche Instrumente des Sozialstaates*, DEUTSCHES VERWALTUNGSBLATT 1073 (2004).

16. RAINER WAHL, *Die Aufgabenabhängigkeit von Verwaltung und Verwaltungsrecht*, in REFORM DES ALLGEMEINEN VERWALTUNGSRECHTS. GRUNDFRAGEN, SCHRIFTEN ZUR REFORM DES VERWALTUNGSRECHTS 207 (Hoffmann-Riem et al, eds., 1993). *For further discussion of*

This explains the regulatory emphasis on continual professional training.[17]

social assistance, see Krause, _Empfiehlt es sich, soziale Pflege und Betreuungsverhältnisse gesetzlich zu regeln?_, in Verhandlungen des zweiundfünfzigsten deutschen Juristentages 103 (1978).

17. See articles 34 to 39 of Law 16/2003, for Spanish legislation on the National Health System.

V

THE PATIENT'S RIGHT TO CHOOSE A DOCTOR

THE patient's right to choose a doctor favors a relationship of trust. This leads to a greater faith in the procedure and, in theory, to a successful provision of the service.[18] In addition, it satisfies the right of the patient to shape the service offered by influencing and participating in the procedure.[19]

This right introduces an element of market competition within those systems that link a doctor's compensation to the number of patients treated. This competitive element may provoke an improvement in the service provided, making it more attractive to a greater number of patients. However, competition has its own risks: Popularity may be based not on the quality of the service but rather on a greater disposition to give in to unreasonable demands, which can lead to greater expenditures. To avoid this outcome one must devise mechanisms of control that avoid unnecessary expenses.[20]

The right to choose cannot be absolute. It usually depends on factors such as the resources available or the number of inhabitants within the relevant area.[21] Since the right is not absolute, health authorities are only obliged to offer *sufficiently varied options* and to *inform* the citizen of those options before the fact.

---

18. ANDREAS WAHL, KOOPERATIONSSTRUKTUREN IM VERTRAGSARZTRECHT 82. (2001).

19. WAHL 83, *supra* note 18.

20. German law controls expenses through a system based on average statistical data. *See* SIMONS 560, *supra* note 11.

21. *See* article 10.13 and articles 14 and 15 of Law 14/1986, on Health Care.

VI
THE RIGHT TO INFORMATION

THE right to information enhances patient participation in medical procedures, and makes it possible for patients to exercise their right to consent. The patient's consent must be sought after providing him with "adequate information."[22] As far as its *content* is concerned, adequate information means all available information regarding relevant medical treatments, including "the aim and nature of the treatment, it risks and its consequences."[23] Relevant consequences include risks specific to the patient, general risks, and contraindications.

As far as *form* is concerned, the relevant information can be provided orally, but it must be included in the medical record of the patient. Additionally, it must be offered in a comprehensive and adequate manner according to the needs of the patient, to enable him to give informed consent.[24] "Medical silence" is thus banished from medical procedures.[25]

Information rights play a double role. They favor the sound administration of health care, by which the patient can participate in his own treatment, conduct useful conversations with his doctor(s), manifest his preferences, and exercise his right to consent with sufficient knowledge. In addition, they may be relevant in determining whether and to what extent a doctor is liable, should an action in tort be brought against him.

---

22. Article 2.2 of Law 41/2002, on patient status.

23. Article 4.1 of Law 41/2002, on patient status.

24. Articles 2, 4 and 10 of Law 41/2002, on patient status.

25. WAHL 122, *supra* note 18.

VII
THE PRINCIPLE OF CONSENT TO HEALTH CARE

THE provision of medical services can certainly be considered a "collaborative" or "cooperative" procedure,[26] for a certain degree of interaction between patient and doctor is always necessary. Furthermore, a patient's right to self-determination would be infringed if he or she were to be excluded from the most important decisions concerning treatment. This would violate the fundamental rights to human dignity,[27] to personal development,[28] and to physical and moral integrity.[29]

These considerations call for the recognition of the right to "informed consent."[30] This right is recognized by Spanish legislation and in the legislation of other countries as well. Medical actions must have the patient's informed consent, that is, the express, voluntary and conscious agreement of the patient, who must be in full control of his faculties and duly informed of every possible risk.[31] As a general rule, patient consent can be given orally, though in exceptional cases a written form is required. In any case, it is always revocable.[32]

This right ensures patients an active role in medical procedures. They are not simply "objects."[33] This defines their *status activus*

---

26. *See generally* SIMONS, *supra* note 11.

27. Article 10.1 of the Spanish Constitution.

28. Article 10.1 of the Spanish Constitution.

29. Article 15 of the Spanish Constitution.

30. WAHL 82, *supra* note 18.

31. *See* Articles 2, 3 of Law 41/2002, on patient status.

32. Articles 8.2, 8.5 of law 41/2002, on patient status.

33. This idea seems to flow from the notion of "human dignity." *See* Matthias Herdegen, in KOMMENTAR ZUM GRUNDGESETZ, Article 1, MN 33 (2005); HANS J. WOLFF & OTTO BACHOF, VERWALTUNGSRECHT I 216 (9th ed., 1974); IGNACIO GUTIÉRREZ GUTIÉRREZ, DIGNIDAD DE LA PERSONA Y DERECHOS FUNDAMENTALES (2005).

processualis in the provision of service procedure. However, the right of consent does not entitle the patient to shape the medical procedure according to his own whim. It does not entitle him to demand a specific treatment, but only to reject the treatment proposed. In other words, it only guarantees that the doctor will not impose a treatment on the patient *against* his will. As a result, a mutual agreement between the doctor and the patient during the process itself will determine a specific treatment.[34] The doctor's therapeutic freedom and the patient's self-determination must run up against each other.[35]

Only in exceptional cases can a doctor go forward with indispensable treatment or surgery without the consent of the patient:[36] for instance, where there exists a serious risk to public health.

---

34. SIMONS 541, *supra* note 11.

35. WAHL 82-84, *supra* note 18.

36. Articles 2.4, 9.2 of Law 41/2002.

VIII

ADMINISTRATIVE PROCEDURE FORMULAS
FOR CONFLICT RESOLUTION

LEGISLATION governing the administrative procedure for the provision of medical services must take into account the possibility of conflicts arising during the procedure; flexible solutions must be offered so that medical procedures are not constantly disrupted.

We have earlier referred to the right to choose or change one's doctor. This right represents a flexible instrument for the resolution of conflicts. If the patient is unable to reach an agreement concerning his treatment, or if he is dissatisfied for any other reason with the service offered, it is always possible to put an end to the problem by simply changing doctors.

In this sense, the right to choose your doctor can be considered a *general* formula for the resolution of conflicts. More *detailed* formulas can be articulated, as in the case of voluntary or mandatory discharge from a hospital.[37] Mandatory discharge is subject to strict administrative procedure requirements, such as an interview with the person concerned (hearing). Within this "cooperative procedure," this is one of the few instances where the exercise of power by the public administration is evident: the differences between the "decision-making procedure" and the "provision of services procedure" are blurred when this measure is taken.

---

37. Article 21 of Law 41/2002.

IX

COOPERATIVE OBLIGATIONS OF THE PATIENT

UNTIL now, we have spoken of the patient's right to participate in the development of his or her medical procedure and to contribute to the determination of its content, through the right to choose and the right of informed consent. These rights must be satisfied by the public organization, which must therefore comply with many specific administrative obligations. The patient, however, is also subject to some obligations.

A general duty of cooperation is imposed upon the patient. Despite the fact that the specific performance of this duty is not possible, its importance should not be underestimated: it has an indirect coercive effect,[38] insofar as the patient who breaks it risks losing other social benefits. It is therefore in the patient's advantage to cooperate. For example, Spanish law offers support for temporarily incapacitated patients, but this support can be suspended if the beneficiary refuses or abandons treatment without justifiable cause, or if he or she fails to turn up for examinations ordered by the doctor in charge.[39]

---

38. SIMONS 551-52, *supra* note 11.

39. Article 102 of the 1974 Social Security General Law. This article is still in force by virtue of the derogatory provisions laid down in the Royal Legislative Decree 1/1994.

X
CONCLUSION

THIS essay has taken two different approaches. First, it has shown that there are no theoretical reasons why the provision of services by the state should be excluded from the concept of "administrative procedure," and that the provision of services by the state poses the same regulatory problems as the adoption of formalized decisions. Second, it has shown that our health system regulation can be explained using the concept of "administrative procedure," and that it can provide useful material for the reconceptualization of provision of services.

The concept of "administrative procedure" must be broadened, because administrative activity cannot be reduced to *formalized decision-making*. The activity carried out by what we have termed "the provider administration" can also be explained and regulated under the concept of "administrative procedure."

CHAPTER VII

US RULEMAKING

Peter L. Strauss*

* Betts Professor of Law, Columbia University, USA.

INDEX

PART I

RULEMAKING, like adjudication, embraces a broad range of possibilities. Rulemaking ranges from the setting of rates for public utilities, to the creation of binding norms to govern private conduct, to the publication of non-binding statements of policy or guidelines to shape understanding and compliance efforts. The APA's definition of "rule" includes the product of each of these activities. Its articulation in 5 U.S.C. §§552-553 of rulemaking procedure – identified by one leading American scholar as "one of the great inventions of modern government"[1] – reflects this diversity by providing three different models of rulemaking procedure: a publication model, a notice and comment model, and a formal hearing model. Unless military or foreign affairs functions are involved, or a matter relating to the government's proprietary functions,[2] one or another of these models applies to all rulemaking that is permitted adversely to affect private interests.

1. THE APA MODELS

A. NOTICE AND COMMENT RULEMAKING

Again it seems useful to start with the central model, which in the case of rulemaking is that of notice and comment (or, as it is often called, "informal") rulemaking. This is the procedure to which Americans generally refer when they speak of rulemaking, and it is

---

1. [Ed.: The author refers to K.C. Davis].

2. The exemption of proprietary functions from rulemaking procedures has been sharply criticized insofar as it bears on matters having an impact on persons outside government – as rules governing "public property, loans, grants, benefits or contracts," 5 U.S.C. §553(a)(2), easily may. Most if not all agencies have responded to these criticisms by providing by regulation that APA rulemaking procedures are to be followed in these cases, despite the formal statutory exception. Where such regulations exist, they may be judicially enforced; that is, if an agency that has such a regulation in place adopts a rule to govern public property, loans, grants, benefits or contracts without following the APA procedures, that rule will be denied legal effect by a reviewing court on the authority of that rule, regardless of the APA exemption.

established by 5 U.S.C. §553. It is the minimum procedure statutorily required for adoption of a rule in the strong sense – that is, for adoption of a rule which if valid will have the force and effect of a statute. Such rules, often described as "substantive" or "legislative" rules, are the bulk of the provisions published in the Code of Federal Regulations. References to a "regulation" in the following pages are references to this kind of rule, that if valid has statutory force and effect on all actors in the legal system – courts as well as agencies and private actors. Like a statute, a regulation's terms may be varied only by the procedures used to create it. The Supreme Court has indicated, with increasing intensity,[3] that Congress must have delegated explicit statutory authority to an agency for it to adopt regulations; however, the delegation itself may be in rather general terms.[4]

Of the APA's procedures, notice and comment rulemaking procedures are those that have been the most strikingly affected by changes since their initial adoption. From passage of the Freedom of Information Act (FOIA), to judicial interpretations significantly departing from original expectations, to the presidential and legislative initiatives requiring the pre-announcement of agendas, and a variety of impact analyses, these initially simple procedures have become considerably more complex.[5] It may nonetheless be sensible to begin, at least briefly, with a description of the initial statutory formulation, on the basis of which one can understand both the continuities and the substantial changes in contemporary rulemaking practice.

Section 553's notice and comment rulemaking procedures begin with the publication of notice of a proposal for rulemaking in the Federal Register, the federal government's daily official gazette.[6] Of

---

3. Chrysler Corp. v. Brown, 441 U.S. 281 (1979).

4. National Petroleum Refiners Assn. v. Federal Trade Comm., 482 F.2d 672 (D.C. Cir.1973), cert. denied 415 U.S. 951 (1974).

5. Extended discussions of these changes appear in P. Strauss, From *Expertise to Politics: The Transformation of American Rulemaking*, 31 Wake Forest L. Rev. 745 (1996); P. Strauss, *Changing Times: The APA at 50*, 63 U. Chi. L. Rev.1389 (1996).

6. Readily searched electronically, and with increasingly useful links, the Federal Register may be found at http://www.access.gpo.gov/su_docs/aces/aces140.html.

course, this publication is likely to occur at a very late stage in the bureaucratic development of the proposal within the agency itself. Under the changes already described it will have been preceded by a brief notice of intended activity in the semi-annual Unified Agenda of Federal Regulations.[7] The section 553 notice begins a period generally 30 to 60 days in length, during which any interested person may submit written comments – "data, views or arguments" – to the responsible agency for its consideration. The agency may provide more elaborate opportunities for public participation if it chooses – for example, oral hearings (generally of a legislative rather than judicial character), opportunities for responsive comment, or a second round of notice. The agency's obligation, "after consideration of the relevant matter presented," is then to publish "a concise general statement of basis and purpose" with any regulation it may decide to adopt.[8] Section 553 provides that, absent special justification, a regulation may not take effect for 30 days. Agencies must use the same procedures if they wish to rescind or amend a regulation.

Overall, the striking characteristic of the section 553 procedure is its informality. What must be contained in the notice is loosely defined; in addition to legal authority and procedural details such as the deadline for filing comments, the notice need only specify "*either* the terms *or* substance of the proposed rule *or* a description of the subjects and issues involved."[9] The notice itself need not appear until late in the rule's development. If public participation is limited to a single round of comment to be filed by a date common to all participants, commenters of necessity will be able only to put forward direct views, not responses or challenges to the data, views or arguments of others who may join in the proceedings. The defined record, initial decision, and bureaucratic separation of staff from decisionmakers that charac-

---

7. Id.

8. 5 U.S.C. §553(c).

9. 5 U.S.C. §553(b) (emphasis added). Note that this language does not require even that the text of the proposed rule, or data the agency believes it has to support its proposed action, be revealed.

terize formal adjudication are completely absent. Finally, the agency's obligation to explain its ultimate conclusions is stated far more permissively than for the case of adjudication. Only a "concise general" statement of basis and purpose is required, and most speakers of English would understand, as was the initial practice, that such a statement could be summary.

B. PUBLICATION RULEMAKING

When an agency or one of its operating divisions adopts "interpretative rules, general statements of policy, or rules of agency organization, procedure, or practice,"[10] section 553 notice and comment procedures need not be followed as a general matter; such procedures might, however, be called for by an agency's governing law. These and similar instruments, such as staff manuals, may be thought of as statements that announce an agency's positions or procedures on matters within its competence but that, unlike regulations, do not have a statute's legal effect. Since the Freedom of Information Act amendments of 1966, section 552(a) (2) of the Act has provided that "[a] final order, opinion, statement of policy, interpretation, or staff manual or instruction that affects a member of the public may be relied on, used, or cited as precedent by an agency against a party other than an agency only if" it has been appropriately published.[11] Thus, the effect they have could better be analogized to that of judicial precedent. Hierarchically inferior agency staff can be expected to regard them as governing law. Yet the agency itself can change its "publication rules"

---

10. 5 U.S.C. §553(b)(A).

11. Section 552(a)(1) contains a similar formula for matters, including "statements of general policy or interpretations of general applicability formulated and adopted by the agency," that are published in the Federal Register. The author's views on the proper place of publication rules in the rulemaking spectrum are set out at P. Strauss, *The Rulemaking Continuum*, 41 Duke L. J. 1463 (1992) and P. Strauss, *Publication Rules in the Rulemaking Spectrum: Assuring Proper Respect for an Essential Element*, 53 Admin. L. Rev. 803 (2001).

as informally as it `makes them.[12] For the agency itself and for any court reviewing agency action, the underlying statute and regulations remain the source of any legal obligation. For a hierarchically superior body like a reviewing court, the agency's views, if well-informed, will be regarded only as constructions entitled to persuasive weight in reaching a conclusion on the legal question involved.[13] From this perspective, the agency's adoption of a publication rule may well have an impact on the positions the agency itself will be able to take, and the burden of explanation it will face should it attempt to vary its view;[14] but for the outside world, the validity of a publication rule does not establish it as the source of fresh legal obligation.

Interpretive rules and other like formulations generally address matters of technical detail one would not expect to warrant the attention of the agency's leadership. They comprise a volume of text and regulatory activity enormously greater than the body of legislative rules. Examples include the Internal Revenue Service's opinions about the meaning of the tax laws, the Nuclear Regulatory Commission's "regulatory standards" informing applicants for nuclear power plant licenses how they may be able to satisfy Commission staff that they have met the technical specifications for licensing, and the Department of the Interior's staff manuals on procedures to be followed in carrying out its various regulatory responsibilities. As the characterization of these documents may suggest, they are frequently the product of responsible staff offices, rather than the agency's political

---

12. United States v. Mead Corp., 533 U.S. 218 (2001).

13. Id.; Pacific Gas & Electric Co. v. Federal Power Comm., 506 F.2d 33 (D.C. Cir. 1974); Skidmore v. Swift & Co., 323 U.S. 134 (1944).

14. For an example of a court unselfconsciously treating a publication rule as binding upon the government, see Anastasoff v. United States, 235 F.3d 1054 (8th Cir. 2000). Facing a conflict in holding between two circuits on an issue of tax law, the government had published "a document styled Action on Decision" announcing its acquiescence in the taxpayer-favoring outcome. This publication rule led an en banc panel of the Eighth Circuit to vacate the government-favoring outcome one of its panels had reached as moot, see p. n. above – an outcome defensible only on the understanding that the government had in some respect bound itself by issuing the document.

leadership – which is, it is believed, the only agency authority properly authorized to adopt regulations. With the emergence of the Internet, too, they are becoming considerably more accessible; 1996 amendments to FOIA, known as the Electronic Freedom of Information Act, require each agency to maintain an electronic reading room. These sites are considerably more accessible than were the physical reading rooms where the indexing and availability required by section 552 were previously effected. As a result, what had been a somewhat obscure and specialized collection of agency documents is now broadly available, and available in readily searched format.[15]

Although lacking the statutory force of regulations, these opinions may carry great weight in the practical world. They shape behavior that never reaches the courts, and may influence decisionmakers with formal responsibility for decision (such as the courts) with the persuasiveness of their origin in an expert and responsible agency. Agencies issue these interpretations and opinions precisely to shape external behavior, reducing to that extent the need for regulatory enforcement. For this reason, consultative procedures are strongly recommended, often followed, and sometimes statutorily required. As notice and comment rulemaking has become more complex, the suspicion has grown that agencies have been tempted to use publication rulemaking as a substitute, and the courts of appeal have been persuaded with some frequency to require the use of section 553 procedures. This question is taken up below. For a proper publication rule, however, all that the APA requires in order to permit the agency to rely on it in its own proceedings against the interest of private parties, and to entitle it to some deference on judicial review, is that the agency's position must be published – a step one would imagine the agency taking to assure visibility in any event, if it wished its position to have influence.

---

15. See, for example, the E-FOIA "reading room" at the National Highway Transportation and Safety Administration, http://www.nhtsa.dot.gov/nhtsa/whatsup/foia/index.html, or the opinions of its General Counsel interpreting its regulations, http://www.nhtsa.dot.gov/cars/rules/interps/.

In addition to publishing its interpretations and policies, each agency must afford "an interested person the right to petition for the issuance, amendment, or repeal of a rule,"[16] including in this instance interpretive rules and the like.

c. FORMAL RULEMAKING

Individual statutes occasionally require rules "to be made on the record after opportunity for an agency hearing."[17] When this is the case, the comment stage and "concise general statement of ... basis and purpose" of informal rulemaking are replaced by a hearing comparable to that provided for initial licensing. On-the-record constraints are applicable, with relatively elaborate provision for "party"[18] participation in evidentiary matters and argumentation. The agency's conclusions must be fully and responsively explained. As in initial licensing, however, neither oral process nor the observance of separation of functions within the agency decisional structure is as rigorously insisted upon as would be the case in ordinary on-the-record adjudication. Like initial licensing – a form of adjudication – formal rulemaking can often be seen to have a mixed character – highly individualist from one perspective (thus, strong procedural and participatory claims), yet polycentric and non-adversary from another. The two procedural sets are essentially identical.

Proceedings to fix permitted rates for a public utility or common carrier are by far the commonest setting for formal rulemaking. For the utility or carrier facing the possibility of being denied a reasonable

_____

16. 5 U.S.C. §553(e).

17. 5 U.S.C. §553(c).

18. The ideas of rulemaking (a procedure for the formulation of general norms) and "parties" are not easily reconciled. As a general matter any person who wishes to is permitted to participate in any rulemaking. At least some formal rulemakings, however – those setting rates for public utilities, for example – require the participation of particular entities, as well as permitting the participation of all.

return on its investment, the claim to formal hearing has a constitutional dimension.[19] Formal rulemaking proceedings are, however, notoriously inconvenient and difficult to manage, given the frequent diffuseness of the issues presented and the large number of parties that may wish to participate.[20] Consequently, courts are reluctant to find that statutes require rules to be formally made. In sharp distinction from their approach to statutory provisions for *adjudicatory* hearings, the courts virtually require a formula including the words "on the record" to appear before they will conclude that the informal rulemaking procedures of section 553 will not suffice.[21]

2. THE TRANSFORMATION OF RULEMAKING

Against the spare provisions of the Administrative Procedure Act, consider both the tremendous importance of rulemaking as an activity in contemporary regulation, and the rich internal – one might even say political – life of government in reaching decisions of magnitude. Since the explosion of environmental, health and safety regulation in the late '60s and early '70s, rulemaking has become the pre-eminent administrative activity in the United States. Which risks among the many possible to address shall be controlled, and how should they be chosen? To what extent, and by what regulatory means? Under what hypotheses about such sensitive issues as, what is the assumed discount rate for calculating the present value of future costs and benefits, or what value should be assigned to human life, or the preservation of wilderness? Consider the issues posed in three prominent rulemakings from among the many: (1) whether and how OSHA will decide that

---

19. ICC v. Louisville & Nashville R. Co., 227 U.S. 88 (1913).

20. R. Hamilton, *Procedures for the Adoption of Rules of General Applicability: The Need for Procedural Innovation in Administrative Rulemaking*, 60 Calif. L. Rev. 1276 (1972).

21. United States v. Florida East Coast Railway Co., 410 U.S. 224 (1973).

the handling of benzene (only one of the many chemicals the petro-chemical industry produces and uses that might have implications for the health of workers and the public generally) will be subject to special precautions (and which precautions, how uniformly applied across the variety of contexts in which it is used); (2) what controls coal-fired electric power plants must employ to prevent emission of soot, heat, or chemicals possibly harmful to the environment; (3) what technology fish processors shall use to avoid the threat of botulism poisoning from imperfectly smoked fish. Each of these decisions raises highly complex questions of risk, physical science, technology, human health, economics, and political will. These questions will engage whoever has the responsibility and opportunity to participate in their resolution and their resolution will affect a wide range of interests in the community. Both the benefits and the costs of particular regulations requiring complex interventions to control the effects of major industrial processes may be estimated in the hundreds of millions of dollars.

Issues like these challenge both any idea that rulemaking can be *simply* a technocratic exercise best protected from the world of politics and left to experts, and its opposite – that these are matters best resolved *strictly* in the world of politics. Constructing a workable middle ground has been complicated by the efforts of stakeholders to secure procedural advantage. The importance of the issues being resolved put enormous pressure on a procedure whose public aspects, slight to begin with, occur so late in policy development; stakeholders inevitably have sought earlier and more influential roles than the public procedure suggests. In view of the high stakes for the community as a whole, one can also understand a certain insistence on regularity and visibility, particularly when rulemaking comes before the courts for their necessarily retrospective review. While not repudiating his distinction between rulemaking and adjudication, the courts have become increasingly aware of the imperfections in the analogy first drawn by Justice Holmes in *Bi-Metallic Investment Co.* between rulemaking and legislative action, and this has led to much more intense judicial supervision of the validity of regulations than of statutes.

Recall Holmes' statement in *Bi-Metallic* that the procedural claims of citizens in respect of legislation are strictly political ones – "their rights are protected in the only way that they can be in a complex society, by their power, immediate or remote, over those who make the rule." This position, joined with the judiciary's profound unwillingness to examine the factual justification for regulatory statutes following the "substantive due process" crisis of the 1930s, produced extremely permissive standards of judicial review of rulemaking. When agency rules were challenged on judicial review – and it did not become clear until 1969 that such challenges could often be made in advance of government-initiated enforcement proceedings[22] – judges presumed their validity just as they would presume the validity of a statute. A challenger would be required to show (on the basis of a record freshly made in court) that the agency's judgment had been arbitrary and capricious in the strongest sense, that no facts could be adduced to support the rule it had adopted.[23] Yet an agency is not an elective body. The ties between federal administrative agencies and the electorate are limited to the periodic election of the American President (a connection that at times has seemed so frail as to escape even the description "remote") and to the possibilities inherent in legislative revision and oversight of agency authority. What, then, was the warrant for according such respect to the products of agency rulemaking, which could "affect the person or property of individuals, sometimes to the point of ruin"?[24]

Presenting a coherent picture of the rulemaking processes resulting from repeated encounters with these difficulties is challenging for a variety of reasons. One's tendency is to see the picture that has emerged from the large-consequence rulemakings just evoked, but relatively few rulemakings in any given year – a few dozen, perhaps – have this dimension. Second, for these high-consequence regulations

---

22. Abbott Laboratories v. Gardner, 387 U.S. 136 (1967).

23. Pacific States Box & Basket Co. v. White, 296 U.S. 176 (1935).

24. Bi-Metallic Investment Co.

(and to a lesser extent for simpler rulemakings) the situation is complicated by the adoption of a hodgepodge of statutes and executive orders imposing various analytic requirements, and the absence to date of any rationalizing effort. Third, among the most prominent high-consequence rulemaking agencies, several (notably, the EPA and OSHA) act under procedural statutes unique to them. Finally, much of the development has its roots in agency anticipation of the demands of judicial review, a subject whose discussion now would be premature. What may be helpful is to present a brief summary, focused just on notice-and-comment rulemaking, and then spend a few pages indicating how various elements of this snapshot developed.

In practical terms today, rulemaking begins as a public procedure with the submission of a proposed element of the semi-annual Unified Agenda of Federal Regulations and its incorporation under OIRA (White House) oversight. There has for a while been talk about creating an even earlier stage for public involvement, the stage at which an agency appraises the various risks that might warrant regulation to choose from among them its best particular targets for possible action. Some agencies – EPA, for example[25] – devote considerable energies to risk appraisal; and for others – OSHA, for example – separate specialized institutions have been created to assist in this work.[26] But no general public process for risk evaluation has yet emerged.

The Unified Agenda description as published includes not only a brief description of the project being undertaken, but also contact information within the agency for members of the public who might wish to become involved. Use of the Internet will increasingly permit citizens to register their interest in matters appearing in the Unified Agenda, for subsequent notifications and other uses. In developing its

---

25. See http://www.epa.gov/ncea/.

26. The National Institute for Occupational Safety and Health is a constituent element of the Center for Disease Control, a distinctly apolitical part of the Department of Health and Human Services, *see* http://www.cdc.gov/niosh/homepage.html, that is made statutorily responsible for advising OSHA – a part of the Department of Labor – on the workplace risks most deserving its attention.

concrete proposal, the agency may invoke the Negotiated Rulemaking Act, discussed below, or simply proceed to do so bureaucratically. Before publishing its proposal, the agency will have drafted any necessary impact analyses under governing statutes (such as the National Environmental Policy Act or the Regulatory Flexibility Act) or presidential executive orders. In the process, it will have amassed a fair amount of data *and* developed both the text of a specific proposal and a somewhat detailed explanation of its (provisional) thinking. For important rulemakings, today, the section 553 notice of proposed rulemaking must contain or make available all this matter: text, explanation, and supporting data. All these, increasingly, are made available – highlighted – on agency web-sites. The opportunity to comment occurs as before, but now with targets both more precise and more extensive. Detailed technical submissions of competing data are not unusual and for rulemakings of wide import media campaigns may produce a flood of comments – hundreds of thousands in a few cases. Increasingly, commenting can occur on the Internet and, with the development of the Internet, increasingly comments are readily available to public view. With the comments in hand, the agency may then be required to develop a *final* impact analysis – which implies discussions within government that interested private parties may anticipate and try to influence. With these processes continuing, comments available for analysis, and rulemaking in any event not a formalistic procedure, participants may seek an opportunity to file responsive comments. If the agency decides after considering the comments to follow a course that could not readily have been predicted from its initial proposal, it is obliged to publish a new notice of proposed rulemaking and repeat this process. If it is going forward with its proposal or making only predictable changes, it will feel obliged to explain its action rather fully, showing its resolution of any issues that comments put significantly in issue. For a major regulation, the statement of basis and purpose will run to dozens and perhaps hundreds of pages in the Federal Register.

It should be evident that this is a transformed procedure, perhaps the most striking development in American administrative law over the past several decades. The transformation occurred without amendment to section 553, which still refers to notice of "*either* the terms *or* substance of the proposed rule *or* a description of the subjects and issues involved,"[27] and to a "concise general statement of basis and purpose." As we will see, it also occurred in the face of the Supreme Court's ostensible and strident insistence that courts not improvise on the APA's provisions, "a formula on which opposing social and political forces have come to rest."[28] The paragraphs following seek to explain that development, albeit under the important handicap that we have not yet encountered extended treatment of the subject of judicial review.[29] The focus here will be at the agency level.

A. BUREAUCRATIC STRUCTURES OF RULEMAKING, THE RULEMAKING "RECORD," AND RULEMAKING DECISION

Significant elements of the changes emerged from the courts' efforts to understand what could be described as the "record" of a rulemaking, against which they could assess its validity on review. If they could not simply presume that the agency knew some state of facts that would support its conclusions, what facts could they conclude that the agency did know, and how should they understand the resolution of any disputes about them? Rulemaking is characterized by institutional processes for consideration and decision of controversial matters. What can be a considerable range of offices staffed with different specialists identify, sharpen, and then propose resolutions for those aspects of the problem that are brought to their attention. They may possess knowledge about these aspects from a wide range of

---

27. 5 U.S.C. §553(b) (emphasis added). Note that this language does not require even that the text of the proposed rule, or data the agency believes it has to support its proposed action, be revealed.

28. Vermont Yankee Nuclear Power Corp. v. National Resources Defense Council, Inc. 435 U.S. 519, 523 (1978), quoting Wong Yang Sung v. McGrath, 339 U.S. 33, 40 (1950).

29. See, in this respect, Chapter VIII, especially VIII (D)(2).

sources and experience, that they don't feel called upon (and perhaps would be unable) to restate every time a question within their expertise arises. Issues surviving this process are negotiated in a politically complex institutional structure. These institutional processes complicate the process of defining a "record" of decision, if they do not deny the possibility altogether.

Such an institutional process has very different presuppositions about appropriate decisionmaking than adjudication. In adjudication, one imagines that the whole issue is placed at a certain time before a discrete individual (or a handful of individuals) valued for judgment, and whose function in relation to the collection of information is relatively passive. She considers identifiable matters, argument and data, in relationship to a unique and defined body of data more-or-less formally placed before her and reaches her individual decision. Although difficulties can be introduced when the adjudicator takes judicial notice of some matter the parties have not placed before her, that practice is constrained. On the whole, everyone knows (without having to rely on the judge to state) what is the basis on which a decision is taken and may be defended. Additionally, the decider is committedly neutral. She will not talk to any contender outside the presence of the others or participate in the rough-and-tumble of political discourse.

The characteristic rulemaking decision, like that of most organizations other than courts when faced with important problems, is institutional. That is, the taking of decisions is not focused on a particular judge-like individual or group of individuals, but occurs within and across the ordinary operating staff of the agency. Responsibilities may be divided within the agency in accordance with interest or expertise in particular aspects of a given problem, perhaps under the supervision of an ad hoc working group. Piecemeal decisions are taken, over time, across the desks of numerous members of agency staff. As they gradually accumulate, only what remains controversial rises through the agency hierarchy. The data that produced resolution of a given aspect may be entirely within the knowledge of a particular employee – her "expertise" – and does not travel with that resolution to later stages. Similarly, controversy may be eliminated or shaped by informal conversations among agency staff whose ordinary roles bear on the particular controversy (but who have no responsibility for the rule as a whole); once those conversations have occurred, traces of the controversy or the basis for its resolution may disappear. The resolution becomes part of what the agency "knows." Even when controversy rises to the level of the agency heads, they may suggest new inquiries or additional approaches that they hope will permit staff to resolve the matter, rather than decide it themselves. That approach often succeeds.

The rulemaking process as a whole also lacks the characteristic isolation adjudication traditionally enjoys from other aspects of an agency's work. Those working on the regulation continue their work on other aspects of the agency's business. They are encouraged to bring to bear whatever they learn, may and do speak with whoever seems relevant to the matters before them, and feel no need either to inform other "parties" of these conversations or to permit their participation in them in any way.[30]

To speak of a "record" in this context, then, is highly artificial – at least, if we are imagining a collection of data all of which was exposed to the interested public for its response and challenge, placed before a single decisionmaker at a given point in time, and uniquely made the basis for her decision. There will have been no single decisionmaker. Much that has been relied upon will not have been collected, certainly will not have been presented to the individual or collegial body formally identified by statute as responsible for the adoption of a regulation. On the other hand, documents will have been submitted to the agency as comments on the rulemaking, and the APA requires that they be attended to. Major studies may have been commissioned, or

---

30. A full and still useful description of a characteristic rulemaking process, as seen from inside an important American administrative agency, appears in W. Pedersen, *Formal Records and Informal Rulemaking*, 85 Yale L. J. 38 (1975). While the rulemaking processes of the Environmental Protection Agency have since been changed by statute – in good part as a result of Pedersen's analysis – agencies continue to make rules today under the statutory procedures that governed the EPA when he wrote this.

other large bodies of data may exist, on which the agency or members of its staff have drawn for decision of one or another aspect of the proceeding. Memoranda will have been written within the agency as decision went forward, indicating resolutions reached, controversies remaining and, in a healthy bureaucracy, the contending positions on those controversies. Meetings may have occurred within the agency or with outsiders, private interests or other government officials, where views are expressed and data provided that could be, and sometimes are, recorded. All of these, if public, could be described as a "record," at least in the sense of their being a body of data bearing on the agency's rulemaking decision, against which its rationality and lawfulness could be tested.

B. THE UNCERTAINTIES OF "LEGISLATIVE" JUDGMENT AND DISPUTES ABOUT GENERAL FACT

In the context of economic regulation, the general propositions on which prescriptive rulemaking turns could be imagined generally to involve the same kinds of judgments about social condition as usually confront legislatures – normative questions about whether this or that behavior should be allowed, that generally do not turn on what might appear to be determinable propositions of fact about the physical world.[31] With the emergence of health, safety and environmental regulation as the dominant setting for rulemaking in the 1960s and 1970s, this changed. What the impact is on human health of prolonged exposure to background radiation of 3 Frem/day may be hard to establish experimentally, but it is nonetheless a question to which it seems there should be a correct and determinable answer, as a matter of fact – in the same way as we could hope to determine whether a traffic light facing Mr. Jones was red or green when he drove through the

_____

31. When economic rulemaking involves particular data, in rulemaking notably, the governing statutes require formal rulemaking.

intersection it controlled. If there are uncertainties, disagreements, or professional judgments about the matter, it would seem relevant to know about them, in the same way as we think we should be aware of differing accounts of the state of the traffic light at that moment. To purport to decide either question by political judgment – by vote – would be strongly objectionable.

At the same time, these are not the same kinds of factual questions. For the traffic light, using a neutral non-expert to make judgments after hearing the testimony of witnesses who can be closely questioned about their opportunities for observation, truthfulness, animus, etc., is a well-established modality. For the question of science fact, as we may call it, neutral non-experts are poor deciders and a viva voce process for acquiring "evidence" is at least inefficient. The scientific community uses ongoing processes of inquiry and criticism under norms of transparency; reaching consensus about remaining uncertainties, and clearly articulating the models or hypotheses being used, help to distinguish the known from the supposed. Both are fact-finding processes, as distinct from means of asserting political will. Yet in their details they are strikingly different fact-finding processes. The changing character of rulemaking brought this problem into strong relief.

c. The impact of open government legislation

Until the mid-1960s, participants in rulemaking lacked any procedural means for forcing the transparency of science fact-finding in rulemaking procedures. Persons outside the agency were essentially limited to what the agency chose to report in its statement of basis and purpose as the factual grounding for its decision. Internal documents, even factual studies, were not public documents, and courts did not require them to be revealed. Traditional rulemaking review, treating rules as deserving no more substantial inquiry into their factual basis than statutes, put few demands on the agency. It might have to supply the file of comments that it had received in the rulemaking; but generally it was free simply to show what it knew that could be regarded as supporting its conclusions. Inquiry into its actual decisionmaking process would not be undertaken.

The Freedom of Information Act,[32] first adopted in 1967 and vastly strengthened in 1974, brought much of the internal documentation of agency rulemaking, and some of its decisionmaking, into public view. While neither intended as a record-enhancing statute[33] nor addressed to the new characteristics of rulemaking facts when it was adopted, FOIA nonetheless dramatically altered rulemaking. It permitted any participant to request "all documents the agency regards as bearing upon its proposed rulemaking in ...," and this request was sufficiently definite to have to be honored. Filing such a request quickly became a mandatory element of competent professional practice. Not all parts of all documents had to be revealed; in particular, predecisional advice given by agency staff to their superiors could usually be withheld as privileged. Yet even for these documents, only advice could be withheld. Factual assertions – data and technical analysis – are not privileged, and the agency's obligation under the FOIA is to edit privileged material out of a document and honor the remainder of the request. Thus agencies could be forced to reveal their factual basis for action. Often enough they would provide the advice portion of memoranda as well, rather than go through the trouble of redaction. Anticipating the requests, they began to organize, and to make available at the outset of rulemakings, data that inevitably would have to be disclosed at some later stage.

The Government in the Sunshine Act,[34] adopted in 1976, made explicit the FOIA's latent judgment about openness in rulemaking. Under this statute, multi-member commissions are required to hold their meetings on advance notice, in public view.[35] The Act's limited

---

32. 5 U.S.C. §552.

33. The statute makes government records available on demand to "any person," and the courts from the outset resisted litigant efforts to tie FOIA requests to judicial review of agency action. National Labor Relations Board v. Sears, Roebuck & Co., 421 U.S. 132 (1975).

34. 5 U.S.C. §552(b).

35. In public view, but not with public participation. Like FOIA, the Sunshine Act's focus is on openness, not additional external controls or decision procedures.

exemptions, quite intentionally, do not permit an agency to close any part of a discussion of ordinary rulemaking. Unlike the FOIA, that is, the Sunshine Act recognizes no privilege whatsoever for predecisional consultations with staff about policymaking; only discussions about decision in on-the-record adjudication are protected in that way. To be sure, the Sunshine Act mechanism does not apply to agencies like the EPA or OSHA, that function with a single individual at their head; only the multi-member commissions are affected. Yet this can be seen as a technical judgment about the difficulty of constructing a "Sunshine" mechanism for a strictly hierarchical decision process lacking collegial elements, or as a result of the President's greater ability to protect agencies attached to the executive branch as distinct from the independent agencies. As a comment on rulemaking, its message is clear.

D. THE "PAPER HEARING"

Judicial interpretation responsive to these changes would draw agency rulemaking away from the simple legislative analogy. Three related elements of the APA's notice and comment rulemaking procedure permitted this: what constituted "notice"; what, an effective opportunity for "comment"; and what, an adequate "statement of basis and purpose," however "general" and "concise." The mood of the 1946 legislature enacting the provisions containing these words, no one could doubt, was highly permissive. Yet the widespread use and enormous impact of rulemaking resulting from environmental, health, and safety legislation was not foreseen at that time. When those developments occurred, these phrases were the obvious pressure points.

The last of them, the findings requirement, was the first to respond to the new circumstances. Faced with the first rules adopted to regulate automobile safety under the National Traffic and Motor Vehicle Safety Act – rules that would contribute tremendously to reshaping the American automobile market – the D.C. Circuit "cautioned" against an overly literal reading of the statutory terms "concise" and "general." These adjectives must be accommodated to the realities of judicial scrutiny. ... We do not expect the agency to discuss every item of fact or opinion included in the submissions made to it ... [but we do expect that the statement] will enable us to see what major issues of policy were ventilated by the informal proceedings and why the agency reacted to them as it did.[36]

What is the "record" in informal proceedings? : The attitude underlying this opinion, that judges were entitled to see and understand what had occurred at the agency level, received major impetus from a 1971 Supreme Court opinion that focused particular attention on the problem of the record in informal agency action. *Citizens to Preserve Overton Park, Inc. v. Volpe*[37] challenged the decision of the federal Secretary of Transportation to provide federal financing for a portion of highway that would inevitably interfere with an important urban park, despite recent federal legislation intended to protect park lands against such uses. In the APA's terms, the Secretary's decision would be characterized as informal adjudication, not rulemaking. Nonetheless, it shared the institutional characteristics of rulemaking. The decision had been reached through a coordinated, informal bureaucratic process, after a number of opportunities for public comment but without any procedure resembling a trial. The Secretary did not issue an opinion explaining his judgment at the time he granted permission to go forward with the project. He attempted to explain it only when review was sought by a group of citizens opposing the project.

The Supreme Court strongly endorsed review of that judgment, describing its appropriate elements in a manner to be examined later

---

36. Automotive Parts & Accessories v. Boyd, 407 F.2d 330, 338 (D.C. Cir. 1968). For trenchant critiques of the impact of this judicial attitude on the agency's performance two decades later, see J. MASHAW & D. HARFST, THE STRUGGLE FOR AUTO SAFETY (Harvard University Press1990); J. Mashaw & D. Harfst, *Regulation and Legal Culture: The Case of Motor Vehicle Safety*, 4 Yale J. Reg. 257 (1987).

37. 401 U.S. 402 (1971). This case is extensively discussed in P. Strauss, Revisiting Overton Park: Political and Judicial Controls Over Administrative Actions Affecting the Community, 39 U.C.L.A. L. Rev. 1251 (1992).

in this essay. It made two observations of particular moment to the present discussion. First, it said that judicial review, while "narrow" (to avoid the substitution of judicial for agency judgment) was to be "thorough," "probing," and "careful" in examining the Secretary's declared basis for his decision against the materials before him. Second, and relatedly, the Court indicated that this review was to occur on the basis of "the record" compiled in the agency in the course of the decisional process. Its call for "thorough," "probing" and "careful" review only reinforced the attitudes already emerging in cases like the D.C. Circuit's review of the automobile safety rules. If this was the judicial responsibility, how much more important that the statement of basis and purpose "enable us to see what major issues of policy were ventilated by the informal proceedings and why the agency reacted to them as it did"!

The Court's confident reference to the administrative "record" is surprising in light of the structural realities of the decision process, an institutional process much like that just described for informal rulemaking. Until FOIA compelled them to acquire it, agencies had no habit of identifying all materials brought to bear on an accumulating decision as it passed through various levels of bureaucratic review. In all likelihood the reference was encouraged by a misunderstanding on the part of the attorney who had argued the case for the government, a young lawyer accustomed to the judicial model of litigation.[38] Nonetheless, the reference was made and – among lawyers and judges equally used to that model – was easily accepted.

Accommodating issues of science fact: Once one began to know what material was being considered by an agency (in addition to the

---

38. Because a major highway project was being suspended during the litigation, the case was argued and briefed in the Supreme Court on an extremely condensed schedule, one usually reserved for the most important affairs of state; this haste doubtless contributed to the government brief's repeated references to "the administrative record" – as if a defined set of papers existed. After the Supreme Court had remanded the case for further proceedings, it quickly became apparent that no such collection existed. Definition of the materials before the various agency personnel sharing responsibility for the decision consumed weeks of litigation effort.

outside comments that long had been a matter of public record), the natural instinct to wish to be able to respond to that material – to confront it, challenge it, contradict it – quickly took shape. The impulse was perhaps especially strong for the increasing body of important rules dealing with health, safety or environmental issues – rules frequently based on disputable conclusions about such general, but factual, questions as the impact of breathing various concentrations of a given substance on human health.

The instinct found expression in a 1973 proceeding involving an EPA rulemaking to set standards for the control of concrete dust.[39] After the rule had been adopted but before it had been judicially reviewed, the EPA (prompted by a court of appeals decision in another case[40]) put in the record for review new information about the methodology it had employed to reach its conclusions. With its information about the agency's data thus enlarged, one of the participants in the rulemaking now persuaded the court to send the rule back to the agency, to allow the filing of new comments critical of the agency's methodology. When the agency appeared to ignore those comments, the court not only insisted that they be responded to, but gave forceful new content to the statutory provisions for "notice" and "comment" by suggesting an obligation to reveal agency data from the outset: "it is not consonant with the purpose of a rulemaking proceeding to promulgate rules on the basis of inadequate data, or on data that ... [are] known only to the agency."

Four years later a similar view was expressed by another court of appeals in reviewing a Food and Drug Administration rule governing the preparation of smoked fish:

> Although we recognize that an agency may resort to its own expertise ... we do not believe that when the pertinent research material is readily available ... there is any reason to conceal the scientific data relied upon from the interested

---

39. Portland Cement Assn v. Ruckleshaus, 486 F.2d 375 (D.C. Cir. 1973), cert. den. 417 U.S. 921 (1974).

40. Kennecott Copper Corp. v. EPA, 462 F.2d 846 (D.C. Cir. 1972).

parties. ... If the failure to notify interested persons of [the material relied on] actually prevented the presentation of relevant comment, the agency may be held not to have considered all "the relevant factors."... One cannot ask for comment on a scientific paper without allowing the participants to read the paper.[41]

Thus was "notice" expanded past the information section 553 mentions to include any data the agency knows that bears on its proposed rule. Similarly, "comment" came to entail an opportunity to challenge that data, in addition to the chance to supply fresh data, argument or views. And the statement of basis and purpose must be full enough to show the agency's reasoning in some detail, including its response to important comments that have been made.

E. THE SIREN CALL OF THE MODEL OF JUDICIAL TRIAL

Taken no farther than the point just described, these developments can be tied, however loosely, to section 553's text and – as important – associated with the processes scientists are accustomed to using to ventilate and resolve disputed matters. Characterized as a "paper hearing," this understanding of rulemaking process was widely accepted;[42] one thoughtful bureaucrat found in its requirements "a great tonic" to the integrity of the rulemaking process within the agency, giving "those who care about well-documented and well-reasoned decision-making a lever with which to move those who do not."[43] While fullness and visibility have necessary costs in time and effort,[44] important

41. United States v. Nova Scotia Food Products Corp., 568 F.2d 240, 251 (2d Cir. 1977).

42. R. Stewart, *The Development of Administrative and Quasi-Constitutional Law in Judicial Review of Environmental Decisionmaking: Lessons from the Clean Air Act*, 62 Iowa L. Rev. 713 (1977).

43. W. Pedersen, *Formal Records and Informal Rulemaking*, 85 Yale L. J. 38, 60 (1975).

44. See J. Mashaw & D. Harfst, n. above; D. Costle, *Brave New Chemical: The Future Regulatory History of Phlogiston*, 33 Admin. L. Rev. 195 (1981); more recent accounts of rulemaking "ossification," p. below, seem considerably less critical of these costs as elements contributing to the turgidity of contemporary rulemaking than of others.

issues warrant such expenditures, and many would concede that the problems of fact-finding in matters complicated by issues of modeling, scientific judgment, and projection[45] require a public procedure of some fullness and visibility.

Perhaps inevitably, however, judges and lawyers more familiar with the models of adversarial legal trial than those of scientific dispute resolution (or, for that matter, legislative inquiry) came to see the issues of ventilation and resolution in lawyers' rather than scientists' or politicians' terms. Two essentially contemporaneous cases dramatized the influence of judicial models on the developing requirements and, in doing so, also served to set limits upon them. The first threatened institutional decision processes with misunderstandings about the nature of rulemaking records; the second, notice-and-comment procedures with judicial requirements for the use of viva voce trial procedures.

"Ex parte contacts": Home Box Office, Inc. v. FCC[46] concerned a Federal Communications Commission rule regulating what programs could be shown by cable antenna systems competing with regular television broadcasters. This was a rule of a more traditional character – fact-finding presented no particular difficulty, but the rule's financial implications for many of the groups participating were substantial. Many participants had not only filed comments, but also approached FCC Commissioners and staff informally to voice their views. An inquiry by the court produced "a document over 60 pages

---

45. Modeling involves the use of computer models or other analytic devices to predict the outcome of complex interactions – for example, the economic impact of a proposed regulation – and is highly dependent on the assumptions of the model as well as the accuracy of the data employed in it. Scientific judgment issues arise in assessing the outcomes of processes that cannot be directly tested, for example the impact on steel used in a nuclear power plant of being exposed to high levels of radiation for forty years. Projection involves the transplanting of data developed in one sphere to another, as when scientists use the results of experiments on mice conducted by administering relatively high doses of a chemical to estimate carcinogenicity in humans at low dosage rates. A highly regarded decision illustrating these problems is Sierra Club v. Costle, 657 F.2d 298 (D.C. Cir. 1981).

46. 567 F.2d 9, cert. den. 434 U.S. 829 (1977).

long which revealed, albeit imprecisely, widespread ex parte communications involving virtually every party [to the rulemaking]."

Was this wrong behavior? While the court was horrified, none of the participants appear to have treated it guiltily, one going so far as to boast of its success in bringing congressional pressure to bear. As we have seen, the "ex parte communication" limitation is one characteristic of on-the-record proceedings, in particular of adjudication; all the statutory provisions concerning it are pointed in that direction. Informal rulemaking, on the other hand, encourages contact and interaction; it imposes no structures of separation on agency decision-making, and no obligation of mutual disclosure among the participants.

For the Home Box Office court, however, the discovery of the rulemaking "record" and the development of the "paper hearing" pointed in another direction:

Even the possibility that there is here one administrative record for the public and this court and another for the Commission and those "in the know" is intolerable. ... [I]mplicit in the decision to treat the promulgation of rules as a "final" event in an ongoing process of administration is an assumption that an act of reasoned judgment has occurred, an assumption which further contemplates the existence of a body of material ... with reference to which such judgment was exercised. Against this matter, "the full administrative record that was before [an agency official] at the time he made his decision,"[47] ... it is the obligation of this court to test the actions of the Commission for arbitrariness or inconsistency with delegated authority. ... As a practical matter, Overton Park's mandate means that the public record must reflect what representations were made to an agency so that relevant information supporting or refuting those representations may be brought to the attention of the reviewing courts by persons participating in agency proceedings. This course is obviously foreclosed if communications are made to the agency in secret and the agency itself does not disclose the information presented.[48]

---

47. The quotation is from Citizens to Preserve Overton Park, Inc. v. Volpe.
48. 567 F.2d at 54.

The opinion continued in this vein for some pages, adding the thought that the "paper hearing" requirements for the disclosure of materials in agency files were important, also, for their promotion of "adversarial discussion among the parties." Explicitly, then, in this court's view, the opportunity to comment had become not only a chance to contribute argument, data or views to which attention must be paid, but also the occasion for challenge and testing of what others had contributed.[49]

The characteristic to note is the extent to which the opinion's rhetoric draws on the instincts of judges, and thus tends to convert rule-making into a species of adjudication.[50] This aspect of the opinion, promptly discredited by the Supreme Court decision next to be discussed, has essentially been disavowed by subsequent courts, who tend to explain *Home Box Office* in terms of the very large financial stakes it involved.[51] Receding from the language about "adversarial comment" and any requirement of one record for all participants, they acknowledge that the public record of rulemaking need not be exhaustive of what the agency may know or have heard; nor need there have been an opportunity for each participant to respond to every item that appears there. But the "paper hearing" idea continues to require that the public record contain all documents that the agency may have

---

49. The court's reaction could be understood as one of the periodic reactions to suspicion about the reality of an agency's professed findings. The difficulty of the court's position as a matter of statutory construction of 5 U.S.C. §553, however, should be evident. The agency is required to provide for only one opportunity for comment. If most or all comments are filed on the final day, it is impossible for any one commenter's submission to include responses to what others are simultaneously saying. Here, again, the court evidently had the elegant rituals of judicial filings in mind. Of course it is also true that (unlike judicial proceedings) the time deadlines for filing rulemaking comments are not jurisdictional. One may file comments, responsive or otherwise, at any time, and the agency is free to consider them. What the designated time period for comments assures is that timely comments will be paid attention to. Later comments need not be so regarded.

50. *See, e.g.*, Action for Children's Television v. FCC, 564 F.2d 458 (D.C. Cir. 1977).

51. This reading was challenged, and the general problem thoughtfully explored, in E. Gellhorn & G. Robinson, *Rulemaking "Due Process": An Inconclusive Dialogue*, 48 U. Chi. L. Rev. 201 (1981).

received in relation to a rulemaking. There also remains a general expectation, grounded in political rather than judicial norms and reinforced by a recommendation of the Administrative Conference of the United States,[52] that significant oral communications about pending rulemakings – particularly any data they may convey – will be noted, and a precis placed in the rulemaking record. This is the regime adopted in the special rulemaking provisions governing proceedings under the Clean Air Act, which most commentators expect to be the model for any future reform of federal rulemaking procedures generally.

Required oral procedures? At about the same time as one panel of judges of the United States Court of Appeals for the District of Columbia Circuit was announcing its judgment in *Home Box Office,* another seemed to be saying, in a case that *did* involve highly contentious judgment about scientific facts in rulemaking, that trial-like adversary procedures might be required to assure their proper determination. The rulemaking outcome depended upon complex findings about the handling and impact of nuclear waste. The agency had in fact used oral proceedings in the rulemaking, and had revealed its data and permitted participants a degree of influence over the proceedings significantly beyond what section 553 required.[53] The court, however, believed the procedures the agency had chosen were not "sufficient to ventilate the issues" as fully as their importance required. Its opinion marked one side of a running debate between two wings of the court. One side believed that judges had the obligation to educate themselves to whatever extent was necessary to review agency results effectively

---

52. Recommendation 77-3, published at 1 CFR 305.77-3, relied on "the widespread demand for open government" as well as the needs of judicial review in recommending the creation of a rulemaking file that would include the texts of all written communications and notes of "significant oral communications;" it rejected, however, the idea of an "opportunity of interested persons to reply" as inconsistent with the idea of rulemaking, and "neither practicable nor desirable." On the Administrative Conference, see p. below.

53. The reader is entitled to know that the author was General Counsel of the Nuclear Regulatory Commission when the case was decided by the court of appeals and briefed to the Supreme Court, so that his view of the case is to some extent, inevitably, that of an advocate.

on their own terms. The other – the voice of this opinion – despaired of judges' capacity to educate themselves effectively on highly technical matters. These judges thus concluded that the desirable judicial role was to require agencies to use procedures that would permit full ventilation, challenge, and explanation at the expert and responsible agency level.[54] Under this "hybrid" model, important issues of fact in rulemaking – facts of a general character, such as the impact of a given level of radiation on human health – would require trial-like oral procedures for their determination. Viva voce examination of scientific experts and the presentation of contending expert points of view, proponents asserted, would permit more informed decision. They claimed that truth was more likely to arise from the contending views and from partisan challenges to expert testimony than from a process considering such disputes only on the papers. Congress had adopted hybrid procedures legislatively for a few particular statutes and agencies, and – although doubts were being expressed about the costs in time and effort it imposed[55] – the courts of appeals seemed poised to require it more generally.

In *Vermont Yankee Nuclear Power Corp. v. Natural Resources Defense Council, Inc.,*[56] the Supreme Court repudiated this development in a sharply worded and unanimous opinion that appeared to forbid the courts of appeals to require *any* procedures beyond those specifically required by section 553. The APA, it reasoned, settled

---

54. See Ethyl Corp. v. EPA, 541 F.2d 1 (D.C. Cir.) cert den 426 U.S. 941 (1976).

55. The most disciplined study was that done for the Administrative Conference of the United States by Professor Barry Boyer; he studied the Federal Trade Commission's experience with hybrid rulemaking procedures a 1974 statute required for its adoption of certain types of rules, concluding they produced little gain in accuracy, fairness, or acceptability of results but a good deal of additional cost and delay. See Boyer, *Report on the Trade Regulation Rulemaking Procedures of the Federal Trade Commission,* 1979 ACUS Ann.Rep. 41; 1980 ACUS Ann.Rep. 33; for more recent studies, *see* T. McGarity & S. Shapiro, Workers at Risk: The Failed Promise of the Occupational Safety and Health Administration (Praeger 1993); W. West, Administrative Rulemaking: Politics and Processes (Greenwood 1985).

56. 435 U.S. 519 (1978).

"long-continued and hard-fought contentions, and enacts a formula on which opposing social and political forces have come to rest."[57] Its rulemaking provisions "established the maximum procedural requirements which Congress was willing to have the courts impose upon agencies in conducting rulemaking procedures. Agencies are free to grant additional procedural rights in the exercise of their discretion, but reviewing courts are generally not free to impose them if the agencies have not chosen to grant them."[58] Permitting courts to determine what would have been "properly tailored" procedures after the fact, the Court reasoned, would involve the courts in assessing outcomes by hindsight, a perspective denied the agencies when they made their procedural choices. The predictable consequence would be to lead agencies to choose excessive formality as the only safe means of avoiding reversal on procedural grounds. And, the Court stressed, the argument for more elaborate procedures rested on a false view of the record of rulemaking: "[I]nformal rulemaking need not be based solely on the transcript of a hearing held before an agency. ... Thus, the adequacy of the "record" in [rulemaking] is not correlated directly to the type of procedural devices employed, but rather turns on whether the agency has followed the statutory mandate of the Administrative Procedure Act or other relevant statutes."[59]

Clearly enough, the Supreme Court's *Vermont Yankee* opinion now forbids courts to require oral procedures in connection with rulemaking. Correspondingly, the *Home Box Office* idea of "adversarial comment" has been rejected. But what of the elements of the "paper hearing" – the expanded notions of "notice," "comment," and "statement of basis and purpose" that the courts of appeals had developed? In fact the extent and context of rulemaking has changed enormously since the APA was adopted in 1946, and statutes such as the Freedom of Information Act reflect new ideas about the procedural context

---

57. Id. at 523.
58. Id. at 524.
59. Id. at 547.

"upon which opposing social and political forces have come to rest." The Supreme Court's casual assumption about the record in *Overton Park*, as we have seen, was a central factor in the development of the "paper hearing" idea; that assumption would have provoked wonder among the APA's drafters. While the Supreme Court's *Vermont Yankee* opinion underscored the differing nature of records in informal rulemaking and on-the-record adjudication, it did not abandon *Overton Park* review and in later cases the Court has reaffirmed it – confirming, in this way, the "paper hearing" approach.[60] Scholars from the outset doubted that *Vermont Yankee* swept as broadly as its language suggested,[61] and the paper hearing ideas can be attached – however loosely – to the language of the APA itself. Permitting fresh understanding of that language as circumstances change exercises a conventional judicial function. The nature of rulemaking, and for that matter of judicial review, have changed since 1946, and the enactment of new statutes such as the FOIA, even if not directly amendments to the APA, signal changing contexts as well. The Court ought not to be taken as having ignored those developments.

F. THE IMPACT OF INCREASING POLITICAL OVERSIGHT

With the institutional character of rulemaking secured,[62] and in step with what seems generally a greater judicial disposition to regard rulemaking as, in significant respects, a political as well as an expert enterprise, the last two decades' developments have focused more on

---

60. Motor Vehicle Manufacturers Assn. v. State Farm Mutual Ins. Co., 463 U.S. 29 (1983).

61. R. Stewart, *Vermont Yankee and the Evolution of Administrative Procedure*, 91 Harv. L. Rev. 1805 (1978); C. Byse, *Vermont Yankee and the Evolution of Administrative Procedure: A Somewhat Different View*, 91 Harv. L. Rev. 1823 (1978); A. Scalia, *Vermont Yankee: The APA, The D.C. Circuit, And The Supreme Court*, 1978 The Sup. Ct. Rev. 345.

62. See, e.g., United Steelworkers of America, AFL-CIO-CLC v. Marshall, 647 F.2d 1189 (D.C. Cir.), cert den 453 U.S. 913 (1981), in which two of the three *Home Box Office* judges joined.

the political control of rulemaking and, correspondingly perhaps, more on the period that precedes publication of a section 553 notice of proposed rulemaking.

Sierra Club v. Costle: These shifts were signaled in 1981 by *Sierra Club v. Costle,*[63] a case involving an EPA regulation setting standards for the emission of sulfur compounds by coal-burning electric power plants. The standards entailed sharp political as well as technical issues.[64] Setting a standard was not simply a matter of fixing an emission level each power plant must achieve, which would be complex in itself. Sulfur emissions can be controlled in several ways: use of low-sulfur coal, pre-treatment (washing) of the coal, the use of either of two available technologies for "scrubbing" the gases produced by burning the coal, or some combination of these measures. These techniques vary in effectiveness and in cost, and their costs depend on whether they are being integrated into the design of a new plant, or retrofitted onto an old one. Coal-fired power plants are located throughout the United States; both air quality and coal quality vary considerably with American geography, as do their significance. Thus, maintaining visual clarity of the desert air near the Grand Canyon may have an importance in addition to the requirements of health. Sulfur compounds, once air-borne, mix with whatever else is in the air and travel in the direction of prevailing winds, slowly precipitating out of the atmosphere as acid rain; any one plant's contribution is merely incremental, *and* downwind users of the air, like downstream users of a river, have to deal with an aggregate result – potentially damaging, yet hard to affix particular responsibility for. Low-sulfur coal is present in some parts of the country but not others; eliminating a market for high-sulfur coal would cost jobs in already impoverished regions.

---

63. 657 F.2d 298 (D.C. Cir. 1981).

64. The story of the rulemaking is well told, with an emphasis on the distortions (as the authors see them) introduced by the political process in B. ACKERMAN & W. HASSLER, CLEAN COAL/DIRTY AIR (Yale, 1981); a shorter account by the same authors appears as Beyond the New Deal: Coal and the Clean Air Act, 89 Yale L. J. 1466 (1980).

Scrubbing would demand expensive equipment that if not universally required would diminish the market for high-sulfur coal. And while washing and burning low-sulfur coal might be sufficient to produce emissions like those achievable by cleaning and scrubbing high-sulfur coal, still cleaner air could be produced by also scrubbing the low-sulfur coal, which is found near the mountains and canyons of the American West where visibility has high value.

It is thus evident that the issues presented were "polycentric," with many essentially political tradeoffs possible. For environmentalists seeking pure air, eastern coal interests with high-sulfur reserves, other areas with low-sulfur reserves, and a President concerned about the general economic impact of imposing a costly and generally unproven technology, the stakes were high. The Clean Air Act obliges the EPA to maintain a rulemaking file including all information or data on which it intends to rely, and it had docketed there the notes of a series of meetings, including several with the President and/or his staff held shortly before the rule was announced. Some of these meetings included coal industry officials and a powerful senator from one of the eastern high-sulfur states, whose cooperation the President needed on many issues. One meeting with the President and his staff was not recorded on this docket. The rule as adopted had been couched in terms tending to favor the eastern interests. Had there been improper political meddling?

Unlike the court of appeals in *Home Box Office*, even despite the special provisions of the Clean Air Act, the panel deciding *Sierra Club v. Costle* sought to respect the non-judicial characteristics of the rule-making process. Informal oral meetings about pending rulemakings would not be forbidden or made the subject of formal recording requirements. As Judge Wald noted:

[T]he very legitimacy of general policymaking performed by unelected administrators depends in no small part upon the openness, accessibility, and amenability of these officials to the needs and ideas of the public.... As judges we are insulated from these pressures ... but we must refrain from the easy temptation to look askance at all face-to-face lobbying efforts, regardless of the forum in which they occur, merely because we see them as inappropriate in the judicial context.[65]

Stressing the President's exclusive constitutional responsibility for exercise of executive authority and the agency's inability to rely on any factual matter not placed in its docket, the court found that the failure to record notes of one of the meetings with the President presented no difficulty.

After all, any rule ... must have the requisite factual support in the rule-making record, and ... the Administrator may not base the rule ... on any "information or data" which is not in the record, no matter what the source. ... Of course, it is always possible that undisclosed Presidential prodding may direct an outcome that is factually based on the record, but different from the outcome that would have obtained in the absence of Presidential involvement. In such a case, it would be true that the political process did affect the outcome in a way the courts could not police. But we do not believe that Congress intended that the courts convert informal rulemaking into a rarified technocratic process, unaffected by political considerations or the presence of Presidential power.[66]

The court was similarly undisturbed by the possibility of congressional pressure inherent in the meetings with the eastern Senator, absent a demonstration that he had introduced extraneous considerations.[67] "Where Members of Congress keep their comments focused on the substance of the proposed rule ... administrative agencies are expected to balance Congressional pressure with the pressures emanating from all other sources."

---

65. 657 F. 2d at 400-01.

66. Id. at 408-09.

67. Such a demonstration had been successfully made in an earlier case, D.C. Federation of Civil Associations v. Volpe, 459 F.2d 1231 (D.C. Cir. 1971), cert. den. 405 U.S. 1030 (1972). There, a member of Congress had demanded that the Secretary of Transportation move forward to authorize construction of a bridge (the decision challenged in the case), and threatened to hold funds for another, unrelated departmental program hostage in the appropriations process until he did so.

Economic and other impact analyses: This acknowledgment of a proper role for political oversight in rulemaking, emphatically echoed by the Supreme Court in later years,[68] has armed the development of the executive orders already discussed, requiring economic impact analyses and annual participation in the setting of a regulatory agenda. Both activities occur during the pre-notice period of rulemaking. The issues about these consultations have turned not on their fact so much as on their transparency, and on the subtle line between the President's desirable influence and his more questionable substitution of a possibly very political judgment to resolve complex scientific issues. Factual analyses prepared by the agency in the course of these processes or submitted to it by other agencies, including the OMB, seem a necessary part of the record generated by a "paper hearing." Insofar as they concern fact, such analyses would not ordinarily be privileged from disclosure under the FOIA. But an FOIA privilege would extend to predecisional discussions about policy choices, the very matter as to which oversight is likely to be the most vigorously exercised and the public's suspicions are likely to be the most aroused.

Practices regarding transparency have varied considerably from President to President. The court in *Sierra Club* placed evident emphasis on an undertaking by the White House of President Jimmie Carter, whose administration was responsible for the rule being reviewed. Under lawyers' advice, the White House had agreed to avoid serving as a "conduit" for essentially private contributions by political "friends." The court hinted that any such involvement would produce more difficult questions. In subsequent Republican administrations, the unwillingness of the White House to make its interventions public (and suspicions that they often reflected corporate input) produced extended political struggles with the Democrat-controlled Senate – that, for example, refused to confirm the first President Bush's choice for the office responsible for administering his executive order, in the absence of clear undertakings on the transparency ques-

---

68. Chevron, U.S.A., Inc. v. Natural Resources Defense Council, Inc., 467 U.S. 837 (1984).

tion. The interventions were criticized, as well, for inducing delay transferring and politicizing rulemaking authority.[69] President Clinton's Executive Order 12,866 made extensive commitments to transparency and timeliness; with those commitments, public controversy over the politicality of the Executive Order's administration appeared to have faded away. The second Bush administration's approach is not yet clear. Through all of this, however, general congressional support for the idea of presidential participation and oversight has been strong. "To what extent in public?" has been the significant question.

Whitman v. American Trucking: The importance of limits on broad political direction may be suggested by *Whitman v. American Trucking Assn,*[70] the Supreme Court's 2001 decision resulting from challenges to another EPA rule about air quality control, referred to in the course of the earlier discussion of delegation. In sustaining the constitutionality of the statute in that case, one question that appears to have held some importance for the Court was whether the EPA was to reach its judgment strictly in terms of scientific judgment about the level of protection "that is 'requisite' – that is, not higher or lower than is necessary – to protect the public health with an adequate margin of safety," or whether it was also permitted to compromise that judgment in light of costs to the national economy. The Court firmly concluded, as had the courts of appeals previously considering this question, that those costs were not, as such, a proper factor to be considered (acknowledging, nonetheless, a certain imprecision in "requisite" and "adequate"). That the Administrator was to be governed by technical considerations bearing on public health protection, one could believe, made her judgment less baldly legislative (or, at least "political") than if it were seen to depend on essentially political trade-offs among a number of factors. Those factors both are less susceptible of "expert

---

69. R. Pildes & C. Sunstein, *Reinventing the Regulatory State*, 62 U. Chi. L. Rev. 1 (1995).
70. 531 U.S. 457 (2001).

judgment" and would extend the Administrator's responsibilities to a broader range of subjects, an extension arguably more threatening to separation of powers concerns. It is easier, that is, to accept a powerful delegate with a responsibility limited to a particular set of concerns in terms of which her actions must be justified, than a delegate made responsible for a broad range of concerns, of whose resolution effective judicial review might be difficult to imagine.

Yet the habit of causing agencies at least to *report on and analyze* issues beyond their immediate responsibilities in important rulemakings, which began with the National Environmental Policy Act,[71] is by now deeply ingrained in the Executive Orders about impact analysis, and a number of statutes building upon them. The Court's opinion contains no direct suggestion that these frameworks (including, under Executive Order 12, 866, presidential requirements for particular bureaucratic arrangements within each agency) raise issues of either constitutionality or legality. Unsurprisingly, given the President's constitutional responsibilities for overseeing all government, one finds in the literature little question or criticism about his power to call for such analyses,[72] although some believe the variety of such analyses required has expanded beyond reason,[73] and others have questioned its effectiveness.[74] So long as the responsible administrator articulates her

---

71. Calvert Cliffs' Coordinating Comm. v. USAEC, 449 F.2d 1109 (D.C. Cir. 1971); S. Taylor, Making Bureaucracies Think: the Environmental Impact Statement Strategy of Administrative Reform (Stanford University 1984). NEPA does not change the agency's mandate, as such, but requires it to engage in a specified inquiry (in this case, about environmental impact), under external supervision, before it pursues its mandate – on the theory that the inquiry itself will produce a more informed pursuit of that mandate. See Robertson v. Methow Valley Citizens' Council, 490 U.S. 332 (1989).

72. See E. Kagan, *Presidential Administration*, 114 Harv. L. Rev. 2246 (2001); P. Shane, *Political Accountability in a System of Checks and Balances: The Case of Presidential Review of Rulemaking*, 48 Ark.L. Rev. 161 (1995).

73. S. Shapiro, *Political Oversight and the Deterioration of Regulatory Policy*, 46 Admin. L. Rev. 1 (1994).

74. R. HAHN, REVIVING REGULATORY REFORM: A GLOBAL PERSPECTIVE (2000) and R. Hahn et al., *Empirical Analysis: Assessing Regulatory Impact Analyses: The Failure of Agencies to Comply with Executive Order 12,866*, 23 Harv. J. L. & Pub. Pol'y 859 (2000) give what is at

judgment in the terms in which the statute authorizing her action commands, and the action is sustainable in those terms, the situation remains as Judge Wald characterized it in Sierra Club above. Despite the commitments to transparency made in E.O. 12,866, it may be remarked, OIRA leaves it to the individual agencies how and to what extent they will make its interventions available; its own practice is to post on its Website a running account of pending matters, with some indications of meetings held or comments made, but no details.[75]

Regulatory Flexibility, Unfunded Mandates, etc.: Support for centralized coordination of rulemaking has been reflected in a number of statutes. These both pick up the "impact analysis" theme and also reflect an increasing practice (notable as well in a variety of executive orders) of requiring rulemakers to take special account of the needs of particular communities or political themes. Thus the Regulatory Flexibility Act,[76] first adopted in 1980 and then much strengthened in 1996, requires agencies to pay special attention to the possible special needs of small businesses affected by important regulations, and to consider alternative approaches that might protect them, especially, from severe economic impacts. Agency compliance with this require-ment, unlike the executive orders, is made subject to judicial review in limited respects. The court reviews to see that the correct inquiry was made; then, with the information it will have generated in the "record" of the rulemaking along with all other information, it asks whether the agency's conclusions were "reasonable" in whatever terms its mandates command.[77] As with the National Environment Policy Act, the mandate of the agency has not been changed by the

---

best a mixed report on the success of E.O. 12,866 (and its predecessors) in causing agencies to perform professionally creditable economic impact analyses, or to produce regulations whose projected economic benefits consistently exceed their projected costs.

75. See http://www.whitehouse.gov/omb/inforeg/regpol.html.

76. 5 U.S.C. §601 ff.; see Associated Fisheries of Maine, Inc. v. Daley, 127 F.3d 104 (1st Cir.1997).

77. Ibid.

Act; but the body of information the agency will have before it in deciding how to pursue that mandate has been considerably expanded, and the importance of new policy concerns is, as it were, "in the air."

The Regulatory Flexibility Act was also the first statutory source of the requirement for published early notice of work that is expected to lead to proposals for rulemaking, in a semi-annual Unified Agenda of Federal Regulation. This attention to the earliest phase of agency rulemaking – how agencies decide on their regulatory priorities – has been picked up in presidential executive orders requiring consultation with OIRA over rulemaking plans, most recently E.O. 12,866, as well as in the continuing "regulatory reform" attention to issues of risk. This is self-evidently a context in which presidential "guidance" can be particularly strong. Since review of such priority judgments is extremely limited, any such guidance is unlikely to encounter much judicial resistance.

Stepping back from a particular agency's choice to attack a particular regulatory target, one can imagine an integrated universe of regulatory activity, having impacts across the private sector as a whole. The fact of these impacts, which must be paid for by the private sector but have no direct reflection in government expenditures, catalyzed the development of required economic impact analysis for "major" rules. It has also fueled efforts to track the overall costs of government regulation for the private sector. Some accordingly argue for limits to that overall required "expenditure," on analogy to the annual appropriations budget for direct governmental expenditures. Achieving a meaningful annual "regulatory budget" has proved elusive – as may be imagined, estimates are extremely varied, political, self-interested, and controversial – but the effort has spawned legislative steps in addition to the President's annual regulatory agenda. The Government Performance and Results Act of 1993[78] requires each agency periodically to develop strategic plans looking at least five years

---

78. Pub.L. 103-62, 107 Stat. 285 (1993); see W. Funk, Governmental Management, a report as part of the ABA's Administrative Law and Regulatory Practice Section APA Project, p. n. above; the report is available at http://www.abanet.org/adminlaw/apa/govmanage0401.doc.

into the future, that could set the parameters for performance measures – objective, quantifiable, and measurable to the extent that is
possible – against which Congress could assess agency performance as
part of the annual appropriations process. Results under the Act are
not yet apparent.

In 1995, the Unfunded Mandates Reform Act added states, localities and tribal governments to small businesses, as entities especially
entitled to have the impact of important regulations on their resources
and concerns taken into account.[79] Ostensibly addressed to the
Congress as much as to agencies, the Act's provisions have somewhat
greater legal force for the latter.[80] They require agencies to analyze
the economic impact of their important actions on the private sector
as well as states, localities and tribal governments. Agencies are to
take special account of, and seek to reduce, any "disproportionate
budgetary effects." They are either to choose the "least costly, most
cost-effective or least burdensome method of achieving" their regulatory objectives that would not be "inconsistent with law," or to explain
why they have not done so. A rule imposing private duties and unsup-
ported by government subvention is easily characterized as an
"unfunded mandate," even though in this context funded mandates
are unknown. The special consultation provisions that are the heart of
the Act's mechanism for achieving consideration of impact, however,
are particularly aimed at states, localities, and tribal governments.

One can add to this picture of increasing analytic complexity
Executive Orders that already have required, or are promised shortly to
require, special consideration of impacts on family life, property rights,
civil justice reform, and energy efficiency. All these are sensible subjects for analysis, but in gross they help one to understand why com-

---

79. 2 U.S.C. §1501 et seq.

80. As addressed to Congress's legislative practices, they are wholly hortatory; agencies act
under OMB supervision and reporting requirements, see. e.g. OMB, Fourth Annual Report to
Congress, Agency Compliance with Title II of the Unfunded Mandates Reform Act of 1995
(1999), and are subject to judicial enforcement only if they wholly omit the required analysis.
Any analysis prepared simply becomes an element of the rulemaking record.

mentators now frequently refer to the "ossification" of rulemaking.[81] At the time of its making, a table prepared for the American Bar Association's Section of Administrative Law and Regulatory Practice as a checklist for government attorneys supervising rulemaking tracked 20 different statutes and executive orders to be accounted for, at 25 different stages of rule development.[82] The great bulk of the entries, including all required impact analysis stages, occur in *advance* of section 553 notice of proposed rulemaking. One can thus understand the comment of a law professor who had served as EPA's general counsel in the Bush administration: "Notice-and-comment rulemaking is to public participation as Japanese Kabuki theater is to human passions – a highly stylized process for displaying in a formal way the essence of something which in real life takes place in other venues."[83]

3. NEGOTIATED RULEMAKING

Under the encouragement of statute[84] and executive order, agencies in some cases develop their rulemaking proposals not internally, but through an external, mediated process known as "negotiated rulemaking." This is formally a process for generating proposals for rulemaking rather than the final rules as such. Thus, it brings the statutory provisions for public rulemaking procedures forward in time, into the development period previously left largely to bureaucratic initiatives. If negotiated rulemaking discussions succeed in developing a consensual proposal subscribed to by representatives of all the inte-

---

81. T. McGarity, *The Courts and the Ossification of Rulemaking: A Response to Professor Seidenfeld*, 75 Tex. L. Rev. 525 (1997); M. Seidenfeld, *Demystifying Deossification*, 75 Tex. L. Rev. 483 (1997); R. Pierce, Jr., *Seven Ways to Deossify Agency Rulemaking*, 47 Admin. L. Rev. 59 (1995); P. Verkuil, *Rulemaking Ossification – A Modest Proposal*, 47 Admin. L. Rev. 453 (1995).

82. M. Seidenfeld, *Rulemaking Table*, 27 Fla. St. L. Rev. 533 (2000).

83. E.D. Elliott, *Reinventing Rulemaking*, 41 Duke L. J. 1480, 1492 (1993).

84. 5 U.S.C. §561

rests possibly affected by the rule and also acceptable to the agency, the notice-and-comment period is unlikely to generate significant opposition, and adoption of the proposal is also thought unlikely to produce judicial review.

The scheme of the Negotiated Rulemaking Act is relatively straightforward. An agency believing that a needed regulation will significantly affect only a limited number of interests, and that a committee representing those interests may be able through good faith negotiations to reach timely consensus on a proposal, may (but cannot be compelled to) establish a committee to that end. It may and frequently does appoint a neutral convenor to help identify the interests affected and suitable representatives. It must publish a notice fully describing the planned undertaking, including committee membership. This notice permits others to submit comments proposing new participants for unidentified or inadequately represented interests. A committee usually has fewer than 25 members, including agency representative(s). The agency also nominates a "facilitator" – often the convenor – to chair meetings and assist negotiations; if the committee does not accept the agency's nomination they may by consensus select their own. Balance in committee membership, public notice of committee meetings, and records of committee actions are all controlled by the Federal Advisory Committee Act. The committee is to report to the agency any proposal on which it reaches consensus which will then be published as a notice of proposed rulemaking. Should it fail to reach full consensus, the committee reports any areas of agreement it has been able to develop, or other matters it considers appropriate. It is understood, but not statutorily required, that participants in the process will not challenge, but rather support, the recommended regulation should it eventually be adopted. In terms, the statute fully preserves the right to judicial review of a resulting rule (but *not* of the negotiation process), which "shall not be accorded any greater deference by a court than a rule which is the product of other rulemaking procedures."[85]

---

85. 5 U.S.C. §570.

Negotiated rulemaking is a common but not predominant practice – depending as it does on several factors: agency initiative to develop the activity, the susceptibility of the matter to a consensual outcome, and securing agreement from all the private interests involved to participate in good faith. Critical responses are mixed, with some claiming indifferent success in reducing costs, time demands, and controversiality as compared to conventional rulemaking, and others asserting that where it has been successful, substantial gains have in fact been made. In departing from the usual hierarchical arrangements common to agency structure, the process courts frustration by agency superiors (who are not involved in the negotiations) of any consensus that might be achieved. Perhaps the most trenchant criticism has been that a mediated process can produce an outcome agreeable to all participants, yet inconsistent with legality. For example, when the EPA appointed a committee to develop standards for wood-burning stoves, it successfully developed a consensus proposal, ultimately adopted as a regulation, that contained a number of consumer protection measures and assignments of responsibility. Although these outcomes were acceptable to all interests involved as a political matter, one critic argued, the EPA could not have defended them as a lawful exercise of its statutory delegations had judicial review been sought.[86] The negotiation process, perhaps unsurprisingly had produced compromises that if closely examined would be found to have been unauthorized. This politically satisfying outcome is hard to square with commitment to the rule of law.

---

86. W. Funk, When Smoke Gets in Your Eyes: Regulatory Negotiation and the Public Interest - EPA's Woodstove Standards, 18 Envtl. L. 55 (1987).

PART II

SOME CONTEMPORARY ISSUES IN AMERICAN RULEMAKING

IN the American legal system, as virtually all others, one can observe a hierarchy of textual instruments created for and/or by the government, and having the force of law or, if not quite that force, significant influence over how citizens and corporations conduct their affairs. This hierarchy might be depicted in the following way:

ONE CONSTITUTION
RATIFIED BY "THE PEOPLE"

HUNDREDS OF STATUTES ENACTED BY
AN ELECTED CONGRESS

THOUSANDS OF REGULATIONS ADOPTED BY POLITICALLY
RESPONSIBLE EXECUTIVE OFFICIALS

Tens of thousands of interpretations and guidance documents issued
by responsible bureaus

Countless advice letters,
press releases, and other statements of understanding generated by individual bureaucrats

* * *

This essay addresses contemporary developments and issues in American law at the third and fourth of these levels. The third, that of "regulations," constitutes hard law that, if valid, is binding upon all actors (including the issuing agency). These regulations correspond to subsidiary legislation or European ministerial regulations having the force of law. The fourth level, that of interpretations and guidance documents, is best thought of as "soft law," to which government adherence is expected but which is not directly enforceable against private actors and may not be enforceable, as well, against the government. The fifth level, occurring in dealings with individual bureaucrats, rarely if ever has any discernable legal influence in the United States (although it may of course influence individuals' decisions) and will not be further addressed here.

The federal Administrative Procedure Act,[1] which creates the general framework for Americanadministrative law at the national level, defines the instruments of both level three and level four as "rules." In general, this essay will refer to rules at the third level as "regulations," and to rules at the fourth level as "interpretive rules," "guidance," or "soft law." "Rulemaking" will refer to the procedures by which either kind of instrument is created. The essay has three principal subdivisions. The first addresses some general structural issues about American public law and institutions. The second turns to contemporary issues concerning regulations; and the third to contemporary issues concerning soft law. Any essay of this character is necessarily brief and general; the reader wishing more detail is referred to the fine technical analyses to be found in Jeffrey Lubbers' *A Guide to Federal Agency Rulemaking*[2] and Cornelius Kerwin's *Rulemaking: How Government Agencies Write Law and Make Policy*,[3] and also to the author's *Administrative Justice in the United States*.[4]

I. THE PRESIDENT, THE CONGRESS, AND AMERICAN ADMINISTRATIVE AGENCIES

The American Constitution radically separates executive and legislative authorities in a manner quite strange to parliamentary systems of government. Under the Constitution, the American Congress has no responsibility for rulemaking beyond its creation by statute of legal authority for executive actions (such as rulemaking), its provision of budgetary support for government actions, its power by statute to

---

1. 5 U.S.C. § 551 et seq.

2. Amer. Bar Ass'n, 2006.

3. CQ Press, 2003.

4. Carolina Academic Press, 2002.

countermand regulations,[5] and its informal oversight of agency actions through investigative hearings and the like. Members of Congress, like any member of the public, may attempt to influence rulemaking outcomes by commentary; but once they have authorized rulemaking to occur, its fruition as a legal matter is strictly an issue for the executive. And the Constitution is explicit that members of Congress are forbidden to hold executive office. Thus, the difference between the second and third levels of the hierarchy sketched above is quite dramatic. Congress legislates; but rulemaking is an executive activity.[6]

Analysts from parliamentary systems draw a distinction between "political" and "administrative" (or bureaucratic) controls of regulatory bodies. They tend to ascribe "political" control to the parliament, and "administrative" control to executive actors, who areunderstood in amore technical than political sense. This is natural in a system in which ministerial and legislative terms of office are interdependent, and only legislators are elected (even if it may be known in advance which person or persons, if elected with majority legislative support, will assume executive office). In parliamentary systems, moreover, executive governance may usually be imagined as collegial in character; a "prime" minister is merely that – the first among equals, whose government depends on continuing consensus among all ministers and the legislators who have elected her, and on whose continued support the survival of her government depends.

This interdependency with the legislature and this collegial character of the executive are not to be found in the United States. Our President and the members of Congress are separately elected, in each case to fixed terms of office. These terms do not coincide – two years for the House of Representatives, six years for the Senate, four years for the President. These terms are also rigorous; the government does not

---

5. That is, if an agency adopts a regulation, Congress's only power of disapproval is by statutory enactment. "Laying before" procedures of a less formal sort are constitutionally unavailable.

6. Federal Courts also adopt regulations, but these concern judicial procedures, evidence, etc., and are not directly addressed to private conduct.

fall on a vote of no confidence. The President is the solitary elected executive official.[7] While his appointments to positions of leadership in the various government departments andagencies requiresenatorial approval, thesepersons, once appointed, are answerable *only* to him; unless Congress uses the stringent process of impeachment, it cannot participate in the removal of any executive official from office, from the President on down. It cannot require senatorial approval of Presidential removals. Political realities do offer some protection, since a President will know that he must secure Senate confirmation of the successor to any person he removes from office. Nonetheless, a cabinet secretary or agency head understands that her continuation in office depends on a President who, in general, can remove her at any time, for any reason, without recourse.[8] The result is to make executive control of administrative actions such as rulemaking "political" as well as "administrative."

One consequence is to dramatize the placement of administrative law, from an American perspective, on the difficult and evanescent boundary between politics and law. One can find this already expressed in the earliest of our great constitutional cases, *Marbury v. Madison*, which established the principal that American courts can review legislation to determine its constitutionality.[9] In doing so, Chief Justice Marshall's opinion famously established the place of the courts in the constitutional order. In the course of his opinion, he sought to distinguish between governmental acts that a court might control by law, and others that were not subject to judicial constraint. He denied

---

7. The Vice President is also elected, of course. Our Vice President, has no defined responsibilities beyond his availability to assume the presidency if required. Moreover, the Vice President is not separately voted for. He or she is a fixture of the ballot for President.

8. In limited circumstances, notably for our independent regulatory commissions such as the Securities and Exchange Commission, Congress has validly provided that agency heads can be removed only "for cause." The effective meaning of this constraint has never been tested. In any event the President would be the one to determine that "cause" existed. His determination could be challenged only in the courts, which would be very likely to defer to any credible explanation. The finding that cause existed does not, and constitutionally could not, require congressional approval.

9. Marbury v. Madison, 5 U.S. (1 Cranch) 137 (1803).

any possibility of judicial review over acts that the President was entitled to *command* from his subordinates. When an official

> "is to conform precisely to the will of the President [h]e is the mere organ by whom that will is communicated. The acts of such an officer, as an officer, can never be examinable by the courts. ... The province of the court is, solely, to decide on the rights of individuals, not to enquire how the executive, or executive officers, perform duties in which they have a discretion. Questions, in their nature political, or which are, by the constitution and laws, submitted to the executive, *can never be made in this court.*"[10]

In the particular case, the official in question was the Secretary of State, and Marshall was drawing a contrast between the administration of foreign affairs (a question in its nature political) and another responsibility of the Secretary of State at the time, to deliver commissions for certain public offices (not a political question, but a matter in which the officer had a legal right).

Are American courts then precluded from reviewing any governmental acts in which the executive has some "discretion"? No. Few if any American analysts would describe decisions about air quality made by the Administrator of the Environmental Protection Agency (EPA)[11] in the way Chief Justice Marshall describes decisions of the Secretary of State about foreign affairs. The Secretary of State is exercising dis-

---

10. *Id.* at 166, 170 (emphasis added).

11. The EPA is an executive agency that is not an element of any cabinet department. Headed by a single Administrator whose appointment requires Senate confirmation and who serves on presidential sufferance, EPA's responsibilities are almost entirely regulatory, and not political in the sense Chief Justice Marshall was expressing. Cabinet departments, headed by Secretaries, often mix regulatory and political responsibilities; the non-regulatory activities are often assigned to internal subdivisions, also headed by presidentially-appointed administrators, whose responsibilities, like EPA's, are almost entirely regulatory. Examples would include the Food and Drug Administration (FDA) in the Department of Health and Human Services, the Occupational Safety and Health Administration (OSHA) in the Department of Labor, and the Federal Aviation Administration (FAA) in the Department of Transportation. Independent regulatory commissions like the SEC, too, have responsibilities that are almost entirely regulatory. The statements in this text, unless otherwise noted, apply to every actor of this kind – EPA, FDA, or SEC.

cretion in its largest sense, one might say *DISCRETION!*, in contexts for which there is no law to apply and which "can never be examinable by the courts." The great Chief Justice did not have in mind "discretion" such as the EPA Administrator is given by statute to decide mixed questions of law and politics. Issues like his determinations about necessary air quality are the everyday focus of administrative law; courts review these determinations for "abuse of discretion" under our federal Administrative Procedure Act.[12] Indeed, we would say that for these acts, the possibility of effective judicial review to justify their legality is *essential*. It is generally expressed as a *sine qua non* of their constitutionality. Generally we assume that such agency determinations reflect *objective judgment* about general propositions of fact (as, for example, what is the degree of hazard posed to human life by given quantities of ozone in the atmosphere) rather than simple *political will*. If standards did not exist permitting a court to assess the legality of the Administrator's decisions and acts concerning these matters, we would say an unconstitutional delegation had been made.[13] These are *not* matters to be decided by politics, and they *are* questions examinable by the courts. And that gives the borderline between politics and law particular significance.

To what extent, then, is our President entitled to command, as a political matter, outcomes whose determination Congress has entrusted to an administrative agency like the EPA? How far down into the structure of government do political operatives penetrate? At what point is the work of government done by a permanent civil service that may act under political supervision, yet has "administration" rather than "poli-

---

12. 5 U.S.C. § 706(2)(A).

13. *See, e.g.,* Ethyl Corp. v. EPA, 542 F.2d 1, 68 (D.C. Cir. 1976) (Leventhal, J., concurring:) ("Congress has been willing to delegate its legislative powers broadly – and courts have upheld such delegation – because there is court review to assure that the agency exercises the delegated power within statutory limits."); Skinner v. Mid-Atlantic Pipeline Co., 490 U.S. 212, 218 (1989) ("[S]o long as Congress provides an administrative agency with standards guiding its actions such that a court could ascertain whether the will of Congress has been obeyed, no delegation of legislative authority trenching on the principle of separation of powers has occurred." (internal quotations omitted)).

tics" as its guiding light? Over the past few decades, two trends have emerged in American administrative law: a growing reliance on rule-making to elaborate the detailed (but often quite significant) elements of regulation, as well as a steadily increasing insistence on political penetration of the agency apparatus and political control of its products.

The increased use of rulemakingis, from one perspective, a natural consequence of our increased awareness of social interdependence and environmental hazard. At the same time as human existence has come to involve more artificial elements of uncertain long-term effect, we have developed greater technological capacities to discern and evaluate risk. The great increase in rulemaking occurred, precisely, at the time of the great outpouring of health, safety and environmental legislation in the United States that marked the 1960's and 1970's. Whatever the Nineteenth Century's contributions to global warming, industrial disease, and other ills, the people of that time had fewer tools with which to detect them (and, perhaps, more immediate and evident hazards to which to respond). The judgments we want to reach in consequence of our growing knowledge about and sensitivity to risk – to continue the example already mentioned, how much ozone is safe to permit in the atmosphere we breathe – involve too much detail to be entrusted to the vote of an elected, generalist legislature's politicians. Inevitably, as the pyramidal figure opening this essay may suggest, we expect political legislatures to set general standards for determinations of this sort, and to leave it to experts – i.e., administration – to find the precise levels for particular substances, like ozone, that those standards make appropriate.

The severance of executive from legislative function in the United States (or, to put it another way, the political irresponsibility of American legislators for rulemaking's particular outcomes) introduces a reinforcing temptation to rely on rulemaking – one that is much celebrated in the American scholarship on "public choice."[14] The only poli-

_____

14. "Public choice" is a scholarly discipline that attempts to apply economic reasoning in the world of politics. Particularly well developed in analyses of legislators' behavior, it tends to explain legislators' choices in terms of their incentives to secure reelection, and what behaviors are most likely to contribute to that. A useful American introduction, somewhat skeptical of the

tical necessity for Congress to earn public credit for "action" is to *appear* to have dealt with a problem. It need not actually have done as much as it might have by way of political resolution of issues. It can then point the finger of blame elsewhere should things not work out so well. In consequence, some of the work that ideally ought to be politically re-solved at the second level of the hierarchy above, is passed on to the third.

We have discovered no effective corrective for this institutional failure. The logical candidate would be a constitutional limitation on Congress's power to confer authority on executive government.[15] In name, there is such a limitation, under the rubric "delegation." The constraints of "delegation" doctrine suffice to prevent the conferring of *DISCRETION!* in contexts where courts will conclude that they must be in a position to determine the legality of government behavior – that is, where they will conclude that for executive power to be tole-rated, there must be law to apply. Government lawyers thus rarely argue in any administrative context that judicial review is unavailable, but instead work to persuade the courts that agency behavior meets the constraints of legality.

While there thus must be "intelligible standards" to which government actors may be held,[16] the test for their existence is extre-mely permissive. One may almost say that it suffices for the govern-

---

normative consequences of treating the political world as a "market," is DANIEL A. FARBER & PHILLIP P. FRICKEY, LAW AND PUBLIC CHOICE: A CRITICAL INTRODUCTION (University of Chicago Press 1991). See also, Daniel A. Farber & Philip P. Frickey, *The Jurisprudence of Public Choice*, 65 TEX. L. REV. 873 (1987).

15. Implicit in this account is a fact about our Constitution: it does not define the government of the United States, but rather only the three principal heads of authority: Congress, President, and Supreme Court. Definition of all the rest – cabinet departments, lower courts, independent agencies, even the precise size of the Supreme Court – is left to statutory determination by Congress under its general authority to enact any statutes "necessary and proper" to accomplish the Constitution's ends. U.S. Const. Art. I Sec. 8. See Peter L. Strauss, *The Place of Agencies in Government: Separation of Powers and the Fourth Branch*, 84 COLUM. L REV. 573 (1984).

16. J.W. Hampton, Jr., & Co., v. United States, 276 U.S. 394, 409 (1928) ("If Congress shall lay down by legislative act an intelligible principle to which the person or body authorized to [set standards] is directed to conform, such legislative action is not a forbidden delegation of legis-lative power.").

ment to acknowledge the need to demonstrate legality under the governing statutes.[17] The courts will then work rather hard to determine *that* issue by interpretation, rather than tell Congress that it had not legislated sufficiently. Our courts have lamented that they lack a judicially manageable standard for identifying legislative insufficiencies.[18] They do work hard to find the "intelligible standard" that is the coin of a valid delegation of lawmaking authority, which then permits them to assess the legality of agency action. Yet this review necessarily accepts broad scope for agency discretion on issues that courts are ill-equipped themselves to decide (e.g., the health or environmental consequences of various concentrations of ozone).

So the resulting regulation embodies a judgment that at the same moment:

– has high social consequence (the choice of one rather than another ozone level may have tremendous economic and other effects on various elements of society);

– has an objective character suggesting the appropriateness of expert determination, but in actuality is incapable of a single "correct" resolution and thus requires significant elements of scientific "judgment";

---

17. In *State of South Dakota v. United States Dept. Of Interior,* 69 F.3d 878 (8th Cir. 1995), the government argued before the Eighth Circuit court of appeals that the court lacked power to review a decision of the Secretary of the Interior in a matter involving permission to an Indian tribe to conduct gambling operations on its reservation because the statute authorizing that decision conferred *DISCRETION!* on the Secretary; there was no law to apply. *Id.* at 881. Astounded, the court then held that the statute was an unlawful delegation of authority. *Id.* at 885. The case was taken to our Supreme Court and, while it was pending, governmentlawyers informed thatCourt thatthe Secretary had now concluded that there *was* law to apply, and that the lower court *could* effectively review the challenged decision for its legality. Without hearing argument, the Supreme Court vacated the Eighth Circuit's opinion and remanded the matter to it for the review that had now been conceded to be proper. Dept. Of Interior v. South Dakota, 519 U.S. 919 (1996).

18. See, e.g., Whitman v. Amer. Trucking, 531 U.S. 457, 474-75 (quoting Mistretta v. United States, 488 U.S. 361, 416 (1989) (Scalia, J., dissenting)) ("[W]e have 'almost never felt qualified to second-guess Congress regarding the permissible degree of policy judgment that can be left to those executing or applying the law.'"); Mistretta, 488 U.S. at 415 (Scalia, J., dissenting) (noting that "the doctrine of unconstitutional delegation... is not an element readily enforceable by the courts").

– is subject to effective judicial review to only a limited degree;

– cannot be laid politically at the feet of Congress or the political party that at the moment may hold the balance of power there; and

– although ostensibly reached by an expert agency (the EPA), might be laid politically at the feet of the President, who appointed the head of the EPA, and who will have his own general concerns about regulatory affairs.

One then readily understands how, as the uses and impacts of rule-making have increased, Presidents have increasingly sought to bring it under their unitary and political control. They have sought to bring politics and will to bear where the governing assumptions are that the exercise of such authority is rationalized by its being an act of judgment.

In its most extreme form, growing in popularity over recent years and characterizing the administration of the most recent President Bush, the claim is that in creating a single, "unitary" executive, our Constitution entitles the President ultimately to decide any matter Congress has made the responsibility of an executive agency.[19] This is a proposition I have addressed at length in another place,[20] and it may be helpful here to quote passages that suggest the outlines of the issues:

---

19. Representative positions taken in the contemporary literature: Constitution confers decisional authority: *see, e.g.*, Steven G. Calabresi & Saikrishna B. Prakash, *The President's Power to Execute the Laws*, 104 YALE L. J. 541, 54950 (1994); Christopher S. Yoo, Steven G. Calabresi, & Anthony J. Colangelo, *The Unitary Executive in the Modern Era, 1945-2004*, 90 IOWA L. REV. 601, 730 (2005); Constitution does not confer decisional authority, but it should be presumed Congress intends it, given the realities of modern administration: *see, e.g.*, Elena Kagan, *Presidential Administration*, 114 HARV. L. REV. 2245, 2251 (2001); Lawrence Lessig & Cass R. Sunstein, *The President and the Administration*, 94 COLUM. L. REV. 1, 2-3 (1994); the President, unless directly authorized, is only an overseer: *see, e.g.*, Cynthia R. Farina, *The Consent of the Governed: Against Simple Rules for a Complex World*, 72 CHI.-KENT L. REV. 987, 987-89 (1997); Kevin M. Stack, *The President's Statutory Powers to Administer the Laws*, 106 COLUM. L. REV. 263, 267 (2006); Peter L. Strauss, *Presidential Rulemaking*, 72 CHI.-KENT L. REV. 965, 984-86 (1997).

20. Peter L. Strauss, *Overseer or "The Decider"? The President in Administrative Law*, 75 GEO.WASH.L.REV 696 (2007).

The Constitution itself is at best ambivalent on the question. On the one hand, the opening words of Article II locate all executive power in the President, and the Philadelphia convention famously and emphatically rejected any idea of a collegial executive.[21] Those who take the strongest perspective on what it means to have a unitary chief executive thus argue that when Congress assigns a matter for decision to a constituent element of the executive branch, it does so only for convenience—that, as a matter of constitutional power, the President has the right to decide it.[22]

On the other hand, the Constitution twice refers to "duties" or "powers" assigned to other officers.[23] Article II in terms gives the President only the right to seek from those officers a written opinion about their exercise of those duties (i.e., it does not say he may command their exercise of the duties assigned to them),[24] and it concludes that he is responsible to see to it that the laws "be faithfully executed"[25]—i.e., as if by others. From this perspective, as some (but not all) Attorneys General have concluded,[26] when Congress creates duties in others, that act creates in the President constitutional obligations not only to oversee,

---

21. *See* Peter L. Strauss, *The Place of Agencies in Government: Separation of Powers and the Fourth Branch*, 84 COLUM. L. REV. 573, 599-602 (1984).

22. *See, e.g.*, Calabresi & Prakash, *supra* note 17; Yoo, Calabresi, & Colangelo, *supra* note 17.

23. U. S. CONST. art. I, § 8, cl. 18 confers on Congress the authority to "make all Laws which shall be necessary and proper for carrying into Execution... all other Powers vested by this Constitution in the Government of the United States, or in any Department or Officer thereof.; U. S. CONST. art. II , § 2, cl. .1 provides that the President "may require the Opinion, in writing, of the principal Officer in each of the executive Departments, upon any subject relating to the Duties of their respective Offices." (emphases added)

24. U. S. CONST. art. II , § 2, cl. 1 (The President "may require the Opinion, in writing, of the principal Officer in each of the executive Departments, upon any subject relating to *the Duties of their respective Offices*[.]") (emphasis added).

25. *Id.* art. II, § 3, cl. 3 (emphasis added).

26. The contrast often given in the literature is between the advice of Attorney General Wirt to President Monroe that

> [the President's role is to give] general superintendence [to those to whom Congress had assigned executive duties, as] it could never have been the intention of the constitution... that he should in person execute the laws himself... [W]ere the President to perform [a statutory duty assigned to another], he would not only be not taking care that the laws were faithfully executed, but he would be violating them himself.

but also to respect, their independent exercise of those duties. Just as he must respect a statutory framework that assigns care for the national parks to the Department of the Interior, and care for the national forests to the Department of Agriculture, on this view, he must respect a statutory framework that assigns actual decision-making about particular issues affecting air quality to the EPA; he is entitled only to his (inevitably political) oversight.

The difference between oversight and decision can be subtle, particularly when the important transactions occur behind closed doors and among political compatriots who value loyalty and understand that the President who selected them is their democratically chosen leader. Still, there is a difference between ordinary respect and political deference, on the one hand, and law-compelled obedience, on the other. The subordinate's understanding which of these is owed, and what is her personal responsibility, has implications for what it means to have a government under laws. I cannot improve on the characterization of the problem given half a century ago by Professor Corwin:

Suppose... that the law casts a duty upon a subordinate executive agency eo nomine, does the President thereupon become entitled, by virtue of his "execu-tive power" or of his duty to "take care that the laws be faithfullyexecuted,"to substitute his own judgment for that of the agency regarding the discharge of such duty? An unqualified answer to this question would invite startling results. An affirmative answer would make all questions of law enforcement questions of discretion, the discretion moreover of an independent and legally uncontrollable branch of the government. By the same token, it would render it impossible for Congress, notwithstanding its broad powers under the "necessary and proper" clause, to leave anything to the specially trained judgment of a subordinate exec-

---

The President and Accounting Officers, 1 Op. Att'y Gen. 624, 624-25 (1823) and the advice of Attorney General Cushing to President Pierce that

> no Head of Department can lawfully perform an *official* act against the will of the President, [because a contrary view would permit Congress so to] divide and transfer the executive power as utterly to subvert the Government, [albeit that] all the ordinary business of administration [is, in statutory terms, placed under the authority of the Departments, not the President, and] may be performed by its Head, without the special direction or appear-ance of the President.

Relation of the President to the Executive Departments, 7 Op. Att'y Gen. 453, 469-71 (1855) (emphasis in original). These opinions, with helpful commentary, may be found in H. JEFFERSON POWELL, THE CONSTITUTION AND THE ATTORNEYS GENERAL 29-34, 131-48(1999); *see also* HAROLD H.BRUFF,BALANCE OF FORCES:SEPARATION OF POWERS LAW IN THE ADMINISTRATIVE STATE 456-59 (2006).

utive official with any assurance that his discretion would not be perverted to political ends for the advantage of the administration in power. At the same time, a flatly negative answer would hold out consequences equally unwelcome. It would, as Attorney General Cushing quaintly phrased it, leave it open to Congress so to divide and transfer "the executive power" by statute as to change the government "into a parliamentary despotism like that of Venezuela or Great Britain with a nominal executive chiefor president, who, however, would remain without a shred of actual power."[27]

This is the concern that motivates this writing. As in earlier scholarship,[28] my own conclusion is that in ordinary administrative law contexts, where Congress has assigned a function to a named agency subject to its oversight and the discipline of judicial review, the President's role—like that of the Congress and the courts—is that of overseer and not decider. These oversight responsibilities, in my judgment, satisfy the undoubted constitutional specification of a unitary chief executive, while avoiding the executive tyranny horn of Corwin's dilemma.

... Our Constitution explicitly gives us a unitary head of state, but it leaves the framework of government almost completely to congressional design. If its text chooses between President as overseer of the resulting assemblage, and President as necessarily entitled "decider," the implicit message is that of oversight, not decision. Congress's arrangements of government are a part of the law that the President is to assure will "be faithfully executed," and the Constitution's text anticipates that thosearrangementswill place "duties" elsewhere in the executive branch, which Congress is given wide scope to define. The size and ambition of contemporary government, in a country dedicated to the rule of law and resolute to defend itself against unchecked individual power, point in the same direction. Congress can, to be sure, give the President decisional authority, and it has sometimes done so. In limited contexts—foreign relations, military affairs, coordination of arguably conflicting mandates—the argument for inherent presidential decisional authority is stronger. But in the ordinary world of domestic administration, where Congress has delegated responsibilities to a particular governmental actor it has created, that delegation is a part of the law whose faithful execution the President is to assure.[29] Oversight, and not decision, is his responsibility.

---

27. EDWARD S. CORWIN, THE PRESIDENT: OFFICE AND POWERS 1787–1957, at 80–81 (4th rev. ed. 1957) (quoting the opinion cited *supra* note 24) (emphasis in original).

28. *E.g.*, Strauss, op. cit. *supra* notes 17 and 18.

29. Illustrative of the stronger view of President Bush's administration is a statement he issued on signing the Postal Accountability and Enhancement Act of 2006, which contained

Of course it would rarely be the President himself who commands, but a political apparatus operating under his immediate control. Recent years have seen both a significant expansion of that apparatus in the White House itself, and much enlarged penetration of "political clearances" into agency bureaucracies. From the administration of President Ford (1974-77) forward, Presidents have created increasingly stringent mechanisms for oversight of agency rulemakings likely to have a significant economic impact. These particular mechanisms, centered in the Office of Information and Regulatory Analysis (OIRA) of the President's Office of Management and Budget, will be discussed further below. Here, one should remark that OIRA's controls are professional and bureaucratic, at least in comparison with those of other White House offices. Lisa Bressman and Michael Vandenbergh's groundbreaking account of the EPA-White House interface from the perspective of EPA political appointees dramatically illustrates the number of White House voices (in both Republican and Democratic administrations) purporting to exercise "presidential control";[30] Elena Kagan, now Harvard Law School's dean, recounted at length her experience of presidential direction of agency rulemaking during the Clinton administration, without ever focusing on OIRA's work.[31]

The increasing scope of political clearance for persons having policy responsibilities has attracted rather less attention, but certainly renders American "administration" more political than would be expected in the strong civil service regimes of many parliamentary democracies. Probably the move in this direction began during the presidency of Jimmy Carter, when a reform of the civil service laws created in the upper echelons of the civil service a Senior Executive Service, those persons responsible for policy direction and other matters involving

---

a statutory provision explicitly requiring a search warrant to open domestic first class mail:

> The executive branch shall construe subsection 404(c) of title 39, as enacted by subsection 1010(e) of the Act, which provides for opening of an item of a class of mail otherwise sealed against inspection, in a manner consistent, to the maximum extent permissible, with the need to conduct searches in exigent circumstances, such as to protect human life and safety against hazardous materials, and the need for physical searches specifically authorized by law for foreign intelligence collection.

That is, as he had inherent authority to act to protect the nation, the statutory provision could be ignored. President's Statement on H.R. 6407, The "Postal Accountability and Enhancement Act," December 20, 2006, 2006 WL 3737548.

30. Lisa Schultz Bressman & Michael P. Vandenbergh, *Inside the Administrative State: A Critical Look at the Practice of Presidential Control*, 105 MICH. L. REV. 47, 47-52 (2006).

31. Op. cit. note 17 supra.

substantial discretion. In the United States as in European democracies, important federal bureaus, elements perhaps of a cabinet department, might be under the direction of a senior civil servant, a permanent government employee rather than a political appointee.[32] The new law made them more subject to reward and punishment, reassignment and direction, than they had previously been. While these persons were still nominally in the civil service (that is, they are permanent employees), it is perhaps not surprising to learn that with the enlarged possibilities of reward and discipline from above, practices of political clearance developed:

- The White House office responsible for vetting appointments within government for, inter alia, political acceptability grew from thirteen to twenty-one during the quarter century between 1982, the second year of the Reagan administration, and 2008, during the second term of the second Bush administration. The office peaked in 2001 with thirty-five employees.[33]

- A Department of Justice investigation found that Monica Goodling, the DOJ's White House Liaison and Senior Counsel to the Attorney General, "improperly subjected candidates for careerpositions [in the Justice Department] to the same politically based evaluation she used on candidates for political positions, in violation of federal law and department policy."[34]

---

32. The classic study of their work, written at about the time of this change, is HERBERT KAUFMAN, THE ADMINISTRATIVE BEHAVIOR OF FEDERAL BUREAU CHIEFS (1981).

33. Compare FEDERAL/STATE EXECUTIVE DIRECTORY 1985 (Carroll Publishing Co. 1985) with CARROLL'S FEDERAL DIRECTORY (Carroll Publishing Co. 2008).

34. U.S. Dep't of Justice, Investigation of Allegations of Politicized Hiring by Monica Goodling and Other Staff in the Office of the Attorney General 1, 135 (2008), available at http://www.usdoj.gov/oig/special/s0801/final.pdf.
   Similar implications arise from presidential reactions to congressional requirements of relevant expertise for important policy positions. In the wake of the Katrina disaster and the deficiencies in Federal Emergency Management Administration management it revealed, Congress passed statutes requiring that the person appointed to head FEMA be a person experienced in the management of complex institutions and disaster management. Department of Homeland Security Appropriations Act, 2007 § 611(11), 6 U.S.C. § 313 In a later statute, it directed that appointees to high office in the United States Postal Commission have similar experience-related backgrounds. Postal Accountability and Enhancement Act of 2006 § 501, 39 U.S.C. § 202. In signing the lengthy statutes including these provisions into law, the President identified these two provisions in particular, as against many he accepted, as unconstitutional infringements of

– Newspapers have reported that Vice President Cheney has attempted to control decisions as slight as the amount of water having to be released from a federal dam to protect threatened fish populations (in competition with the needs of farmers in a drought-stricken region) suggested the placement of White House political operatives deep within agency bureaucracies.[35]

– A presidential executive order following quickly upon the Democratic Party's winning back control of Congress in 2006 essentially required every agency to place control over its rulemaking operations, not in the hands of the agency head, but a White House appointee.[36]

– The administration of the second President Bush has been dogged throughout its length with accusations of the political bending of science,[37] rom refusals to permit government analysts to testify concerning their results, to thumb-on-the-scales influence over determinations ranging from the protection of an endangered whale species to the precise level of ozone most appropriate for national air quality standards.

All of this, one might understand, is intimately connected with presidential claims to dominate, as of right, the work of executive government – then turned not to administrative, but to political ends.

This intense politicization of what had been imagined as expert, administrative processes is from a certain perspective not surprising. It can be thought a consequence of legislative irresponsibility in Congress, of the increasing practical importance of regulation to the

---

his authority to nominate or appoint anyone he chose. Statement by President George W. Bush Upon Signing H.R. 5441, 2006 U.S.C.C.A.N S49, S52 (Oct. 4, 2006) ("[the statute] purports to limit the qualifications of the pool of persons from whom the President may select the appointee in a manner that rules out a large portion of those persons best qualified by experience and knowledge to fill the office. The executive branch shall construe [section 611] in a manner consistent with the Appointments Clause of the Constitution."); Statement by President George W. Bush Upon Signing H.R. 6407, 2006 U.S.C.C.A.N. S76 (December 20, 2006) (making an almost identical statement).

35. Jo Becker & Barton Gelman, *Leaving No Tracks on Environmental Policy*, WASH. POST, June 27, 2007, *available at* 2007 WLNR 12054552.

36. Exec.Order No. 13,422, 72 Fed. Reg. 2763 (Jan. 23, 2007).

37. THOMAS O. MCGARITY & WENDY E. W AGNER, BENDING SCIENCE: HOW SPECIAL INTERESTS CORRUPT PUBLIC HEALTH RESEARCH (2008).

American economy (and hence to politicians), and of the American habit, common in recent decades, of putting one political party in power in the White House and the other in power in Congress. For Presidents facing a politically hostile Congress, the incentive – the need – to take active control of the permanent government bureaucracy is clear.

The difficulties, of course, are those suggested byCorwin, and byhistory's experiencewith overpowerful chief executives. Congress's creation of power in discrete executive branch bodies might not seem so threatening to civil liberties. Even though there is a democracy deficit – such agencies are politically responsible only through their tie to presidential appointment – these are dispersed authorities. Each agency acts in a delimited area of not only responsibility but also technical expertise, and they exercise their limited authority using procedures that are both transparent and subject to judicial oversight. It is harder to accept the argument that the power to decide *all* the manifold policy decisions Congress has committed to government agencies lies in the hands of a single autocrat acting behind closed doors and, one may fear, under the influence more of power politics than of expert judgment.[38] Congress, after all, has placed the responsibilities in the agencies, not the President, and made them subject (as he ordinarily is not) to judicial as well as political controls.

In an important mid-Twentieth Century decision for the Supreme Court involving President Truman's effort to claim an enlarged executive authority to deal with an emergency of the Korean War (in a context that had nothing to do with presidential direction of rulemaking), Justice Hugo Black famously remarked in his majority opinion for the Court that "the President's power to see that the laws are faithfully executed refutes the idea that he is to be a lawmaker."[39] Our courts nonetheless accept agency rulemaking, which is unmistakably lawmaking. They see agency decisions as agency, not presidential, lawmaking. It is

---

38. Todd D. Rakoff, *The Shape of the Law in the American Administrative State*, 11 Tel-Aviv U. Stud. L. 9 (1992).

39. Youngstown Sheet & Tube Co. v. Sawyer, 343 U.S. 579, 587 (1952).

perhaps not difficult to see the challenges that the arguments for such a strong "unitary executive" pose to this accommodation.

I conclude this section with remarks taken from an informal paper on the President and the Rule of Law:[40]

[Recently,] Neal Katyal published in the Yale Law Journal an essay entitled "Internal Separation of Powers: Checking Today's Most Dangerous Branch from Within."[41] Faced with a broken Congress, he argued – and it is hard to doubt that Congress is broken – the restraints of law on a President's political ambition must come from within the Civil Service.

Much maligned by both the political left and right, bureaucracy serves crucial functions. It creates a civil service not beholden to any particular administration and a cadre of experts with a long-term institutional world view.

Fans of "Yes, Minister" will recognize this as not simply a possible American view. ... Our laws have created it, beginning with the Civil Service Reform Act of 1883, which first created a professionalized federal civil service, but does one not see all around the signs of increasing politicization in the civil service – the use of political tests as well as, in lieu of, expertise? ... Posing our problem as one of choosing between the rule of law or the rule of men imagines the impossible. Even with the rule of law, we will at best have both. The question is how we can keep the politics in check – and this is perhaps above all else an issue of integrity.

II. NOTICE AND COMMENT RULEMAKING

In 1946, Section 553 of the federal Administrative Procedure Act created a generalized "notice and comment" procedure for adopting regulations. This provision is quoted in its entirety in the margin, and reference will be made to its provisions in the following pages.[42] Note its simplicity.

---

40. Peter L. Strauss, The President and the Rule of Law (Nov. 2007) (unpublished manuscript).

41. Neal Kumar Katyal, *Internal Separation of Powers: Checking Today's Most Dangerous Branch from Within*, 115 Yale L.J. 2314 (2006).

42. 5 U.SC. § 553. Rule making
    (a) This section applies, accordingly to the provisions thereof, except to the extent that there is involved—

The sole statutory definition of our "notice and comment" rule-making, this provision requires only three procedural elements involving the public, each described in very permissive terms.

1. Subject to exceptions for emergencies, in-house matters, and minor details, agencies must give the public advance notice that they are considering adopting a regulation. As defined, the required notice is to be of a very general kind. In addition to indicating the public procedures to be used, the notice must refer to the legal authority claimed to adopt the regulation, and to "*either* the terms *or* substance of the proposed rule *or* a description of the subjects and issues involved." (Emphasis added.)

---

(1) a military or foreign affairs function of the United States; or

(2) a matter relating to agency management or personnel or to public property, loans, grants, benefits, or contracts.

(b) General notice of proposed rule making shall be published in the Federal Register, unless persons subject thereto are named and either personally served or otherwise have actual notice thereof in accordance with law. The notice shall include—

(1) a statement of the time, place, and nature of public rule making proceedings;

(2) reference to the legal authority under which the rule is proposed; and

(3) either the terms or substance of the proposed rule or a description of the subjects and issues involved.

Except when notice or hearing is required by statute, this subsection does not apply—

(A) to interpretative rules, general statements of policy, or rules of agency organization, procedure, or practice; or

(B) when the agency for good cause finds (and incorporates the finding and a brief statement of reasons therefor in the rules issued) that notice and public procedure thereon are impracticable, unnecessary, or contrary to the public interest.

(c) After notice required by this section, the agency shall give interested persons an opportunity to participate in the rule making through submission of written data, views, or arguments with or without opportunity for oral presentation. After consideration of the relevant matter presented, the agency shall incorporate in the rules adopted a concise general statement of their basis and purpose. When rules are required by statute to be made on the record after opportunity for an agency hearing, sections 556 and 557 of this title apply instead of this subsection.

(d) The required publication or service of a substantive rule shall be made not less than 30 days before its effective date, except—

(1) a substantive rule which grants or recognizes an exemption or relieves a restriction;

(2) interpretative rules and statements of policy; or

(3) as otherwise provided by the agency for good cause found and published with the rule.

(e) Each agency shall give an interested person the right to petition for the issuance, amendment, or repeal of a rule.

2. Where such notice is given, it must provide any interested member of the public with an opportunity for written or oral commentary, at the agency's choice. An individual may become an interested person simply by participating in this process; there is no eligibility test. The language suggests that nothing more need be given than an opportunity to volunteer one's own views, in the normal manner of a legislative hearing rather than a judicial trial.

3. Finally, after considering the comments, in adopting a regulation, the agency is to give a "concise general statement of [its] basis and purpose." Congress in adopting this language gave no reason to think it expected more than this quite permissive and undemanding language suggests.

I have written elsewhere how the explosion of rulemaking in the latter part of the 20th Century, accompanying greatly increased health, safety and environmental regulation requiring difficult judgments about risks presented by modern technology, contributed to a transformation of this simple procedure into a much more complex one.[43] As would have surprised the drafters of 1946, notice and comment rulemaking now effectively requires

– Quite detailed indications of the proposal, with the corollary that if the agency is persuaded by comments or other developments to take a course other than that initially proposed, it may have to resubmit the new course as a further proposal for comment. "Logically entailed" is the stated criterion, and reviewing courts are sometimes quite demanding in applying this criterion.

– The agency must reveal the data known to it on which its decisions may be based, so that they as well as the proposal may be commented upon. This development might be viewed as a natural outgrowth of American Freedom of Information legislation,[44] which from the mid-60's dramati-

---

43. Peter L. Strauss, *Statutes that Are Not Static: The Case of the APA*, 14 J. Contemp. Leg. Issues 767 (2005); Peter L. Strauss, *From Expertise to Politics: The Transformation of American Rulemaking*, 31 WAKE FOREST L. REV. 745 (1996).

44. 5 U.S.C. §552. A good general source on the Freedom of Information Act is Patricia M. Wald, *The Freedom of Information Act: A Short Case Study in the Perils of Legislating Democratic Values*, 33 EMORY L.J. 649 (1984).

cally expanded the rights of citizens to have access to information in government possession. However, the Freedom of Information Act does not purport to amend section 553's requirements for rulemaking, and this judicial development of what is in effect a greatly expanded notice requirement is very difficult to square with the way "notice" is defined in the text of that section.

– Perhaps drawing again on the same impulse, the agency must be prepared to identify the full "record" ofitsrulemaking, generallyincluding (as a product ofcommonagency regulations) some account of oral communications informally received as well as the comments filed in the process.

– The "concise general statement of ... basis and purpose" has become, at least for important rulemakings, an elaborate rationale running dozens of pages in length, elaborating the agency's reasoning in general and in reaction to particular comments. Reviewing courts will consider a statement that does not persuasively deal with the most important comments inadequate. Since the "most important comment" category is determined only after the fact, during judicial review sought by those asserting that they were not attentively heard, the agency must effectively anticipate all complaints about its attentiveness to comments that might be made. This contributes greatly to the lengthiness of its explanations.

– Judicial review is generally available immediately upon adoption of the regulation, without having to wait for its enforcement. This obviously permits those who might be directly affected by the rule to seek to postpone (if not to defeat) its application by seeking review. The review may occur on a wider range of issues and at less risk to their enterprises than would be involved if they awaited and then resisted its enforcement. At least as important, however, it also permits review on behalf of people or groups who might think the regulation insufficiently rigorous to protect their interests. These persons could never raise this kind of issue at the enforcement stage.

– Judicial review of a regulation's validity is considerably more rigorous than judicial review of the constitutionality of legislation. This is so whether one is considering the adequacy of its factual underpinning, or the rationality (and explanation) of the judgments it entails. In 1946 no such distinction would have been drawn. The judicial touch for review of regulations as of statutes was light indeed. Now, the two kinds of review are seen as entirely distinct enterprises and the sobriquet for judicial review of important rules is "hard look."

Although our Supreme Court seemed to have decided in 1978 that only those procedural requirements for notice and comment rulemaking that could properly be ascribed to the 1946 Congress could be enforced,[45] all of these developments have in fact survived to the current day. The 1978 opinion is taken as a barrier to the *judicialization* of rulemaking, but *not* to developments that have made its procedures more transparent, and review of its outcomes more balanced and thorough, than the 1946 Congress would have anticipated.

In recent decades, both new statutes and presidential initiatives embodied in executive orders[46] have added to the complexities of rulemaking, at least those rulemakings likely to have a significant economic or other impact.

– A new statutory procedure, more applauded by scholars than used by agencies, envisions the development of rulemaking proposals through a consensual process of mediated discussion among stakeholders, "negotiated rulemaking," rather than by bureaucratic actors alone.[47] To work, the number of discrete stakeholders or their representatives must be relatively few, and their willingness to compromise substantial.

---

45. Vt. Yankee Nuclear Power Corp. v. Natural Res. Def. Council, 435 U.S. 519, 545-46 (1978). Readers are entitled to know that the author, then General Counsel to the United States Nuclear Regulatory Commission, was an author of the government's brief in the case.

46. An Executive Order is a presidential document published in the Federal Register and directed to federal agencies – in effect one of the means by which the President fulfills his responsibility to take care that the laws are faithfully enforced. It is "law" for agencies in the sense that they understand their obligation to comply and may rationalize their actions in its terms, but such an order is rarely if ever judicially enforceable and generally lacks direct force on individuals outside government. Consultation in its development is commonplace, but no statutory procedure controls its promulgation; all that is "required" is the President's signature on a document so designated and submitted to the Government Printing Office for publication. Executive orders are consecutively numbered, now approaching 14,000.

47. Philip J. Harter, *Assessing the Assessors: The Actual Performance of Negotiated Rulemaking,* 9 N.Y.U. Envtl. L.J. 32, 33 ("[N]egotiated rulemaking is a process by which representatives of the interests that would be substantially affected by a rule, including the agency responsible for issuing the rule, negotiate in good faith to reach a consensus on a proposed rule.").

– The Regulatory Flexibility Act, amended by the Small Business Regulatory Enforcement Fairness Act (SBREFA),[48] requires special consideration of the impact of regulations on smaller businesses and of possible adjustment of the requirements imposed on them to accommodate their lesser resources. A subsidiary element, notable for increasing the transparency of pending government action, requires semi-annual publication of a "regulatory agenda" (not unlike the EU Commission's workplans) both giving notice of rulemakings expected to be undertaken and identifying agency contacts with whom interested persons can register any concerns.

– The Unfunded Mandates Relief Act, principally addressed to controlling the phenomenon of federal legislation requiring state expenditures to achieve its ends, without federal subvention, requires identification and special analysis of regulations that require significant private expenditure for their implementation.[49]

– The Electronic Freedom of Information Act,[50] inter alia, directs web implementation of rulemaking procedures. While the governmental response to this is very much a work in progress, inhibited by funding failures and inter-agency rivalries,[51] the notice and comment process is increasingly available by Internet. The Regulatory Agenda mentioned above, and all proposals for rule-making may be found there through a unified, government-wide site; comments may (but need not be) filed electronically; and all the materials of rulemaking – underlying studies, proposals, comments, etc. – are increasingly available through a single federal data management service.

– The Paperwork Reduction Act and its amendments,[52] like E-FOIA and other measures, by assigning certain coordination and control responsibilities to the Office of Information and Regulatory Analysis (OIRA), which is part of the President's Office of Management and Budget (OMB) – the principal bureaucra-

---

48. 5 U.S.C. §§ 801-808 (amending 5 U.S.C. §§ 601-612 (1980)).

49. Unfunded Mandates Reform Act of 1995, Pub. L. No. 104-4, 109 Stat. 48 (codified in scattered sections of 2 U.S.C.).

50. 5 U.S.C. § 552.

51. Achieving the Potential: The Future of Federal E-Rulemaking (ABA Section of Administrative3 Law and Regulatory Practice, 2008).

52. Paperwork Reduction Act of 1980, Pub. L. No. 96-511, 94 Stat. 2812 (1980); Paperwork Reduction Reauthorization Act of 1986, Pub. L. No. 99-500, 100 Stat. 1783-335 (1986); Paperwork Reduction Act of 1995, 44 U.S.C. §§ 3501-3520.

tic body through which the President coordinates executive branch activities[53] –
have in effect accepted the responsibilities the President has given that office to
oversee governmental rulemaking.

– Through a series of executive orders and associated OMB guidance documents – most recently and most prominently E.O. 12,866[54] – the President has
added considerable structure to the period that precedes the publication of a
notice of proposed rulemaking, as well as somewhat complicated the notice and
comment process itself.

- Integrated with SBREFA's Regulatory Agenda, and as amended by
  President Bush in January 2007,[55] the Executive Order requires annual
  development, apparently subject to OIRA approval, of a regulatory plan;
  this occurs under the responsibilityof a "regulatory policy officer" in each
  agency who is to be a presidential appointee. Unless the agency head specifically overrides her judgment, development of a regulation cannot proceed without the approval of the regulatory policy officer. These processes are not transparent. This is one of those elements that, in my judgment, signals significantly increased presidential and political power over
  agency rulemaking.
- Associated with agency choices of their targets for regulation, OMB has
  developed increasingly stringent and detailed guidance on such subjects as
  risk assessment and peer review.[56] Both the instructions and resulting
  agency analyses are public documents; to the extent they invite controversy they extend the rulemaking process, but the transparency involved is
  a public policy benefit.

---

53. For example, executive branch requests for legislation, emphatically including annual
requests for budget appropriations, must be coordinated with and cleared by OMB. It also over-
sees all communications with Congress, such as testimony or commentary on proposed legislation. Its staff, traditionally permanent civil servants but in this instance ones working directly
for and with the White House, oversee management issues from an executive branch perspective (a congressional body, the Government Accountability Office, does the same, independently, from the legislative perspective).

54. Exec. Order No. 12,866, 58 Fed. Reg. 51,735 (Sept. 30, 1993), *amended by* Exec. Order
No. 13,258, 67 Fed. Reg. 9,385 (Feb. 26, 2002) and Exec. Order No. 13,422, 72 Fed. Reg. 2,703
(Jan. 18, 2007).

55. Exec. Order No.13,422, 72 Fed. Reg. 2,703 (Jan. 18, 2007).

56. OFFICE OF MANAGEMENT AND BUDGET, PROPOSED RISK ASSESSMENT BULLETIN (2006),
http://www.whitehouse.gov/omb/inforeg/proposed_risk_assessment_bulletin_010906.pdf;
OFFICE OF MANAGEMENT AND BUDGET, FINAL INFORMATION QUALITY BULLETIN FOR PEER
REVIEW (2004), http://www.whitehouse.gov/ omb/inforef/peer2004/peer_bulletin.pdf.

– Once a particular target for regulation has been chosen, agencies are responsible for analyzing the potential impact of their regulatory proposals along a
variety of dimensions. In addition to statutory requirements to analyze impact
on small business[57] and the environment,[58] executive orders have called for analysis of potential impact on such matters as family values,[59] federalism values,[60] and
the national economy. The last of these is directly controlled by EO 12,866 and
receives the most emphasis. The stringency of OIRA's oversight under EO
12,866 varies considerably with the extent to which such impact is expected.

   - Essentially three categories of regulation are identified, minor, significant,
     and major – the most important identified as regulation likely to impose
     an annual cost of $100,000,000 on the economy, or having some other
     unusual degree of importance for the nation. A few hundred of the seve-
     ral thousand regulations adopted annually fit this description. For them,
     OIRA's requirements for analysis are intense. The result is to produce, in
     effect, variable procedures for notice and comment rulemaking, depen-
     ding on the importance of the initiative involved. This seems a natural
     and welcome outgrowth of the increasing importance of rulemaking.
   - For the more significant regulations, the Executive Order is explicit about
     a number of matters implied in the judicial developments of the preceding
     decades not readily found in the statutory language:
         - that notice of proposed rulemaking should include draft regulatory text;
         - that 60 days should normally be available for comment;
         - that data on which the agency relies must be available for public com-
         ment; and
         - that (via the analysis EO 12,866 independently requires) a relatively
         elaborate explanation of the agency's rationale should be given.

   - Again for significant regulations, the agency's draft analysis of economic
     impact, following detailed guidance that OIRA has provided,[61] must be
     cleared with OIRA before publication of the notice of proposed rule-

57. Small Business Regulatory Enforcement Fairness Act, 5 U.S.C. §§ 801-808 (amending
Regulatory Flexibility Act, 5 U.S.C. §§ 601-612 (1980)).

58. National Environmental Policy Act of 1969 § 102, 42 U.S.C. §§ 4332.

59. Exec. Order No. 12,606, 52 Fed. Reg. 34,188 (Sept. 2, 1987), *revoked by* Exec. Order No.
13,045, 62 Fed. Reg. 19,885 (Apr. 21, 1997).

60. Exec. Order No. 13,132, 64 Fed. Reg. 43,255 (August 4, 1999).

61. OFFICE OF MANAGEMENT AND BUDGET, CIRCULAR A-4, REGULATORY ANALYSIS (2003),
http://www.whitehouse.gov/omb/circulars/a004/a-4.pdf.

making. (The agency must also inform OIRA in a summary way of rules it concludes do not require this treatment, and OIRA has authority to disagree and require the analysis to be done.) This draft analysis is a public document that becomes a part of the rulemaking record, along with certain elements of OIRAcommunications – not aperfectlytransparent process, but considerably more transparent than one finds in respect of other White Houseagency relations. The transparency (along with the professionalism of OIRA staff and the consistently high intellectual qualifications of its leadership, which is subject to senatorial confirmation in office) was a part of the political price the White House understood it must pay for congressional acceptance of the office and its processes.

- Once notice of proposed rulemaking has been published and comments received, the agency must produce a final analysis for clearance by OIRA before adopting a final regulation. This analysis is, again, a public document that becomes a part of the rulemaking record. This process has been the occasion for ostensibly political interference on occasion, when it has become evident OIRA has insisted on changes in regulatory content in respects committed to agency, not presidential, judgment,[62] or has simply refused for months, even years, at a time to clear for release a regulation the agency is ready to issue in final form.[63]

---

62. *See* David C. Vladeck, *Unreasonable Delay, Unreasonable Intervention: The Battle to Force Regulation of Ethylene Oxide*, in Peter L. Strauss, ed., ADMINISTRATIVE LAW STORIES (Foundation Press 2006) (discussing OSHA's delay is issuing ethylene oxide standards, at the direction of OIRA); Gen. Accounting Office, Rulemaking: OMB's Role in Reviews of Agencies' Draft Rules and the Transparency of Those Reviews, GAO-03-929, at 9, http://www.gao.gov/new.items/d03929.pdf (OIRA had an effect on almost a third of the draft rules it reviews and that at OIRA's recommendation, EPA removed manganese from a list of hazardous wastes.); *Waxman Threatens to Cite Johnson With Contempt Over Documents*, INSIDE THE EPA, June 20, 2008, 2008 WLNR 11540109 (EPA administrator Stephen Johnson withholding documents related to the EPA's ozone standard: "Waxman's investigation aims to put a spotlight on the contentious ozone rulemaking, which President Bush personally ordered amended hours before it was due for release."); Letter from Patrick Leahy, Chairman, S. Comm. on the Judiciary, to William A. Roderick, Deputy Inspector General, U.S. Envt'l Prot. Agency (July 25, 2008), *available at* http://leahy.senate.gov/issues/Judiciary/072508LeahyToEPAIG.pdf (asking Roderick to investigate "[w]hether EPA's decision with respect to California waiver from the Clean Air Act was made in accordance with the technical and legal conclusions of its own staff or whether the White House improperly interfered with EPA decision-making")

63. Letter from Henry A Waxman, Chairman, H. Comm. on Oversight and Govt. Reform, to Susan A. Dudley, Administrator, Office of Info. and Regulatory Affairs (Apr. 30, 2008), http://oversight.house.gov/documents/20080430103958.pdf. ("for over a year, the Office of

– Under the Congressional Review Act, legislation adopted during the Clinton administration shortly after the Republicans won control of both houses of Congress for the first time in decades, major regulations cannot be effective before Congress has had a limited period in which to consider disapproving them.[64] To be effective, however, a resolution of disapproval must meet the procedural requirements of legislation – it must be passed in identical form by both houses and then signed by the President. This has happened only once, during the transition from the Clinton to the Bush administration, when the President asked to sign the resolution of disapproval was different from the President in office when the regulation was adopted. It is unlikely to happen under other political circumstances.

From this lengthy resume of changes to the simple model of notice and comment rulemaking given by Section 553, it is possible to extract some present-day issues facing American notice and comment rulemaking.

In the judicial arena, a number of Supreme Court Justices (not yet a majority) and some scholars have expressed doubts about doctrinal developments of previous decades that have given those *favoring* regulation access to the courts comparable to that enjoyed by those to whose behavior regulations are directed. These developments include the availability of pre-enforcement review, permissive standing requirements, and a willingness to find somewhat abstract questions "ripe" for judicial review. The current intensity of review and its availability at an early stage is thought to have brought about the "ossification" of agencyrulemaking– overly elaborate, time-consuming and expensive rulemaking procedures, and excruciatingly long (emphatically not "concise general") statements of basis and purpose. Some also ascribe to this ossification an increasing agency reliance on less formal

---

Information and Regulatory Affairs has blocked the National Marine Fisheries Service from issuing a rule to protect [right] whales from being killed by ships. According to documents obtained by the Committee, the rule's delay appears to be due to baseless objections by White House officials.")

64. 5 U.S.C. § 801; *See* Daniel Cohen & Peter L. Strauss, *Congressional Review of Agency Regulations*, 49 ADMIN. L. REV. 95 (1997).

means of making policy – e.g., guidance or other forms of soft law – rather than rulemaking.

The rejoinders to these concerns are numerous: that ossification is a reflection of the importance of rulemaking; that it is in general limited (as one may concede it should be limited) to the highconsequence rules that are most in public view; that ossification these days can be laid at least equally at thefeet of theexecutiveoversight provisions like EO 12,866, about the general soundness of which there seems overall acceptance; that close attention and lengthy processes are warranted for regulations that have a large impact on the economy or particular industries; and that the twosided review possible *only* with pre-enforcement review and broad "standing" rules has advantages far outweighing its costs. Knowing that the statement of basis and purpose will be closely examined in relation to the information and views in the rulemaking record, as plangently remarked by a former EPA official, arms those within the agency who care about reasoned decision-making (i.e., acts of judgment) with a weapon with which to influence those who do not (i.e., prefer acts of will).[65] Knowing that a regulation may be reviewed for doing too little to protect public interests, as well as for doing too much to interfere with private ones, is an antidote to the capture that can result from, as James Landis once put it, the machine-gun impact of daily encounters with the regulated.[66]

Legislatively, the largest challenge would be a rerationalization of rulemaking to consolidate – and at the same time could hopefully simplify – many of the developments that have occurred. Procedures for rulemaking, and perhaps the occasions for an intensity of judicial review as well, should vary with the importance of the regulation

---

65. William F. Pedersen, Jr., *Formal Records and Informal Rulemaking*, 85 YALE L.J. 38, 59 (1975).

66. Staff of Subcomm. on Administrative Practice and Procedure to the Senate Comm. on the Judiciary, 86th Cong., Report on Regulatory Agencies to the President-Elect, at 71 (1960) (written by James M. Landis) ("The daily machinegun-like impact on both agency and its staff of industry representation that makes for industry orientation on the part of many honest and capable agency members as well as agency staffs.").

involved. Rulemaking is not legislation; it suffers correspondingly from a "democracy deficit." Such a deficit *not* cured by the attentions of an elected President acting behind closed doors and perhaps on behalf of undisclosed interests. Rather, as Judge Harold Leventhal once cogently put it, it is compensated for by a level of transparency it its formation, and by a judicial review considerably more intense than legislation ever undergoes.[67]

The mind-numbing variety of requirements that now apply in rulemakings, even the most important, needs to be pared down and simplified.[68] The "impact analysis" rubric has been with us now since the 1970's, when "environmental impact analysis" was first required as a legislative matter. Now, in addition to this and the economic impact analysis of EO 12,866, we have federalism impact, risk assessment, and regulatory flexibility, to name only the most prominent. Some – economic impact perhaps especially – pretend to an objectivity of analysis that is no better than a chimera.[69] Careful, forward thinking policy analysis, to can help single-mission agencies rise above a narrowly focused perspective – to think outside the box – is important. Its intensity should properly vary with the importance of the undertaking. Both full transparency and proper resources (monetary and management) for its performance and oversight must be assured. On the other hand, a false precision, institutional arrangements that threaten to empower the exercise of covert political will over judgment, and a welter of poorly articulated "impact" concerns, should be avoided.

Careful attention needs to be paid to the developing world of e-government. Transferring rulemaking documentation from paper to the Internet promises great gains in transparency and accessibility. But care must be taken to assure uniform practice, universal deposit of documents, ready searchability, and effec-

---

67. Ethyl Corp. v. EPA, 542 F.2d 1, 68 (D.C. Cir. 1976) (Leventhal, J., concurring:)

68. Mark Seidenfeld, *A Table of Requirements for Federal Administrative Rulemaking*, 27 FLA. ST. U.L. REV. 533, 536 (2000).

69. Sidney A. Shapiro & Christopher H. Schroeder, *Beyond Cost-Benefit Analysis: A Pragmatic Reorientation*, 31 Harv. Envtl. L. Rev. (forthcoming 2008).

tive management. Congress to date has been sparing of both the funds that could permit this and attention to effective management approaches. Development has been troubled in consequence.

Having a great volume of material available on-line and thus widely accessible could transform rulemaking in either (or both) political or judicial directions. On the political side, one now sees the possibility of e-mail campaigns in which rulemaking comes to be seen as a kind of plebiscite, one subject to all the distortions "grass roots" uses of the Web are prey to. Judges may be tempted by these developments to impose a more adversarial view of rulemaking. Having comments filed by others available on the Internet (that is, not simply as paper submissions simultaneously made to a Washington bureau and consequently hard to access, read and index) will multiplythe occasions for demanding an opportunity to respond – not currently an element of the process. Judges, tempted by their internalized preferences for the model of trials, may agree, making the procedure more adversarial. Either development would strike this author as undesirable, although very possible.

Better treatment and integration of the pre-notice period might permit some response to these issues. When the Commission of the European Union develops legislative proposals, the author found,[70] it uses a comment-like process at an early stage to develop its information base, assess political temperatures, and the like. That kind of approach, not unlike the idea behind "negotiated rulemaking" in America, permits the more flexible development of proposals, ones that are likely to reflect consensus and developed technical knowledge. The regulatory agenda and regulatory plans, our analogy to the work plans of the EU's DGs, need to be better integrated into the electronic resources and other elements of contemporary rulemaking; they need to become more transparent in their management and less subject to simple political interference.

For our new President, the issues are primarily those of reestablishing the line between "will" (simple power politics) and judgment. We have rationalized the creation of regulations by agencies, rather

---

70. Peter L. Strauss, *Rulemaking in the Ages of Globalization and Information: What America Can Learn From Europe, and Vice Versa,* 12 COLUM. J. EUR. L. 645 (2006).

than legislation by Congress, on the understanding that regulations are made transparently, in accordance with legislative standards, and under close judicial supervision for their rationality. Covert conversations with the White House, the introjection of presidential agents within agencies who (without legislative sanction) are ostensibly handed control of the rulemaking apparatus, the frequent bending of science to political ends,[71] presidential insistence on deciding matters Congress has assigned to the judgment of expert agencies – all these developments threaten our rule-of-law culture. If our new President could find a way back to oversight as an administrative rather than a political activity, he might possiblystem this tide. Impact analysis, including its attention to the front end of regulatory planning, needs to continue; but its susceptibility to political intrigue must somehow be cabined.

The "regulatory policy officer" element of Executive Order 12,866, added by President Bush in 2007, can perhaps serve as an illustration of the contending views and fears about these issues. Recall that he newly empowered these subordinate officials to control rulemaking activities, diminishing the ostensible connection between them and their agency superior and increasing White House control over them. The White House, for its part, has been insistent that this is merely a minor step to more effective management, one that does not alter the political balance between the bureaucracy of the agencies and the politicians of the executive branch. Others, including the author, have seen this as another reflection of the strong "unitary President" theory of the current administration, with its hazards to the place of law in regulation. The House of Representatives has now twice voted to denyfunding to the activities of the regulatory policy officers, apparently finding them an opaque source for implementing political judgments of the White House and distorting expert bureaucratic judgments. The first of these legislative efforts failed when a Senate committee removed the proposed statutory language without explanation or public discussion. The Senate action followed a concerted lobbying effort by industrial interests; a White House offi-

71. THOMAS O. MCGARITY & WENDY E. W AGNER, BENDING SCIENCE: HOW SPECIAL INTERESTS CORRUPT PUBLIC HEALTH RESEARCH (2008).

cial also argued to the Senate that such an action would prevent the President from exercising his inherent constitutional authority to control the executive branch as our "unitary executive." Of course, what the Constitution says is that no money may be spent by the government without a congressional appropriation to support it, and those who wrote the Constitution understood perfectly well that the power of the purse was the means by which the English Parliament had brought that country's chief executive, a pretender to inherent absolute power, under control. The official's claim, then, was laughable. At this writing, the House again has before it a measure that would prohibit the use of government money to support regulatory policy officers;[72] the outcome this time around is not clear.

III. GUIDANCE AND OTHER FORMS OF SOFT LAW

"Soft law" is a common phenomenon in any developed legal culture. Statutes and regulations invariably leave room for interpretation and discretion. This is perhaps especially the case when (as currently in the United States) it is thought preferable for the legal obligations of regulated industry to be expressed in general terms giving standards to be met (ends to be achieved), rather than as precise courses of conduct to be followed ("command and control"). Using standards rather than rules leaves room for the regulated to find the most efficient means of meeting the legal demands on its conduct. Absent considerations of morality, this is the course more consistent, as well, with human freedom.

If it is better for a manufacturer be told that it must achieve given levels of pollution control rather than told precisely what machinery to use, however, we can also expect the manufacturer to seek and value official guidance about means of doing so that government officials may already have determined will suffice to reach the proper levels. This does not exclude initiative to find a better way, but for those who perhaps lack the resources for such research it gives an assurance

---

72. "House Panel Trying Again to Block Spending On Bush-Appointed Regulatory Policy Officers," BNA DAILY REPORT FOR EXECUTIVES, July 1, 2008, p. A-17.

how to comply with their legal obligations. When I was General Counsel to the Nuclear Regulatory Commission, an entire bureau of the agency was charged with producing this kind of guidance about nuclear safety issues, where performance standards had been set by regulation. The regulations were adopted by the Commission itself; but the guidance documents were informally produced by staff, often in close discussions with those affected, under only the most general supervision of the Commissioners. The volume of guidance vastly exceeded the volume of regulations. One can find the same relationships at the Federal Aviation Administration, the Food & Drug Administration, or virtuallyanyhealth-safety-environmental regulatorattemptingto regulateby providing standards to be met rather than precise courses of conduct to be followed.

Soft law created in the form of instructions to staff also provides some assurance of regularity in the behavior of government officials, benefitting both the regulated and agency leadership. If an agency depends on inspectors to accomplish its responsibilities in the field, both the agency's leadership and those whose premises get inspected will value the existence of instructions helping the instructors understand how they are to perform their duties. "Staff manuals" and similar instructions are public documents. Although not directly enforceable in judicial actions against street-level bureaucrats, they provide frameworks for citizen expectation, for management discipline, and for non-judicial correction of deviations.

Soft law also usefully emerges when the regulated seek governmental advice about proposed courses of conduct. How a given item is to be treated by customs officials, whether certain activities must be considered work time under federal fair labor legislation, what should be the tax treatment of various transactions, how a regulation of the National Highway Transportation Safety Administration requiring automobiles to contain airbags will be interpreted – these are all matters about which citizens may ask for government advice. If the public then can readily learn about this advice, it can influence their behavior. In the Information Age, such advice is widely available to the public; indeed, government officials are strongly encouraged – if not legally required – to make it present and readily searchable. And this seems normatively the better course, both as an enhancement of transparency and as a discouragement to covert favoritism or even corruption. While, again, one expects regularity of behavior and these developments encourage it, it would be excessive to make such advice, if given, a precedent enforceable on future occasions. That consequence would make officials refuse to advise, or at the least require elaborate bureaucratic clearances before doing so.

All this has been true for many years. With the increasing complexity of notice-and-comment rulemaking procedures, however, another element appears to have entered the picture: agencies using soft law in an effort to accomplish what one might expect to have been accomplished by the adoption of regulations. That is, as rulemaking becomes more "expensive," it appears that agencies have attempted to accomplish their ends at lower cost to themselves, where that seemed possible.[73] I have written extensively in another place about these developments, urging the importance of finding a means of preserving the valuable contributions soft law makes to legality while perhaps controlling these abuses.[74] Here it may suffice to note several ways in which the contrasts between regulations and soft law have been dealt with in recent American legal developments.

– When an agency adopts a *regulation* embodying a certain view of its constitutive statue, courts reviewing that view follow a regime that has become known as the *Chevron*[75] twostep. Initially they determine, independently (albeit with appropriate attention to all the traditional tools for ascertaining legislative meaning, which can of course include some respect for the manner in which responsible officials have treated

---

73. The FDA, for instance, reduced the number of regulations it adopted by fifty percent from the early 1980s to the mid-1990s. During this same time period there was a corresponding dramatic increase in the number of guidance documents issued by the FDA– in the 1990s, the FDA released four times as many guidance documents per year than in the previous decade. See Todd. D. Rakoff, *The Choice Between Formal and Informal Modes of Administrative Regulation,* 52 ADMIN. L. REV. 159, 167-68 (2000).

74. Peter L. Strauss, *Publication Rules in the Rulemaking Spectrum: Assuring Proper Respect for an Essential Element,* 53 ADMIN. L. REV. 803 (2001).

75. Chevron U.S.A., Inc. v. Natural Resources Defense Council, 467 U.S. 837 (1984).

it) whether the meaning assigned by the agency is a *possible* meaning, one that the language can support. Here one may say they are acting as "deciders" of a statutory issue. After concluding that the assigned meaning is a possible one, however, they become not deciders but overseers; the question at the second step is whether the particular meaning that the agency has assigned is a reasonable one – it being presumed that Congress has assigned that task to the agency. Courts are responsible to control the agency action for reasonableness, but they are also to respect the primary authority Congress has conferred on the agency.[76]

Now suppose, however, that the agency reaches its interpretation not by adopting a regulation, but by some form of "soft law." The agency is no longer exercising a delegated authority to "make law," following defined public procedures. In a more recent case, *United States v. Mead Corp.*,[77] the Court essentially limited its *Chevron* approach to cases in which it could be seen that an agency was acting to make law following the means that Congress had designated for the purpose. In the "soft law" context (*Mead* itself involved relatively informal advice about the customs treatment of certain imports), the government's view could be no more than a weight on the scales of an irreducibly judicial judgment, and the extent of that weight would depend on the variety of considerations that might make the agency view persuasive.[78] I find this contrast reasonable and easy to understand, but a reader of American legal literature would be astounded to find the extent to which *Chevron, Mead,* and other cases following on them are the subject of continuing and quite intricate dispute.[79]

---

76. Peter L. Strauss, *Overseers or "The Deciders": The Courts in Administrative Law*, 75 U. CHI. L. REV. 815 (2008).

77. 533 U.S. 218 (2001).

78. Skidmore v. Swift & Co., 323 U.S. 134, 140 (1944) ("The weights [an agency's] judgment in a particular case will depend upon the thoroughness evident in its consideration, the validity of its reasoning, its consistency with earlier and later pronouncements, and all those factors which give it power to persuade, if lacking power to control.").

79. See, e.g., JERRY L. MASHAW , GREED, CHAOS AND GOVERNANCE (Yale Univ. Press 1999); Cynthia R. Farina, *Statutory Interpretation and the Balance of Power in the Administrative*

– Suppose the soft law involved is an agency interpretation, not of a statute but of the agency's own regulations – a situation that the introductory remarks to this section may persuade the reader is both inevitable and desirable. Long established judicial doctrine accords such interpretations extraordinary force; they must be accepted unless demonstrably unreasonable – outside the possibilities of the regulatory language, or the like.[80] If one is thinking in terms of the locus of both responsibility and knowledge, this makes eminent sense. But it perhaps also creates a perverse incentive for agencies. When Congress legislates, delegating authority to an agency, it knows that it is giving up substantial power over future uses of that authority; this knowledge gives it an incentive to legislate as precisely and as fully as it can. But when an agency adopts a regulation that it may later interpret, it is giving up no such power. Some have seen in this reality an encouragement to "promulgate mush," as one appellate judge colorfully put it, and then interpret and reinterpret these indefinite regulations as the occasion warrants, secure in the knowledge that possible interpretations will have to be accepted by a reviewing court.[81]

How to respond to this unfortunate incentive? Professor John Manning has powerfully argued that the long established doctrine must be abandoned, as inconsistent with American ideas about separation of powers.[82] In its place, one should substitute an approach like

---

State, 89 COLUM. L. REV. 452 (1989); Jonathan T. Molot, *The Judicial Perspective in the Administrative State: Reconciling Modern Doctrines of Deference with the Judiciary's Structural Role*, 53 STAN. L. REV. 1 (2000); Cass. R. Sunstein, *Law and Administration After Chevron*, 90 COLUM. L. REV. 2071 (1990); Peter L. Strauss, *One Hundred Fifty Cases Per Year: Some Implications of the Supreme Court's Limited Resources for Judicial Review of Agency Action*, 87 COLUM. L. REV. 1093 (1987); Peter L. Strauss, *Overseers or "The Deciders": The Courts in Administrative Law*, 75 U. CHI. L. REV. 815 (2008).

80. Bowles v. Seminole Rock & Sand Co., 325 U.S. 410, 414 (1945) ("the ultimate criterion is the administrative interpretation, which becomes controlling weight unless it is plainly erroneous or inconsistent with the regulation."); Thomas Jefferson Univ. v. Shalala, 512 U.S. 504 (1994) , Auer v. Robbins, 519 U.S. 452 (1997).

81. Paralyzed Veterans of Am. v. D.C. Arena L.P., 117 F.3d 579, 584 (D.C. Cir. 1997).

82. John F. Manning, *Constitutional Structure and Judicial Deference to Agency Interpretations of Agency Rules*, 96 COLUM. L. REV. 612, 682-83 (1996).

that of *Mead.* The Court of Appeals for the District of Columbia, the country's premier administrative law court, has adopted a "one bite" rule – that a regulation once interpreted may not be reinterpreted without fresh notice and comment rulemaking. But one can see that this may substitute inappropriate rigidity for inappropriate flexibility, and other courts (including, it appears, the Supreme Court)[83] have accepted the possibility of reinterpretationin the same "soft law" form as the original. In my judgment, memorialized in the piece mentioned in beginning these observations about guidance,[84] the better approach is to treat all soft law interpretations, whether of statutory or regulatory commands, in the respectful butindependentmanner commanded by *Mead.* Additionally, one can imagine a court saying to an agency more readily than it could to Congress (for political reasons) that the agency had not been sufficiently diligent in creating the regulation being interpreted – that more detail was required for the regulation itself to be valid. This would respond to the "promulgate mush" issue, but one could fear it would open an inappropriate avenue for adventurous judges to insert their own politics; and to date no significant move in this direction appears in the cases.

– Another troublesome issue that has arisen with some frequency in the D.C. Circuit, less in other courts, responds to the perception that agencies are using soft law in circumstances that require regulations – i.e., the use of notice and comment procedures. When as a practical matter guidance will direct private conduct, that court has characterized it as "binding" – that is, as having the force of law and therefore requiring the procedures used to create regulations: notice and comment procedures. This approach imperils not only evasive but also beneficial uses of soft law. An agency must fear that every time it uses soft law that might influence private conduct, there is the risk that a court will think the influence so great as to require formal procedures.

---

83. Shalala, 512 U.S. at 515.

84. Peter L. Strauss, *Publication Rules in the Rulemaking Spectrum: Assuring Proper Respect for an Essential Element,* 53 ADMIN. L. REV. 803 (2001).

Two regrettable consequences ensue. First, agencies become much more reluctant to give advice, creating realms of secret "law" and depriving the public of the regularity that attends knowing how an agency expects it to act. Second, when they do give advice, agencies may announce that their advice cannot be relied upon, in an effort to protect themselves from being told the advice required notice-and-comment rulemaking procedures.[85] Why would one wish either of these outcomes?

Almost all of the cases requiring the use of notice and comment procedures rather than soft law, in my judgment, could as readily have been decided on their substantive merits. That is, the cases could usually have been resolved not on the grounds of procedural insufficiency, but more simply on the ground that the existing body of regulations and statutes did not support the guidance being given. The likely influence of the advice on private conduct should be taken as a signal, not that more rigorous procedure is required for giving it, but rather that judicial review of the merits of the advice is appropriate. The analogy would be to declaratory judgment procedures, or the regular practice of pre-enforcement review of regulations discussed above. Courts have tended to deny, however, that "proper" guidance is "final agency action," or action "ripe" for judicial review – two characterizations required for judicial review to be obtained. Then only the

---

85. Appalachian Power Co. v. E.P.A., 208 F.3d 1015, 1022 (D.C. Cir. 2000) ("the elements of the Guidance petitioners challenge consist of the agency's settled position, a position it plans to follow in reviewing State-issued permits, a position it will insist State and local authorities comply with in setting the terms and conditions of permits issued to petitioners, a position EPA officials in the field are bound to apply."). One may contrast the announcement posted on the web site of the National Highway Transportation Safety Administration: "NHTSA's Chief Counsel interprets the statutes that the agency administers and the regulations that it promulgates. The Chief Counsel's interpretations, issued in the form of letters responding to questions from the motor vehicle industry and the public, represent the definitive view of the agency on the questions addressed and may be relied upon by the regulated industry and members of the public. Besides being accessible online, these interpretations are also available to the public in the agency's technical reference library in Washington." http://www.nhtsa.dot.gov/portal/site/nhtsa/menuitem.4d1e17245efafde89ec0f210dba046a0/ This is a desirable outcome; but it runs the risk of having the interpretations characterized as "binding" and consequently requiring notice and comment procedures for their adoption.

grounds of procedural insufficiency remain. Some cases have seen their way past these barriers in an intelligent way, [86] however. In my judgment, this approach poses much less of a threat to continued use of a regulatory tool that, as discussed above, often has very great value to the public as well as to agency leadership.

– Much healthier responses to "soft law" issues have been emerging in recent years. Agencies have often engaged those who will be affected by soft law in discussions about it – an informal adaptation of "notice and comment" procedures without the elaborations of recent years. For the Food and Drug Administration, "Good Guidance practices" of this order have been statutorily required.[87] OMB has been administratively encouraging such practices for all significant guidance, establishing guidelines for federal agencies to follow when creating and disseminating important guidance.[88] Part of these guidelines state that agencies must provide easy access to a list of all of an agency's significant guidance documents in electronic form. Through the Internet, then, much data about agency views is readily available through a brief computerized search that years ago might have required hours of expensive professional time to discover, perhaps less reliably.

In addition to its contestable politicizing provisions, such as the heightened powers given regulatory policy officers, President Bush's recent amendments to EO 12,866, EO 13,422, not only established the requirements just mentioned, nailing down the accessibility of this important information, but also added major guidance documents to the list of agency actions requiring impact analysis procedures. The general reaction to these aspects of the order, in comparison with the others already mentioned, has been quite favorable.

---

86. See National Automatic Laundry & Cleaning Council v. Shultz, 443 F.2d 689 (D.C. Cir. 1971); Floersheim v. Weinburger, 346 F. Supp. 950, 954-55 (D.D.C. 1972).

87. 21 U.S.C. § 371(h).

88. Guidelines for Ensuring and Maximizing the Quality, Objectivity, Utility, and Integrity of Information Disseminated by Federal Agencies, 67 Fed. Reg. 369 (Office of Mgmt. and Budget, Jan. 3, 2002).

Even such slight and readily justified measures, of course, impose costs of time and resources on agencies that are increasingly challenged to find the means with which to fulfill their statutory mandates. Budgetary stringencies and the increasing complexity and sensitivity of tasks agencies are asked to accomplish give what appear to be sound policy development measures like these as well as those concerning risk assessment or peer review of scientific judgments in the regulation context – a double edge. In the different context of mass programs for individual benefits, commentators have written of the need to find "flivver"[89] justice, where the "Rolls Royce" model is unsustainable. The same challenges exist here.

89. A flivver is an aging automobile, that was probably quite cheap even when new – a Citröen 2 CV, for example.

CHAPTER VIII

THE DEVELOPMENT OF GERMAN APA'S STANDARD PROCEDURE: TOWARDS A COMPREHENSIVE PROCEDURAL CONCEPT*

Jens-Peter Schneider*

* Professor, University of Osnabrück, Germany.

INDEX

I thank my research assistant *Andreas Tiedge* for his extremely helpful draft translation of this paper's German version.

I

ADMINISTRATIVE PROCEDURE AS AN INFORMATION AND COMMUNICATION SYSTEM TO IMPLEMENT AND DEVELOP THE LAW

P UBLIC administrations are social systems processing information, acting communicatively and making decisions under a primarily rule-based structure.[1] Their decisions and actions become reality through administrative procedures. From a legal point of view, administrative procedures are a flexible mode of implementing administrative law which allows for creativity by the administrator, because their abstract rules are often not self-executing. Instead, administrative law statutes must be supplemented by specific rules and applied to particular cases by public administrations. Depending upon the extent of the discretion vested in the administration, procedures can range from a strictly determined application of the law to an important medium for concrete creation of law.[2] Thus, administrative actions even in individual cases do not only implement legislative decisions but may also take part in developing the law. In the German legal literature this creative aspect of implementation or development is called "legal concretizing." In strictly determined application of the law, the legislature has prescribed a particular result. In the case of legal concretizing, the administrative procedure determines its own result.

---

1. RAINER PITSCHAS, VERWALTUNGSVERANTWORTUNG UND VERWALTUNGSVERFAHREN: STRUKTURPROBLEME, FUNKTIONSBEDINGUNGEN UND ENTWICKLUNGSPERSPEKTIVEN EINES KONSENSUALEN VERWALTUNGSRECHTS 28(1990).

2. Rainer Wahl, *Verwaltungsverfahren zwischen Verwaltungseffizienz und Rechtsschutzauftrag*, in 41 VERÖFFENTLICHUNGEN DER VEREINIGUNG DER DEUTSCHEN STAATSRECHTSLEHRER [VVDStRL] 151 *passim* (1983); Eberhard Schmidt-Aßmann, *Der Verfahrensgedanke im deutschen und europäischen Verwaltungsrecht* in II GRUNDLAGEN DES VERWALTUNGSRECHTS [II GlVwR] § 27 note 65 (Hoffmann-Riem et al, eds., 2008), ; GUNNAR FOLKE SCHUPPERT, VERWALTUNGSWISSENSCHAFT 794 (2000); HERMANN HILL, DAS FEHLERHAFTE VERFAHREN UND SEINE FOLGEN IM VERWALTUNGSRECHT 282 (1986).

In dynamic societies featuring a division of labor and complex social systems, substantive law becomes less determinative in certain important and technical areas, ceding way to administrative law. Administrative procedure law therefore acquires functions for democratic legitimation of the exercise of state power. This tendency is enhanced by replacing concrete legal programming with statutes setting rather abstract objectives and goals and thereby reducing the possibilities of judicial control.[3]

Characterizing procedure law as functionally auxiliary for the realization of substantive administrative duties does not imply any disregard for its relevance. To the contrary, it actually reveals administrative procedure law's substantive weight.[4] Speaking of administrative procedure law as auxiliary is only problematic when that term indicates a generally subordinate position in regard to substantive law.[5]

Administrative procedure concretizes and develops law by reaching decisions. Administrative decisions may differ in their nature. According to § 9[6] of the German Administrative Procedure Act of 1976 (APA)[7] the statutory standard procedure applies only to decisions about

---

3. Wahl 158 *passim, supra* note 2; SCHUPPERT 805 *passim, supra* note 2; also Franz Reimer, *Das Parlamentsgesetz als Steuerungsmittel und Kontrollmaßstab*, in I GRUNDLAGEN DES VERWALTUNGSRECHTS § 9 note 84 *passim* (Hoffmann-Riem, et al, eds., 2006); Hoffmann-Riem, *Eigenständigkeit* in I GlVwR§ 10 note 56 *passim;* HEIKE JOCHUM, VERWALTUNGSVERFAHRENSRECHT UND VERWALTUNGSPROZESSRECHT: DIE NORMATIVE KONNEXITÄT VON VERWALTUNGSVERFAHRENS- UND VERWALTUNGSPROZEßRECHT UND DIE STEUERUNGSLEISTUNG DES MATERIELLEN VERWALTUNGSRECHTS (2004).

4. *See* Federal Constitutional Court [Bundesverfassungsgericht – BVerfG] in: Neue Zeitschrift für Verwaltungsrecht [NVwZ] 1041 *passim;* Neue Juristische Wochenschrift [NJW] 2613 (2006).

5. Schmidt-Aßmann, *Verfahrensgedanke*, in II GLVwR § 27 note 64 *supra* note 2.

6. APA § 9: "Definition of administrative procedure: For the purposes of this Act, administrative procedure shall be the activity of authorities having an external effect and directed to the examination of basic requirements, the preparation and adoption of an administrative act or to the conclusion of an administrative agreement under public law; it shall include the adoption of the administrative act or the conclusion of the agreement under public law."

7. Verwaltungsverfahrensgesetz [VwVfG], I Federal Law Gazette [Bundesgesetzblatt – BGBl.] 102 (2003), as amended by Act of May 5th, 2004 Art. 4 (8) I BGBl 718 (2004). For a translation of the German APA as at July 1st, 2004 into English see: http://www.bmi.bund.de/

the issuance of administrative acts in concrete and individual cases as defined in APA § 35[8] as well as about concluding public law contracts pursuant to APA § 54[9]. Nevertheless, the scope of legal scholarship ought not to be limited to such a narrow understanding of administrative procedure when taking a systematic approach to administrative law[10]. Although they do not fulfill the requirements set by the statutory definition of the term "administrative procedure" in APA § 9,[11] decisions concerning administrative rule-making and planning, concluding private law contracts, and simple disbursements are equally significant. Agency-devised ways of cooperatively reconciling conflicting interests are similarly important elements of administrative procedure. New processes primarily aimed at generating knowledge for the administration stem from the realization that a growing number of administrative decisions can only be made in a state of uncertainty about their legal basis as well as their consequences[12]. These processes are only latently connec-

---

Internet/Content/Common/Anlagen/Gesetze/Gesetze__Sprachen/VwVfg__en,templateId=ra w,property=publicationFile.pdf/VwVfg_en.pdf. All translations in the footnotes of this article have been taken from this source.

8. APA § 35: "Definition of an administrative act: An administrative act shall be any order, decision or other sovereign measure taken by an authority to regulate an individual case in the sphere of public law and intended to have a direct, external legal effect. A general order shall be an administrative act directed at a group of people defined or definable on the basis of general characteristics or relating to the public law aspect of a matter or its use by the public at large."

9. APA § 54: "Admissibility of an agreement under public law: A legal relationship under public law may be constituted, amended or annulled by agreement (agreement under public law) in so far as this is not contrary to legal provision. In particular, the authority may, instead of issuing an administrative act, conclude an agreement under public law with the person to whom it would otherwise direct the administrative act."

10. Eberhard Schmidt-Aßmann, *Das Allgemeine Verwaltungsrecht als Ordnungsidee*, in GRUNDLAGEN UND AUFGABEN DER VERWALTUNGSRECHTLICHEN SYSTEMBILDUNG Ch. 6 note 48 (2nd ed., 2004), *see also* Wolfgang Hoffmann-Riem, *Verwaltungsverfahren und Verwaltungsverfahrensgesetz – Einleitende Problemskizze*, in, VERWALTUNGSVERFAHREN UND VERWALTUNGSVERFAHRENSGESETZ 9, 51 *passim* (Hoffmann-Riem & Schmidt-Aßmann eds., 2002).

11. *See supra*, note 6.

12. *Detailed in this regard*: Hans Christian Röhl, *Ausgewählte Verwaltungsverfahren*, in II GlVwR § 30 note 24, *supra*, note 2.

ted to actual decision-making. Nonetheless, they should be included in any evaluation of the administrative process; their production of knowledge is related to the administrative state, not an end in itself.

"All law is concerned with interests. Consequently, interests are a basic category of legal thinking."[13] This also holds true for administrative procedure because one of its functions is to develop law. Administrative procedure is supposed to balance public and private interests. It must particularly be able to engage in balancing when facing multipolar and multidimensional constellations of interests. In such cases, public administration cannot simply execute one party's interests. It has to optimize the interests of all persons concerned with the case according to the law.[14]

Balancing interests requires information. Information is necessary to spot all legally relevant interests in a case, and to identify each legitimate and permissible way of dealing with them. From a strictly decision-oriented point of view, administrative procedure can thus be understood as a structured process of choice between different alternatives through acquiring and processing information.[15] It often takes place under the auspices of large administrative agencies. Although some matters may be decided individually, any specific clerk's decision

---

13. Eberhard Schmidt-Aßmann, *Zur Reform des Allgemeinen Verwaltungsrechts: Reformbedarf und Reformansätze*, in REFORM DES ALLGEMEINEN VERWALTUNGSRECHTS 37 (Hoffmann-Riem et al, eds. 1993),

14. Wolfgang Hoffmann-Riem, *Ökologisch orientiertes Verwaltungsverfahrensrecht: Vorklärungen*, in 119 ARCHIV DES ÖFFENTLICHEN RECHTS [AöR]. 590, 593 *passim* (1994); Jens-Peter Schneider, *Kooperative Verwaltungsverfahren: Problemebenen der Kooperation in multilateralen Interessenstrukturen, aufgezeigt am Beispiel von Nachvollziehender Amtsermittlung, Vorhaben- und Erschließungsplan sowie Konfliktmittlung*, in 87 Verwaltungsarchiv [VerwArch] 38 *passim* (1996); Friedrich Schoch, *Der Verfahrensgedanke im allgemeinen Verwaltungsrecht: Anspruch und Wirklichkeit nach 15 Jahren VwVfG*, in 25 DIE VERWALTUNG (DV) 21 *passim* (1992); concerning the general problem of protection of interests via procedural law, *see* MATTHIAS SCHMIDT-PREUß, KOLLIDIERENDE PRIVATINTERESSEN IM VERWALTUNGSRECHT: DAS SUBJEKTIVE ÖFFENTLICHE RECHT IM MULTIPOLAREN VERWALTUNGSRECHTSVERHÄLTNIS (2nd ed., 2005).

15. See Schmidt-Aßmann Ch 6, note 47, *supra* note 10; *see also* Christoph Gusy, *Die Informationsbeziehungen zwischen Staat und Bürger*, in II GlVwR § 23 Rn. 33 *passim, supra*, note 2.

is not that clerk's responsibility but is ascribed to the agency as a whole. Accordingly, other members of the agency, particularly high-ranking superiors, can exert influence on individual decisions during the process.[16] Under modern-day conditions, information and communication technologies also play an increasingly important part, albeit an implicit and subtle one.[17] Administrative procedure law may neither disregard the influence of such technologies[18] nor underestimate the power of individual clerks in decision-making.[19]

To fulfill its informational function, administrative procedure law requires predecisional communication between actors inside and outside of public administration.[20] Administrative procedures do not provide unlimited opportunities for communication. Instead, they are selectively restricted to prearranged, legally relevant topics, actors and times of communication.[21] Despite these strict limitations, however, the goals which structure administrative procedure — particularly the bipolar objectives of efficiency and legal protection — should not be forgotten in structuring communications.[22] A balance between the democratic, legitimate, and effective advancement of public welfare on

---

16. Concerning the structure of such interior administrative procedures *see* Jens-Peter Schneider, *Strukturen und Typen von Verwaltungsverfahren*, in II GlVwR § 28 note 107 *passim supra*, note 2.

17. *See Gabriele Britz*, II GlVwR § 26 note 59 *supra*, note 2.

18. Detailed in this regard: Thomas Vesting, *Die Bedeutung von Information und Kommunikation für die verwaltungsrechtliche Systembildung*, in II GlVwR § 20 note 2 *passim*.

19. *See* Pitschas 30, 35, 47 *supra*, note 1; *see also* Winfried Brohm, *Die Dogmatik des Verwaltungsrechts vor den Gegenwartsaufgaben der Verwaltung*, in 30 VERÖFFENTLICHUNGEN DER VEREINIGUNG DER DEUTSCHEN *STAATSRECHTSLEHRER [VVDStRL] 245, 286 (1972)*.

20. *Jan Ziekow, Der Einfluss des neuen Steuerungsmodells auf das Verwaltungsverfahren und seine gesetzliche Regelung*, in VERWALTUNGSVERFAHREN UND VERWALTUNGSVERFAHRENS-GESETZ 349 *passim* (Hoffmann-Riem & Schmidt-Aßmann eds., 2002); Hill 210 *passim*, *supra* note 2; HUFEN, FEHLER IM VERWALTUNGSVERFAHREN note 46 (4th ed. 2002); Schmidt-Aßmann Ch 6 note 47, *supra* note 10; *see also* Matthias Schmidt-Preuß, *Gegenwart und Zukunft des Verfahrensrechts*, in NVwZ 489, *supra*, note 4.

21. Gusy *Informationsbeziehungen*, II GlVwR § 23 note 33, *supra*, note 15.

22. Wahl *Verwaltungsverfahren*, 153 *passim*, *supra*, note 2; Schuppert, *Verwaltungswissenschaft*, 801 *passim*, *supra* note 2; Schmidt-Aßmann, *Verfahrensgedanke*, in II GlVwR § 27 note 85 *passim*, *supra*, note 2.

one side and the legal protection guaranteed as a fundamental right[23] on the other must be found. The acceptance and analysis of comments and assistance in the information gathering process may not always be undertaken from a merely efficiency or efficacy point of view.[24] Administrative procedure serves the purpose of articulation as well as information-gathering.[25] In the context of public notice and comment procedures, the traditionally subjective understanding of procedural legal protection in Germany is currently in a state of transition. Due to the influence of European law, a movement towards objectively-granted legal protection, not requiring subjective standing as a condition of rights protection, is becoming significant in some areas of administrative law. This new concept becomes apparent in broad public participation in the administrative process.

The goal of information gathering is linked to the other functions of administrative procedure. First of all, administrative procedure coordinates complex and intricate government components by allocating different levels of consultation rights to them[26] (coordinatory function). Second, cooperative administrative procedure fulfills complicated administrative duties by integrating public and private procedural contributions in cooperative procedures[27] (integration function). Finally, converting the hearts and minds of both the regulated industry and the public or to gain acceptance by all parties for the decision at the end of the procedure is an increasingly important procedural function in controversial areas such as environmental law and risk regulation.[28]

---

23. German Basic Law Art. 19 (4) (Grundgesetz für die Bundesrepublik Deutschland - GG), (1949) Federal law gazette (Bundesgesetzblatt - BGBl.) III no. 100-1, as last amended by Act of August 28th, 2006, I BGBl 2034, *supra*, note 7.

24. *Regarding the constitutional requirements for administrative procedural law see* Schmidt-Aßmann, *Verfahrensgedanke*, in II GlVwR § 27 note 31 *passim*, *supra*, note 2.

25. Schmidt-Preuß, *Verfahrensrecht*, in NVwZ 489, *supra*, note 4.

26. Schneider, *Strukturen und Typen*, in II GlVwR § 28 note 91 *passim*, *supra*, note 16.

27. *Idem* § 28 note 38; *see also* SCHUPPERT 810 *passim*, *supra* note 2.

28. Hoffmann-Riem 29, *supra*, note 10; SCHUPPERT, *Verwaltungswissenschaft*, 815 *passim*, *supra*, note 2; Thomas Würtenberger, *Akzeptanz durch Verwaltungsverfahren*, in Neue Juristische Wochenschrift [NJW] 257 *passim* (1991).

II
SELECTED MODIFICATIONS OF THE STANDARD PROCEDURE ACCORDING TO APA

A. INTRODUCTION

WHEN examining the myriad objectives of agencies through the lens of institutional design,[29] some German legal scholars question administrative procedure law's ability to fulfill its goals. The APA serves as the primary resource for this endeavor. Conceptually, the APA's underlying procedural principle can be described as classical rule-based and hierarchical administration.[30] Eberhard Schmidt-Aßmann identified its typical features as follows:[31]

– Command and control administration;

– Unilateral decisions about particular cases;

– Aiding in the implementation of substantive administrative law;

– Firmly defined procedural roles: citizens as defenders of their rights seeking protection of legitimate expectations on one side, and administrative authorities solely committed to furthering public interests on the other;

– Disregard of the internal structures and heterogeneities of multi-level and multipolar administrations in national federations as well as within the EC.

---

29. *See* Andreas Voßkuhle, *The reform approach in the German Science of Administrative Law: The "Neue Verwaltungsrechtswissenschaft,"* in THE TRANSFORMATION OF ADMINISTRATIVE LAW IN EUROPE 89 (Ruffert ed., 2006).

30. On this Weberian conceptualisation of public administration, *see* Jens-Peter Schneider, *Regulation and Europeanisation as Key Patterns of Change in Administrative Law*, 309, *supra*, note 29.

31. Schmidt-Aßmann, *Verfahrensgedanke*, II GlVwR § 27 Rn. 13, *supra* note 2; Schmidt-Aßmann, *Verwaltungsverfahren und Verwaltungsverfahrensgesetz: Perspektiven der System-bildung*, in VERWALTUNGSVERFAHRENSGESETZ 430 *passim, supra*, note 10.

– In spite of these constraints, the standard procedure according to APA § 9 et seq. serves as the starting point for all systematic evaluations of administrative law today, including this paper. In addition, several key modifications of standard procedure codified in the APA and leges speciales will be broken down into elements, which will provide a basis for the development of a comprehensive administrative procedure concept.[32]

The German APA includes rules for only some particular phases of administrative procedure. This narrow scope has to be abandoned, though, when assessing administrative procedure from a general perspective. Instead, all procedural legal thinking must consider the broad reach of and the lack of functional limits on administrative procedure. In particular, *preliminary* proceedings such as concept design must be included. The same applies for *post-decisional* phases such as decision control, decision enforcement, decision monitoring and - consecutively - decision alteration or annulment by the administration itself.[33]

B. PRELIMINARY PROCEEDINGS

According to APA § 22,[34] the commencement of administrative proceedings calls for a discretionary decision by an agency unless the

---

32. For a detailed analysis *see* Schneider Strukturen und Typen, in II GlVwR § 28 *passim*, *supra*, note 16. Further insight can be generated by a comparison with EU and member states' administrative procedural law. Due to space restraints, an in-depth analysis like this cannot be made in this publication. The fundamental research necessary for this is yet to be rendered; for England, Spain and the Netherlands see the contributions in I VERWALTUNGSRECHT IN EUROPA (Jens-Peter Schneider ed.,. 2007). The forthcoming second volume will contain corresponding presentations for France, Poland and the Czech Republic. *See also* Schmidt-Aßmann, *Verfahrensgedanke*, in II GlVwR § 27 note 18 *passim, supra*, note 2.

33. Schmidt-Aßmann, *Ordnungsidee*, Ch. 6 note 158 *passim, supra,* note 10; *see also* Karl A. Bettermann, *Das Verwaltungsverfahren*, in 17 VERÖFFENTLICHUNGEN DER VEREINIGUNG DER DEUTSCHEN STAATSRECHTSLEHRE (VVDStRL), 118 *passim* (1959).

34. APA § 22: Commencement of proceedings: The authority shall decide after due consideration whether and when it is to instigate administrative proceedings. This shall not apply when the authority by law:

law requires that agency to act *ex officio* or upon application. In exercising discretion, administrative authorities generally act *ex officio* and according to the principle of expediency. These provisions highlight the amount of control over administrative procedure that is vested in administrative agencies. Furthermore, their prevalence in administrative procedure technically distinguishes it from all court proceedings, including those in the area of administrative law. In reality, though, administrative authorities are oftentimes prompted to institute proceedings ex officio, by other administrative agencies or even private citizens. Allowing private parties to rouse agencies to action can tap new reserves of information and increase attention to the interests of the public.[35] In spite of their possible impact, private communications and lawsuits were not taken into account during the drafting of the APA, or during the addition of later amendments.

Preparation for the formal institution of administrative procedure is not regulated by the APA as well. While the lack of formal structure for preparatory processes might be acceptable when dealing with mere factual acts (acts which do not create binding precedent, as, for example, when the agency or public administration distributes informational literature), it certainly is not when facing more complex subjects. There is a demand for the precise structuring and ordering of administrative procedure, and for citizens to be given advice well in advance and extensively informed about the scope and nature of regulation.

Such deliberations did not, however, find their way into the APA until 1996. In licensing procedure, APA § 71c[36] defines today the administration's prepara-

---

1. must act *ex officio* or upon application;
2. may only act upon application and no such application is submitted.

35. *See also* Gusy, *Informationsbeziehungen,* inII GlVwR § 23 note 69 *passim* , *supra,* note 15.

36. APA § 71c: Special provisions governing formal proceedings before committees:
(1) If the formal administrative procedure takes place before a committee (section 88), each member shall be entitled to put relevant questions. If a participant objects to a question, the committee shall decide as to the question's admissibility.
(2) Only committee members who have attended the oral hearing may be present during discussions and voting. Other persons who may attend are those employed for training

tory duties.[37] On a more general level, rights to disclosure and information prior to applying for admission to a profession have been recognized as basic rights by the courts.[38] The goal of information provision was to guarantee equal opportunities, especially in regard to Art. 12 of the German Basic Law, *i.e.*, freedom of profession. Whether the increasing number of freedom of information acts on both the federal and the state level will play an equally important role remains to be seen.[39]

Several areas of administrative law feature further specific preliminary requirements, for example, according to the principle of investigation, the information to be gathered by the administrative procedure may be decided in advance. Often, the purpose of these requirements is to to condition the subsequent exercise of discretion in administrative procedure.

One can see this limitation at work in environmental law, where mandatory scoping is used to structure and focus fact-finding. "Scoping," the technical term for the community process of determining which issues will be addressed in the environmental impact assessment, is used to establish the analytical frame for environmental impact assessment[40] and strategic environmental assessment.[41]

---

purposes by the authority forming the committee, subject to the chairman's approval. The results of the voting must be recorded.

(3) Any participant may reject a member of the committee who is not entitled to take part in the administrative proceedings (section 20) or who may be prejudiced (section 21). A rejection made before the oral hearing must be explained in writing or recorded. The explanation shall not be acceptable if the participant has attended the oral hearing without making known his reasons for rejection. Decisions as to rejection shall be governed by section 20, paragraph 4, second to fourth sentences.

37. The authorities are supposed to give advice to as well as consult with future applicants in order to accelerate proceedings. Possible acceleratory measures are accumulated in APA § 71 (2) in the form of a check-up list.

38. Federal Administrative Court [Bundesverwaltungsgericht – BverwG], Die Öffentliche Verwaltung [DÖV] 121 *passim.* (2004)

39. *See* Schneider, *Strukturen und Typen*, in II GlVwR § 28 note 58 *passim, supra*, note 16.

40. Environmental Impact Assessment Act § 5 [Umweltverträglichkeitsprüfungsgesetz – UVPG],I BGBl,1757, 2797 (2005), as last amended by Act of October 23rd, 2007 Art. 2 I BGBl 2470 (2007). *See, in this regard,* JENS-PETER SCHNEIDER, NACHVOLLZIEHENDE AMTSERMITTLUNG BEI DER UMWELTVERTRÄGLICHKEITSPRÜFUNG – ZUM VERHÄLTNIS ZWISCHEN DEM

One can also see the power of structuring administrative decisions in public procurement law, where particularly complex contracts must be finalized in great detail before final competitive bids are submitted.[42] Finally, German telecommunications law demands a hearing of all parties involved before starting either bidding procedures for awarding frequencies.[43]

Beyond the above statutory provisions, informal preliminary procedures and negotiations are commonly used to prepare formal procedures. Such practices are problematic under the rule of law due to the factual precommitments made and the powerful influence of these preliminary negotiations on the final decision. The courts nevertheless accept them under certain circumstances:[44] informal dealings must be warranted by the facts, the competent authorities must be involved in the negotiations, and their considerations must lead to passable results. All in all, the subsequent "formal" procedure may not become

---

PRIVATEN TRÄGER DES VORHABENS UND DER ZUSTÄNDIGEN BEHÖRDE BEI DER SACH-VERHALTSERMITTLUNG NACH DEM UVPG 142 *passim* (1991).

41. Environmental Impact Assessment Act § 14f; *see in this regard* Reinhard Hendler, *Das Gesetz zur Einführung einer Strategischen Umweltprüfung*, in NVwZ 977 *passim*, *supra* note 4.

42. *See* Art. 29 directive 2004/18/EC of March 31st 2004 on the coordination of procedures for the award of public works contracts, public supply contracts and public service contracts, (2004) Official Journal of the European Union, L 134, 114, 135; *in this regard see* Matthias Knauff, *Neues europäisches Vergabeverfahrensrecht: Der wettbewerbliche Dialog*, in Vergaberecht [VergabeR] 287 *passim* (2004).

43. *See* Telecommunications Act § 61 (1) (1) [Telekommunikationsgesetz – TKG] I BGBl.) 190 (2004), as last amended by Act of December 21st, 2007 Art. 2, I BGBl 3198 (2007).

44. *See* Michael Fehling, *Informelles Verwaltungshandeln*, in II GlVwR § 38 note 69 *passim*, *supra* note 2; FEHLING, VERWALTUNG ZWISCHEN UNPARTEILICHKEIT UND GESTALTUNGS-AUFGABE 316 *passim* (2001); *see also* FERDINAND O. KOPP & ULRICH RAMSAUER, VERWALTUNGSVERFAHRENSGESETZ: KOMMENTAR [VwVfG:K],Intro. note 96 (9th ed., 2005); Rainer Wahl, *Die Einschaltung privatrechtlich organisierter Verwaltungseinrichtungen in den Straßenbau*, in DVBl 517 *passim* (1993); Wolfgang Hoffmann-Riem, *Selbstbindungen der Verwaltung*, in 40 VVDStRL 187 *passim* (1982); EBERHARD BOHNE, DER INFORMALE RECHTSSTAAT: EINE EMPIRISCHE UND RECHTLICHE UNTERSUCHUNG ZUM GESETZESVOLLZUG UNTER BESONDERER BERÜCKSICHTIGUNG DES IMMISSIONSSCHUTZES 144 *passim* (1981); from the judicature, *see also* Federal Administrative Court, 45 Entscheidungen des Bundesverwaltungsgerichts (BVerwGE), 309 *passim*.

a mere empty hull. Flexible compensation arrangements are another potential solution in these circumstances. The level of scrutiny in judicial review would then depend on the degree of compensational participation in the "formal" procedure and on how well procedural transparency (*i.e.*, documentation etc.) was maintained.[45]

All of these considerations do not detract from the basic statutory concept of instituting procedures on set occasions in order to reach certain decisions. What does knock holes in this principle, though, is an increasing number of investigative or surveillance procedures initiated on a scheduled, regular basis, independent of any specific occasion.[46] These procedures are not directed specifically towards an administrative decision; instead, their goal is the mere accumulation of information. Nonetheless, they are latently connected with the decisional procedures this paper focuses on. Information gathering can have considerable repercussions as it offers easily accessible and public information about aspects which tended to play a subordinate role in administrative decision-making due to lack of information.

For example, environmental surveys occur independent of a specific cause in air pollution control, noise reduction and landscaping plans.[47] Due to recent EC law influences, in the future such surveys will have to be conducted more often and more in-depth than in the past. In EC financial law, systematic finance control procedures concerning EC structural funds are initiated independently of specific causes as well.[48] It can lead to the institution of concrete financial correc-

---

45. *Detailed in this regard, see* Fehling, *Unparteilichkeit*, 325 *passim, supra* note 16.

46. *For a detailed analysis of these types of procedures, see* Röhl *Verwaltungsverfahren*, in II GlVwR § 30 note 40 *passim, supra* note 12; *see also* Schneider, *Strukturen und Typen*, in II GlVwR § 28 note 155 *passim, supra* note 16,

47. *Regarding the following details, see* Ulrich Stelkens, *Von der umweltgerechten zur umweltbestimmten Planung*, in Natur und Recht [NuR] 362 *passim* (2005).

48. *More detailed in this regard, see* Jens-Peter Schneider, *Verwaltungsrechtliche Instrumente des Sozialstaates*, in 64 VVDStRL 238, 262 *passim*; Bettina Schöndorf-Haubold, *Gemeinsame Europäische Verwaltung: die Strukturfonds der Europäischen Gemeinschaft*, in, DER EUROPÄISCHE VERWALTUNGSVERBUND 25, 45 *passim* (Schmidt-Aßmann & Schöndorf-Haubold eds., 2005); RUDOLF MÖGELE, DIE BEHANDLUNG FEHLERHAFTER AUSGABEN IM FINANZIERUNGSSYSTEM DER GEMEINSAMEN AGRARPOLITIK 108 *passim* (1997).

tion proceedings. Further examples for systematically initiated proceedings can be found in food control[49] and tax procedure.[50]

C. COOPERATIVE FACT FINDING

In conceptualizing procedure as a process of predecisional information gathering and processing,[51] fact-finding becomes a major topic of procedural legal thinking. APA §§ 24, 26[52] establish an inquisitorial

---

49. Jens-Peter Schneider, *Vollzug des Europäischen Wirtschaftsrechts zwischen Zentralisierung und Dezentralisierung – Bilanz und Ausblick*, in Europarecht [EuR], supplement 2, 149 (2005).

50. *See* Schneider, *Strukturen und Typen*, in II GlVwR § 28 note 164 *passim*, *supra* note 16.

51. *See supra* I.

52. APA § 24: "Principle of investigation:
(1) The authority shall determine the facts of the case ex officio. It shall determine the type and scope of investigation and shall not be bound by the participants' submissions and motions to admit evidence.
(2) The authority shall take account of all circumstances of importance in an individual case, including those favourable to the participants.
(3) The authority shall not refuse to accept statements or applications falling within its sphere of competence on the ground that it considers the statement or application inadmissible or unjustified";
APA § 26: "Evidence:
(1) The authority shall utilise such evidence as, after due consideration, it deems necessary in order to ascertain the facts of the case. In particular it may:
  1. gather information of all kinds,
  2. hear the evidence of participants, witnesses and experts or gather statements in writing or electronically from participants, experts and witnesses,
  3. obtain documents and records,
  4. visit and inspect the locality involved.
(2) The participants shall assist in ascertaining the facts of the case. In particular they shall state such facts and evidence as are known to them. A more extensive duty to assist in ascertaining the facts, and in particular the duty to appear personally or make a statement, shall exist only where the law specifically requires this.
(3) Witnesses and experts shall be obligated to make a statement or furnish opinions, when the law specifically requires this. When the authority has called upon witnesses and experts, they shall receive compensation or remuneration upon application in accordance with the appropriate provisions of the Judicial Remuneration and Compensation Act (Justizvergütungs- und -entschädingungsgesetz, JVEG)."

model of fact-finding for standard procedure. Thereby, private party participants shall have no steering or controlling powers regarding the factual context established in the investigation.[53] APA § 26 merely leaves them the opportunity to assist the administration in finding the relevant facts. Unless specifically provided for, the administration also cannot ensure that private party participants deliver this sort of assistance. The lack of assistance by private party participants can therefore only function as an excuse for defective fact-finding on the part of the administration in certain circumstances.

Specific administrative law often departs from this basic model. It upgrades participatory opportunities to obligations forming major structural components of cooperative administrative procedure. This is particularly common in application requirements prior to receiving public benefits. A basic model for this can be found in §§ 60 et seq. of the Social Code part I[54]. It features context-specific contributory obligations[55]. The boundaries of these obligations derive from the principle of proportionality. The negative consequences of failing to comply are arranged in a clearcut way. There are also incentive provisions which include discretionary retroactive grants of benefits when the private entity finally complies with its contributory obligations.

Non-distributive administrative law provides further examples: German taxpayers, for instance, are supposed to give full particulars about any facts possibly leading to tax liability.[56] Environmental law adds a further dimension to contributory obligations. Environmental impact assessment, for example, has privatized parts of the fact-finding-process in such a way that the applicant needs to

---

53. Schneider, *Nachvollziehende Amtsermittlung* II GlVwR 92, *supra* note 12.

54. ERSTES BUCH SOZIALGESETZBUCH – ALLGEMEINER TEIL [SGB I] I BGBl 3015 (1975), as last amended by Act of December 19th, 2007 Art. 2 (15), I BGBl 3024 (2007).

55. For a detailed analysis See Ralf Kreikebohm & Friedrich v. Koch, *Das Verhältnis zwischen Sozialleistungsempfängern und Sozialleistungsträgern*, in SOZIALRECHTSHANDBUCH 298 *passim* (3rd ed., v. Maydell & Ruland eds., 2003).

56. Abgabenordnung (AO) § 90, (2002) I BGBl. 3866 (2002; I BGBl. 61 (2003), as last amended by Act of April 8th, 2008 Art. 4, I BGBl. 666 (2008). For a detailed annotation *see* Hans B. Brockmeyer, in Klein (ed.), ABGABENORDNUNG (8th ed., Klein ed., 2003).

supply information even on relevant issues outside his own sphere. This obligation is not limited to issues advantageous to the applicant's goals, but includes all
environmental impacts potentially conflicting with his or her plan.

However, the necessary willingness to cooperate is both present
and risky due to the taxpayers' and applicants' inevitable incentive to
provide a convenient, which may ultimately mean incomplete, depiction of the facts. This may undermine administrative authorities'
objective of being comprehensively informed when deciding cases.
Additionally, third party citizens' legal interests – eventually constitutionally protected as basic rights – in equal taxation and protection
from harmful environmental impacts can be affected. These problems can be solved in part by preliminary procedures structuring and
concretizing the private obligations in a context-specific way and by
providing for the necessary regulatory investigations by public
authorities (reconstructive inquisitorial fact-finding).[57] When facing
multipolar procedural situations, cooperative fact-finding supported
by mediation can become an option as well.[58] It is particularly able to
safeguard administrative neutrality and thus suits complex circumstances well. Readjustments based on third parties' opportunities to
participate in later procedural phases play an important role in any
case.

D. THIRD PARTY AND PUBLIC PARTICIPATION

The APA's standard procedure is bipolar in principle. It focuses on
the relationship between administrative agencies on the one hand and

---

57. *More detailed in this regard, see* Schneider, *Nachvollziehende Amtsermittlung*, 117 *passim*,
supra note 12.

58. Schneider, *Kooperative Verwaltungsverfahren 61*, *supra* note 14; Hermann Pünder, *"Open
Government leads to Better Government"* – *Überlegungen zur angemessenen Gestaltung von
Verwaltungsverfahren, in* NuR 72 *passim*, *supra* note 47.

regulated entities or private partners in public law contracts on the other. It does not, however, reflect the reality of many types of administrative actions.

For instance, requesting the police to intervene against creators of legally relevant hazards is directly aimed at stopping them. Being addressees of such administrative acts does, however, automatically make the perpetrators procedural parties.

More complex problems arise under the traditional doctrine when public administration makes decisions that merely collaterally affect third parties. Several possibilities come to mind: the least critical are procedures yielding parallel impacts.

Examples for these are co-benefits deriving from promotive actions towards third parties[59] or co-injuries deriving from interventions against them.[60] More problematic are conflict-laden situations such as applications for building or emission permits affecting third parties negatively.[61] This field needs to be segmented once more into small scale, manageable conflicts such as construction conflicts in the neighborhood, as in zoning and building regulation, and large scale conflicts with heightened repercussions, as are typical in environmental management.

Administrative procedure law reacts to each of these factual relationships in diverse ways. These range from claiming a violation of subjective rights for granting participatory rights over allowing all interested persons and interest groups to participate to finally letting the whole public take part. German law traditionally pursues a very

---

59. *E.g.*, employees and business partners of subsidized corporations.

60. *E.g.*, family members in case of expulsion of an alien.

61. *For an empirical study, see* Sybille Stöbe, *Verhandeln und Argumentieren als Kommunikationsstrategien (in) der Verwaltung: Die staatliche Mittelinstanz in der Umweltpolitik*, in VERHANDELN UND ARGUMENTIEREN: DIALOG, INTERESSEN UND MACHT IN DER UMWELTPOLITIK 183 *passim* (v. Prittwitz ed., 1996),

62. *See* Schneider, *Strukturen und Typen*, in II GlVwR § 28 note 86 *passim, supra*, note 16.

narrow approach in this respect. Judicial review is limited to a small number of claimants. This limitation stems from a classic subjective view of legal protection and from statutory minimization of invalidation due to procedural defects. Both of these traditions have nowadays come under pressure as EU and international public law increasingly influence national administrative law.[62]

In environmental law, for instance, the Aarhus Convention demands participation opportunities for all of the public involved as well as comprehensive legal protection. Despite the clear intent of the convention, several important voices in the German political debate pled for a minimalist implementation of these provisions. Some even tried to control public participation by substituting representatives of the public in order to accelerate and tighten procedures. Other proposals include partially abandoning investigatory hearings.[63]

In the background of these fragmented legal developments and discussions lies a profound conflict about the actual function of third party or even public participation.[64] Often it is reduced to a mere source of antecedent individual legal protection and an extension of administrative knowledge. Such a view does not just overlook the potential to foment popular and commercial acceptance through participation, it also fails to utilize possibly immense sources of democratic legitimation for administrative decisions. This failure is even more regrettable in situations where administrative decisions are not strictly determined by statutory law. In order to realize the potential of third party participation, the concept of democratic legitimation of administrative action must be extended.[65] Of course, the democratic function of third party and public participation complements rather

---

63. *Idem* § 28 note 83.

64. *See also* ANDREAS FISAHN, DEMOKRATIE UND ÖFFENTLICHKEITSBETEILIGUNG (2002).

65. *See* Hans-Heinrich Trute, *Die demokratische Legitimation der Verwaltung*, in I GlVwR § 6 note 15; *see also* JENS-PETER SCHNEIDER, BERUFLICHE SCHULEN ALS STIFTUNGEN MIT TEIL-PRIVATISIERTEN LEITUNGSGREMIEN: ANFORDERUNGEN DES DEMOKRATIEPRINZIPS UND DES GEBOTS STAATLICHER SCHULAUFSICHT 38 *passim* (2004).

than supersedes its traditional functions of rights protection and information gathering.

E. CONSULTATION OF OTHER ADMINISTRATIVE AGENCIES AND INTERNAL PROCEDURAL GRADUATION (THE STAGES OF ADMINISTRATIVE PROCEDURE)

The responsible administrative agency and all participants are subject to standard procedure[66] according to APA § 13.[67] The administrative agency presiding over the procedure is characterized by APA § 9, 1 (4)[68] as affecting the outside world when performing public duties.

---

66. For a detailed analysis, see Frank Alpert, *Zur Beteiligung am Verwaltungsverfahren nach dem Verwaltungsverfahrensgesetz des Bundes: Die Beteiligtenstellung des § 13 Abs.*, in 1 VwVfG, *supra*, note 7.

67. APA § 13: "Participants:
    (1) Participants shall be:
        1. those making and opposing an application,
        2. those to whom the authority intends to direct or has directed the administrative act,
        3. those with whom the authority intends to conclude or has concluded an agreement under public law,
        4. those who have been involved in the procedure by the authority under paragraph 2.
    (2) The authority may ex officio or upon request involve as participants those whose legal interests may be affected by the result of proceedings. Where such result has a legal effect for a third party, the latter may upon request be involved in the proceedings as a participant. If the authority is aware of such third parties, it shall inform them that proceedings have commenced.
    (3) A person who is to be heard, but is not a participant within the sense of paragraph 1, does not thereby become a participant."

68. *See* APA § 1, *supra* note 6.
    "(1) This Act shall apply to the administrative activities under public law of the official bodies:
        1. of the Federal Government and public law entities, institutions and foundations operated directly by the Federal Government,
        2. of the Länder and local authorities and other public law entities subject to the supervision of the Länder where these execute federal legislation on behalf of the federal authorities, where no federal law or regulation contains similar or conflicting provisions.
    (2) This Act shall also apply to the administrative activities under public law of the authorities referred to in paragraph 1, no. 2 when the Länder of their own authority execute fede-

The statutory allocation of substantive and procedural jurisdiction is decisive; departures from these allocations are strictly sanctioned.[69] Administrative agencies that are merely consulted internally, for instance, are not classified as "parties" to the administrative procedure, thereby lacking procedural rights. According to § 13 (3), they also lack procedural rights. In accordance with the APA's procedural concept, they are only alluded to marginally in the provisions relating to standard procedure.[70] APA § 71d and 71e[71] for the first time established the participation of other administrative authorities in 1996. The goal of adding these provisions was to accelerate complex authorization procedures by permitting all administrative agencies involved[72]

---

ral legislation within the exclusive or concurrent powers of the Federal Government, where no federal law or regulation contains similar or conflicting provisions. This shall apply to the execution of federal legislation enacted after this Act comes into force only to the extent that the federal legislation, with the agreement of the Bundesrat, declares this Act to be applicable.

(3) This Act shall not apply to the execution of federal law by the Länder where the administrative activity of the authorities under public law is regulated by a law on administrative procedure of the Länder.

(4) For the purposes of this Act "authorities" shall comprise any body which performs tasks of public administration."

69. Hermann Pünder, *Verwaltungsverfahren*, in ALLGEMEINES VERWALTUNGSRECHT § 13 note 2 (13th ed., Erichsen/Ehlers eds., 2006).

70. Heinz J. Bonk & Heribert Schmitz, in VwVfG:K § 13 note 6, *supra* note 44; *See also* Winfried Kluth, in II VERWALTUNGSRECHT: EIN STUDIENBUCH § 59 note 54 (6 th ed., Wolff et al. eds., 2000).

71. APA § 71d: "Concurrent procedure:

(1) Where it is necessary to involve public agencies in an approval procedure, the competent authority shall gather the opinions of such agencies concurrently, where this is feasible and warranted, and especially where this is requested by the applicant, and shall set a time limit for reporting (concurrent procedure).

(2) Any comments made after expiry of the time limit shall be disregarded, unless the matters raised are already or should already have been known to the approving authority or have a bearing on the legality of the decision."

APA § 71e: "Application conference: At the request of the applicant, the authority shall convene a meeting to include all other parties affected by the application as well as the applicant."

72. *Regarding the determination and differentiation of these agencies, see* JAN ZIEKO & THORSTEN SIEGEL, GESETZLICHE REGELUNGEN DER VERFAHRENSKOOPERATION VON

participate at the same time in so-called "Sternverfahren," in which the structure of the administrative procedure stands out like a star.[73] Technically, this entails a cooperative, albeit not necessarily legally binding procedural arrangement. All administrative agencies involved are to meet for one comprehensive conference dealing with the requests received.

Consultation rights of other administrative agencies thus mainly depend on the specific administrative statute applicable in each case. Specific administrative statutes generally distinguish between non-binding, merely advisory statements and hearings on the one hand and compulsory consent requirements binding the presiding authority on the other. Provisions requiring consent yield a merely internal grad-uation of procedure. Externally, the citizen still faces a unitary and exclusively competent presiding administrative authority.[74] Cons-truing mandatory consent as an internal act makes independent hear-ings before resolution of a statement unnecessary.[75] This may lead to imperfectly informed administrative agencies deciding whether to agree. Procedural discretion, however, leaves room for flexible, appro-priate ways of dealing with such lack of information like informal hear-ings for instance. To improve the quality of such decisions, this discre-tion ought to be utilized accordingly[76].

BEHÖRDEN UND ANDEREN TRÄGERN ÖFFENTLICHER BELANGE: EMPIRISCHE UNTERSU-CHUNGEN MIT RECHTLICHEN EINFÜHRUNGEN (2001).

73. "Star procedure," used figuratively because of the amount of rays going out from a star.

74. Besides this, German administrative law also includes several instances of external procedu-ral graduation. These feature independent decision-making on each stage, e.g. in granting par-tial licenses (Teilgenehmigung) and advance notices (Vorbescheid). *See* Schneider, *Strukturen und Typen*, in II GlVwR § 28 note 102, *supra* note 16.

75. *Critical in this respect* Klaus Lange, *Innenrecht und Außenrecht*, in, REFORM DES ALLGE-MEINEN VERWALTUNGSRECHTS 307 *passim* (Hoffmann-Riem et al. eds., 1993).

76. Lange, *Innenrecht und Außenrecht* 314 *supra* note 47, *prefers a general analogy to the hea-ring requirement of APA § 28.*

F. INTERNAL PROCEDURE PREPARING FINAL
EXTERNAL DECISIONS

A decision by the administration is necessary to terminate procedures; it presupposes an internal administrative decision-making process within the competent agency. Albeit closely connected functionally to the inter-agency consultation procedures mentioned above, this decision-making process is not to be confused with them. Their close connection can be observed particularly well when former parts of administrative agencies, having assumed an existence of their own outside the traditional ministerial hierarchy, begin to overpromote the specific public issues they are responsible for in the government's decision making process.[77]

The APA only deals with internal predecisional procedures where they become apparent in external procedural acts.[78] Exclusion of biased officials, observing time limits for rulings as in APA § 48 (4),[79]

---

77. *See* Lange, *Innenrecht und Außenrecht*, 321, *supra* note 75.

78. HILL, *Das fehlerhafte Verfahren*, 286 *passim, supra* note 2.

79. APA § 48: "Withdrawal of an unlawful administrative act:

(1) An unlawful administrative act may, even after it has become non-appealable, be withdrawn wholly or in part either retrospectively or with effect for the future. An administrative act which gives rise to a right or an advantage relevant in legal proceedings or confirms such a right or advantage (beneficial administrative act) may only be withdrawn subject to the restrictions of paragraphs 2 to 4.

(2) An unlawful administrative act which provides for a one-time or continuing payment of money or a divisible material benefit, or which is a prerequisite for these, may not be withdrawn so far as the beneficiary has relied upon the continued existence of the administrative act and his reliance deserves protection relative to the public interest in a withdrawal. Reliance is in general deserving of protection when the beneficiary has utilised the contributions made or has made financial arrangements which he can no longer cancel, or can cancel only by suffering a disadvantage which cannot reasonably be asked of him. The beneficiary cannot claim reliance when:

1. he obtained the administrative act by false pretences, threat or bribery;

2. he obtained the administrative act by giving information which was substantially incorrect or incomplete;

3. he was aware of the illegality of the administrative act or was unaware thereof due to gross negligence.

In the cases provided for in sentence 3, the administrative act shall in general be withdrawn with retrospective effect.

and considering the results of official hearings are some examples of the internal predecisional procedures that the APA requires. Most important, though, is adequate reasoning and format for the decision. The control-oriented perspective typical for jurisprudence narrows itself even more in this case, focusing merely on the decision's presentation, rather than its production.[80] The internal process used to reach the decision is only judicially evaluated in cases where the alleged procedural defects are not harmless in nature. Although predecisional processes are not an absolutely unregulated part of administrative practice, the judiciary only actually reviews them in a very select number of cases. Naturally, a strong focus on the presentation of administrative decisions leads to increased rationality during decision-making procedures as well.[81] But that is an indirect effect.

Extreme selectivity in judicial review of predecisional process has its advantages. It leads to legal stability, yet it also enables democratically legitimized chief officers to flexibly tackle any challenges the

---

(3) If an unlawful administrative act not covered by paragraph 2 is withdrawn, the authority shall upon application make good the disadvantage to the person affected deriving from his reliance on the existence of the act to the extent that his reliance merits protection having regard to the public interest. Paragraph 2, third sentence shall apply. However, the disadvantage in financial terms shall be made good to an amount not to exceed the interest which the person affected has in the continuance of the administrative act. The financial disadvantage to be made good shall be determined by the authority. A claim may only be made within a year, which period shall commence as soon as the authority has informed the person affected thereof.

(4) If the authority learns of facts which justify the withdrawal of an unlawful administrative act, the withdrawal may only be made within one year from the date of gaining such knowledge. This shall not apply in the case of paragraph 2, third sentence, no. 1.

(5) Once the administrative act has become non-appealable, the decision concerning withdrawal shall be taken by the authority competent under section 3. This shall also apply when the administrative act to be withdrawn has been issued by another authority."

80. *Regarding the differentiation between decision production and presentation,* see NIKLAS LUHMANN, RECHT UND AUTOMATION IN DER ÖFFENTLICHEN VERWALTUNG: EINE VERWALTUNGSWISSENSCHAFTLICHE UNTERSUCHUNG 51 *passim* (1966); Wolfgang Hoffmann-Riem, in SOZIALWISSENSCHAFTEN IM ÖFFENTLICHEN RECHT 8 *passim* (Hoffmann-Riem ed., 1981); *detailed in this regard,* Hans-Heinrich Trute, *Methodik der Herstellung und Darstellung verwaltungsrechtlicher Entscheidungen,* in METHODEN DER VERWALTUNGSRECHTSWISSENSCHAFT 293 *passim* (Schmidt-Aßmann & Hoffmann-Riem eds., 2003).

81. *See:* Trute (note 52), Herstellung und Darstellung, p. 308 *passim.*

administration is facing. Occasionally, the law demands context-specific procedural adjustments strengthening rationality and transparency of internal administrative decision-making.[82]

Accordingly, specific administrative statutes feature various and remarkable efforts at structuring internal predecisional procedure.[83] Most significant among these are preliminary and intermediate procedures with the sole purpose of formally preevaluating particularly relevant issues to the procedure. In planning-approval procedure, intermediate evaluation according to APA § 73 (9)[84] is not

---

82. *See* Hoffmann-Riem, *Eigenständigkeit*, in: Hoffmann-Riem/Schmidt-Aßmann/ Voßkuhle, GlVwR, vol. 1, § 10 note 30 *passim*; TRUTE, HERSTELLUNG UND DARSTELLUNG, p. 293 *passim*.

83. *See also* TRUTE, HERSTELLUNG UND DARSTELLUNG, p. 313 *passim*.

84. APA § 73: "Hearings:
(1) The project developer shall submit the plan to the hearing authorities to enable the hearing to be held. The plan shall comprise the drawings and explanations to clarify the project, the reasons behind it and the land and structures affected.
(2) Within one month of receiving the complete plan the hearing authorities shall gather the opinions of those authorities whose spheres of competence are affected by the project and shall make the plan available for inspection in those communities on which the project is likely to have an impact.
(3) Within three weeks of receiving the plan, the communities referred to in paragraph 2 shall make the plan available for inspection for a period of one month. This procedure may be omitted where those affected are known and are given the opportunity to examine the plan during a reasonable period.
  (3a) The authorities referred to in paragraph 2 shall report their opinions within a period to be stipulated by the hearing authority, and not to exceed three months. Comments made after the date set for discussion shall be disregarded, unless the matters raised are already or should already have been known to the planning approval authority or have a bearing on the legality of the decision.
(4) Any person whose interests are affected by the project may, up to two weeks after the end of the inspection period, lodge objections to the plan in writing or in a manner to be recorded with the hearing authority or with the community. In the case referred to in paragraph 3, second sentence, the period for lodging objections shall be determined by the hearing authority. Following the closing date for lodging objections, no objections shall be allowed except those which rest on specific titles enforceable under private law. This fact shall be noted in the announcement of the inspection period or in the announcement of the closing date for lodging objections.
(5) Those communities in which the plan is to be made public shall give advance notice of the fact according to local custom. The announcement shall state:
  1. where and for what period the plan is open to inspection;
  2. that any objections must be lodged with the authorities mentioned in the announcement within the time limit set for that purpose;

mandatory but merely allowed. In the case of distinct agencies, the administrative agency responsible for hearing has to submit an independent statement regarding the hearing to the agency making the final decision. But – as is usually the case – If the administrative agency responsible for hearing is identical with the agency ultimately deciding whether to approve the plan, the intermediate

---

3. that if a participant fails to attend the meeting for discussion, discussions may proceed without him;

4. that:

a) those persons who lodge objections may be informed of the dates of meetings for discussion by public announcement,

b) the notification of decisions on objections may be replaced by public announcement, if more than 50 notifications have to be made or served.

Persons affected who do not reside locally but whose identity and residence are known or can be discovered within a reasonable period shall, at the instigation of the hearing authority, be informed of the plan's being made available for inspection, with reference to sentence 2.

(6) Following the closing date for lodging objections, the hearing authority shall discuss those objections made to the plan in good time, and the opinions of the authorities with regard to the plan, with the project developer, the authorities, the persons affected by the plan and those who have lodged objections to it. The date of the meeting for discussion must be announced at least a week beforehand in the manner usual in the district. The authorities, the project developer and those who have lodged objections shall be informed of the date set for discussion of the plan. If apart from notifications to authorities and the project developer more than 50 notifications must be sent, this may be replaced by public announcement. Public announcement shall be effected, notwithstanding sentence 2, by publishing the date of the meeting for discussion in the official journal of the hearing authority, and also in local daily newspapers with wide circulation in the district in which the project may be expected to have its effect. The period referred to in the second sentence shall be calculated from the date of publication in the official bulletin. In other respects, the discussion shall be governed by the provisions concerning oral hearings in formal administrative proceedings (section 67, paragraph 1, third sentence, paragraph 2, nos. 1 and 4 and paragraph 3, and section 68) as appropriate. Discussion shall be concluded within three months of the closing date for lodging objections.

(7) Notwithstanding the provisions of paragraph 6, second to fifth sentences, the date of the meeting for discussion may already be fixed in the announcement in accordance with paragraph 5, second sentence.

(8) If a plan already open for inspection is to be altered, and if this means that the sphere of competence of an authority or the interests of third parties are affected for the first time or more greatly than hitherto, they shall be informed of the changes and given the opportunity to lodge objections or state their points of view within a period of two weeks. If the change affects the territory of another community, the altered plan shall be made available for inspection in that community; paragraphs 2 to 6 shall apply as appropriate.

(9) The hearing authority shall issue a statement concerning the result of the hearing and shall send this, together with the plan, the opinions of the authorities and those objections which have not been resolved, to the planning approval authority, if possible within one month of the conclusion of the discussion."

procedure is omitted.[85] Intermediate steps can thus become obsolete by virtue of procedural design. An example of mandatory intermediate evaluation can be drawn from environmental impact assessment law. §§ 11 and 12 of the Environmental Impact Assessment Act demand an integrated description of a project's various effects on the environment and, based on that description, an environmental impact assessment. The environmental impact assessment is to be incorporated into the final ruling granting approval. This ruling naturally relies on many different factors, not simply environmental ones. Even so, the environmental impact assessment stands out amongst the factors on account of its transparent documentation.[86]

---

85. Kopp & Ramsauer, VwVfG, § 73 note 107 *supra*, note 16; Hansjochen Dürr, inVwVfG:K § 73 note 108 *supra* note 44.

86. *Regarding this, see* Heinz-Joachim Peters & Stefan Balla, GESETZ ÜBER DIE UMWELTVERTRÄGLICHKEITSPRÜFUNG: HANDKOMMENTAR § 12 note 35 (3rd ed., 2006).

III

CONTINUATION AND FUNCTIONAL EXTENSIONS
OF ADMINISTRATIVE PROCEDURES

A. GENERAL INTRODUCTION

NOTIFICATION of the parties involved follows the internal administrative decision. By virtue of their external effects, statutory law arranges a standard procedure regulation for these actions as well. APA § 41 (1)[87] provides for notification of concerned parties for every administrative act.[88] APA §§ 43 (1)[89] then declares that administrative

---

87. APA § 41: "Notification of an administrative act:
 (1) An administrative act shall be made known to the person for whom it is intended or who is affected thereby. Where an authorised representative is appointed, the notification may be addressed to him.
 (2) A written administrative act shall be deemed notified on the third day after posting if posted to an address within Germany, and an administrative act sent electronically shall be deemed notified on the third day after sending. This shall not apply if the administrative act was not received or was received at a later date; in case of doubt the authority must prove the receipt of the administrative act and the date of receipt.
 (3) An administrative act may be publicly promulgated where this is permitted by law. A general order may also be publicly promulgated when notification of those concerned is impracticable.
 (4) The public promulgation of an administrative act in written or electronic form shall be effected by advertising the operative part in accordance with local custom. Promulgation shall state where the administrative act and its statement of grounds may be inspected. The administrative act shall be deemed to have been promulgated two weeks after the date of advertising in accordance with local custom. A general order may fix a different day for this purpose but in no case may this be earlier than the date following advertisement.
 (5) Provisions governing the promulgation of an administrative act by service shall remain unaffected."
88. Administrative acts may be issued in written, electronic, verbal, or any other form, APA § 37 (2).
89. APA § 43: "Validity of an administrative act:
 (1) An administrative act shall become effective vis-à-vis the person for whom it is intended or who is affected thereby at the moment he is notified thereof. The administrative act shall apply in accordance with its tenor as notified.

acts may not go into effect prior to notification of concerned parties. According to APA § 9,[90] administrative procedure itself is directed at issuing administrative acts or concluding public law contracts. In contrast to the concept embodied in the statute, administrative procedure and the procedural rights associated with it do not end doctrinally in the instant of notification. Although disputed by some scholars of administrative law, the procedure's conclusion occurs when the appeals of litigation of the administrative act have expired or been exhausted or a public law contract goes into effect.[91] Accordingly, the principal decision and the decision on administrative appeal form for the purpose of judicial review one and the same entity pursuant to Administrative Courts Act (ACA) § 79.[92] Rights to access records also do not lapse with the publication of administrative action.

The idea of procedure is even more all-encompassing from a steering- and impact-oriented point of view.[93] From this perspective, procedure continues in the implementation of its results, their control and – eventually – revision, and ultimately in the learning process as the agency examines the outcome of the decision. This perspective also recognizes the creation of recursive procedural chains. Those procedural chains are made up of interrelated complex decisions either relying on or modifying each other. Observing post-decisional phases of procedure like these enables legal scholars to identify and

---

(2) An administrative act shall remain effective for as long as it is not withdrawn, annulled, otherwise cancelled or expires for reasons of time or for any other reason.
(3) An administrative act which is invalid shall be ineffective."

90. *See supra* note 6.

91. Federal Administrative Court, 82 Entscheidungen des Bundesverwaltungsgerichts [BVerwGE] 336 *passim*; concurring: Wolfgang Clausen, inVwVfG:K § 13 note 11, § 9 note 30 *passim*; Kopp & Ramsauer, VwVfG, § 9 note 23a, 30 *supra* note 16; dissenting: Paul Stelkens & Heribert Schmitz, in: VwVfG:K § 9 note 182 *passim supra* note 44.

92. Verwaltungsgerichtsordnung (VwGO), (1991) I BGBl. 686 (1991), as last amended by Act of June 17th, 2008 § 62 (11) I BGBl 1010 (2008).

93. Schmidt-Aßmann, *Ordnungsidee*, Ch. 6 note 155 *supra* note 10; Wolfgang Hoffmann-Riem, *Ermöglichung von Flexibilität und Innovationsoffenheit im Verwaltungsrecht: Einleitende Problemskizze*, in, INNOVATION UND FLEXIBILITÄT DES VERWALTUNGSHANDELNS 60 *passim* (Hoffmann-Riem & Schmidt-Aßmann eds., 1994).

evaluate reciprocity between these phases and the original procedure. Such reciprocity can, of course, have helpful as well as burdensome effects. Many different forms of a functional outline of administrative procedure can thus be uncovered. This does not mean, though, that jurisprudence need not separate different layers of administrative decisions. In order to preserve post-decisional insulation from judicial review, for instance, such a separation may be indispensable doctrinally.

B. CONTINUATION BY VIRTUE OF AN ADMINISTRATIVE APPEAL PROCEDURE AND PROCESS-ADJACENT HEALING ADMINISTRATIVE PROCEDURES

1. The Dual Nature of Administrative Appeal Procedure

The most apparent form of continuation of administrative procedure can be found in appeal procedures initiated after the issue of a merely provisional principal decision. According to ACA § 68, an appeal to a higher administrative authority must be filed before a suit in an administrative court can be lodged, unless otherwise provided.[94] Therefore administrative appeal in procedure is both a requirement prior to seeking a quashing or a mandatory order at court and a preliminary proceeding to court procedures. At the same time, appeal procedure is a continuation of the original administrative procedure, eventually modifying the first decision and thereby becoming an integrated part of it.

---

94. In the interest of administrative efficiency several German "Länder" have used in recent times new derogatory powers to reduce the need to file objections: *See* Schneider, *Strukturen und Typen*, in II GlVwR § 28 note 128 *supra* note 16.

2. Curative Procedures Accompanying Judicial Proceedings

Besides appeal administrative proceedings, a second possible continuation of the principal procedure was installed in 1996 by amending APA § 45 (2). § 45 (2)[95] now provides for curing procedures to take place simultaneously with judicial proceedings at the trial court. Prior to 1996, curing of procedural defects was barred after an action was brought to court. This had been criticized on efficiency grounds.

The new statute is particularly revolutionary as curative proceedings are a purely administrative procedure. The competent administrative authority presides over it. The administrative court dealing with the action brought forward is not involved directly. Nevertheless, curative procedure now runs parallel to the court's legal proceedings. This inevitably leads to novel dialogue between administrative law courts and administrative authorities. Curative procedures accompanying court actions thus constitute yet another remarkable example of movement toward dialog with agencies in the administrative law courts.[96] The courts' new cooperative approach has enormous repercussions for legal studies in administrative procedure as well. Yet, doctrinal differences between the parallel procedures prevail even in the face of the

---

95. APA § 45: "Making good defects in procedure or form:

(1) An infringement of the regulations governing procedure or form which does not render the administrative act invalid under section 44 shall be ignored when:

1. the application necessary for the issuing of the administrative act is subsequently made;
2. the necessary statement of grounds is subsequently provided;
3. the necessary hearing of a participant is subsequently held;
4. the decision of a committee whose collaboration is required in the issuing of the administrative act is subsequently taken;
5. the necessary collaboration of another authority is subsequently obtained.

(2) Actions referred to in paragraph 1 may be made good up to the final court of administrative proceedings.

(3) Where an administrative act lacks the necessary statement of grounds or has been issued without the necessary prior hearing of a participant, so that the administrative act was unable to be contested in good time, failure to observe the period for legal remedy shall be regarded as unintentional. The event resulting in restoration of the status quo ante under section 32, paragraph 2 shall be deemed to occur when omission of the procedural action is made good."

96. Other instances include recent changes to interim injunctions and the new possibility of complementing deliberations about how to exercise discretion provided for in ACA § 114 (2).

discursive restructuring of administrative procedure. In particular, there is an inevitable and fundamental difference between the role of administrative authorities actively and politically managing issues and that of administrative law courts reactively and neutrally resolving disputes.[97]

The insertion of APA § 45 (2) created some concern regarding its constitutionality under the German Basic Law. Constitutional concerns did not win general recognition.[98] Nevertheless, it is apparent that any hearing conducted so long after the administrative action and in such a conflict-ridden situation as in the curative procedure suffers from restrictions arising from litigational tactics.[99] Complying with minimum requirements for curative proceedings accompanying judicial proceedings thus becomes all the more significant. In case of defective hearing procedures, for instance, the administrative authority at first needs to explicitly prompt the concerned person to submit a statement on the subject matter. An authority entirely competent for decision-making then has to consider the statement submitted as impartially as possible. Lastly, the whole process needs to be documented. This can take place by supplementing the reasoning of the decision with further considerations.[100]

---

97. Eberhard Schmidt-Aßmann, in SCHOCH ET AL, VERWALTUNGSGERICHTSORDNUNG, KOMMENTAR, intro. note 177 (1996); dissenting Rainer Pitschas, *Verwaltung und Verwaltungsgerichtsbarkeit im staatlichen Modernisierungsprozeß*, in VERWALTUNGSVERFAHREN UND VERWALTUNGSPROZEß IM WANDEL DER STAATSFUNKTIONEN 56 (Blümel & Pitschas eds., 1997).

98. Michael Sachs, in VwVfG:K § 45 note 112 *passim*; Heinz J. Bonk, *Strukturelle Änderungen des Verwaltungsverfahrens durch das Genehmigungsverfahrensbeschleunigungsgesetz*, in NVwZ 320 *passim*, *supra* note 4; *for a critical opinion, see* Christian-Dietrich Bracher, *Nachholung der Anhörung bis zum Abschluß des verwaltungsgerichtlichen Verfahrens?: Zur Verfassungsmäßigkeit von § 45 Abs. 2 VwVfG*, in DVBl 534 *passim*; Armin Hatje, *Die Heilung formell rechtswidriger Verwaltungsakte im Prozeß als Mittel der Verfahrensbeschleunigung*, in DÖV 477 *passim* (1997).

99. Kopp/Ramsauer (note 16), VwVfG, § 28 note 80, § 45 note 33 *passim*; Friedhelm Hufen, *Heilung und Unbeachtlichkeit grundrechtsrelevanter Verfahrensfehler? Zur verfassungskonformen Auslegung der §§ 45 und 46 VwVfG*, in NEUE JURISTISCHE WOCHENSCHRIFT [NJW] 2160, 2165 (1982); *Heilung und Unbeachtlichkeit von Verfahrensfehlern*, in JURISTISCHE SCHULUNG [JuS], 313, 317 (1999), *aptly speaks of "psychological non-appealability" in this context. For an even more poignant comment see former Federal Administrative Court judge* Jörg Berkemann, *Verwaltungsprozeßrecht auf "neuen Wegen"?*, in DEUTSCHES VERWALTUNGSBLATT (DVBl), 446 *passim* (1998); *"Farce" Very graphic: Administrative Court (Verwaltungsgericht – VG) Berlin*, in NJW 1063, 1064 (2003).

100. Kopp & Ramsauer, VwVfG § 28 note 81 *passim supra* note 16.

3. Defect Repair Procedures Concerning Planning Approval

Planning approval law features certain peculiarities due to its inherent bias toward upholding complex plans already made.[101] In this context the distinction between plan amendments curing substantive shortcomings of plans and supplementary procedures making up for limited procedural omissions becomes crucial. Both classes of procedures attempt to repair defects. Typically, they follow judicial proceedings which uncover said defects. They can, however, also take place simultaneously with judicial proceedings just like the curative procedures described above. To ensure parallel proceedings, the administrative authority responsible for planning approval must proactively initiate repair procedure at an early point in the litigation.

C. IMPLEMENTATION OF ADMINISTRATIVE PROCEDURE RESULTS

Administrative decisions have to be implemented. If the decision reached at that point is not self-executing, implementation will occur either through tangible administrative measures or by private citizens. Tangible administrative measures can appear as construction (in the case of approved plans concerning infrastructure measures), as disbursements (in the case of administrative acts granting cash benefits), or in any other beneficiary tangible way. Implementation by private citizens takes place, for example, in the case of using an administrative permission, as can be illustrated by a house builder making use of a building permit. Problems with private implementation may, however, arise in cases of non-beneficiary administrative acts, such as orders to remove illegal buildings. These problems can be overcome by enforcement procedures. Traditional legal thought generally separates implementation and execution phases from primary administrative

---

101. Hans D. Jarass, *Aktuelle Probleme des Planfeststellungsrechts: Plangenehmigung, Planergänzung, ergänzendes Verfahren*, in DVBl 795 *passim* (1997).

procedure.[102] In administrative science, however, the understanding of decision implementation as part of a broad, unitary and oftentimes recursive decisional process is canonical.[103] Scholars of administrative law concerned with the concept of steering therefore ought to integrate these phases in their considerations as well.[104]

Decisions can also be implemented formally in other ways than administrative execution. Environmental law, in particular, features a variety of approaches to monitoring facilities after they have been deemed to comply with permission requirements.[105]

Federal Emission Control Act §§ 20, 26 et seq., 52,[106] for instance, equips the authorities with specific monitoring powers including investigation, interdiction of operations, temporary shutdown or even permanent closure. Despite these extensive options and abilities, monitoring powers are oftentimes criticized for its practical irrelevance due to capacity overload. Often, complaints by neighbors or interested parties must spur the agency to begin installation monitoring procedures.[107] Internally motivated procedures hardly ever occur in cases governed exclusively by German administrative law. European financial aid regulation, in contrast, demands systematic regulation based on venture-oriented standards for quality and quantity of spending.[108]

---

102. FRANZ-JOSEPH PEINE, ALLGEMEINES VERWALTUNGSRECHT note 18 (8th ed., 2006).

103. Bernd Becker, *Entscheidungen in der öffentlichen Verwaltung*, in ÖFFENTLICHE VERWALTUNG IN DEUTSCHLAND 435 *passim* (2nd ed., König & Siedentopf eds., 1997); Werner Thieme, *Einführung in die Verwaltungslehre* 142 *passim* (1995).

104. *See also* Schmidt-Aßmann, *Ordnungsidee* Ch. 6 note 161 *supra* note 10; Hoffmann-Riem, *Flexibilität und Innovationsoffenheit*, in INNOVATION UND FLEXIBILITÄT, 29 *passim supra* note 7.

105. *Regarding the following passage, see* Hans-Joachim Koch, in, UMWELTRECHT § 4 note 166 *passim* (2nd ed., Koch, ed., 2007); *Klaus Jankowski*, idem, § 10 note 84 *passim*.

106. Bundes-Immissionsschutzgesetz (BImSchG), I BGBl.3830 (2002), as amended by Act of October 23rd, 2007 Art. 1, I BGBl. 2470 (2007).

107. HANS-JOACHIM KOCH ET AL., ANLAGENÜBERWACHUNG IM UMWELTRECHT: ZUM VERHÄLTNIS VON STAATLICHER ÜBERWACHUNG UND EIGENKONTROLLE (1998).

108. *Regarding structural fund law, see:* Schneider, *Instrumente* 263 *supra* note 20; *regarding the law on agricultural subsidies, see* CATHARINA MEYER-BOLTE, AGRARRECHTLICHE CROSS COMPLIANCE ALS STEUERUNGSINSTRUMENT IM EUROPÄISCHEN VERWALTUNGSVERBUND (2006).

D. FUNCTIONAL EXTENSIONS OF PROCEDURES AND INCREASED FLEXIBILITY OF DECISIONS IN LATER ADMINISTRATIVE PROCEDURES

The procedures discussed above dealt with continuations of administrative procedure. Yet administrative procedures independent from and subsequent to earlier proceedings actually are of similar interest to procedural legal studies. Subsequent procedures review, annul, modify and tie in with decisions made earlier in a specific way. Although they are doctrinally categorized as separate layers of administrative procedure, primary and subsequent proceedings are linked to each other in many different ways. The consequent freedom to alter decisions becomes especially apparent in subsequent procedures which either finalize the primary decision's binding force and its non-appealability or actually override those virtues in whole or in part. Various ways of increasing flexibility in decision making are thus open to the administration. Subsequent procedures for retrospectively reviewing primary decisions must be systematically distinguished from those permitting an adjustment to later developments. An example of the former is the APA § 48[109] procedure to repeal originally unlawful administrative acts. Instances of the latter include monitoring, subsequent orders, and procedures according to APA § 49[110] allowing to revocate

---

109. *See infra*, note 51.

110. APA § 49: "Revocation of a lawful administrative act:
  (1) A lawful, non-beneficial administrative act may, even after it has become non-appealable, be revoked wholly or in part with effect for the future, except when an administrative act of like content would have to be issued or when revocation is not allowable for other reasons.
  (2) A lawful, beneficial administrative act may, even when it has become non-appealable, be revoked in whole or in part with effect for the future only when:
    1. revocation is permitted by law or the right of revocation is reserved in the administrative act itself;
    2. the administrative act is combined with an obligation which the beneficiary has not complied with fully or not within the time limit set;
    3. the authority would be entitled, as a result of a subsequent change in circumstances, not to issue the administrative act and if failure to revoke it would be contrary to the public interest;

originally lawful administrative acts if for instance certain conditions stipulated in that act have been ignored by the addressee. Furthermore, subsequent examinations can either be initiated *ex officio* or upon request of a concerned party. Finally, one must distinguish between examinations that are potentially beneficiary to the addressee and such that are not.

1. RESUMPTION OF PROCEEDINGS ACCORDING TO APA § 51

Persons affected by non-appealable administrative acts may be entitled to a resumption of proceedings under APA § 51 in certain cases.[111] Such resumption

---

4. the authority would be entitled, as a result of an amendment to a legal provision, not to issue the administrative act where the beneficiary has not availed himself of the benefit or has not received any benefits derived from the administrative act and when failure to revoke would be contrary to the public interest, or
5. in order to prevent or eliminate serious harm to the common good.
Section 48 paragraph 4 applies *mutatis mutandis*.
(3) A lawful administrative act which provides for a one-time or a continuing payment of money or a divisible material benefit for a particular purpose, or which is a prerequisite for these, may be revoked even after such time as it has become non-appealable, either wholly or in part and with retrospective effect,
1. if, once this payment is rendered, it is not put to use, or is not put to use either without undue delay or for the purpose for which it was intended in the administrative act;
2. if the administrative act had an obligation attached to it which the beneficiary either fails to satisfy or does not satisfy within the stipulated period.
Section 48 paragraph 4 applies *mutatis mutandis*.
(4) The revoked administrative act shall become null and void with the coming into force of the revocation, except where the authority fixes some other date."
111. APA § 51: "Resumption of proceedings:
(1) The authority shall, upon application by the person affected, decide concerning the annulment or amendment of a non-appealable administrative act when:
1. the material or legal situation basic to the administrative act has subsequently changed to favour the person affected;
2. new evidence is produced which would have meant a more favourable decision for the person affected;
3. there are grounds for resumption of proceedings under section 580 of the Code of Civil Procedure.
(2) An application shall only be acceptable when the person affected was, without grave fault on his part, unable to enforce the grounds for resumption in earlier proceedings, particularly by means of a legal remedy.

requires either ex post changes in the factual or legal situation or new information calling for a reevaluation of the primary decision's accuracy. The APA's creators regarded resumption of proceedings as a doctrinally new and independent administrative procedure. Resumption was never seen as an immediate continuation to primary proceedings, despite the highly similar subject matter.[112]

2. Repeal Procedures According to §§ 48 and 49 of the APA

Equally significant are the increased availability of various types of decisions offered in §§ 48 and 49 of the APA,[113] even if all subsequent modifications are constrained by the principle of protection of confidence (legitimate expectations). §§ 48 and 49 allow for the repeal of the binding effect of administrative acts on the authority that announced them initially.

At the same time, those burdened by non-appealable administrative acts are equipped with the narrow opportunity to obtain a repeal. APA § 48 in this context is applicable for originally illegal acts, whereas APA § 49 is supposed to provide for adjustment of decisions originally compliant with the law to changed factual circumstances. It thus specifically creates space for future developments in administrative decisions, increasing administrative flexibility.[114] The APA usually provides for claims for compensation as a remedy for the concerned parties. Therefore, fiscal policy may indirectly restrain the administration

---

(3) The application must be made within three months, this period to begin with the day on which the person affected learnt of the grounds for resumption of proceedings.
(4) The decision regarding the application shall be made by the authority competent under section 3; this shall also apply when the administrative act which is to be anulled or amended was issued by another authority.
(5) The provisions of section 48, paragraph 1, first sentence and of section 49, paragraph 1 shall remain unaffected.".

112. Michael Sachs, in, VwVfG:K § 51 note 28, § 48 note 252, 255 *supra* note 44.

113. *See supra* note 51.

114. Specific administrative law is even more fruitful in this regard: *See* Friedrich Schoch, *Der Verwaltungsakt zwischen Stabilität und Flexibilität*, IN INNOVATION UND FLEXIBILITÄT DES VERWALTUNGSHANDELNS 199, 242 (Hoffmann-Riem & Schmidt-Aßmann, eds., 1994).

from undertaking an objectively necessary or justified revision of a decision it made earlier.[115]

3. MODIFICATIONS TO PLANNING APPROVAL DECISIONS ACCORDING TO APA § 76

The procedure to modify planning approval decisions prior to completion of the planned project is regulated in a nuanced fashion by APA § 76,[116] which differentiates between essential and nonessential changes. The latter can be defined as changes that leave the process and result of balancing structurally and substantially untouched.[117] If essential changes are being made, new planning approval proceedings compliant with APA §§ 74 and 75[118] become

---

115. *See* Hoffmann-Riem, *Flexibilität und Innovationsoffenheit*, in INNOVATION UND FLEXIBILITÄT 62 *supra* note 93.

116. APA § 76: "Changes to the plan before the project is finished:
(1) If the approved plan is to be changed before the project is finished, a new approval procedure shall be required.
(2) If the changes to the plan are of negligible importance, the planning approval authorities may waive the need for a new procedure where the interests of others are not affected or where those affected have agreed to the change.
(3) If, in the cases referred to in paragraph 2, or in other cases of a negligible change to a plan, the planning approval authority conducts an approval procedure, then no hearing and no public notification of the planning approval decision is required."

117. Federal Administrative Court, (1990) Neue Juristische Wochenschrift (NJW), p. 925 (926).

118. APA § 74: "Decisions on planning approval, planning consent:
(1) The planning authority shall consider and decide on the plan (planning approval decision). The provisions concerning decisions and contesting decisions in formal administrative proceedings (sections 69 and 70) shall apply.
(2) The planning approval decision shall contain the decision of the planning approval authority concerning the objections on which no agreement was reached during discussions before the hearing authority. It shall impose upon the project developer the obligation to take measures or to erect and maintain structures or facilities necessary for the general good or to avoid detrimental effects on the rights of others. Where such measures or facilities are impracticable or irreconcilable with the project, the person affected may claim reasonable monetary compensation.

mandatory. In modifications, however, the new planning approval process is limited in scope to the changes intended. Although it is independent of the original planning approval proceedings, the out-

---

(3) Where it is not yet possible to make a final decision, this shall be stated in the planning approval decision; the project developer shall at the same time be required to submit in good time any documents still missing or required by the planning approval authority.

(4) The planning approval decision shall be sent to the project developer, those people known to be affected by the project and those people whose objections have been dealt with. A copy of the decision, together with advice on legal remedies and a copy of the plan as approved, shall be open for inspection in the communities concerned for two weeks, the place and time at which the plan may be inspected being made known in accordance with local custom. With the end of the inspection period, the other parties affected shall be regarded as having been notified, which fact shall be made known in the announcement.

(5) If apart from the project developer more than 50 notifications have to be made under paragraph 4, this may be replaced by public announcement. Public announcement shall be effected by publishing the operative part of the decision of the planning approval authority, as well as advice on legal remedies and a reference to the fact that the plan is open to public inspection pursuant to paragraph 4, second sentence, in the official bulletin of the competent authority, and also in local daily newspapers with wide circulation in the district in which the project may be expected to have its effect. Any impositions shall be indicated. At the end of the period of public inspection, those affected by the decision and those who have lodged objections to it shall be regarded as having been notified, which fact shall be indicated in the public announcement. Between the time of the public announcement and the end of the period during which legal remedies may be sought, those affected by the decision and those who have lodged objections may make written requests for copies of the decision; this shall likewise be indicated in the public announcement.

(6) Planning consent may be issued in place of a planning approval decision where
    1. there is no impairment of the rights of others or where those affected have declared in writing that they consent to the utilisation of their property or of some other right, and
    2. agreement has been reached with those public agencies whose spheres of competence are affected.

Planning consent has the same legal effects as planning approval except for the predetermining legal effect with regard to later expropriation; the granting of such consent shall not be governed by the provisions on planning approval procedures. Re-examination in preliminary proceedings is not required prior to the filing of an action with the administrative court. Section 75, paragraph 4 applies mutatis mutandis.

(7) Planning approval and planning consent are not required in cases of minor significance. Such cases are deemed to exist where
    1. no other public concerns are affected, or the required decisions on the part of authorities have already been taken and are not in conflict with the plan, and
    2. rights of others are not affected, or the relevant agreements have been reached with those affected by the plan."

come of the second procedure merges with the first decision to form a unitary plan.[119] When the change is not essential, the agency has discretion to decide how to proceed. Its options are to engage in informal proceedings, as provided for in APA § 76 (2), or in shortened planning approval procedures according to APA § 76 (3). Both of these proceedings are independent from the prior procedure, yet they

---

APA § 75: "Legal effects of planning approval:

(1) Planning approval has the effect of establishing the admissibility of the project, including the necessary measures subsequently to be taken in connection with other installations and facilities, having regard to all public interests affected thereby. No other administrative decisions, in particular consent issued under public law, grants, permissions, authorisations, agreements or planning approvals are required. Planning approval legally regulates all relationships under public law between the project developer and those affected by the project.

    (1a) Flaws in the weighing of public and private interests touched by the project shall be deemed to be significant only where they have clearly exerted an influence on the outcome of deliberations. Significant flaws in weighing public and private interests shall result in the annulment of the decision on planning approval or of planning consent only where such flaws cannot be rectified by means of modifications to the plan or by a supplementary procedure.

(2) Once the decision on planning approval has become non-appealable, no claims to stop the project, to remove or alter structures or to stop their use will be allowed. If unforeseeable effects of the project, or of structures built in accordance with the approved plan, on the rights of another become apparent only after the plan has become non-appealable, the person affected may demand that measures be undertaken or structures erected and maintained to counteract the detrimental effects. Such measures shall be imposed on the project developer by a decision of the planning approval authority. If such measures or the installation of such structures are impracticable or irreconcilable with the project, a claim may be made for reasonable monetary compensation. If measures or structures within the meaning of sentence 2 become necessary because of changes which occur on a neighbouring piece of land after the planning approval procedure has been concluded, the costs arising shall be borne by the owners of the adjacent land, unless such changes are the result of natural occurrences or force majeure; sentence 4 shall not apply.

(3) Applications seeking to enforce claims to the erection of installations or structures or for reasonable compensation in accordance with paragraph 2, second and fourth sentences shall be made to the planning authority in writing. These shall only be acceptable if made within three years of the date on which the person affected became aware of the detrimental effects of the project resulting from the non-appealable plan, or of the installations. They may not be made once thirty years have passed from the creation of the situation shown in the plan.

(4) If work is not commenced on the project within five years of the plan becoming non-appealable, it shall become invalid."

119. Heinz J. Bonk & Werner Neumann Federal Administrative Court, 75 Entscheidungen des Bundesverwaltungsgerichts [BverwGE] 214, 223, in: VwVfG:K § 76 note 5, 15, *supra* note 44.

both also utilize participatory and balancing results of earlier planning approval procedures. This reliance serves to legitimate the reduction of procedural requirements laid out in APA §§ 76 (2), (3).[120] The modification process makes for a remarkable example of administrative procedures' increased flexibility.

4. SUBSEQUENT ORDERS

Subsequent orders are yet another significant instrument for increasing the options available in administrative decisions.[120] When placing a burden on one or more parties, they are void if not specifically warranted by either valid reservation in the initial decision or statutory law. Specific administrative law features several provisions allowing for subsequent orders.[122] The substantive legal standards for subsequent orders, most importantly those derived from the principle of proportionality, cannot be discussed in any further detail here.[123] The article will instead dwell on the legal structure of subsequent ordering procedures. Subsequent orders are issued after an independent administrative procedure, yet the subsequent order and the primary administrative act constitute only one single administrative act.[124] Their merger accordingly produces a composite subs-

---

120. *Regarding the Federal Highway Act [Bundesfernstraßengesetz – FStrG]*, I BGBl. 1206 (2007), see Federal Administrative Court, Neue Juristische Wochenschrift [NJW] 925 *passim* (1990); Kopp & Ramsauer, VwVfG, § 76 note 12 *supra*.note 16.

121. Schoch, *Verwaltungsakt*, in INNOVATION UND FLEXIBILITÄT 241 *supra* note 93; HANS-JOACHIM KOCH ET AL, ALLGEMEINES VERWALTUNGSRECHT, § 6 note 48 *passim* (2003).

122. *E.g.*, Federal Immission Control Act § 17 (1); Atomic Energy Act § 17 (1) (3) [Atomgesetz – AtG], I BGBl. 1565 (1985), as amended by Act of February 26th, 2008 Art. 4, I BGBl. 215 (1985) (2008); Water Resources Act § 5 [Wasserhaushaltsgesetz – WHG], I BGBl. 3245 (2002), as last amended by Act of May 10th, 2007 Art. 2, I BGBl 666 (2007); Genetic Engineering Act § 19 (1) (3) [Gentechnikgesetz – GenTG] I BGBl. 2066 (1993), as amended by Act of April 1st, 2008 Art. 1, I BGBL.499 (2008); Restaurant Business Act § 5 [Gaststättengesetz – GastG] I BGBl. 3418 (1998), as last amended by Act of September 7th, 2007 Art. 10, I BGBl. 4426 (2007).

123. *In detail, see* HANS-JOACHIM KOCH, in GEMEINSCHAFTSKOMMENTAR ZUM BUNDES-IMMISSIONSSCHUTZGESETZ § 17 note 59 *passim*, (Koch & Scheuing eds., 1994); KARSTEN SACH, GENEHMIGUNG ALS SCHUTZSCHILD: DIE RECHTSSTELLUNG DES INHABERS EINER IMMIS-SIONSSCHUTZRECHTLICHEN GENEHMIGUNG 116 *passim* (1994).

124. Paul Stelkens & Ulrich Stelkens, in VwVfG:K § 36 note 9b, § 35 note 32a, *supra* note 44.

tantive regulation. Subsequent ordering procedure thus serves as yet another validation of the assumption that administrative procedures add flexibility to decisions.

5. SYSTEMATIC SURVEILLANCE OF THE EFFECTS OF DECISIONS

Surveilling and monitoring decisions systematically is an important component of administrative procedure law open to revision and aiming at generating new knowledge.[125] Statutory law to date, however, does not feature a comprehensive structure for systematic monitoring of administrative activities. Unlike the monitoring procedures discussed above, decision surveillance and monitoring does not deal with tangible implementation of decisions but with evaluating their subsequent factual effects.[126] While procedures monitoring permission rulings can motivate decision surveillance by uncovering operative shortcomings as discussed above, they are certainly not equipped to motivate decision surveillance on a systematic basis. The impetus behind introducing systematic decisions surveillance and monitoring can in large parts be attributed to EC Law.

6. CONTINUATION OF PROCEDURE IN CONCATENATED PERMISSIONS

Granting *temporary* permissions can serve as the functional equivalent of monitoring the effects of decisions.[127] By virtue of the decisions' sunset provision, the subject matter is automatically surveyed repeatedly in new and independent administrative procedures.

---

125. *See* Hoffmann-Riem, *Flexibilität und Innovationsoffenheit*, in INNOVATION UND FLEXIBILITÄT 63 *passim*, *supra* note 7; Karl-Heinz Ladeur, *Risikooffenheit und Zurechnung – insbesondere im Unweltrecht*, in Idem 111.

126. Regarding different types of monitoring, see Anke Sailer, Bauplanungsrecht und Monitoring: Die Umsetzung der Plan-UP-Richtlinie in das deutsche Recht 133 *passim* (2006).

127. *See* Hoffmann-Riem, *Flexibilität und Innovationsoffenheit,* in INNOVATION UND FLEXIBILITÄT 61 *supra* note 7.

A chain of permission rulings can develop from that. Such chains are often found in broadcasting law. Other parts of statutory law, such as installation permissions, utilize it infrequently.[128] Nonetheless, permission chains can be observed particularly in installation permission practice,[129] as complex installations permission more often than not takes place in external procedures featuring temporary licenses and provisional decisions. Also, operational and commercial considerations often increase the need for permission modification. This in turn leads to the institution of *modification* permission proceedings[130]. Sequential permissions like these functionally establish continuing legal obligations and ultimately lead to a procedural continuum. They thereby serve as a fine example of increased flexibility and functional extension of the administrative procedure.

---

128. According to the German Federal Immission Control Act (similar to the US Clean Air Act) § 12 (2), for instance, limitations are only provided for upon the request of the operators of installations. *See also* HANS D. JARASS, BUNDES-IMMISSIONSSCHUTZGESETZ § 12 note 16 *passim* (6th ed., 2005).

129. *See* Schoch, *Verwaltungsakt*, in INNOVATION UND FLEXIBILITÄT, 240 *passim supra* note 28.

130. *E.g.*, German Federal Immission Control Act (similar to the US Clean Air Act) §§ 15, 16; *See also* Martin Führ, *Wesentliche Änderung von Industrieanlagen: Praktische Auswirkungen des neuen § 16 BImSchG*, in ZEITSCHRIFT FÜR UMWELTRECHT [ZUR] 293 *passim* (1997); Jens-Peter Schneider, *Interessenverarbeitung in flexibilisierten Genehmigungsverfahren*, in VOM HOHEITSSTAAT ZUM KONSENSUALSTAAT: ÖKONOMISCHE ANALYSE DER FLEXIBILISERUNG VON GENEHMIGUNGSVERFAHREN 80 *passim* (Schmidtchen & Schmidt-Trenz eds., 1999); REINHARD SPARWASSER ET AL, UMWELTRECHT: GRUNDZÜGE DES ÖFFENTLICHEN UMWELTSCHUTZ-RECHTS § 10 note 250 *passim* (regarding immission control law), § 7 note 208 *passim* (regarding atomic energy law) (5th ed., 2003).

CHAPTER IX

ADMINISTRATIVE PROCEDURE IN SPAIN: CURRENT SITUATION AND PERSPECTIVES ON CHANGE

Luciano Parejo[*]

[*] Professor of Administrative Law, Carlos III University, Madrid, Spain.

INDEX

T HE current state of administrative procedure in Spain is far from satisfactory. The present rules for administrative action are deficient and filled with loopholes. Most of these deficiencies stem from the fact that Spain is a highly decentralized country. The Spanish Constitution of 1978 introduced the concept of "uniform" or "common administrative procedure" as a tool to structurally allocate the normative powers of the State and of the seventeen Autonomous Communities. However, this body of "common" administrative procedure was not concretely identified by State legislation until 1992 (by means of Act 30/1992 (Nov. 26), on Common Administrative Procedure) and the final result did not sufficiently clarify this intricate subject. In addition, Spanish legislation has not fully internalized the fact that Spain is a member state of the European Union, and that as a result, the Spanish bureaucracy and its agencies are functionally a "European" administrative organization. The implementation of EU Law by Spanish agencies and departments has currently had little if any impact on the regulation of administrative procedure.

The current structural model of the "common administrative procedure" must be rethought, and in this process this article will: (1) extract all the consequences that are implicit in the constitutional model of State; (2) internalize the functional consequences of the "administrative" process of implementing EU Law; and (3) build a new model of relations between the citizen and the public administration.

I

AN ASSESSMENT: DEFICIENCIES AND LOOPHOLES
IN THE PRESENT STATUTORY REGULATION OF THE
"COMMON" (OR UNIFORM) ADMINISTRATIVE
PROCEDURE

A. THE SPANISH CONSTITUTION AND
ADMINISTRATIVE PROCEDURE

At the time of the creation of the 1978 Spanish Constitution,[1] the categories "legal regime of public administration" (organization and

---

1. Spain is a highly decentralized country. The Constitution (C.E.) (ratified in a national referendum on December 6, 1978) sets the basic rules for the allocation of power between the

structure) and "administrative procedure," while not absolutely distinct, occupied different domains. Accordingly, these categories were regulated by different pieces of legislation.[2] Against this historical background, the Spanish Constitution (art. 148.1.18) uses these two terms as different conceptual entities, and largely assumes the existing organizational and structural model of government and public administration. This model focuses on those aspects of the executive branch that are mainly related to the administrative action seen as an "ad extra" activity, that is, the activity that has an influence on the sphere of interests and rights of the citizen. Under this conceptual model, administrative procedure is important in administrative activity because the institutional role of administrative agencies is largely perceived in a quasi-judicial manner: At the end of a formal and sequential administrative procedure, the agency *says* what the Law is.

For this reason, the Constitution (art. 103) emphasizes the "dynamic" perspective of Public Administration in order to make sure

---

State (the "federal" layer of government) and the seventeen Self-Governing Communities or Regions (*Comunidades Autónomas*). In the domain of administrative procedure, Art. 149.1.18 of the Constitution states that "the State shall have exclusive competence over the following matters: ...18. Basic rules of the legal system of Public Administrations and the status of their officials which shall, in any case, guarantee that all persons under said administrations will receive equal treatment; the common administrative procedure, without prejudicing the special features of the Self-governing Communities' own organizations; legislation on compulsory expropriation; basic legislation on contracts and administrative concessions and the system of liability of all Public Administrations." Thus, the Constitution introduced for the first time in Spanish Administrative Law the concept of *procedimiento administrative común*, which may be translated into English as "uniform" or "common administrative procedure." This term designates the basic rules and principles on administrative procedure that must be respected by all levels and units of government (the State, the regions and the local government entities) and in any type of "special" or "sectoral" procedures. On their side, the Regions may establish specific legal prescriptions on administrative procedure, based on their organizational features. The final, practical result is two-fold: (1) Contrary to what would happen in a typical "unitary" or centralized country (for instance, France or Portugal), in Spain there is not a unique, national regulation of administrative procedure; but (2) contrary to what would happen in a typical federal country (for instance, the United States) in Spain there are not eighteen different Administrative Procedure Acts (the national and the regional ones).

2. The two major pieces of legislation in this area are the Administrative Procedure Act (*Ley de procedimiento administrativo*) of July 17, 1958 (LPA), and the Act on the Legal Regime of the State Government (*Ley de régimen jurídico de la Administración del Estado*) of 1955 (LRJAE).

that its entire activity is subordinated to the Law.[3] It stresses the importance of judicial control of the rulemaking procedures (art. 106.1)[4] and the right of individuals to be compensated for all damage suffered as a consequence of governmental activity (art. 106.2).[5]

Thus, it is no surprise that the Constitution (art. 105) states that several aspects of administrative action may only be regulated by legislative acts, and not by administrative regulation, such as the participation of individuals and groups in rulemaking procedures and the format of administrative decision-making procedures.[6]

Clearly, in the Spanish constitutional context, "administrative action" (as executive activity) and "procedure" (seen as an obligatory and sequential course of action) are deeply intertwined. Pre-constitutional pieces of legislation continued to uphold the linkage between action and procedure for almost fifteen years after the enactment of the Constitution,[7] but the Constitution eventually led to a misunderstanding: that "common" administrative procedure consisted of the

---

3. C.E. Art. 103 "1. The Public Administration shall serve the general interest in a spirit of objectivity and shall act in accordance with the principles of efficiency, hierarchy, decentralization, deconcentration, and coordination, and in full subordination to the law.

The organs of State Administration are set up, directed, and coordinated in accordance with the law.

The law shall lay down the status of civil servants, their (prior) entry into the civil service in accordance with the principles of merit and ability, the exercise of their right to union membership, the system of incompatibilities, and guarantees regarding impartiality in the discharge of their duties."

4. C.E. Art. 106.1 "The Courts shall check the power to issue regulations and ensure that the rule of law prevails in administrative action, and that the latter is subordinated to the ends which justify it."

5. C.E. 63Art. 106.2 ("Private individuals shall, under the terms laid down by law, be entitled to compensation for any harm they may suffer in any of their property and rights, except in cases of force majeure, whenever such harm is the result of the operation of public services.").

6. C.E. Art. 5 ("The law shall make provision for: the hearing of citizens, directly, or through the organizations and associations recognized by the law, in the process of drawing up those administrative provisions which affect them; the access of citizens to administrative files and records, except to the extent that they may concern the security and defense of the State, the investigation of crimes and the privacy of persons; the procedures for the taking of administrative action, with due safeguards for the hearing of interested parties when appropriate.").

7. See supra note 3.

general regulation of various administrative procedures but not that of administrative action.

Unfortunately, this incorrect identification of "common" administrative procedure was confirmed in 1992, when the national parliament eventually approved the key statute on this matter, Act 30/1992 (Nov. 26, amended in 1999), on the legal regime of Public Administration and on the Uniform (or Common) Administrative Procedure (hereinafter "Act 30/1992"). This piece of legislation has aggravated the problematic differentiation of the concepts "legal regime of Public Administration" and "common administrative procedure."

This confusion helps describe the conceptual orientation of different features of Act 30/1992, such as the regime of "tacit" administrative decisions or the lack of substantive regulation of administrative activity that is not formalized (i.e., "*informal*" activity).

These features can be explained by the fact that the constitutional system has not been completely interpreted by statute. As a result, the rules governing the legal regime of public administration and the rules governing administrative procedures are not fully in line with constitutional determinations. Consequently, this article starts from the insight that Act 30/1992 does not represent the totality of the "uniform" or common administrative procedure required by the Constitution.

It is necessary to go beyond the current situation, and to "constitutionalize" administrative procedure, updating the legislation on this matter. This rethinking of administrative procedure must be accomplished in light of the deep changes that have taken place in the organization and functioning of the public administration. The structure and functions of administrative procedure should be reformulated through the lens of a comprehensive understanding of the procedural vision of administrative action.

B. EUROPEAN UNION LAW AND
ADMINISTRATIVE PROCEDURE

As a result of the current unsatisfactory development of the constitutional provisions on administrative procedure, Spanish administrative procedure has not been fully adapted to the requirements of EU
Law. For instance, Act 30/1992 does not fully recognize the general
principles of administrative procedures found in the case law of the
ECJ. Moreover, the Act does not regulate in a satisfactory manner the
complex inter-governmental relations of coordination and cooperation, which are triggered by the implementation of EC Law, both
horizontally (among the public administrations of the member States)
and vertically (with the EC agencies and bodies). Monitoring coordination and cooperation is especially important in a decentralized State.
Domestic regulation simply ignores the reality that public administration in Spain is not only the institutional instrument for the implementation of the "internal" general interest (as defined by the "domestic" law), but has become also (and increasingly) an "indirect" public
administration of the EC.

C. "FORMAL" ADMINISTRATIVE DECISION
(ADJUDICATION) AND STATUTORY REGULATION
OF THE DIFFERENT TYPES OF ADMINISTRATIVE
PROCEDURES

Act 30/1992 does not achieve its limited goals; it aims to become
the "locus" of general prescriptions for all different administrative
procedures, despite the heterogeneous nature of sectoral governmental activity, but falls short. For instance, the administrative procedure in the domain of public procurement is enshrined in specific
legislation on the matter (*Act on the regulation of contracts of the
public sector,* of 2007), and not in Act 30/1992. The existence of
separate statutes for particular areas of administrative action, such as

procurement, is an example of the tension between "general regulation of administrative procedure" and regulation of sectoral administrative activity.

It is difficult to justify this state of regulatory decentralization, not
only in the light of the Constitution, but also in the light of the
requirements of EC Law, since the European legal order requires that
any and all "adjudicatory power" should behave according to a uniform body of basic rules, in order to ensure equal access to the public
markets of public procurement awards.

This separation of certain sectors from the common administrative procedure is unnecessary because it is artificial, something that
becomes evident in the regulation of the validity of administrative
decisions. Thus, the 2007 Act on public procurement (cited earlier)
regulates the validity of public contracts and the preparatory and preliminary decisions of those contracts (articles 31 to 36), but on the
other hand refers to Act 30/1992 for the procedure to annul and suspend the enforcement of the decisions rendered by public procurement adjudicatory bodies.

D. THE CURRENT REGULATION OF ADMINISTRATIVE PROCEDURE IS UNSUITABLE FOR CORRECT GOVERNANCE OF UNILATERAL AND "FORMAL" ADMINISTRATIVE ACTION

Act 30/1992 follows a model inherited from pre-constitutional
legislation, with an understanding of administrative procedure as
mainly a procedural relation between a specific administrative
agency and a citizen or a group, singled out on the basis of a concrete
and clearly defined characteristic. Under this idea: (1) the agency
implements the law with due respect for the procedural rights of the
individual (a clear analogy to the judicial paradigm of decision-making); (2) the administrative relation is established by "conflicting"
interests; and (3) the institutional role of the agency may be charac-

terized as "a party and a judge." From this perspective, the most important concern of the law is the validity of the preliminary and intermediate decisional steps, and of the final decision on the merits of a particular case.

This approach ensures the requirements of the due process clause (as enshrined in art. 1.1 and 9.3 of the Constitution), but underesti mates several important aspects of the administrative process. For instance, the informal activity of administrative agencies is not substantively regulated, and factors like third-party interests or the potential intervention of other public administrations are neglected. Finally, Act 30/1992 is unable to effectively govern complex decision-making processes in public administration (for instance, governmental programs that are jointly implemented by several public administrations or levels of government).

E. THE GAP BETWEEN RULES ON ADMINISTRATIVE PROCEDURE AND THE PRESENT STATE OF ORGANIZATION OF AND INSTRUMENTS FOR ADMINISTRATIVE ACTION

Act 30/1992 pays limited attention to crucial aspects of public administration, such as administrative organization and internal operation of the different administrative units. Each level of government is characterized by the Law of a distinct and autonomous legal personality, precisely to make possible its "unilateral" action *vis-à-vis* an individual or a group. For that reason, the Act is only concerned with the process of creating administrative units and organs, determining their competencies and establishing the conditions for their operation. Moreover, the provisions of Act 30/1992 on these matters are overly sparse and general, unable to fulfill the goal of fixing a general regulation regarding them.

Thus, from the beginning there was a gap between the general regulation set out in Act 30/1992 and other partial regulations set out in other laws, and between the internal dimension of administrative agencies (rules on organization and functioning) and the external dimension (rules on "uniform" or common administrative procedure). This gap is especially clear in determining the appropriate definition of "administrative agency" and in the decision-making process of administrative collegiate bodies. Other evidence of this gap is the fact that the provisions of Act 30/1992 on the application of new technologies in public administration have become largely outdated in the light of new, specific legislation on the matter (Act 11/2001 (June 22)), which falls outside the "system" of the said Act.

II
REMEDYING THE PRESENT SITUATION: RETHINKING "UNIFORM" ADMINISTRATIVE PROCEDURE IN SPAIN

A. FRAMEWORK

IN the Spanish legal system, administrative procedure is determined not only by the Constitution, but also by EC and international law. For this reason, the constitutional provisions on fundamental rights and civil liberties must be interpreted in the light of applicable international treaties and agreements. The internal regime of administrative procedure must be in accordance with international legal sources.

In the constitutional model (arts. 103.1[8] and 106[9]), the public administration has a two-fold reality. From the subjective perspective, it is an organization serving the general interest. From the objective perspective it is an activity aimed at the realization of said interest. From both perspectives, administrative procedure is an essential element of public administration. The current procedural regime should be adapted to the heterogeneous goals and perspectives of modern administrative action. However, this adaptation cannot be performed at legislators' whim, without taking into account the system of constitutional values and principles. The intertwining of "legal regime" and "uniform administrative procedure" is of great significance, and

---

8. C.E. Art. 103.1: The Public Administration shall serve the general interest in a spirit of objectivity and shall act in accordance with the principles of efficiency, hierarchy, decentralization, deconcentration, and coordination, and in full subordination to the law.").

9. C.E. Art. 106 ("The Courts shall check the power to issue regulations and ensure that the rule of law prevails in administrative action, and that the latter is subordinated to the ends which justify it. Private individuals shall, under the terms laid down by law, be entitled to compensation for any harm they may suffer in any of their property and rights, except in cases of force majeure, whenever such harm is the result of the operation of public services.").

should be resolved by means of two separate pieces of state legislation. Each one should contain the necessary uniform regulation of both aspects (the legal regime on the one hand, and administrative procedure on the other) and should act as the "foundation" or basic statute for subsequent, more precise regulations. The national parliament should identify the "basic" legal regime of the several public administrations and levels of government, the "uniform" administrative procedure, and leave room for specific regulations to be developed by local legislation.

B. THE RENEWAL OF ADMINISTRATIVE PROCEDURE

1. THE UNIFORM ADMINISTRATIVE PROCEDURE AND THE CONSTITUTION

The Spanish Constitution does not define the concept "administrative procedure," although it is present in its text (art. 105).[10] Nor does it define the concept of common "uniform administrative procedure" (*procedimiento administrativo común*), mentioned in art. 149.1.18, for the purpose of allocation of legislative power between central state and sub-state units (Autonomous Communities). This loophole has been filled by the case law of the Spanish Constitutional Court, which, in a series of decisions, has identified the material content of uniform administrative procedure.[11] Under this case law, uniform administrative procedure is the group of rules and principles governing the essential features of the decision-making process of administrative agencies, and the validity and enforce-

---

10. C.E. Art. 105 ("The law shall make provision for...the procedures for the taking of administrative action, with due safeguards for the hearing of interested parties when appropriate.").

11. *See, e.g* STC 157/1985 of Nov. 15, 1985 ; STC 50/1999 of Apr. 6, 1999; STC 251/2006 of July 25, 2006.

ability of administrative decisions (*actos administrativos*). It also covers the mechanisms for the revision of said administrative decisions, as well as guarantees to individuals in the decision-making process (right to be heard, right to defense, etc.). However, the national parliament cannot cover every aspect of this domain, for it may only regulate rules deemed to be "in common" in order to ensure "uniformity" in the action of the several levels and units of government and public administration. What is more, "uniform administrative procedure" and "administrative organization" are different, though intertwined, concepts.

In light of the constitutional case law, it is possible to correctly identify the concept of common or "uniform administrative procedure": (1) this notion consists of a complete and "commonplace" set of rules which are self-executing and do not require any further legal implementation, and for these reasons are binding and directly applicable to any administrative action; (2) these rules are universal, in the sense that they bind all of the action of the different levels and layers of government and public administration, but are restricted to what are supposed to be strictly "uniform" requirements of the Constitution, and an idea connected to the equality of all citizens; (3) it is a multifunctional concept, because it works independently of the features of the acting administrative organization and of the sectorial regulation; (4) to a certain extent, it is also a "residual" regulation, because there exist separate constitutional provisions on specific administrative matters, such as "expropriation," the "liability of public administration," and "public contracts." The separate rules on these matters are the natural place to establish procedural guarantees to the individual who faces these forms of administrative action.

In short, "uniform administrative procedure" has its own domain and includes not only the "nuclear" elements that have been mentioned earlier, but also common minimum guarantees in sectoral administrative action, where the Constitution has not established a specific ground for federal, as opposed to local, competence.

2. Uniform Administrative Procedure and EU Law

The fact that Spain is a member state of the EU has transformed the several domestic Spanish public administrations and levels of government into "indirect" administrations of the EC, and this radical feature has determined that all the requirements, guarantees, and principles of administrative procedure that have been spelled out in European rules (including directives, regulations, and laws) and the case law of the ECJ are fully applicable in Spain. This development triggers some important consequences in our field of discussion: (1) the national "administrative procedure" must adequately serve not only the "domestic" general interest, but also the European one; and (2) the EC Law requirements on administrative procedure, which are common to all member States, must also be taken as components of "uniform" administrative procedure in Spain.

What is more, the EC elements on administrative procedure prevail over the purely "domestic" provisions, and the latter must be adapted and interpreted in light of these European standards. As a consequence, domestic administrative procedure must be ready to absorb and internalize the growing impact of the different institutional and procedural regulations established by EC Law.

The EC influence on the domestic regulation of administrative procedure comes not only from binding legal materials, but also from "soft law." For instance, the non-binding Charter of Fundamental Rights, signed at Nice on December 7, 2000 (and introduced in the Primary EC Law by the new Treaty of Lisbon) establishes several provisions in the domain of administrative procedure, such as good administration, access to files and documents, and the right of petition. These elements must be taken into consideration when interpreting Spanish constitutional law.

C. SOME ASPECTS THAT REQUIRE CHANGES

1. THE "GOVERNMENT-CITIZEN" RELATIONSHIP

From a constitutional perspective, administrative action is correct as long as it respects some principles that are implicit in the Constitution, such as the principles of transparency, participation, and responsible performance. However, the current "uniform" administrative procedure does not openly declare these principles, and when it takes those principles it transforms them into purely procedural rights and duties.

If, under the Constitution, the determination of the basic conditions that ensure the equality of all citizens *vis-à-vis* the government is within the competence of the State, then uniform administrative procedure should rely on the true status of the government-citizen relationship. This status must be based on the fundamental position of the citizen as a holder of constitutional rights and duties (for instance, the right to participate directly in public affairs, enshrined in art. 23.1).[12]

2. THE "GOVERNMENT-TO-GOVERNMENT" RELATIONSHIP

From the perspective of the territorial structure of Spain, the relationships between the several territorial levels of government (central administration, autonomous communities, and local governments) are of crucial importance in the domain of administrative procedure, because the procedure usually involves different levels of public administration. From this perspective, Act 30/1992 sets out a system of inter-administrative relationships. This regulation is unsatisfactory because it only covers certain features or general principles, and produces confusion between the procedural or "dynamic" dimension and the institutional aspects of the administrative process. The Act only stresses certain features of inter-agency regulation, such as the duties

---

12. C.E. Art. 23.1 ("Citizens have the right to participate in public affairs, directly or through representatives freely elected in periodic elections by universal suffrage.").

of mutual assistance and cooperation, and these duties are regulated in a rather murky way and do not produce specific consequences in the domain of administrative procedure (for instance, when a given legal rule states that a given decision must be taken jointly by two or more public administrations).

3. The Structure of the Procedure

Uniform administrative procedure is certainly ambiguous in its present form, due to confusion between the "uniform" and "general" elements of administrative procedure. The administrative procedure that is "uniform" should be differentiated from the elements that are merely steps in the "dynamic" or sequential development of the procedure, and in this sense some techniques should be eliminated. For instance, governmental "silence" or inaction is automatically interpreted as a real, *tacit* administrative decision (a technique known as "administrative silence," *silencio administrativo*), if public administration does not make a formal decision within a specific time-span or deadline. Eliminating the "tacit" decision would recognize the fact that administrative activity is so heterogeneous that imposing a "general" or "universal" deadline for adopting a decision on all agencies is simply unreasonable. In most cases, the general interest is poorly served by a mere "tacit" decision and may require a decision that is more complex than a "yes" or "no" reply. In addition, this technique is too rough and simplistic, and is therefore incapable of producing legal certainty for an individual.

4. A Uniform Legal Regime for the Validity and Enforcement of Administrative Decisions

The conceptual category of the administrative decision (*acto administrativo*) urgently needs updating. This concept is outdated from the perspective of increasingly complex and diverse administrative action in our changing and risk-prone society. This situation should no longer surprise anyone because the traditional idea of the *acto administrativo* or administrative decision has been based on the conceptual paradigm of the government as "the organization that applies the law to a specific case" (similar to the quasi-judicial paradigm of the decision-making process). In my view, the administrative decision category should not be based on a single model, but instead should result in different types of administrative decisions: partial decisions, provisional decisions, and so on.

Another element in need of revision is the fact that, under the current rules on uniform administrative procedure, the system of judicial revision of administrative decisions depends on whether the decision is favorable or unfavorable to the citizen. However, the terms of this duality (favorable/positive vs. unfavorable/negative) are rather ambiguous from the point of view of the addressees of the decision, something that is made clear in the domains of subsidies and of administrative penalties.

CHAPTER X

IMPLICATIONS OF THE LAW ON ADMINISTRATIVE PROCEDURE FOR GENERATING KNOWLEDGE IN PUBLIC ADMINISTRATION

Winfried Kluth* and Jana Nuckelt**

* Professor of Administrative Law, University of Halle, Germany.

** Research Assistant of Administrative Law, University of Halle, Germany.

INDEX

I N our modern knowledge-based society, the administration is faced with many difficulties and challenges that arise from the overwhelming quantity and variety of information available, from the constantly rising standards for the evaluation and processing of information, and from limited, highly regulated budget resources. This article analyzes the traditional structure of administrative proceedings and examines whether acquired knowledge may be utilized for developing a law governing the generation and administration of information in the public sector, and if so, how. Three factors need to be taken into account from the perspective of national law as well as European Community law: 1) the importance of the principle of administrative investigation, 2) the role of third persons (citizens, as well as other authorities, including experts) in the process of generating knowledge, and 3) the information duties of the administration in relation to citizens and companies. The procedural law may take the existing legal instruments for generating and processing of information as a starting point. However, in many isolated instances, further development and improvement of the legal and technological frame is necessary.

I
STATE AND ADMINISTRATION IN THE KNOWLEDGE-BASED SOCIETY

It is one of the characteristics of our time that both the life of the individual and the functioning of the economy, the society, and the state[1] are affected by the basic conditions of our knowledge-based society.[2] The challenging increase in information, combined with ever-increasing requirements for information evaluation and processing, leads one to wonder whether these developments are advantageous to the individual, society, and the state. Private individuals, entrepreneurs, and even the state certainly can appreciate the convenience produced by the possibility that modern technology allows to communicate, gather information, and exchange expert knowledge from the office or the living room anywhere in the world. In some companies today, work is done around-the-clock in global real time. Electronic stock exchanges require decisions from every corner of the globe to be transmitted within a split second.

In stark contrast, the institutional sector of public administration rarely, if ever, takes such quick action. As a consequence of the legal requirements concerning public budget expenditure and the award of contracts, as well as chronically limited resources in general, the administration is rarely able to provide itself with cutting edge technology when it is first released, or even whilst still current. Besides this basic mechanical problem, as we will see, the increase in information and knowledge gives rise to substantial challenges for the public administration in many other respects.

As of yet, administrative law has only partially responded to these challenges. In the past few years, it has attempted to develop e-government in the area of electronic administrative proceedings.[3] However, this development is still ongoing. From the citizens' perspective, the laws on the administration of information and data protection have simply been reactions to new technological developments.[4] Yet, these developments comprise only a few, although significant, segments pertinent to this subject matter. For this information to be useful to other agencies of the administration in their various tasks, it is necessary to implement changes well beyond the mere improvement of dissemination of information not only within the public administration itself but also in its relationship with private partners.

In order to cope with the changes brought about by the increase in the generation and administration[5] of information based on the division of labor, the law of administrative procedure is essential. The law of administrative procedure is not only a formal frame of administrative action, but also the medium of information transmission. For the state and its administration, which are inevitably affected by the rapid development of new knowledge, new technology, and all the related risks, the gathering of new and updated information becomes ever more crucial. The establishment of an organizational and procedural base for the generation of information that complies with the required administrative duties and responsibilities is therefore vital. Against this background, great hopes are placed in the study of public administration.[6]

Since this article cannot exhaustively deal with the subject matter, it will focus on the currently established relationship of the law on administrative procedure with the generation of information. Hence, it is the objective of this article to analyze the traditional structure of administrative proceedings, which focuses on the influence of administrative procedure law on the generation of information and the decisions which are based on this information from a different perspective and to examine whether and how the acquired experience may be utilized for developing a law governing the generation and administration of information in public administration.

II
DEFINITION OF TERMS AND SPECIFICATION
OF THE OBJECT OF INVESTIGATION

AT the beginning of this investigation, some terms must be defined. These include the terms data, information, and knowledge, which function as key terms. Referring to the works of Willke[7], the subsequent considerations are based on the following understanding:

A. DATA, INFORMATION AND KNOWLEDGE

1. DATA

Data are the raw material of all knowledge. They may be described as "observable differences," since all data require an instrument that enables their observation and subsequent differentiation.[8] For example, a brick falls from the roof of a house onto the street or a Russian citizen works in a German factory.

Additionally, in order to be usable, data must be encoded, and therefore also must be presented in a certain established form, characterized by figures, language, text, or pictures. In recent years, significant changes have taken place with regard to both the observation instruments available[9] as well as the development of encoding methods, releasing a proverbial flood of information into today's world.

2. INFORMATION

Information is system-specific processed data, and as such constitutes an intermediate product of knowledge. Data become information through integration into a relevant context that applies to a certain system.[10] In this manner, different information is obtained from the same data concerning a major project in connection with different areas of environmental law and the law governing the admission of technical installations on the basis of different legal contexts. The relevance of the context reveals that new information may emerge by passing on data to other institutions operating in a different context. Vice versa, the passing on of information also requires that the transmitting and receiving institutions ascertain the appropriate legal contexts for the data. At this point, the specific requirements for the management of information become apparent. To continue with our examples, the brick is a danger for people on the street and the Russian worker needs authorization to work legally in Germany.

3. KNOWLEDGE

Knowledge is the refinement of information through practice. Knowledge, in this sense, evolves when information is integrated into a practical context and a new or changed practice arises.[11] This concept of knowledge is not purely theoretical; instead, it is specifically focused on the actions and control of organizations. The obtained information is integrated into a second relevant context. The second criterion of relevance is based on normative and empirical patterns, in which the suitability for the intended purpose is expressed. In our examples, the local administration can obligate the owner of the house to repair his roof. Similarly, the Russian worker has to apply for a work permit or to leave the country, and the owner of the factory may be held responsible for his foreign employees. The context of responsibility and obligation in which the information is placed constitutes knowledge.

With every increase in knowledge, there is a corresponding increase in ignorance.[12] This important insight serves as a reminder to the state and the administration to act with caution and reserve when the exercise of power is based on knowledge, particularly concerning far-reaching plans and when rights are at stake.

This distinction deviates from the traditional understanding insofar as factual knowledge at the data level and specialized knowledge at the information level are defined by the relevant context. The *knowing what* is clearly differentiated from the knowing how and more importance is attached to the latter.[13]

4. IMPLICIT AND EXPLICIT KNOWLEDGE

The distinction between implicit and explicit knowledge, as introduced by Polanyi[14] in 1958, is an important aspect of the peculiarities of knowledge both in and of organizations. While explicit knowledge is an articulated, documented, and therefore generally accessible knowledge, implicit knowledge is characterized by certain rules and experiences that are unarticulated yet obeyed. These implicit rules contribute to the functioning of organizations. This phenomenon is also addressed by the term "administrative culture."[15] However, it is problematic to equate implicit knowledge with irrational knowledge.[16] Implicit knowledge, unlike irrational knowledge, may be converted into explicit knowledge.

5. INSTITUTIONAL KNOWLEDGE

Closely related to implicit knowledge is the knowledge of organizations or institutional knowledge, although these phenomena are not identical. Institutional knowledge is contained in regulatory systems established and maintained without regard to specific individuals, and therefore anonymously. It is found in organizations of every kind, from the Catholic Church, which has a tradition of more than two thousand years, to States, associations, enterprises, and families.[17]

Institutional knowledge corresponds to the recognition of institutions as bodies capable of action.[18] According to the German *Amtswalter* theory,[19] organizations can only act via persons. The acts of the natural person are considered acts of the organization, so that it is the organization and not the natural person responsible for them. At the same time, the information the natural person possesses is in effect information (knowledge) belonging to the organization. Nevertheless, this does not mean that only persons are capable of action and therefore that it is the persons who act voluntarily. Instead, the actions are determined by the internal peculiarities of an organization and externally imposed on each member.[20] The decisive factor for attributing actions to the institution is the consistency of the underlying system of action, which is determined by the internal institutional knowledge, based on practical understanding, which is the focus of this article.[21] The organization can avail itself of the long-term experience of all of its members and employees, as stored in the internal rules of the organization. In this way, the organization knows more than any individual person acting for the organization. When these people obey the internal rules of an organization, they are inadvertently taking advantage of the accumulated knowledge and experience.

B. GENERATING KNOWLEDGE

This article will focus on the generation of knowledge.[22] The expression "generating knowledge" comprises the entire process: beginning with the gathering of data, through processing the information, and culminating in its conversion into knowledge (in the practical sense, as defined above). Generating knowledge includes external processes – in particular, obtaining the data – as well as the internal processes of placing the data in context.

The process of generating knowledge is determined both by the structure of the organization and by its procedure. In this respect, the organizational structure is characterized by different organizational types,[23] while the procedure is determined by different procedural methods and by procedural law.[24]

The following sections examine the specific interactions between the structural framework, determined by the law regarding the organization of the administration, and the procedural framework, determined by organizational and procedural law, and their implications on knowledge generation.

C. ATTRIBUTION OF KNOWLEDGE

Finally, the attribution of knowledge has to be mentioned.[25] It plays an important role in organizations characterized by decentralized gathering of knowledge. To examine the attribution of knowledge, one must explore the relationship between the descriptive and the normative. The question is whether the descriptive knowledge extant, if not brought together within the confines of the organization, is also relevant at the normative level, and if so, to what extent it can be considered grounds for action. Closely related to this is the establishment of the duties of the legislature and the administration, and the processes and parameters they should use to organize of information.[26] This topic, which so far has been discussed mainly from the viewpoint of liability law,[27] will not be extensively discussed here.

III

RESPONSIBILITY OF THE ADMINISTRATION UNDER THE RULE OF LAW AND THE PRINCIPLE OF ADMINISTRATIVE INVESTIGATION FOR THOROUGH ACQUISITION OF INFORMATION AS A BASIS FOR DECISIONS

A. BACKGROUND

UNDER the principle of administrative investigation, the decision-making authority in any procedure is obliged to clarify the facts relevant to its decision ex officio. With regard to the administrative procedures described in section 9 of the *Verwaltungsverfahrensgesetz* or Administrative Procedure Act (APA),[28] section 24 of that act[29] lays down the principles of administrative investigation by taking into account basic principles already in effect at that time.

Several special provisions, such as section 86 of the Verwaltungsgerichtsordnung (Rules of the Administrative Courts - VwGO), section 88 of the Abgabenordnung (Fiscal Code - AO), section 20 of the Sozialgesetzbuch X (Social Security Code X - SGB-X), section 76 of the Finanzgerichtsordnung (Tax Court Code - FGO), and section 103 of the Sozialgerichtsgesetz (Rules of the Social Courts - SGG), comprise specific forms of administrative investigation.[30] This principle applies analogously to the other administrative procedures as a basic principle of administrative law.[31] Thus, the principle of administrative investigation constitutes a part of the comprehensive principles of administrative procedure.

When concerning the direct execution of Community law, the same European Community law considers the official duty to investigate all relevant facts a basic legal principle. According to Art. 41 of the Charter of Fundamental Rights of the European Union[32] (hereinafter CFR), this duty forms an integral part of the right to good administration. The Commission's investigative rights comprise the right of access to data as provided for in Art. 284 EC[33] at the level of primary law, and as provided for at the level of secondary law of special investigation authorizations, for example, in Articles 4 and 17 of EC Regulation 1/2003.[34] As far as the indirect execution of European Community law and national law implementing Community law are concerned, according to the case law of the European Court of Justice, section 24 of the APA is to be applied as a basic principle, and compliance must be ensured in the national execution of European Community law.[35]

The investigation of the facts of a case as thoroughly as possible is an indispensable precondition for correct application of the law and, is therefore a requirement for legitimacy of administrative actions as stipulated in Article 20 ¶ 3 of the *Grundgesetz* (Basic Constitutional Law - GG).[36] This seemingly simple idea, as a goal of administrative procedure, is far from easy to implement practically and legally. Several obstacles occur, in light of current efforts to accelerate and simplify administrative procedures, cooperation, transparency, and data protection. The different goals that guide the process of investigation into the facts of a case are partially contradictory. A more simple procedure may result in a less accurate investigation and cooperation with private actors runs the risk of biasing the administrative procedure and decision towards private interests. It is the task of the agency governing the procedure to settle this conflict to the greatest possible extent permitted by its discretionary power.

The complexity of the practical and legal requirements for the investigation of the facts of a case is expressed only rudimentarily in the wording of section 24.1 of the APA. In particular, this provision suggests the existence of previously fixed facts of a case, which may need further investigation.[37] Contrary to this, a more contemporary view is that the facts of the case themselves are linked inseparably to and produced by administrative procedure.[38] Thus, the modern administrative lawyer refers to a process of acquiring and processing information in which the agency governing the procedure and other interested parties participate in different roles. Additionally, in light of the undisputed relevance of the acquisition of information on basic rights,[39] the factual and legal aspects of investigation of the facts of a case are inextricably intertwined. Thus, the official duty to investigate, as established by the principle of administrative investigation, is already manifestly dependent and restricted at the legal level. In particular, it does not follow that the administration has unlimited competence to acquire information from the principle of administrative investigation itself.[40]

There is another determining factor for the realistic evaluation of fact investigation as part of the official daily routine, which must not be underestimated: in regular administrative procedures a remarkable economy of investigational efforts can be observed. This is caused by a shortage of staff as well as a lack of time and must be regarded as a reaction to increased legal requirements - perhaps better said, obstacles – concerning the acquisition of information. As a consequence, not all of the evidence and expert opinions will be considered and the information given by interested parties is presumed true or false even if the procedural requirements for such assumptions are not fulfilled.[41]

B. RANGE OF THE CONTENT OF THE DUTY TO INVESTIGATE INTO THE FACTS

Although the second sentence of APA § 24 ¶1 leaves the manner and breadth of investigations into the facts of a case to official discretion, against the background of the first sentence of that section it must be assumed that the aim is complete (*i.e.,* as far as possible in terms of the factual and legal situation) investigation of the facts of a case. In this respect, the factual and legal peculiarities of the object of a procedure and the cause for the official action (ex officio or upon application) are the decisive circumstances. In such context, discretion in administrative procedure works as discretion for clarification.[42]

Only the facts relevant to a decision should be investigated. In order to discover which facts still merit investigation, one may apply the procedure whereby certain facts are presumed to be true in order to ascertain the facts necessary to the decision.[43] The facts of the case that have already been investigated are legally assessed. Facts irrelevant to the decision according to this analysis may be excluded from further investigation.[44]

Particularly in those cases in which the administration acts upon application,[45] it may base its decision on the facts presented by the applicant inasmuch as they appear to be typical circumstances with no concrete indication of any special circumstance requiring a special assessment of the case.[46] This is especially common in tax procedure law, which is controlled by administrative regulations in order to ensure the principle of equality.[47]

Once the personal and financial expenditures connected with the factual investigation of a case are considered alongside the chronically empty state of public accounts and the consequent orientation towards the principles of thrift as well as cost-effectiveness,[48] the question arises as to what extent these costs affect the determination of the scope of factual investigations and the administrative work plan. A certain input of resources not falling below a minimum standard is particularly required in cases in which one would otherwise have to assume an infringement of the duty to execute rules according to GG Art. 20 ¶ 3.[49] In several areas, the adoption of practices used in tax procedure law due to lack of resources is possible. These practices include, for example, urging the contending parties to reach a settlement or issuing an administrative decision while reserving the right to reexamine it later.[50]

Since investigations may take a long time, can be very complex, and may need to be revisited (see section 26 paragraph 1 No. 3 of the APA),[51] the acquired information must be stored in consistent, complete, and correctly filed records. For example, even parts of files which are later proven to be factually incorrect cannot be removed from a file unless there is a claim for deletion under the data privacy law, *Bundesdatenschutzgesetz* § 20 ¶ 2 and § 35 ¶ 2 (Federal Data Protection Act - BDSG).[52] The new, correct information must be included in the record as well.

C. RULES ON THE BURDEN OF PROOF

The law on administrative procedure in APA §§ 24 and 26 does not explicitly establish a burden of proof for the involved parties, as is characteristic in civil procedure. For this reason, it has been argued[53] that there is no burden of proof in the law of administrative procedure. Not even the burden of participation on the persons involved or the possibility of a motion to take evidence[54] could change the dictated outcome. On the contrary, the substantial burden of proof is relevant only if, despite all official attempts of investigation, the facts of a case still cannot be determined. On the other hand, according to a more recent opinion,[55] the burden of proof can be seen as in favor of the interested parties even in cases in which the interested parties have a substantial burden of proof, as long as it is impossible for the agency to supply evidence to the contrary. Since, in the end, the substantial burden of proof is the decisive factor linking both opinions, the dispute concerns terminology rather than the matter itself.

Therefore, if it depends significantly on the sharing of the substantial burden of proof (objective burden of determination), the question revolves upon which principles give rise to this shared burden between the administration and the persons involved. There are some explicit provisions on the burden of proof, such as BDSG § 8 ¶ 4[56] and § 48 ¶ 3 of the *Baugesetzbuch* (Federal Building Code – BauGB).[57] Leaving aside such explicit provisions, the decision hangs on the facts of whom a provision favors (also called the principle of the provision-favored person),[58] to whose sphere of disposition and responsibility the unproven fact belongs (theory of spheres),[59] and, taking the substantive law into account, to whom the risk of the administrative decision[60] is assigned in cases of a *non liquet*.[61]

Notwithstanding these basic rules, it is possible that the burden of proof shifts not only due to explicit provisions but also due to general criteria.[62] The analogous application of §282 of the *Bürgerliches Gesetzbuch* (Civil Code – BGB) is particularly relevant here.[63] Under that section, the facts must be distinguished in order to determine where the obstruction of evidence occurs. The burden of proof does not automatically shift. The predominant opinion in § 282 cases generally states that a decision is made according to the substantial burden of proof.[64]

INCLUSION OF THIRD PERSONS IN THE PROCESS
OF GENERATING INFORMATION

A. DUTY TO COOPERATE OF APPLICANTS AND
OTHER PERSONS INVOLVED

CONTRARY to the idea of having the burden of proof on a particular party, the principle of administrative investigation is meant to guarantee that the administrative decision is reached independently of the parties' arbitrariness.[65] The persons involved are generally exempted from investigating the facts of a case. Nevertheless, the inquiry into the facts as stipulated by section 24 paragraph 1 sentence 1 of the APA does not take place in an area without law. Rather, access to excessive information causes interferences with the legal sphere of citizens. Therefore, the question arises whether in these cases the public authority governing the administrative procedure needs to be legally authorized to find the facts of a case and, if so, where these required authorizations may be found. Additionally, the manner in which the procedure may be affected if certain information is not accessible to the administration needs to be clarified.

Today, it is common understanding that the first sentence of § 24 ¶ 1 of the APA does not empower the agency to carry out fact-finding measures affecting fundamental rights.[66] What is required is either a specific authorization or the consent of the affected. Moreover, APA § 26 ¶ 2,[67] which requires the persons involved to cooperate in the fact-finding process, provides an obligation but not an authorization to interfere.[68] The text of the third sentence of APA §26 ¶2 supports this view. Corresponding authorizations may be found primarily in substantive law. Here the provisions of the law concerning police and public order are of special significance. In the area of environmental law a growing number of cooperation and information duties is established as well.[69] Therefore, together with Pitschas, it may be assumed that the state and the citizen carry a common responsibility for the generation of knowledge.[70]

The burden of participation[71] in APA § 26 ¶ 2 leaves it to the discretion of the interested party to cooperate in official fact-finding. This primarily applies, as sentence 2 illustrates, for the facts and evidence lying in the sphere of the interested party. The administration may speed up participation by setting a deadline.[72] In case of a refusal to participate, there is no loss of material rights due to nonparticipation because the burden of participation is merely procedural.[73] However, when evaluating the evidence, the administration may indirectly sanction the interested party when the refusal to participate results in missing or incomplete facts. Possible sanctions include putting an application aside or delaying the process,[74] feigning the withdrawal of the application,[75] assuming that missing or incomplete facts weigh against that party,[76] or even finding contributory fault[77] and refusing to hear offered evidence.[78] In terms of procedural law, the refusal to participate may also be sanctioned through special provisions mandating formal or substantive forfeiture of rights.[79]

Further, independent duties of participation may arise from provisions contained in special acts. An interested party may be required to appear in person, to give information, to obtain an expert opinion, to present documents, or to permit inspection of documents as well as to permit a visit by the public authority to the location in question, a search, or an investigation by a public health officer.[80]

The necessary elements of the respective rules will determine whether additional official fact-finding measures are allowed and whether interested parties must carry out their own means of investigation on the basis of substantive legal competences to act, such as the general clause of police law.[81] These decisions are most often disputed in cases where there is only a faint suspicion of danger.[82]

Sections 24 and 26 of the APA do not provide a basis for requiring interested parties to bear the costs of fact-finding. In general, the administration bears these costs. In some instances, especially those in which the procedure is open via application on the part of the involved party, it is possible to pass on the costs to the applicant. As a rule, the interested parties are responsible for the costs of fact-finding in proportion to their participation, according to APA § 26 ¶ 2, except where a legal claim for reimbursement exists.[83]

The increased transfer of information-gathering and knowledge-generation duties to the interested parties embodied in substantive law[84] gives rise to the displacement of public investigation and thus leads to an increased shift of responsibility from the administration towards the applicant. A similar problem occurs when these substantive provisions in effect oblige the persons involved to incriminate themselves.[85] Such self-incrimination for the benefit of the administration is generally[86] objected to under APA § 26.

No less important, provisions of European Community law may prescribe certain participation duties for the persons involved. For instance, the Directive on the Recognition of Professional Qualifications[87] (DPRQ) establishes specific information duties for service suppliers and individuals willing to exercise their freedom to establish cross-border traffic. For instance, according to DRPQ Art. 7 ¶ 1[88], a service supplier can be required to notify and inform authorities of existing insurance coverage when first traveling into another member state with the intent to supply services. Furthermore, the responsible public authorities of the host member state may require the service supplier to furnish the recipient of the service with certain information, as per DRPQ Article 9 lit. (a)–(f).[89] If the responsible authority of a host member state has to decide on an application to pursue a regulated profession in the sense of DRPQ Art. 3 ¶ 1 lit. (a), it may demand the presentation of detailed documents and certificates according to DRPQ Art. 50 ¶ 1 and DRPQ Annex VII.[90]

B. PARTICIPATION DUTIES OF OTHER AUTHORITIES

Many provisions stipulate the participation of other entities in an administrative procedure. In general, actions not corresponding to the public authority governing the procedure are not considered outwardly directed actions and, hence, are not procedural actions in the sense of APA § 9.[91] Because the action of another authority is usually only

an internal, preparatory act, no parties other than the relevant authorities are involved under the conditions of APA § 13.[92]

There are many current examples of such duties to participate. Official
communication and investigation duties are stipulated in section 68 of the
Arzneimittelgesetz (Medicine Act – AMG).[93] According to BauGB § 36,[94] there
is a duty to participate, and in particular to agree or assent, placed on the local
administration in proceedings conducted by a higher administrative authority.
Further requirements of participation can also arise as in the case of section 72 of
the Aufenthaltsgesetz (Residence Act - AufenthG),[95] for example. The administrative assistance explicitly stipulated in section 4 APA[96] should be distinguished
from instances where participation duties are required of other authorities.

At the level of European Community law, Article 8 DRPQ[97] lays
down rules governing the administrative cooperation between the
responsible authorities of the home member state and the host member state with regard to the exchange of information concerning the
legality of establishment and the good conduct of a service supplier.
This information is to be transferred according to Article 56 DRPQ[98].
Subject to this provision, the authorities of the home member state
and of the host member state work together closely and provide mutual administrative assistance. Accordingly, in Article 28 of the Directive on Services in the Internal Market[99] (subsequently cited as SD),[100]
member states are to provide mutual administrative assistance and to
take the measures necessary for effective administrative cooperation.

C. UTILIZATION OF EXTERNAL EXPERTISE

If the responsible agency lacks the necessary expertise to reach an
informed decision, the remedy may be investigations carried out by
private experts.[101] Compare, for instance, § 24 AMG, or § 13 of the
9th *Bundesimmissionsschutzverordnung*[102] (Federal Emissions Protection Regulation – BimSchV).[103] This solution is increasingly
used.[104] When hiring private experts,[105] the administration must

ensure that the expert keeps within the legal limits of generating information.[106] In many cases, the consultation of an expert specifically focused on a given procedure is not necessary. To the contrary, the administration may also introduce into the proceedings an expert opinion created in the scope of a different administrative procedure by giving that expert the possibility to comment.

Given that it has its basis in the principle of administrative investigation, the use of private expertise presents the danger of excessive dependence on private experts in decision-making. Such dependence endangers the democratic legitimacy of the decision insofar as one takes the classic democratic understanding of the Federal Constitutional Court[107] as a basis. Consequently, the principle of democracy also determines the process of a cooperative generation of knowledge, for instance, in the scope of application of section 4b BauGB[108].[109]

A private expert opinion presented by an interested party to substantiate their statement of facts is not expert evidence in the sense of APA § 26 ¶ 2 No. 2, which pertains to an official request for an opinion. On the assumption that private actors always pursue their own interests to some degree,[110] the administration needs to be able to examine and evaluate the product of consultation on the basis of its own expertise. This independent evaluation is a minimum requirement for shifting the burden of generating knowledge onto private persons.[111] Currently, due to budget bottlenecks, there is a reduction in specialized staff in the public administration. Rules stipulated in special laws also state specific requirements with regard to the instruction of private experts; compare, for example, AMG § 65 ¶ 4.[112]

V

THE DUTY OF THE ADMINISTRATION TOWARDS CITIZENS AND COMPANIES VIS-À-VIS INFORMATION

A. INFORMATION AS A BASE FOR THE USE OF FREEDOM

FREE access to information is guaranteed by the freedom of information stipulated in GG Art. 5 ¶ 1[113]. The ability to fight the infringement of fundamental laws is increased through legislation increasing and modifying legal claims, specifically claims for the release of information. On the one hand, this aligns with the high value of freedom of opinion, media, and information in a democracy. But it also plays an important role in the scope of application of other fundamental rights. Two important rights which are bolstered by freedom of information are the right to know one's own descent in the context of the general right of personality (GG Art. 2 ¶ 1 in connection with Art. 1 ¶ 1[114])[115] and the granting of information indispensable for an economic activity according to GG Art. 12 ¶ 1[116] (in other words, information for planning). The presence of fundamental rights means that the government increasingly has to justify any limitations on the right of the access to information.

Conflicting objectives are present in the restrictions of information following from the right to informational self-determination (or privacy) and the right of access to information guaranteed by the freedom of information. The necessary balance is provided by the area-specific principles of the law on data protection.

Eventually, the claim for equal opportunity participation in private access to information administrated by the state must be taken into account, which follows from the right of individual liberty in connection with GG Article 3 ¶ 1[117]. In this respect, the specific need for information, the degree to which one is affected, and integration in official decision processes may constitute legitimate criteria with which to differentiate between requesting parties.

According to current understanding, private applicants, in general, also need to be granted complete rights to inspect files and gain information in areas in which the state collects and provides information.[118] The principle of secrecy, although valid as a rule, functions as a limit, as do the law on data protection, the right to privacy, and other important public interests.

Respective rules are provided for in the Informationsfreiheitsgesetz (Freedom of Information Act – IFG) of the federation and in the respective Acts of the federal States, as well as in sector-specific provisions (compare APA § 73 ¶ 3[119] and Umweltverträglichkeitsprüfungsgesetz [Act on Assessment of Environmental Effects – UVPG] art. 9,[120] with the third sentence of BImSchG § 10 ¶ 3 in connection with § 10 of the 9th BImSchV)[121]. Because of these limits, the claim for access to information often presents itself as a claim for participation in generating information.

The widening informational claims of citizens, together with the rules on administrative transparency, decisively stem from European directives such as the Directive on the Freedom of Access to Information on the Environment.[122] A similar provision may also be detected in the Charter on Fundamental Rights of the European Union. According to Art. 8 § 1 of this Charter,[123] every person has the right to protection of his or her personal data. Art, 11 ¶ 1 ensures the freedom to receive and pass on information and ideas.[124] Art. 41 ¶ 2[125] guarantees the right of access to any files and documents of the European Parliament, Council, and Commission related to the requesting party. Art. 255 ¶ 1 EC[126] also guarantees free access to documents of the European Parliament, Council, and Commission for every natural or juridical person with a place of residence in a member state of the European Union. At the level of secondary Community law, for instance, SD Arts. 7 and 22[127] require member states to ensure that information is easily accessible for service suppliers and recipients. This provision reduces the transaction costs for cross-border activity and aids the vindication of the respective basic freedoms.

B. CHANGE IN THE BASIC UNDERSTANDING OF ACCESS TO INFORMATION AND DUTY TO INFORM

Nowadays, the deliberate use of information in order to regulate conduct (information-based state action) and the granting of access to information are among the standard instruments of state action. Yet state conduct with regard to information is also becoming more and more complex and technologically refined. This technological complexity does not manifest itself only in access to personal data held by the government via the Internet. The omnipresence of information and communication, as well as the rapid progress of information technology, lead to the limits of classic sovereign regulatory concepts, which because of their long procedural course are often technologically outstripped when finally entering into force. The use of indefinite legal terms as well as delegation of the power to issue regulations is also helpful only to a limited extent.

The law governing access to information, which in many areas has been improved, reduces the informational superiority of the state a great deal with its manifold opportunities to gain information. The individual-related information activity of the state refers to supplying information (see, for example, the second sentence of APA§ 25,[128] SGB I § 15, and the second sentence of AO § 89),[129] consultation of citizens on the handing in of declarations or filing of applications (for instance, the first sentence of APA § 25, SGB I §§ 14, 16, and the first sentence of AO § 89),[130] as well as granting of inspection of files (APA § 29).[131]

Although the publication duties of the administration have increased, the existing legal order concerning information is deficient with respect to the organization of private access to proceedings of the executive and with respect to the principle of limited file publicity. For this reason, a new and more appropriate administrative procedure law governing information must take these developments into account.[132]

C. LIABILITY ISSUES

Liability issues arise when the administration does not comply with the requirements for the state organization of knowledge. In this respect, the question of to what extent relying on state liability law may offer a solution to this problem arises. It is possible to rely on instances of official liability according to BGB § 839 in connection with the first sentence of GG Art. 34[133] or on liability under administrative law obligations according to BGB sections 280 I, 249.[134] Another possibility is liability based on principles of reliance, which derives from protection of confidence. The latter may be regarded as a product of the GG Art. 20 ¶ 3 principle of a state governed by the rule of law and fundamental rights. The final option would be to apply the principle of loyalty and good faith.

However, to rely on any of these to solve the problems arising from a breach of the requirements for the organization of information is flawed. With regard to the injunctive relief usual to official liability under BGB § 839, redress for mistakes when dealing with information and positive knowledge is impossible because there is only a claim for money payment but no restitution in kind. Liability arising from an administrative law obligation does not provide a convincing solution, due to its limited scope of application and the lack of a relevant duty to organize information. Similarly, liability based on reliance proves unsatisfactory because the elements of a rule of confidence related to a poorly functioning organization constitute a low standard of protection and the confidence in such an organization will be difficult to articulate as a legal position. Moreover, the principle of loyalty and good faith is only used in exceptional cases because a particularly egregious act of frustration of legitimate expectations with regard to the organization of information is necessary.

Nevertheless, *Henning*[135] tries to grasp the more recent developments in civil law concerning the establishment of duties to organize knowledge in the public law by means of state liability. The liability of the administration in cases where the administration decided on the basis of incorrect information (facts) will force the administration to avoid such mistakes and to optimize the generation of information.

The question whether it is possible to draw on the preexisting forms of state liability cannot currently been resolved. Instead, the article will now outline the practical legal issues and current tendencies of development in Germany with regard to the organization of information.

The legal practice established the following principles with regard to information.[136] First, the usual addressee of a knowledge provision is generally neither the administrative agency, nor a single administrative official, but the internally responsible functioning unit. Moreover, in general, knowledge concerning the elements of a rule constitutes a state of consciousness. The functioning units do not themselves have the necessary mens rea of knowledge; the knowledge of their employees must be attributed to them. In addition, the knowledge of current high-level officials and other representative positions conferred in accordance with the by-laws is always attributed to the functioning unit. This is analogously valid for officials and representative persons appointed in accordance with the by-laws that have already retired. The knowledge of other persons, at any rate, is attributable to the organization if these persons carry out an outstanding function, which generally has to consist of the independent and decisive handling of the facts of the case with respect to the specific knowledge provision. In practice, there are rare cases where insufficiencies in the taking in, passing on, storing of, and organization of information make knowledge that no one in the functioning unit had access to attributable to the functioning unit. Generally, the functioning unit should be considered to be "knowing." However, this fiction should generally not apply towards the public administration in the case of a tortfeasor without a special legal relationship.

VI
SUMMARY AND OUTLOOK

THE transition to a knowledge-based society, which may be observed in many areas of society and the economy, has also reached the public administration and affects administrative procedure as well. This article has pointed out that procedural law, when coping with this development, can transcend the existing instruments of generating and processing information. Nonetheless, in many different areas, further development and improvement of the legal and technological frame is necessary. In addition, a change in perspective must occur. In other words, what is needed is the analysis, interpretation, and application of existing provisions from the viewpoint of their relevance for generating knowledge and administrating information. Having said this, there is no paradigm change intended in the central tasks of administrative procedure. What is called for is a widening of the context and a shifting of the vocabulary that deals with all aspects of the increased significance of access to information and regulation of information for both the citizen and the administration.

Besides the classic administrative procedure and the established laws on freedom of information, future work must particularly focus on the information duties of authorities towards citizens and companies as established by the laws such as the new SD. These new developments illustrate the great significance information may have for the practice of freedom; the practical relevance of this insight must surely increase in the future.

NOTES

1. *On the distinction between state and society in the field of knowledge, see* B. Faßbender, *Wissen als Grundlage staatlichen Handelns, in* IV HANDBUCH DES STAATSRECHTS § 76 n. 58 (Isensee & Kirchhof, eds., 2007).

2. *See* H. MOHR, WISSEN – PRINZIP UND RESSOURCE (1999). *For discussion of the thesis that it was the knowledge-based state which created the knowledge-based society, see* B. Faßbender, *supra* note 1, § 76 n. 4. This still applies today to research that mainly takes place in public institutions.

3. M. EIFERT, ELECTRONIC GOVERNMENT (2006). *See also* W. KLUTH, I VERWALTUNGSRECHT § 58 n. 18 (Wolff et al., eds., 12th ed. 2007).

4. *For a comprehensive background on this topic, see generally* M. KLOEPFER, INFORMATIONSRECHT (2002).

5. In this context, the expression "administration of knowledge" does not primarily comprise archival storage, but rather working with this knowledge in a comprehensive sense. This includes the use of knowledge for the fulfillment of administrative tasks as well as its being passed on to society. *On the law of archives, compare* F. SCHOCH, DIE VERWALTUNG 39 (2006) 463 ff.

6. *For instance,* P.-T. STOLL, GENERIERUNG UND TRANSFER STAATLICHEN WISSENS IM SYSTEM DES VERWALTUNGSVERFAHRENS 29 (Spieker & Collin, eds., 2008); B.P. PRIDDAT, GENERIERUNG UND TRANSFER STAATLICHEN WISSENS IM SYSTEM DES VERWALTUNGSVERFAHRENS 283 (Spieker & Collin, eds., 2008); P.-J. JOST, GENERIERUNG UND TRANSFER STAATLICHEN WISSENS IM SYSTEM DES VERWALTUNGSVERFAHRENS 319 *passim* (Spieker & Collin, eds., 2008); D. BECK, GENERIERUNG UND TRANSFER STAATLICHEN WISSENS IM SYSTEM DES VERWALTUNGSVERFAHRENS 336 *passim* (2008) .

7. H. WILLKE, SYSTEMISCHES WISSENSMANAGEMENT (1998); H. WILLKE, SYSTEMTHEORIE I: GRUNDLAGEN (7th ed., 2006); H. WILLKE, SYSTEMTHEORIE II: INTERVENTIONSTHEORIE (4th ed., 2005); H. WILLKE, SYSTEMTHEORIE III: STEUERUNGSTHEORIE (3d ed., 2001). *See also* N. LUHMANN, DIE WISSENSCHAFT DER GESELLSCHAFT (1990).

8. H. WILLKE, EINFÜHRUNG IN DAS SYSTEMISCHE WISSENSMANAGEMENT § 28 f. (2004); H. WILLKE, DYSTOPIA. STUDIEN ZUR KRISIS DES WISSENS IN DER MODERNEN GESELLSCHAFT § 15 (2002).

9. In particular, scientific-technological development is important, because it opened up numerous new opportunities to gain knowledge. DNA analysis is a good example of an area in which the legal context of criminal prosecution was affected by the possibility to derive important information on the suspect from only small traces of body cells. New opportunities for prosecution arose which required adjustment of legal requirements.

10. H. WILLKE, EINFÜHRUNG IN DAS SYSTEMISCHE WISSENSMANAGEMENT, *supra* note 8, at 31 f. See also K.-E. SVEIBY, WHAT IS INFORMATION? (1998), *available at* http://www.sveiby.com/Portals/0/articles/Information.html.

11. H. Willke, Einführung in das systemische Wissensmanagement, *supra* note 8, at 33 *passim*. *On the dimensions of knowledge within a theory of socio-economic control, see* A. Etzioni, Die aktive Gesellschaft. Eine Theorie gesellschaftlicher und politischer Prozesse 157 (1975).

12. H. Willke, Systemtheorie III: Steuerungstheorie, *supra* note 7, at 355 *passim*; H. Willke, Studien zur Krisis des Wissens in der modernen Gesellschaft, *supra* note 8, at 29, 35, 49, 67. *See also* M. Schulte, Generierung und Transfer staatlichen Wissens im System des Verwaltungsverfahrens 250 (2008).

13. H. Willke, Einführung in das systemische Wissensmanagement, *supra* note 8, at 34. The plethora of currently electronically available data and information is worthless if there is no ability and no concept for their exploitation and application.

14. M. Polanyi, Personal knowledge. Towards a Post-Critical Philosophy (1958); *hereto* H. Willke, Einführung in das systemische Wissensmanagement, *supra* note 8, at 35.

15. *On this topic* R. Fisch & D. Beck, *Organisationskultur als kritischer Faktor des Verwaltungsmanagements, in* Jahrbuch des Kammer- und Berufsrechts 117 (W. Kluth, ed., 2006, 2007).; G. Endruweit, Organisationssoziologie 137 (2d ed., 2004). *See also* W. Kluth ed., Verwaltungskultur (2000).

16. *But see* B. Faßbender, *supra* note 1, § 76, n. 8 ff.

17. H. Willke, Systemtheorie III: Steuerungstheorie, *supra* note 7, at 313. *See also* C. Argyris & D.A. Schön, Organizational Learning II. Theory, Method, and Practice 12 (1996).

18. H. Willke, Systemtheorie I: Grundlagen, *supra* note 7, at 169 *passim*.

19. *Hereto* W. Kluth, 3 Verwaltungsrecht § 83 n. 24 (5th ed., 2004).

20. H. Willke, Systemtheorie I: Grundlagen, *supra* note 7, at 170 *passim*, 173.

21. H. Willke, Systemtheorie I: Grundlagen, *supra* note 7, at 175 *passim*.

22. *For further discussion, see* G.-M. Hellstern, The Public Sector – Challenge for Coordination and Learning 271 (Kaufmann, ed., 1991).

23. *See* G. F. Schuppert, Verwaltungswissenschaft 579 (2000).

24. *On the tasks of procedural law, see* Kluth, *supra* note 3, § 58 n. 8, 44; Schuppert, *supra* note 23, at 794.

25. *For more detail on this, see* P. Buck, Wissen und juristische Person (2001); B. Henning, Wissenszurechnung im Verwaltungsrecht (2003). *See also* Kluth, *supra* note 19, § 83 n. 58.

26. Kluth, *supra* note 19, § 83 n. 67, 74.

27 *On the issue of liability for incorrect (private) expert opinions, see* E. Hofmann, Generierung und Transfer staatlichen Wissens im System des Verwaltungsverfahrens 166, 175 (2008).

28. "For the purposes of this Act, administrative procedure shall be the activity of authorities having an external effect and directed to the examination of basic requirements, the preparation

and adoption of an administrative act or to the conclusion of an administrative agreement under public law; it shall include the adoption of the administrative act or the conclusion of the agreement under public law."

29. "(1) The authority shall determine the facts of the case ex officio. It shall determine the type and scope of investigation and shall not be bound by the participants' submissions and motions to admit evidence.

(2) The authority shall take account of all circumstances of importance in an individual case, including those favourable to the participants.

(3) The authority shall not refuse to accept statements or applications falling within its sphere of competence on the ground that it considers the statement or application inadmissible or unjustified."

30. The content of these articles is similar to APA art. 29.

31. G. ENGELHARDT, 24 KOMMENTAR ZUM VERWALTUNGSVERFAHRENSGESETZ 4 (1999).

32. "Right to good administration: 1. Every person has the right to have his or her affairs handled impartially, fairly and within a reasonable time by the institutions, bodies, offices and agencies of the Union.

2. This right includes: (a) the right of every person to be heard, before any individual measure which would affect him or her adversely is taken;

(b) the right of every person to have access to his or her file, while respecting the legitimate interests of confidentiality and of professional and business secrecy;

(c) the obligation of the administration to give reasons for its decisions.

3. Every person has the right to have the Union make good any damage caused by its institutions or by its servants in the performance of their duties, in accordance with the general principles common to the laws of the member states.

4. Every person may write to the institutions of the Union in one of the languages of the Treaties and must have an answer in the same language."

33. Article 284: The Commission may, within the limits and under conditions laid down by the Council in accordance with the provisions of this Treaty, collect any information and carry out any checks required for the performance of the tasks entrusted to it.

34. Council Regulation (EC) No 1/2003 of 16 December 2002 on the implementation of the rules on competition laid down in Articles 81 and 82 of the Treaty, OJ (2003) L 1/1. Article 17: Investigations into sectors of the economy and into types of agreements 1. Where the trend of trade between member states, the rigidity of prices or other circumstances suggest that competition may be restricted or distorted within the common market, the Commission may conduct its inquiry into a particular sector of the economy or into a particular type of agreements across various sectors. In the course of that inquiry, the Commission may request the undertakings or associations of undertakings concerned to supply the information necessary for giving effect to Articles 81 and 82 of the Treaty and may carry out any inspections necessary for that purpose. The Commission may in particular request the undertakings or associations of undertakings concerned to communicate to it all agreements, decisions and concerted practices. The Commission may publish a report on the results of its inquiry into particular sectors of the economy or particular types of agreements across various sectors and invite comments from interested parties.

2. Articles 14, 18, 19, 20, 22, 23 and 24 shall apply mutatis mutandis.

35. For a more detailed discussion of the impact of Community law on the finding of the facts by the German administration, see S. Wittkopp, Sachverhaltsermittlung im Gemeinschaftsverwaltungsrecht 66 (1999); *On European law in German administrative lawsuits, see also S. Kuntze*, VBlBW 5 (2001).

36. W. Berg, 9 Die Verwaltung 161, 165 (1976) ("(3) The legislature shall be bound by the constitutional order, the executive and the judiciary by law and justice"); *see also* M. Nierhaus, Beweismass und Beweislast. Untersuchungsgrundsatz und Beteiligtenmitwirkung im Verwaltungsprozeß 259 (1989); Engelhardt, *supra* note 31, § 24 n. 9 *passim*; P. Stelkens & D. Kallerhoff, Verwaltungsverfahrensgesetz. Kommentar § 24 n. 1 (Stelkens et al., eds., 6th ed., 2001).

37. *For a critical view, see* F. Hufen, Fehler im Verwaltungsverfahren. Ein Handbuch für Ausbildung und Praxis (4th ed., 2002).

38. *For another perspective, see* R. Pitschas, Reform des Allgemeinen Verwaltungsrechts 219 *passim* (1993).

39. *See infra* Part V.1.

40. Limits on fact-finding arise with regard to information that must not be taken into consideration because of a prohibition of exploitation (for instance, § 51 BZRG [Bundeszentralregistergesetz – Federal Act on the Central Register], § 153 V, VI GewO [Gewerbeordnung – Industrial Code]) or that has been gained by applying untoward methods of facts-finding and evidence (for example, interrogations prohibited by § 136a StPO [Strafprozessordnung – Code of Criminal Procedure]).

41 *See* P. Stelkens, NVwZ 1982, 81 ff.; F. Schoch, Innovation und Flexibilität des Verwaltungshandelns 199, 226 (1994); F. Hufen, *supra* note 38, 2002, marginal note 119.

42. Stelkens & Kallerhoff, *supra* note 37, § 24 n. 26.

43. Engelhardt, *supra* note 31, § 24 n. 64 ff.

44. BVerwGE 39, 36; 61, 295 (304).

45. Particularly for the application of procedural rules, there is often provided special explanations, submission, and evidence duties; compare, for instance, §§ 27, 31 BImSchG (Bundesimmissionsschutzgesetz – Law Concerning the Protection against harmful Effects on the Environment through Air Pollution, Noise, Vibrations, and Similar Factors), §§ 65, 67 BauO LSA (Bauordnung des Landes Sachsen-Anhalt – Building Code of the Federal State Saxony-Anhalt).

46. HeVGH, NVwZ-RR 1991, 357 (358); Stelkens & Kallerhoff, *supra* note 37, 2001, § 24, marginal note 26; W. Clausen, Verwaltungsverfahrensgesetz (VwVfG): Kommentar, (2004).

47. R. Seer, Steuerrecht § 22 (18th ed., 2005).

48. *See* G. Gaentzsch, DÖV 952 (1998,).

49. The details are disputed. *Compare* W. Berg, 9 Die Verwaltung 161, 181 (1976); Stelkens & Kallerhoff, *supra* note 37, § 24 n. 36; Engelhardt, *supra* note 31, § 24 n. 116.

50. Engelhardt, *supra* note 31, § 24, marginal note 118; *On the practice of the law on tax procedure, see* Seer, *supra* note 48, at 796, 860.

51. "(1) The authority shall utilise such evidence as, after due consideration, it deems necessary in order to ascertain the facts of the case. In particular it may: [...] 3. obtain documents and records."

52. BVerfG, NJW 1983, 2135; *Engelhardt*, in: Obermayer (note 30), 1999, § 24, marginal note 111. See on the keeping of records in general *G. Püttner*, Verwaltungslehre, 3rd edition 2000, 298 *passim*.

53. Stelkens & Kallerhoff, *supra* note 37, § 24 n. 54. *On the distribution of the material burden of proof, see* S. Wittkopp (note 32), 1999, 34 *passim*.

54. This motion is provided for by APA § 24 ¶ 1.

55. Engelhardt, *supra* note 31, § 24 n. 297.

56. "(4) If, in the case of automated processing, several bodies are entitled to store the data and the injured person is unable to ascertain the controller of the filing system, each body shall be liable."

57. "(3) Where doubt exists in connection with an entitlement which has been registered, the real-location department shall without delay set a time-limit within which the party registering the entitlement shall furnish substantiation. Where this period expires without substantiation being furnished, the party shall no longer be involved until such time as substantiation is furnished."

58. BVerwGE 44, 265; 77, 102 (121 f.); BVerwG, NVwZ-RR 1990, 165; *W. Berg*, JuS 1977, 23; Stelkens & Kallerhoff, *supra* note 37, § 24 n. 55; F.O. KOPP & U. RAMSAUER, VwVfG. VERWALTUNGSVERFAHRENSGESETZ: KOMMENTAR § 24 n. 42 (10th ed., 2008).

59. *For further discussion and citations, see* M. Nierhaus, *supra* note 37, at 430 *passim*.

60. BVerwG, NVwZ 1988, 434.

61. *See also.* Stelkens & Kallerhoff, *supra* note 37, § 24 n. 55; *Engelhardt*, *supra* note 31, § 24 n. 301.

62. *Engelhardt*, *supra* note 31, § 24 n. 308 *passim*.

63. "Section 282 BGB
Damages in lieu of performance for breach of a duty under section 241 para. 2
   If the obligor breaches a duty under section 241 para. 2, the obligee may, if the requirements of section 280 para. are satisfied, demand damages in lieu of performance, if he can no longer reasonably be expected to accept performance by the obligor."

64. Engelhardt, *supra* note 31, § 24 n. 311 & § 26 n. 166.

65. F.O. Kopp & U.Ramsauer, *supra* note 52, § 24, n. 6.

66. Engelhardt, *supra* note 30), 1999, § 24 n. 15; HUFEN, *supra* note 38, n.144.

67. "(2) The participants shall assist in ascertaining the facts of the case. In particular they shall state such facts and evidence as are known to them. A more extensive duty to assist in ascertaining the facts, and in particular the duty to appear personally or make a statement, shall exist only where the law specifically requires this."

68. W. Clausen, *supra* note 47, § 26 n. 36; Engelhardt, *supra* note 30), § 26, n. 152; Stelkens & Kallerhoff, *supra* note 37, § 26 n. 42; P. Stelkens, NuR 261 (1983).

69. W. ERBGUTH & A. SCHINK, 6 GESETZ ÜBER DIE UMWELTVERTRÄGLICHKEITSPRÜFUNG: KOMMENTAR (2d ed., 1996); B. BENDER ET AL., UMWELTRECHT. GRUNDZÜGE DES ÖFFENTLICHEN UMWELTSCHUTZRECHTS § 43 n. 116 (4th ed. 2000).

70. R. Pitschas, *supra* note 39, at 25.

71. On the cooperation duties of interested parties in general, see K. Grupp, VerwArch. 1980, 44 ff.; H. Mösbauer, Der Betrieb 1985, 410 ff.; R. Köhler-Rott, BayVBl. 1999, 711 *passim*.

72. Engelhardt, *supra* note 31, § 26, n. 153; Stelkens & Kallerhoff, *supra* note 37, § 26 n. 49.

73. F.O. Kopp & U. Ramsauer, *supra* note 52, § 24, marginal note 12d.

74. BVerwG, DVBl. 1997, 609.

75. Engelhardt, *supra* note 31, 1999, § 26 n 160.

76. BVerwG, NJW 1986, 270; BVerwGE 77, 240 (247).

77. BGH, NJW 1992, 2769 (2770).

78. BVerwG, NJW 1993, 1542.

79. Engelhardt, *supra* note 31, § 26 n. 163.

80. *For further discussion of the legal basis, see* W. Clausen, *supra* note 47, § 26 n. 36; F.O. Kopp & U. Ramsauer, *supra* note 52, 2008, § 26 n. 44a; Engelhardt, *supra* note 31, 1999, § 26, marginal notes 181*passim. On the cooperation of interested parties, see also* S. Wittkopp, *supra* note 32, at 35 *passim*.

81. *Compare, for instance,* section 11 NdsGefAG, section 8 PolGNW, section 9 RhPfPOG, section 13 SOG LSA, section 12 ThürPAG.

82. HeVGH, NVwZ 1993, 1009 (1010); bwVGH, ZfW 1994, 407; A. Schink, DVBl. 1989, 1182 (1186 *passim.*); T.B. Petri, DÖV 1996, 443 *passim.*; W.-R. Schenke & J. Ruthig, VerwArch. 87 (1996) 329 (345, 359); W. Weiß, NVwZ 1997, 737 *passim*.

83. BVerwG, NVwZ 1984, 724.

84. See, for example, section 67 paragraph 2 BauO LSA, sections 22 paragraph 2, 63b, 66 AMG or sections 6 paragraph 1, 10 paragraph 2 No. 5, 15 paragraph 3 No. 4 GenTG.

85. I. SPIEKER, GENERIERUNG UND TRANSFER STAATLICHEN WISSENS IM SYSTEM DES VERWALTUNGSVERFAHRENS 190 *passim* (2008).

86. *See* Stelkens & Kallerhoff, *supra* note 37, § 26 n. 60, 63.

87. Directive 2005/36/EC of the European Parliament and the Council of 7 September 2005 on the recognition of professional qualifications, OJ (2005) L 255/22. *For more detail on this directive, see* W. Kluth & F. Rieger, EuZW 486 *passim.* (2005).

88. "1. Member States may require that, where the service provider first moves from one Member State to another in order to provide services, he shall inform the competent authority in the host Member State in a written declaration to be made in advance including the details

of any insurance cover or other means of personal or collective protection with regard to professional liability. Such declaration shall be renewed once a year if the service provider intends to provide temporary or occasional services in that Member State during that year. The service provider may supply the declaration by any means."

89. "In cases where the service is provided under the professional title of the Member State of establishment or under the formal qualification of the service provider, in addition to the other requirements relating to information contained in Community law, the competent authorities of the host Member State may require the service provider to furnish the recipient of the service with any or all of the following information: (a) if the service provider is registered in a commercial register or similar public register, the register in which he is registered, his registration number, or equivalent means of identification contained in that register; (b) if the activity is subject to authorisation in the Member State of establishment, the name and address of the competent supervisory authority; (c) any professional association or similar body with which the service provider is registered; (d) the professional title or, where no such title exists, the formal qualification of the service provider and the Member State in which it was awarded; (e) if the service provider performs an activity which is subject to VAT, the VAT identification number referred to in Article 22(1) of the sixth Council Directive 77/388/EEC of 17 May 1977 on the harmonisation of the laws of the Member States relating to turnover taxes - Common system of value added tax: uniform basis of assessment (1); (f) details of any insurance cover or other means of personal or collective protection with regard to professional liability."

90. "1. Where the competent authorities of the host Member State decide on an application for authorisation to pursue the regulated profession in question by virtue of this Title, those authorities may demand the documents and certificates listed in Annex VII. The documents referred to in Annex VII, point 1(d), (e) and (f), shall not be more than three months old by the date on which they are submitted. The Member States, bodies and other legal persons shall guarantee the confidentiality of the information which they receive.

2. In the event of justified doubts, the host Member State may require from the competent authorities of a Member State confirmation of the authenticity of the attestations and evidence of formal qualifications awarded in that other Member State, as well as, where applicable, confirmation of the fact that the beneficiary fulfils, for the professions referred to in Chapter III of this Title, the minimum training conditions set out respectively in Articles 24, 25, 28, 31, 34, 35, 38, 40, 44 and 46.

3. In cases of justified doubt, where evidence of formal qualifications, as defined in Article 3(1)(c), has been issued by a competent authority in a Member State and includes training received in whole or in part in an establishment legally established in the territory of another Member State, the host Member State shall be entitled to verify with the competent body in the Member State of origin of the award:
(a) whether the training course at the establishment which gave the training has been formally certified by the educational establishment based in the Member State of origin of the award;
(b) whether the evidence of formal qualifications issued is the same as that which would have been awarded if the course had been followed entirely in the Member State of origin of the award; and (c) whether the evidence of formal qualifications confers the same professional rights in the territory of the Member State of origin of the award.

4. Where a host Member State requires its nationals to swear a solemn oath or make a sworn statement in order to gain access to a regulated profession, and where the wording of that oath

or statement cannot be used by nationals of the other Member States, the host Member State shall ensure that the persons concerned can use an appropriate equivalent wording."

91. "For the purposes of this Act, administrative procedure shall be the activity of authorities having an external effect and directed to the examination of basic requirements, the preparation and adoption of an administrative act or to the conclusion of an administrative agreement under public law; it shall include the adoption of the administrative act or the conclusion of the agreement under public law."

92. "(1) Participants shall be:
    1. those making and opposing an application,
    2. those to whom the authority intends to direct or has directed the administrative act,
    3. those with whom the authority intends to conclude or has concluded an agreement under public law,
    4. those who have been involved in the procedure by the authority under paragraph 2.

(2) The authority may ex officio or upon request involve as participants those whose legal interests may be affected by the result of proceedings. Where such result has a legal effect for a third party, the latter may upon request be involved in the proceedings as a participant. If the authority is aware of such third parties, it shall inform them that proceedings have commenced.

(3) A person who is to be heard, but is not a participant within the sense of paragraph 1, does not thereby become a participant."

See also W. Kluth, *supra* note 3), § 59 n. 54; F.O. Kopp & U. Ramsauer, *supra* note 52, § 9 n. 8.

93. "Section 68
Obligation to inform and to report

(1) The federal and Land authorities and agencies responsible for the implementation of the present Act shall
    1. inform each other of the authorities, agencies and experts responsible for the enforcement of the Act and,
    2. in instances of contravention and suspected contravention of the provisions contained in the medicinal product legislation for the individual sphere of responsibility, report to each other immediately and support each other's investigative activities.

(2) The authorities specified in sub-section 1
    1. shall furnish the competent authority of another Member State of the European Union with information, upon reasonable request, and shall transmit to it the necessary certificates and documents in so far as necessary to monitor compliance with the medicinal product-related regulations in force,
    2. shall investigate all of the facts of which it is informed by the requesting authority of another Member State and shall inform said authority of the results of the investigation.

(3) The authorities specified in sub-section 1 shall provide the competent authorities of another Member State with all of the information which is necessary to monitor compliance with the medicinal product-related regulations in force in that Member State. In cases of infringement or suspected infringement, the competent authorities of other Member States, the Federal Ministry, the Federal Ministry of Agriculture, Food and Consumer Protection, as well as the European Medicines Agency, in so far as medicinal products intended for administration to animals are concerned, and the Commission of the European Communities may also be informed.

(4) The authorities specified in sub-section 1 may, if necessary for the implementation of requirements stipulated in medicinal product-related legislation, also inform the competent authorities of other states and the competent offices at the Council of Europe. States Parties to the Agreement on the European Economic Area which are not Member States of the European Union shall be informed through the Commission of the European Communities.

(5) Communication with the competent authorities of other states, Council of Europe offices, the European Medicines Agency, and with the Commission of the European Communities shall be the prerogative of the Federal Ministry. The Federal Ministry may transfer this power to the competent Higher Federal Authority or, by means of an ordinance with the approval of the Bundesrat, to the competent higher authorities of the Laender. Furthermore, in individual cases, the Federal Ministry can transfer the above-mentioned power to the competent higher authority of the Land if the latter gives its consent. The higher authorities of the Laender are authorised to transfer the powers specified in sentences 2 and 3 to other authorities. In so far as medicinal products intended for administration to animals are concerned, the Federal Ministry of Agriculture, Food and Consumer Protection shall supersede the Federal Ministry. In such a case, the ordinance shall be promulgated pursuant to sentence 2 in agreement with the Federal Ministry.

(6) In the cases provided for in sub-section 3 sentence 2 and sub-section 4, personal data shall not be transmitted if so doing will have an adverse effect on interests of the affected person which are worthy of protection especially if, on the side of the recipient, an adequate standard of data protection is not guaranteed. Personal data may be transmitted, even if the recipient cannot guarantee an adequate standard of data protection, if necessary for reasons of health protection."

94. "Section 36
Participation of Local authorities and higher Administrative Authorities

(1) Concerning the admissibility of projects referred to in Sections 31 and 33 to 35, the building authority decides in consent with the local authority. A consensual decision is also required if the decision concerning the admissibility of projects referred to in Sections 31 and 33 to 35 is reached on the basis of a procedure different from the usual building authority procedure; this does not apply for projects referred to in Section 29 para. 1, which fall within the competency of the mining authorities. If the admissibility of a project falls within the scope of Section 30 para. 1, the *Länder* are obliged to guarantee that the Local authorities are able to decide upon measures of construction planning according to Sections 31, 33, 34 and 35 timely before the project is executed. In the cases stipulated in Section 35, paras. 2 and 4, the *Länder* governments are authorised to determine by means of statutory regulation that the consent of the higher administrative authorities is required either generally or for certain cases.

(2) The consent of the local authorities and the assent of the higher administrative authorities can only be denied on the basis of the reasons resulting from Sections 31, 33, 34 and 35. The consent of the local authorities and the assent of the higher administrative authorities are presumed if they are not explicitly denied within two month after the receipt of the request. A request to the local authority is considered equal to a submission to the local authority is case that the law of the respective *Land* stipulates this submission. The authority responsible according to the law of the respective *Land* can substitute the consent of the local authority in case of it being denied illegitimately."

95. "Section 72

Requirements for the involvement of authorities

(1) Permission to enter the Federal territory (Section 11 (2) may only be granted with the consent of the foreigners authority which is competent for the intended place of residence. The foreigners authority which has deported or expelled the foreigner is generally to be involved.

(2) The foreigners authority shall decide whether deportation to a specific state is prohibited pursuant to Section 60 (7) only after involving the Federal Office for Migration and Refugees.

(3) Geographic restrictions, requirements and conditions, time limits pursuant to Section 11 (1), sentence 3, orders pursuant to Section 47 and other measures against a foreigner who is not in possession of a required residence title may only be amended or lifted by a different foreigners authority in consultation with the foreigners authority which ordered the measures. Sentence 1 shall not apply if the foreigner's residence is restricted to the region for which the other foreigners authority is competent in accordance with the provisions of the Asylum Procedure Act.

(4) A foreigner against whom legal proceedings are instituted by a public authority or preliminary investigations are instituted under criminal law may only be expelled or deported in consultation with the competent public prosecutor's office. A foreigner who qualifies as requiring protection within the meaning of the Act to Harmonise Protection for Witnesses may only be expelled or deported in consultation with the Office for the Protection of Witnesses.

(5) Section 45 of Book Eight of the Social Code shall not apply for departure facilities and facilities which serve as temporary accommodation for foreigners who are granted a residence permit for reasons of international law or on humanitarian or political grounds.

(6) Before deciding on grant, extension or repeal of a residence title according to Section 25, para. 4a and on determination, annihilation or abbreviation of a departure deadline according to Section 50, para. 2a, the Public Prosecutor's Department responsible for the criminal procedure according to Section 25, para. 4a or the responsible Criminal Court must be engaged, except in cases of Section 87, para. 5 No. 1. In case the Public Prosecutor's Department responsible for the criminal procedure is unknown to the foreigners authority, the police authorities responsible must be engaged before deciding on determination, annihilation or abbreviation of a departure deadline according to Section 50, para. 2a."

96. "4. Authorities' duty to assist one another

(1) Each authority shall, when requested to do so, render assistance to other authorities (official assistance).

(2) It shall not be deemed official assistance when:

1. authorities assist each other in the course of a relationship in which one issues directives to another;
2. assistance involves actions which are the task of the authority approached.

5. Circumstances permitting and limits to official assistance

(1) An authority may request official assistance particularly when:

1. for legal reasons it cannot itself perform the official action;
2. for material reasons, such as the lack of personnel or equipment needed to perform the official action, it cannot itself do so;
3. to carry out its tasks it requires knowledge of facts unknown to and unobtainable by it;

4. to carry out its tasks it requires documents or other evidence in the possession of the authority approached;

5. it could only carry out the task at substantially greater expense than the authority approached.

(2) The authority approached may not provide assistance when:

1. it is unable to do so for legal reasons;

2. such assistance would be seriously detrimental to the Federal Republic or to a *Land* thereof. The authority approached shall not be obliged to submit documents or files nor to impart information when proceedings must be kept secret either by their nature or by law.

(3) The authority approached need not provide assistance when:

1. another authority can provide the same assistance with much greater ease or at much lower cost;

2. it could only provide such assistance at disproportionately great expense;

3. with regard to the tasks carried out by the authority requesting assistance, it could only provide such assistance by seriously jeopardising its own work.

(4) The authority approached may not refuse assistance on the grounds that it considers the request inappropriate for reasons other than those given in paragraph 3, or considers the purpose to be achieved by the official assistance inappropriate.

(5) If the authority approached does not consider itself obliged to provide assistance, it shall so inform the authority making the request. If the latter insists that official assistance be provided, the decision as to whether or not an obligation to furnish such assistance exists shall be taken by the supervisory authority with overall competence in the matter or, where no such authority exists, the supervisory authority competent in matters with which the authority of whom the request is made is concerned.

6. Choice of authority

If more than one authority comes into question as a possible provider of official assistance, assistance shall where possible be requested of an authority of the lowest administrative level of the administrative branch to which the authority requesting assistance belongs.

7. Execution of official assistance

(1) The admissibility of the measure to be put into effect by official assistance shall be determined by the law applying to the authority requesting assistance; the official assistance shall be carried out in accordance with the law applying to the authority of which the request is made.

(2) The authority requesting assistance shall be responsible vis-à-vis the authority from which assistance is requested for the legality of the measure to be taken. The authority of which assistance is requested shall be responsible for the execution of the official assistance.

8. Cost of official assistance

(1) The authority requesting assistance shall not be liable to pay the authority from which official assistance is requested any administrative fee for such assistance. It shall, however, reimburse the latter for individual expenses in excess of thirty-five (35) euros upon request. If authorities belonging to the same legal entity provide each other with assistance, no expenses shall be reimbursed.

(2) If the authority from which official assistance is requested undertakes an official action for which fees are charged, then that authority shall be entitled to such fees paid by a third party (administrative charges, fees, expenses)."

97. "Article 8

Administrative cooperation

1. The competent authorities of the host Member State may ask the competent authorities of the Member State of establishment, for each provision of services, to provide any information relevant to the legality of the service provider's establishment and his good conduct, as well as the absence of any disciplinary or criminal sanctions of a professional nature. The competent authorities of the Member State of establishment shall provide this information in accordance with the provisions of Article 56.

2. The competent authorities shall ensure the exchange of all information necessary for complaints by a recipient of a service against a service provider to be correctly pursued. Recipients shall be informed of the outcome of the complaint."

98. "Article 56

Competent authorities

1. The competent authorities of the host Member State and of the home Member State shall work in close collaboration and shall provide mutual assistance in order to facilitate application of this Directive. They shall ensure the confidentiality of the information which they exchange.

2. The competent authorities of the host and home Member States shall exchange information regarding disciplinary action or criminal sanctions taken or any other serious, specific circumstances which are likely to have consequences for the pursuit of activities under this Directive, respecting personal data protection legislation provided for in Directives 95/46/EC of the European Parliament and of the Council of 24 October 1995 on the protection of individuals with regard to the processing of personal data and on the free movement of such data and 2002/58/EC of the European Parliament and of the Council of 12 July 2002 concerning the processing of personal data and the protection of privacy in the electronic communications sector (Directive on privacy and electronic communications. The home Member State shall examine the veracity of the circumstances and its authorities shall decide on the nature and scope of the investigations which need to be carried out and shall inform the host Member State of the conclusions which it draws from the information available to it.

3. Each Member State shall, no later than 20 October 2007, designate the authorities and bodies competent to award or receive evidence of formal qualifications and other documents or information, and those competent to receive applications and take the decisions referred to in this Directive, and shall forthwith inform the other Member States and the Commission thereof.

4. Each Member State shall designate a coordinator for the activities of the authorities referred to in paragraph 1 and shall inform the other Member States and the Commission thereof. The coordinators' remit shall be:

(a) to promote uniform application of this Directive;
(b) to collect all the information which is relevant for application of this Directive, such as on the conditions for access to regulated professions in the Member States. For the purpose of fulfilling the remit described in point (b), the coordinators may solicit the help of the contact points referred to in Article 57."

99. Directive 2006/123/EC of the European Parliament and the Council of 12 December 2006 on services in the internal market, OJ (2006) L 376/36.

100. "Article 28

Mutual assistance – general obligations

1. Member States shall give each other mutual assistance, and shall put in place measures for effective cooperation with one another, in order to ensure the supervision of providers and the services they provide.

2. For the purposes of this Chapter, Member States shall designate one or more liaison points, the contact details of which shall be communicated to the other Member States and the Commission. The Commission shall publish and regularly update the list of liaison points.

3. Information requests and requests to carry out any checks, inspections and investigations under this Chapter shall be duly motivated, in particular by specifying the reason for the request. Information exchanged shall be used only in respect of the matter for which it was requested.

4. In the event of receiving a request for assistance from competent authorities in another Member State, Member States shall ensure that providers established in their territory supply their competent authorities with all the information necessary for supervising their activities in compliance with their national laws.

5. In the event of difficulty in meeting a request for information or in carrying out checks, inspections or investigations, the Member State in question shall rapidly inform the requesting Member State with a view to finding a solution.

6. Member States shall supply the information requested by other Member States or the Commission by electronic means and within the shortest possible period of time.

7. Member States shall ensure that registers in which providers have been entered, and which may be consulted by the competent authorities in their territory, may also be consulted, in accordance with the same conditions, by the equivalent competent authorities of the other Member States.

8. Member States shall communicate to the Commission information on cases where other Member States do not fulfil their obligation of mutual assistance. Where necessary, the Commission shall take appropriate steps, including proceedings provided for in Article 226 of the Treaty, in order to ensure that the Member States concerned comply with their obligation of mutual assistance. The Commission shall periodically inform Member States about the functioning of the mutual assistance provisions."

101. *General on expert consultation of the state and its constitutional limits A. Voßkuhle*, in Isensee & Kirchhof (eds.), III HANDBUCH DES STAATSRECHTS, § 43 (3rd ed., 2005), especially. marginal notes 54 *passim*.

102. "Article 13

Expertise

(1) The authority responsible for approval obtains expertise of experts as far as this is necessary in order to determine whether the requirements for approval are met. If possible, the expert should be commissioned before the project is given notice of (Section 8). As far as Section 4b para. 2 requires to have parts of the security report attached to the request, which equal chapters II No. 1 and 3, III, IV and V No 1 to 3 of the annex of the disturbance-enactment, the obtaining of an expertise is normally necessary for the assessment of the data given in the request. Furthermore, experts can be consulted with consent of the submitter if it is likely to hereby accelerate the approval process.

(1a) The decision whether the submitted documents should be reviewed by external experts has to account for the location registry according to the EC Directive No. 761/2001 of the European Parliament and the Council of Europe (dated March 19th 2001) concerning the voluntary inclusion of organisations into a community system for environment management and environment auditing (EMAS).

(2) An expert opinion submitted by the submitter is to be reviewed as a miscellaneous document according to Section 10 para. 1, 2nd sentence Bundes-Immissionsschutzgesetz. In case the party responsible for the submitted project commissions the opinion in accordance with the responsible authority or to an expert who is designated for the respective area by the authority responsible according to Länder regulations, the submitted expert opinion is to be considered as expertise within the meaning of paragraph 1; this also applied to expertise provided by an expert meeting the requirements of Section 29a para. 1, 2nd sentence Bundes-Immissionsschutzgesetz."

103. *See* P. SCHOLL, DER PRIVATE SACHVERSTÄNDIGE IM VERWALTUNGSRECHT (2005). *See also* Stelkens & Kallerhoff, *supra* note 37, § 26 n. 68 *passim.*; E.-H. Ritter, *Organisationswandel durch Expertifizierung und Privatisierung im Ordnungs- und Planungsrecht, in* VERWALTUNGSORGANISATION ALS STEUERUNGSRESSOURCE 207 (Schmidt-Aßmann & Hoffmann-Riem, eds., 1997); E. HOFMANN, GENERIERUNG UND TRANSFER STAATLICHEN WISSENS IM SYSTEM DES VERWALTUNGSVERFAHRENS 166 *passim* (2008); U. di Fabio, VerwArch 81 193, 210 (1990).

104. *On the danger of neglect of current state knowledge and state independence related to that neglect, see* A. Voßkuhle, *in* Isensee & Kirchhof *supra* note 85, § 43, marginal note 53.

105. *On the procedural scope of instructing private persons see* W. KLUTH, *supra* note 3, § 59, marginal notes. 55 *passim.*

106. *For such a case (involvement of a private detective via an alien's registration office in order to reveal a fictitious marriage), see* OVG Hamburg, ZAR 2007, 248 *passim. On this, see generally* P. Scholl, *supra* note 106, at 185; W. Kluth, *supra* note 3, § 59 n. 95 *passim.*

107. *See, e.g.,* BVerfGE 83, 60 (71 *passim*); 93, 37 (67). *On the development of the democratic principle in the law on administrative organization, see also* Kluth, *supra* note 19, § 81 n. 134 *passim.*

108. "Section 4b BauGB
Inclusion of Third Parties

In order to accelerate the town plannung procedure, the local authority can transfer the preparatory work and implementation of procedural steps according to Sections 2a to 4a to a third party."

109. *For details on this over-generally formulated provision lacking all control effect, see* W. Schrödter, *in* BauGB § 4b n. 1 *passim* (H. Schrödter, ed., 7th ed, 2006).

110. *On this aspect, see* A. Voßkuhle, *supra* note 85, § 43 n. 50 *passim.*

111. Kluth, *supra* note 3, 2007, § 60, marginal notes 99 *passim;* P. Scholl, *supra* note 106, 191 *passim.*

112. "Section 65, paragraph 4 AMG

Eligible for appointment as a private expert for the testing of samples left behind pursuant to sub-section 1 sentence 2 shall only be a person who

1. has the expert knowledge pursuant to Section 15. The practical experience pursuant to Section 15 sub-sections 1 and 4 can be replaced by practical experience in the control and assessment of medicinal products in medicinal product control laboratories or in other similar medicinal product institutes,

2. is reliable enough to perform his/her duties as an expert for the testing of official samples and

3. has adequate premises and facilities at his/her disposal for the intended testing and assessment of medicinal products."

113. "Article 5
Freedom of Expression

Everyone has the right freely to express and to disseminate his opinion by speech, writing and pictures and freely to inform himself from generally accessible sources. Freedom of the press and freedom of reporting by radio and motion pictures are guaranteed. There shall be no censorship."

114. "Article 1 paragraph 1 GG

The dignity of man is inviolable. To respect and protect it is the duty of all state authority."

115. BVerfGE 79, 256 *passim*.

116. "Article 12 para. 1

All Germans have the right freely to choose their trade or profession their place of work and their place of training. The practice of trades and professions may be regulated by law."

117. "Article 3

All persons are equal before the law."

118. *Fundamental hereto* SCHERZBERG, DIE ÖFFENTLICHKEIT DER VERWALTUNG (2000).

119. "Within three weeks of receiving the plan, the communities referred to in paragraph 2 shall make the plan available for inspection for a period of one month. This procedure may be omitted where those affected are known and are given the opportunity to examine the plan during a reasonable period."

120. "Article 9 UVPG
Involvement of the Public

(1) The competent authority shall hear the public on the project's environmental impacts on the basis of the documents presented pursuant to Article 6. The hearing procedure shall be conducted pursuant to the requirements of Article 73 paras 3 to 7 of the Act on Administrative Procedures (Verwaltungsverfahrensgesetz). If the developer alters the documents required pursuant to Article 6 in the course of the procedures, the public need not be heard a second time as long as no additional or other significant effects on the environment are to be feared.

(2) The competent authority shall make available the decision on the approval of the project and the grounds for decision to those concerned, where names are known, and those on whose objections a decision was made. If the project is dismissed those concerned whose names are known and those who made objections shall be informed.

(3) Notwithstanding paras 1 and 2, the public shall be involved in the advance procedure by

    1. the project being announced publicly,

    2. the documents required pursuant to Article 6 being made available for inspection for a reasonable period of time,

    3. an opportunity being given for the public to express its opinion,

    4. the public being informed about the decision.

Involving the public does not constitute legal claims. Pursuit of claims in subsequent approval procedures shall not be affected."

121. "Section 10 of the 9th Bundesimmissionschutzverordnung
Interpretation of Submission and Documents

(1) The request enclosing documents containing information about the facilities impact on the neighbourhood and on the public must be submitted to the responsible authority and, as far as necessary, to a appropriate office near the location of the facility. Furthermore, all relevant documents in the authorities possession containing information on the facilities' impact and recommendations on the limitation of those impacts have to be displayed publicly. In case the authority obtains additional documents or official statements containing such information before the decision is reached, those have to be made accessible to the public according to the regulation of Bund and Länder concerning the access of environmental information.

In case the project concerns a facility due to a environmental compatibility test, the documents submitted on the implementation of this test have to be displayed likewise; furthermore, the request and the documents are to be displayed in those local authorities which will be affected most likely by the project. As far as a display of the documents according to Section 4b para. 1 and 2 leads to a disturbance within the scope of Section 4b para. 3, a presentation according to 4b para. 3 has to be displayed instead. The request and the documents have to be accessible during office hours.

(2) Third parties must be handed a copy or transcript of the description according to Section 4 para. 3, first sentence if requested.

(3) A far as the documents contain company secrets, the summary according to Section 10 para. 2, second sentence of the Bundesimmisionsschutzgesetz must be displayed instead. In case the authority does not consider it necessary to label the documents as company secrets, it has to consult he submitter before reaching a decision on this issue."

122. *On the Council directive (EEC) 90/313 on free access to information on the environment,* OJ (1990) L 158/56 and the German Act on the freedom of information on the environment; *see R. Röger,* Umweltinformationsgesetz. KOMMENTAR (1995) with further citations.

123. According to Art. 51 I Charter on fundamental rights, the charter applies in the relation between citizens and organs as well as institutions of the European Union and – insofar as these exclusionary carry out European Union law – Member States. Yet, as long as it has not been integrated into the Treaties it cannot be enforced before court.

124. "Article 11
Freedom of expression and information

1. Everyone has the right to freedom of expression. This right shall include freedom to hold opinions and to receive and impart information and ideas without interference by public authority and regardless of frontiers.

2. The freedom and pluralism of the media shall be respected."

125. "Article 41, paras. 1 and 2
Right to good administration

1. Every person has the right to have his or her affairs handled impartially, fairly and within a reasonable time by the institutions and bodies of the Union.

2. This right includes:

- the right of every person to be heard, before any individual measure which would affect him or her adversely is taken;
- the right of every person to have access to his or her file, while respecting the legitimate interests of confidentiality and of professional and business secrecy;
- the obligation of the administration to give reasons for its decisions."

126. "Article 255 para. 1 EC

1. Any citizen of the Union, and any natural or legal person residing or having its registered office in a Member State, shall have a right of access to European Parliament, Council and Commission documents, subject to the principles and the conditions to be defined in accordance with paragraphs 2 and 3."

127. "Article 7 SD
Right to information

1. Member States shall ensure that the following information is easily accessible to providers and recipients through the points of single contact:

(a) requirements applicable to providers established in their territory, in particular those requirements concerning the procedures and formalities to be completed in order to access and to exercise service activities;
(b) the contact details of the competent authorities enabling the latter to be contacted directly, including the details of those authorities responsible for matters concerning the exercise of service activities;
(c) the means of, and conditions for, accessing public registers and databases on providers and services;
(d) the means of redress which are generally available in the event of dispute between the competent authorities and the provider or the recipient, or between a provider and a recipient or between providers;
(e) the contact details of the associations or organisations, other than the competent authorities, from which providers or recipients may obtain practical assistance.

2. Member States shall ensure that it is possible for providers and recipients to receive, at their request, assistance from the competent authorities, consisting in information on the way in which the requirements referred to in point (a) of paragraph 1 are generally interpreted and applied. Where appropriate, such advice shall include a simple step-by-step guide. The information shall be provided in plain and intelligible language.

3. Member States shall ensure that the information and assistance referred to in paragraphs 1 and 2 are provided in a clear and unambiguous manner, that they are easily accessible at a distance and by electronic means and that they are kept up to date.

4. Member States shall ensure that the points of single contact and the competent authorities respond as quickly as possible to any request for information or assistance as referred to in paragraphs 1 and 2 and, in cases where the request is faulty or unfounded, inform the applicant accordingly without delay.

5. Member States and the Commission shall take accompanying measures in order to encourage points of single contact to make the information provided for in this Article available in other Community languages. This does not interfere with Member States' legislation on the use of languages.

6. The obligation for competent authorities to assist providers and recipients does not require those authorities to provide legal advice in individual cases but concerns only general information on the way in which requirements are usually interpreted or applied.

Article 22 SD
Information on providers and their services

1. Member States shall ensure that providers make the following information available to the recipient:

(a) the name of the provider, his legal status and form, the geographic address at which he is established and details enabling him to be contacted rapidly and communicated with directly and, as the case may be, by electronic means;

(b) where the provider is registered in a trade or other similar public register, the name of that register and the provider's registration number, or equivalent means of identification in that register;

(c) where the activity is subject to an authorisation scheme, the particulars of the relevant competent authority or the single point of contact;

(d) where the provider exercises an activity which is subject to VAT, the identification number referred to in Article 22(1) of Sixth Council Directive 77/388/EEC of 17 May 1977 on the harmonisation of the laws of the Member States relating to turnover taxes – Common system of value added tax: uniform basis of assessment;

(e) in the case of the regulated professions, any professional body or similar institution with which the provider is registered, the professional title and the Member State in which that title has been granted;

(f) the general conditions and clauses, if any, used by the provider;

(g) the existence of contractual clauses, if any, used by the provider concerning the law applicable to the contract and/or the competent courts;

(h) the existence of an after-sales guarantee, if any, not imposed by law;

(i) the price of the service, where a price is pre-determined by the provider for a given type of service;

(j) the main features of the service, if not already apparent from the context;

(k) the insurance or guarantees referred to in Article 23(1), and in particular the contact details of the insurer or guarantor and the territorial coverage.

2. Member States shall ensure that the information referred to in paragraph 1, according to the provider's preference:

(a) is supplied by the provider on his own initiative;

(b) is easily accessible to the recipient at the place where the service is provided or the contract concluded;

(c) can be easily accessed by the recipient electronically by means of an address supplied by the provider;

(d) appears in any information documents supplied to the recipient by the provider which set out a detailed description of the service he provides.

3. Member States shall ensure that, at the recipient's request, providers supply the following additional information:

(a) where the price is not pre-determined by the provider for a given type of service, the price of the service or, if an exact price cannot be given, the method for calculating the price so that it can be checked by the recipient, or a sufficiently detailed estimate;

(b) as regards the regulated professions, a reference to the professional rules applicable in the Member State of establishment and how to access them;

(c) information on their multidisciplinary activities and partnerships which are directly linked to the service in question and on the measures taken to avoid conflicts of interest. That information shall be included in any information document in which providers give a detailed description of their services;

(d) any codes of conduct to which the provider is subject and the address at which these codes may be consulted by electronic means, specifying the language version available;

(e) where a provider is subject to a code of conduct, or member of a trade association or professional body which provides for recourse to a non-judicial means of dispute settlement, information in this respect. The provider shall specify how to access detailed information on the characteristics of, and conditions for, the use of non-judicial means of dispute settlement.

4. Member States shall ensure that the information which a provider must supply in accordance with this Chapter is made available or communicated in a clear and unambiguous manner, and in good time before conclusion of the contract or, where there is no written contract, before the service is provided.

5. The information requirements laid down in this Chapter are in addition to requirements already provided for in Community law and do not prevent Member States from imposing additional information requirements applicable to providers established in their territory.

6. The Commission may, in accordance with the procedure referred to in Article 40(2), specify the content of the information provided for in paragraphs 1 and 3 of this Article accordingto the specific nature of certain activities and may specify the practical means of implementing paragraph 2 of this Article."

128. "The authority shall cause statements or applications to be made or corrected when it is clear that these were not submitted or were incorrectly submitted only due to error or ignorance. It shall, where necessary, give information regarding the rights and duties of participants in the administrative proceedings."

129. "Section 89, second sentence of the Abgabenordnung
Consulting and Information

The tax authority informs, as far as necessary, on the parties rights and duties in administrative procedure."

130. "Section 89, first sentence of the Abgabenordnung
Consulting and Information

Tax authorities shall encourage statements, requests and corrections of requests if it is obvious that those have been submitted incorrectly or not all just because of lack of knowledge or by mistake."

131. "(1) The authority shall allow participants to inspect the documents connected with the proceedings where knowledge of their contents is necessary in order to assert or defend their

legal interests. Until administrative proceedings have been concluded, the foregoing sentence shall not apply to draft decisions and work directly connected with their preparation. Where participants are represented as provided under sections 17 and 18, only the representatives shall be entitled to inspect documents.

(2) The authority shall not be obliged to allow the inspection of documents where this would interfere with the orderly performance of the authority's tasks, where knowledge of the contents of the documents would be to the disadvantage of the country as a whole or of one of the *Länder*, or where proceedings must be kept secret by law or by their very nature, i.e. in the rightful interests of participants or of third parties.

(3) Inspection of documents shall take place in the offices of the record-keeping authority. In individual cases, documents may also be inspected at the offices of another authority or of the diplomatic or consular representatives of the Federal Republic of Germany abroad. The authority keeping the records may make further exceptions."

132. M. Kloepfer, *supra* note 4, § 4 n. 35a.

133. "Article 34 GG
Liability in the event of a breach of official duty

If any person, in the exercise of a public office entrusted to him, violates his official obligations to a third party, liability rests in principle on the state or the public authority which employs him. In the case of willful intent or gross carelessness the right of recourse is reserved. With respect to the claim for compensation or the right of recourse, the jurisdiction of the ordinary courts must not be excluded."

134. "Section 280 para. 1 BGB
Damages for breach of duty

If the obligor breaches a duty arising from the obligation, the obligee may demand damages for the damage caused thereby. This does not apply if the obligor is not responsible for the breach of duty.

Section 249 BGB
Nature and extent of damages

(1) A person who is liable in damages must restore the position that would exist if the circumstance obliging him to pay damages had not occurred.

(2) Where damages are payable for injury to a person or damage to a thing, the obligee may demand the required monetary amount in lieu of restoration. When a thing is damaged, the monetary amount required under sentence 1 only includes value-added tax if and to the extent that it is actually incurred."

135. B. Henning, Wissenszurechnung im Verwaltungsrecht – am Beispiel der verwaltungsverfahrensrechtlichen Regelungen der Ausschlussfristen bei der Rücknahme und dem Widerruf von Verwaltungsakten 153 (2003).

136. *For the relevant case law, compare, for instance,* OVG Berlin, NJW 2156 (1983) with OVG Magdeburg, LKV 545, 546(2000); VG Cologne, NVwZ 1984, 537; and BGHZ 135, 354, 359.

THE PRINTING OF THIS BOOK, THE
SECOND OF THE GLOBAL LAW PRESS,
WAS COMPLETED ON 19 APRIL

2   0   1   5

www.ingramcontent.com/pod-product-compliance
Lightning Source LLC
Chambersburg PA
CBHW081800200326
41597CB00023B/4091